SALVATION

SALVATION

I have waited for thy salvation, O Lord,

GENESIS 49:18

THE APOSTOLIC FOUNDATION
OF THE
CHRISTIAN CHURCH

Volume Ten

JOHN METCALFE

THE PUBLISHING TRUST
Church Road, Tylers Green, Penn, Buckinghamshire, U.K.

Printed and Published by the
John Metcalfe Publishing Trust
Church Road, Tylers Green
Penn, Buckinghamshire, U.K.

–

Distributed by Trust Representatives
and Agents world-wide

–

–

First Published 2004

–

ISBN 1 870039 88 2

–

**This work is available at less than the
cost of production through subsidies on
the part of the John Metcalfe Publishing
Trust. The Author waives all royalties in
favour of the Trust, a Registered Charity.**

CONTENTS

INTRODUCTION

SALVATION

INTRODUCTION

IF one were to say 'Let God have the last word', I will tell you what that word would be: *Salvation*! Salvation is God's last word; it is inextricable from the name of Jesus; from the nature of his work; and from the effect of his presence.

Salvation has trembled in the air ever since Christ departed from this world; it is still whispered from heaven; from outside of this world; and it will yet linger at the door of the heart till this world is no more.

Oh, yes: *Salvation* is pre-eminent, it is mightily effectual, it is all of God, and it is nearer than when we first believed. Believe it: *Salvation* is the last word.

But how few have any idea what *Salvation* really means, or what is entailed in it. I entreat you, permit me to open the matter as it is in truth, namely, as it is revealed in the new testament; conveyed by the Saviour of the soul; and taught experimentally by the ministry of the Spirit of God.

Beyond all doubt *Salvation* answers to the deepest cry of the soul, the most profound anguish of the heart that can sound or arise from the inmost being of man. To the destitute, wretched, poor and needy, this one great common necessity stands above and towers over everything else: 'Lord, save us: we perish.'

And he does: above all else this characterizes the new testament of our Lord and Saviour Jesus Christ. This is what is paramount in the evangel. It is the sound that distinguished the church—the *ecclesia*—from the beginning.

Without this resonance, everything is void: nothing is valid: only emptiness remains. *Salvation*! It is God's first word, and it is his last word. O earth, earth, earth, Hear the word of the LORD!

Basically, Salvation means 'safety' or 'soundness' in both old and new testaments. Thus the English translation gives an excellent equivalent to both the Hebrew and the Greek.

'Salvation' as an English word in itself, is derived from the Latin *salvare*, to save; and *salvus*, safe. We use the words Salve, salvable, salvation, salvage, safe, safety, from the same Latin source.

All these variations, however, convey the basic thought of 'rescue, deliverance, freedom', or else of 'preservation, reservation, and protection'. In a word, either of being *saved* from harm or *kept* from harm.

If so, then the very term *Salvation* predicates danger. A *Salve* implies a wound or sore. *Salvage* suggests shipwreck. *Safety* postulates peril. *Save* indicates danger.

Thus the very fact of salvation – in any shape or form – presupposes threatening enemies or calamities. Likewise soundness would be meaningless unless corruption were a hazard. The cry 'Save' indicates that one is in jeopardy.

The desperate signal S.O.S. cries out for a Saviour. So that always behind the word *Salvation* abides the threat of disaster. Otherwise one would neither need saving, nor require salvation, no, nor cry for a Saviour.

In this lies the essence of the word *Salvation*: it is that the Saviour should deliver us out of the hand of the enemy, and save us from perishing.

However in spiritual things the dangers and enemies are invisible. Indeed they are not so much a disaster to one in this world: the real calamity falls in the next world.

It is not now in time, but after death in timeless eternity that the dreadful storm breaks endlessly about the head of an erstwhile heedless mankind.

But beyond death the eye cannot pierce. Hence when in this life all is calm, carefree, and prosperous, then the procrastinator murmurs in false security 'peace and safety'. Yet – should nothing intervene – at the inevitable onset of old age and death, too late, destruction falls with a sickening and everlasting inevitability.

Now, secure on earth, the cry is, 'I will pull down my barns, and build greater'. But, O, so soon God calls down from heaven, 'Thou fool, this night thy soul shall be required of thee'.

Prudent enough in the things of this world, worldly foresight collapses in horror when awakened by the imminence of death and the world to come, the more so when all unexpected – in youth and vigour – the grim reaper scythes down the living with shocking suddenness.

What! As if death were an impassable wall of granite of which not the slightest heed need be taken?

So that when the summons comes, either by decay and age, or, in mid stride, all unawares, far from a wall of granite, death proves to be but a flimsy veil.

Death? a mere tissue so rudely torn aside as a thing of nought, through which the soul is ejected with a precipitous eruption out of time into eternity, and from the world that is seen into the unseen world beyond the veil.

The illusion that this world is not alien to the soul is shrouded from men, deluded through worldliness, by a kind of spiritual veil. Just as with the heavenly and eternal things of the world to come, the senses of mankind lie beneath a kind of thick blanket of darkness literally impenetrable to natural perception.

Between these two illusions the world goes on oblivious of danger. Besides all this, the very air men breathe seems to be filled with a soporific atmosphere which leaves mankind quite stupefied as to the desperately urgent need of salvation.

It is not religion—much less the evangel—that is the opiate of the masses: what has put man to a sleep heavier than that caused by opium is the notion that there is no world to come, then no danger, no life beyond this.

The very atmosphere of the age is impregnated with the false assurance that this life is all that there is; that after it there is nothing but oblivion. The world breathes in this air, and inhales the illusory security it exudes.

Whence it follows that mankind stands in dire need to be awakened to this *spiritual* danger. To hear and give heed to the soul-penetrating cry 'Awake thou that sleepest, and arise from the dead, and Christ shall give thee light'.

Without such an awakening there can be no salvation. How can there be, with nothing but a dead, slumbering indifference, even though – and that rarely enough – it be with an open bible lightly clasped in and gently slipping from the hand of the sleeper.

Of necessity the cry for salvation *must* be preceded by an awakening to the awful danger in which the soul stands, yet to which, hitherto, it was blindly unaware. The salvation of the soul is dependent upon the breaking in through the inmost parts of the enormity of the jeopardy in which one stands.

As if on a narrow neck of land, the ground crumbling beneath one's feet, an ocean, fathomless and infinite, on either side, one for everlasting safety, the other for eternal perdition.

It is this suddenly alarmed consciousness of impending disaster, this awakening to immortal danger, this realization of catastrophic peril, that wrings out the cry from the soul, 'What must I do to be saved?'

To such, salvation is no mere dead letter, no unreal description in the bible, *it is a dire necessity of life and death urgency*. It wrenches from the inmost being the agonizing prayer, 'Save, Lord: I perish'.

But if it is certain that nothing less than such a conviction brings forth the awakening cry to be saved, it is equally true that nothing can measure the sweetness of the sight of the Saviour, and the sound of the grace of God that brings salvation.

This appears within and echoes throughout the heart: 'Be of good cheer; thy sins be forgiven thee.'

This joy unspeakable, and full of glory, outpoured with the sure inward witness of the remission of sins, and salvation of the soul, is to eat the flesh of the Son of man, and to drink his blood, John 6:53: *it is Salvation*.

From within springs up a well of living water unto everlasting life, answering to the power of real and vital religion.

It has always been so. Hence the ancient prophet cried many hundreds of years before Christ came 'Therefore with joy shall ye draw water out of the wells of salvation'.

One of the most conspicuous things about a saved people is their joy. They are a happy people. Their happiness is not in vain pleasures, trifling superficialities and sensual gratifications which perish with the using.

Their joy is not in worldly diversions and meaningless pre-occupations by which they avoid facing the real issues of life and death.

Their happiness is that they have faced these realities, their joy is that they have seen every issue met, satisfied, and discharged in and by the Saviour on the cross. That he is risen from the dead. And that he has appeared to them in a spiritual and experimental way to the salvation of their souls.

The joy of such a people is that every question about life; death; God; man; time; eternity; immortality; heaven; hell; whence one came; what one is; why one is here; whither one goes: every question about God; Father, Son, and Holy Ghost.

Every question about how God has revealed himself; how he brings one to himself; every question about the unseen world: angels; Satan; demons; the glory; the underworld; Every question!

What God has done; is doing; will do; how the world began; how it will end; the old world before the flood; about Abraham, Isaac, Jacob, the children of Israel; the church–the *ecclesia*–how it began, what it is, what has happened to it, what to do in consequence: every question has been happily and joyfully resolved.

And resolved through the revelation of Jesus Christ, the Saviour; and resolved in a way of eternal salvation.

Such a joyful people are ready to die; willing to die: 'to depart, and to be with Christ; which is far better.'

They look forward to death because they know that immediately they are to be with Christ, who has made known to them the ways of life, who shall fill them with joy and gladness, at whose right hand are pleasures for evermore.

Certainly Christ is known now. But then they know that this is nothing compared to the glory that is to be revealed. The very thought is bliss: what shall be the reality?

The inward union passes all expression: how can the heart ever conceive of what is laid up for them by the love of God on the other side of death?

No wonder that *Salvation* is pre-eminent. No truth so advanced, no doctrine so profound, but that the ring of salvation vibrates throughout its utterance.

This salvation is wrought by the Saviour. It is achieved at the cross. It is declared in the evangel. It is experienced in the heart of sinners. It resonates in the assembly of the people of God.

The voice of joy and of salvation reaches out to the sound of the trumpet in the resurrection.

Foretold and prefigured in the old covenant, fulfilled by the Saviour in the new testament, the Holy Ghost from heaven bears witness to the trump of jubilee in the consummation of the salvation of God in that glorious and everlasting inheritance and rest of the saints in the world to come, whereof we speak.

Hence it is obvious that *salvation* is a word which reaches forward to a positive work of deliverance from every enemy and obstacle that hinders the pathway of the pilgrim people of God.

However, though so positive, actually the saving work of God has a negative aspect: it looks back, it views that *from* which one has been saved.

Whilst the word *does* convey what the saints have been saved *for*, in reality the greater emphasis is upon what sinners have been saved *from*. The positive work implied in the word *salvation* is the saving and delivering work of the Saviour.

The negative aspect inherent in *salvation* stresses that which the Saviour overcame: it sees the vanquished foe, it beholds the broken prison walls, it views the fallen chains, the bars of iron broken asunder, and the gates of brass swinging wide.

Therefore one is saved *from* rather than *to* something. Of course salvation sets before the joyful soul the most delightful prospect, but *in itself* it views the way in which this was done: by the slaying of the foe; by the overcoming of every obstacle; and by deliverance from all dangers.

We are saved out of the hand of them that hate us; we are saved from our sins; we shall be saved from wrath through him.

All this looks back and records our enslaved state, the Saviour's conquering work, our being set free from the hand of the captor, and deliverance from the realm of bondage. *That* is salvation.

The sinner saved by grace rejoices in salvation and is overcome by love for the Saviour.

Salvation looks back and sees the thick darkness in the valley of the shadow of death, now at such distance behind, over against the radiant beams of the Light of life shining before one's face.

Salvation views the Saviour himself, who has opened blind eyes, caused the deaf to hear, the tongue to be loosed, the leper to be cleansed, the lame man to leap as an hart, and the dead to be raised to life.

8

But, overcome with love, salvation never for one moment forgets the incalculable price to the Saviour, forever testified in the five wounds engraved in his hands, feet, and side, mute witnesses of untold suffering.

The pre-eminence of *Salvation* is indicated by the frequency of its occurrence in both the old and new testaments.

In fact the Greek is virtually an equivalent meaning to the Hebrew form. In the new testament 'Salvation'–in its various grammatical variations–occurs some one hundred and ninety-one times, that is, in but twenty-seven books.

Twenty-seven books, the largest two having no more than twenty-eight chapters, the smallest four each being composed of no more than one single chapter. Taking the entire number, no less than seventeen books have less than ten chapters: yet in so small a compass *nearly two hundred occurrences of 'Salvation'*.

The first time that the old testament word *yeshuah*–salvation–occurs in scripture is in Genesis 49:18, when Jacob on his deathbed prophesies concerning each of his sons and their issue, namely, the twelve tribes of Israel.

In Genesis 49:1-17 he foretold the future of the first seven tribes. Then in verses 19-27 he prophesied concerning the remaining five.

Between these two prophecies there is a tiny parenthesis. In fact, seven words. They are not words referring to his sons, neither to their twelve tribes, nor are they addressed to any one of his offspring. They are words spoken by ancient–and dying–father Jacob to God himself.

The form of address, the very style, changes completely from what preceded, just as it is wholly different from what follows. It is a sudden interjection, apparently disconnected by the large prophecies that preceded and followed so small an interposition.

This heartfelt cry to God out of the depths of Israel's being broke out in the midst of his twelvefold prophecy: 'I have waited for thy *salvation*, O LORD', Genesis 49:18. Here is the first occurrence of *yeshuah*, *salvation*, in the old testament, and hence in the bible itself.

The chosen seed in righteous Abel, preserved in translated Enoch, brought through the flood in believing Noah, singularly manifest in the elect patriarchs Abraham and Isaac, found expression in the expiring breath of ancient Jacob.

'These all died in faith', records the epistle to the Hebrews: but *what* faith! In the twilight chapters of Genesis, just before the last rays fade from the first book of the bible, the old patriarch Jacob is gathered to his fathers.

Yes, but like them, with hope deferred, faith unfulfilled, the promise yet afar off, and the Saviour but a distant and heavenly vision: then, were they disconsolate? Was Jacob disappointed? Listen: 'I have *waited* for thy salvation, O LORD.'

Then, this is Israel's dying testimony. And if so – mark well – *the salvation for which he waited must be found after death, beyond the grave, and looked for in a better resurrection.*

Exactly the interpretation of the writer of the epistle to the Hebrews in the eleventh chapter. Salvation is seen on the other side of a river infinitely deeper than Jordan, and in a heavenly country immeasurably higher than the earthly inheritance of the land of Israel.

Jacob's dying interjection shows that the true seed of Abraham looked for – and looks for – a salvation not in this body, but from it; not in this world, but out of it; not in Canaan, but in glory; not in time, but in eternity.

Dying Israel waited – and, dead, would wait – for a Saviour not from Jerusalem below, but of a holy city all of translucent gold, glowing lambent with the glory of God and of the Lamb, which shall never pass away world without end. Amen.

In the very midst of Jacob's expiring moments he cries, 'I have waited for thy salvation, O LORD'.

Centred amidst his fleshly heirs, sadly having spoken of seven out of the twelve natural sons from his own loins, the old father with his dying breath bursts out with this expression, nothing to do with Dan, nor with Gad.

Indeed, neither had it the least connection with *any* of his fleshly children or their worldly inheritance.

Yet for all that, this is the true expression of Jacob's spiritual life and heavenly vision. Such words sprang from the inward work and divine hope of God in the inner man of dying Jacob.

Then, it is the outpouring of his interior life of faith. And, in the midst of the carnal and natural seed of the circumcised children of Israel, dying Jacob was conscious that the most had neither part nor lot in the matter.

Salvation is not in the course of nature to the children of Israel, the seed of Isaac and of Abraham: '*For they are not all Israel, which are of Israel*: neither, because they are the seed of Abraham, are they all children: but, In Isaac shall thy seed be called.

'That is'–meaning, the spiritual interpretation of *in Isaac shall thy seed be called*, is–'that is, They which are the children of the flesh, these are not the children of God: but the children of the promise are counted for the seed', Romans 9:6-8.

Then, salvation is neither in nor by the course of natural generation by birth of the seed of Abraham, Isaac, and Jacob.

But it is by grace to the spiritual Israel of God–irrespective of blood, or of the will of the flesh, or of the will of man–

a salvation freely bestowed upon the heirs of the faith of Abraham which he had yet being uncircumcised.

This elect seed of Abraham, of like precious faith with him, called out from both Jew and Gentile alike, is the true Israel in the sight of God.

No matter whatever age, whether circumcised or uncircumcised – because *these* are those whom Jacob encompassed when he cried, peering into the future on his deathbed, 'I have waited for thy salvation, O Lord'.

Although other Hebrew words have been translated 'Save', or 'Salvation' in the English bible, this is not desirable. In fact the word used by Jacob – *yeshuah* – embodies *the* central concept, together with two or three other variations in the same family of words.

Indeed, the name Joshua – from Jehovah and *yeshuah* combined – occurs some two hundred times, being rooted and grounded in the basic concept first uttered by dying Jacob: *yeshuah, salvation.*

It is a remarkable fact that, following on from Genesis 49:18, which gives the first occurrence of this group of words, the next most significant book appears to be the book of Judges.

If so, one of the first lessons to learn is that – quite to the contrary of natural sentiment or assumption – the character of a Saviour is in the nature of a Judge. Salvation is by judgment! Thus Israel was delivered. And thus the Saviour saves.

Above all, however – far beyond Judges – *the* experimental book on salvation is that of the Psalms, and certainly the words 'Save', 'Saviour', and 'Salvation' abound throughout the psalter.

Here is heard the cry for a Saviour, the prayer for the salvation of God, and the supplication to be saved. The psalms express the experiences preceding, the joy in receiving, and the thanks-giving following the experimental reception of supernatural, divine, and heavenly salvation.

Isaiah wonderfully foreshadows the Saviour and that salvation of the LORD for which Jacob–still–yearned so earnestly. The book is full of references, openings, and anticipations of the Saviour and of the saving grace of God.

This is so more than any other of the major prophets, although Jeremiah has much to foretell of a coming salvation. But then, major or minor, each in his measure, so is the case with all the prophets.

Like dying Jacob, every one of the prophets–with all the elect seed of Abraham in successive generations–waited for the salvation of the LORD, and for the coming Saviour.

'I have waited for thy salvation, O LORD', cried the patriarch, his feet upon the threshold of the grave, his soul between the portals of death, and his departure from this world and age lying just at hand.

And this is the cry taken up by all the prophets unto John the Baptist, prophesying, foretelling, prefiguring, and signifying the Saviour and the salvation for which the faithful looked from the beginning of the world.

That is, until the coming of John the Baptist, the forerunner, who was to go before the coming of Christ, straightway preparing the way of the LORD.

When John was but eight days old, his father Zacharias, filled with the Holy Ghost, prophesied of the fulfilment of the long-ings of the ancient patriarchs, the dawning cry in Abraham, the reiteration through Isaac, and the lingering yearning of Jacob:

13

'Blessed be the Lord God of Israel; for he hath visited and redeemed his people, and *hath raised up an horn of salvation* for us in the house of his servant David; as he spake by the mouth of his holy prophets, which have been since the world began', Luke 1:68-70.

This consummates the realization of all the waiting, through such long ages and over so many generations, even from time preceding that first moment in which the word *yeshuah* passed into the Word of God in the first book of the bible from the lips of his dying servant Israel: 'I have waited for thy *salvation*, O LORD.'

Now at last that salvation was at the threshold with the birth of the baptist forerunner, heralding the coming of the promised Messiah, purposed before the foundation of the world, and promised by the mouth of his holy prophets which have been since the world began.

Thus in the fulness of time there came to pass the birth of the Saviour, the one mediator between God and men, even Jesus Christ, there being none other name given among men whereby we must be saved.

'Thou shalt call his name JESUS: for he shall save his people from their sins', Matthew 1:21.

The name JESUS is the new testament equivalent of the old testament Hebrew, in which the divine name JEHOVAH was woven into one with the word *salvation*, YESHUAH, so as to make the Hebrew name JEHOSHUA, or, to transfer that to the Greek, JESUS.

How *this* name answers to Jacob's dying cry, 'I have waited for thy salvation'–*yeshuah*– 'O LORD'–*Jehovah*.

This first occurrence in the new testament shows that *the waiting was over*, salvation was to be fulfilled, and the deliverer had come forth out of Zion. 'Thou shalt call his name JESUS'–*Jehoshua*–'for he shall *save* his people from their sins.'

14

Then this is 'Jehovah salvation' indeed, for *he*, Jehovah, shall save *his*, Jehovah's, people from their sins. If so, not only was the Saviour of the LORD, but the Saviour *was* the LORD.

Hence Mary cries, 'My spirit hath rejoiced in *God* my Saviour', and the angel of the LORD reiterates 'Unto you is born this day in the city of David a Saviour, which is Christ *the Lord.*'

Thus it was that ancient Simeon, to whom it had been revealed by the Holy Ghost that he should not see death, till he had seen the Lord's Christ, coming into the temple, saw the infant Jesus being brought in by Joseph and Mary.

He took up the young child into his arms, even as he prayed, 'Lord, now lettest thou thy servant depart in peace, according to thy word: *for mine eyes have seen thy salvation.*'

Then, as saith the angel of the Lord, 'Unto you is born this day in the city of David a Saviour, which is Christ the Lord.'

A Saviour who can reach in the perfection of his humanity to mankind, for he 'is born this day'. A Saviour who can reach in the eternity of his divine Sonship to God, for he is 'God our Saviour'.

A Saviour who can bring guilty sinners to God, reaching to God and man in his one person, for 'he shall save his people from their sins'.

Hence that which declares his person and his work, that form of sound words, called the Evangel, is said to be 'the power of God unto *salvation*'.

For by the Saviour, through the evangel, God hath *saved* us, and called us with an holy calling, not according to our works, but according to his own purpose and grace, which was given us in Christ Jesus before the world began.

This is now made manifest by the appearing of our *Saviour Jesus Christ*, who hath abolished death, and brought life and immortality to light through the evangel.

How shall we escape if we neglect so great salvation? For God our Saviour, even Christ the Lord, has become the author of *eternal salvation* unto all that obey him.

For the grace of God that *bringeth salvation* hath appeared to all men, teaching us that, denying ungodliness and worldly lusts, we should live soberly, righteously, and godly, in this present world.

And not only so, but earnestly looking for that blessed hope, and the glorious appearing of *the great God and our Saviour Jesus Christ*, who gave himself for us, that he might redeem us from all iniquity.

Jesus Christ is the long-awaited Saviour: he who saves us from our sins, and delivers us from the wrath to come, who is even now in heaven, 'from whence also we look for the Saviour'.

For Christ was once offered to bear the sins of many; and unto them that look for him shall he appear the second time *without sin unto salvation.*

This refers to the second coming of Christ, up until which he must reign, that is, in heavenly glory, until all his enemies be made his footstool. Then he shall come again to bring in their everlasting destruction.

But these, his enemies, are *our* enemies, and, if so, *those from whom we must be delivered, if we are to be saved.* This deliverance is called, The Salvation of God.

When Christ comes again in judgment, and when, all his enemies destroyed, he creates all things new in the glorious inheritance of the saints, those myriads who have been saved by grace, raised from the dead, transported to glory, cry with one accord:

'Salvation to our God which sitteth upon the throne, and unto the Lamb', Revelation 7:10.

Through the salvation of God, and of their Saviour Jesus Christ, all their enemies were overcome, and they became overcomers. By grace, through faith, they were saved from every one of their foes, and from all the calamities and tribulations that beset them upon their earthly pilgrimage.

Then, to grasp the *nature* of salvation, every enemy and adversity that stands in the way of being saved must be discerned, the Saviour must be revealed in his victory, and the resultant salvation of God must be applied experimentally.

And who is sufficient for these things? But our sufficiency is of God.

By the sending of able ministers of the new testament, each and every one of the hidden spiritual and invisible enemies and obstacles is clearly revealed in the preaching of the word of God.

And so is the victory of the Saviour over all, that by the ministry of the Spirit this victory is conveyed to the believing heart. 'This is the victory that overcometh the world, even our faith', I John 5:4.

Then it is a solemn charge incumbent upon the ambassadors of Christ to enumerate all that stands in the way of the salvation of the sinner, besides enlarging by the Holy Ghost upon the victory of the Saviour.

'This is a faithful saying, and worthy of all acceptation, that Christ Jesus came into the world *to save sinners.*'

'Neither is there salvation in any other.' But salvation from what? Salvation from whom? The truth of the evangel reveals and makes this otherwise incomprehensible reality known, and makes it known to the lost.

Then, following this, there appears the revelation of Jesus
Christ as Saviour, the salvation of God being applied spiritually
and experimentally to the heart of every one of those brought
to saving faith.

This gives deliverance to all who are brought to know and
feel their bondage to sin, Satan, and the judgment of the wrath
to come.

It is these enemies and adversities that the following pages
proceed to open and expound in order, and from which the
Saviour frees every single one brought of God to cry by faith for
salvation: 'for there is none other name under heaven given
among men, whereby we must be saved.'

PART ONE

SALVATION FROM SIN

PART ONE

SALVATION FROM SIN

I
Wilful Sins

'THIS is a faithful saying, and worthy of all acceptation, that Christ Jesus came into the world to save sinners; of whom'–saith Paul–'I am chief', I Timothy 1:15.

He calls himself the chief of sinners? But he is Paul the apostle, formerly Saul of Tarsus, who had lived according to the straitest sect of the Jewish religion, a Pharisee: 'touching the righteousness which is in the law, blameless.' Then what does he mean by describing himself in such terms?

He does not mean that he was, or had been, a criminal. Criminals break the laws of society. But Saul of Tarsus did not. He does not mean that he was, or had been, an outcast. Outcasts are rejected by society. But Saul of Tarsus was not. Then how can he be–or have been–the chief of sinners?

Because he means *religious* sinners. These are the worst, in the sight of God. And Saul of Tarsus had been the worst of these.

But one may object, But his life, and the lives of the religious, are so pure! Yes, and whited sepulchres are equally pure. But what is inside? *Death* is inside. And as to religious sinners, God saith, 'Their throat is an open sepulchre'.

Then, there can be nothing but putrefaction and death *within*. And this, despite the whitened outward appearance.

Another may object, But the speech of Saul of Tarsus, and the speech of the religious, is so pious. But God saith, 'This people honoureth me with their lips, but their heart is far from me.'

Yet a further person may complain, But Paul was of the stock of Israel, an Hebrew of the Hebrews, circumcised the eighth day, a Jew indeed!

To which God answers, 'He is not a Jew, which is one outwardly; neither is that circumcision, which is outward in the flesh: but he is a Jew, which is one inwardly; and circumcision is that of the heart, in the spirit, and not in the letter; whose praise is not of men, but of God.'

One who is inwardly dead in the sight of God, yet professes a veneer of religion in the sight of man, is worse to God than any criminal or outcast. And of these worst, Saul of Tarsus was the worst of all: 'the chief of sinners.' Nevertheless, he found mercy. Or rather, mercy found him. How?

Blind to the spiritual revelation of Jesus Christ; void of faith; a stranger to love; having a false hope; hating the doctrine of Christ in the evangel; at enmity against God's people, *towards God Saul was dead, blind, and in thick darkness.*

But not in his own eyes, no, nor even in his own conscience: to himself, his zeal for God marked him out as exemplary. But afterwards, he discovered himself to have been 'the chief of sinners'.

Hating the true disciples of Christ as the epitome of the enemies of true religion, fuming with persecuting zeal on the Damascus road, suddenly a light above the brightness of the sun shone round about him.

Out of the midst of that unbearable brightness came a voice. Too blinding and intense to see the heavenly speaker, all that could be seen was the effulgent glory shining from the person who spake. Who was it? *'I am Jesus whom thou persecutest.'*

This was the unapproachable light of Christ, radiating from his person in the heavenly glory.

And the voice was that of Jesus, whom Saul persecuted in his own true disciples, for their holding fast and confessing Jesus to be the Son of God, the Saviour, loving and obeying the truth of Christ in the evangel.

And as it was then, so it is now. Uniquely, Saul saw and heard without. But we who are saved together with Saul see and hear within. 'Blessed are they that have not seen, and yet have believed.'

The brightness of Jesus' glory so exceeded in light that his person could not–and cannot–be made out for the shining of his radiance. But his voice, sounding from that light, was unmistakable: 'My sheep hear my voice.' *That* stopped Saul of Tarsus. *To condemn him?* No. *To save him!*

Saul did nothing. Up to that very second, he was raging and fuming against Jesus Christ, his evangel, and his disciples. *Then Christ did it all.* 'And the grace of our Lord was exceeding abundant with faith and love which is in Christ Jesus', I Timothy 1:14.

Now *this* is to experience salvation from sin, though the sinner was once completely blind to the nature of those sins so obnoxious to the wrath of God. Nevertheless, 'Christ Jesus came into the world to save sinners', I Timothy 1:15.

For he *shall* save his people from their sins. Save them from the guilt of them; save them from the power of them; and save them from the presence of them.

Yes, but what does the word of God, the testimony of Jesus, the witness of the Holy Ghost, and the doctrine of the apostles, mean by sin?

With the figures and types of the old testament, in the sin offering and the trespass offering, sins were either against God, or against man. The priest must judge as to whether they were done wittingly, or in ignorance.

Judge, that is, unless it should be the intended, blatant, wilful rebellion of the unforgivable sin, the great transgression. That was condemned already. Then, there remained no more sacrifice for sins.

However, the offerings were but a figure of the offering up of Christ on the behalf of sinners, so as to take away their sins by bearing them in his own body on the tree.

Whether those sins were against God or man, or done wittingly or unwittingly. For with the coming of the Saviour Jesus Christ, the Son of God, the shadows fled away, and the true substance, salvation itself, finally appeared.

There is a sin unto death, and there is an unforgivable sin. Notwithstanding in the new testament remission of sins is preached in the name of Jesus Christ.

First by the apostles, then, according to the apostles' doctrine, by those called of God, sent of Christ, and anointed by the Holy Ghost, to proclaim free salvation through the forgiveness of sins, to sinners bound under guilt.

To such souls the Saviour is revealed of God, and the salvation of God by Jesus Christ is proclaimed as the jubilee of deliverance and liberty experimentally to their hearts.

There are a number of words which describe sin or sins in various manifestations in the scriptures, such as Offence; Fall; Trespass; Iniquity; Transgression; Uncleanness; Defilement; Error; Rebellion; Debt; Fault; Unrighteousness; and Perversity.

That is, among other aspects of sin which genders the wrath of God, such as, for example, Carnality; Unbelief; Worldliness, and so on.

All these should be searched out with profit in the Hebrew and Greek respectively, and the soul's experience examined in the light which now shines from heaven.

This reveals whether such ills and iniquities have been discovered by the conviction which comes from God, and, in consequence, been forgiven and purged by the spiritual revelation of the Saviour disclosed so as to deliver from all iniquity.

This being so, and it is necessarily so, then it follows that 'he that hath this hope in him purifieth himself, even as he is pure', and 'the path of the just is as the shining light, that shineth more and more unto the perfect day'.

Nevertheless, since 'He shall save his people from their sins' and 'Christ Jesus came into the world to save sinners', and since 'Salvation from Sin' is the present question, attention is now to be focused upon the meaning of the central word for 'sin' in the new testament.

The Greek *hamartia* is that which the Holy Ghost singles out to give the essential meaning. This word occurs—together with its cognate forms—on some two hundred and sixty-nine occasions. In itself alone, the single word *hamartia* appears about one hundred and seventy-four times.

The origin of this word is associated with the throwing of a spear or javelin, or the shooting of an arrow. That is, when the aim is faulty and results in failure. It misses the mark.

Then, here are four factors: First, the aim taken. Next, the throw made. Third, the arc described by the flight. Last, the striking short of, aside from, or beyond the target.

This concept appears to have been at the heart of the original Greek in the word *hamartia*, which became expanded in general use whenever and wherever the figure applied.

In the Greek of the new testament *hamartia* is applied to two realms. Firstly, the will: to sin, to do wrong, to err. Secondly, the word may mean sin itself, the constitutional state of mankind in the Fall.

The grammatical form, and the context in which the word is used, determine the precise meaning. Firstly, as to the action of the will, 'to miss the mark, to err, to be guilty of wrong'. Secondly, 'a condition or state': born in sin, John 9:34; die in sin, John 8:21; be made sin, II Corinthians 5:21.

To take first the use of *hamartia*, '*to miss the mark, err, to sin*', in relation to the action–or classes of action–of the will, it is necessary to lay down certain premises.

For example, there must be obligation. Such volitions are obligatory, not optional. Then, the ground of obligation should be clarified. Next, from obligation, accountability necessarily follows. In the nature of obligation, an account must be rendered, for good or ill.

Finally, it is essential to understand the classes of action of the will, and that in every instance these are voluntary and not involuntary, intended and not necessitated.

Man in his nature is both responsible and accountable. That is, constitutionally he is *obliged* both to God and his fellows.

Obligation is inherent in his nature: human nature. If so, man in his being has light, and light shines upon his being.

To this light, his *will* is obliged to respond according to the utmost of his capacity, and that both continually and increasingly. Failure to do this is to miss the mark.

The light which is within the being of mankind is set forth in Romans 1:19. 'That which may be known of God is manifest *in* them.'

This refers to an interior light in the consciousness, the light from God which shines within: this is '*manifest* in them'. However denied, ridiculed, or abused, it can never quite be extinguished.

Undeniable in childhood, though wilfully ignored for a lifetime, its flickering candle shall surely flare again through the darkness at the last, a grim reminder at death of the long abuse and denial of 'that which may be known of God', virtually from the cradle to the grave.

'That which may be known of God' which 'is manifest' in human nature, is both constitutional and inherent.

It is the inward light of consciousness, of which God bears witness to man, saying that it is 'the work of the law'–not the law: the *work* of it–'written in their hearts, their conscience also bearing witness, and their thoughts the meanwhile accusing or else excusing one another', Romans 2:15.

The inward manifestation of 'that which may be known of God' appears in the interior of the soul as the first truths which dawn with the awareness of reason, obligation, and accountability.

Here is an interior light that glows deep in the conscious awareness. It is not reasoned or thought out: it *is*; just as one's being *exists*. Moreover, whether one will or not, it is reflected in the conscience.

This light manifests that God is; that he has rights; that one is under absolute obligation to him and his rights to render that which is due to him. Equally, one's fellows have rights, and that these place one under obligation to fulfil those rights, both to the individual and to all humanity.

Moreover, it is written in the heart that life does not cease with death; that eternity does not terminate with time; that one is accountable; that there will be a day of reckoning; that in that day one will be called to account for the volitions and deeds willed and done in the body.

From this light come the questionings of the troubled soul in the dawning of awareness: What am I? Who am I? Where am I from? Where am I going? What is death? What is beyond death? Who is God? Where is God? How may God be known?

These first truths—as it were a dimly flickering candle in the dark obscurity of the consciousness—provide the first glimmering light that awakens such troubled questionings. This is what is manifest deep in the interior soul of man: it is 'that which may be known of God.'

Moreover the light which is of God shines *upon*—as well as *within*—the being of mankind. The first was subjective. This, the last, is objective: 'For the invisible things of him from the creation of the world are clearly seen, being understood by the things that are made, even his eternal power and Godhead', Romans 1:20.

Consider the creation of the heavens and the earth. Consider the infinite variety discernible by touch: what range of substances! What varied textures! By taste: how abundant and bewildering are the flavours savoured by the tongue!

By scent: how diverse are the scents of the wood, the field, the river, the sea, the habitations of man, the range in food and drink, the scent peculiar to differing birds and animals—and how keen *their* nose to detect them—even within a given breed.

By sight: the firmament, the stars and planets above; the clouds in such diversity; sunset and sunrise, rain and shine, the mountains and hills, the earth and field, the woods and deserts, the seas and rivers; the form of things, of man and beast, of faces and features; of colour and shade: What multiplicity!

And what of sound? The range of octaves, below, across, and above what may be audible to man. Yet, if only within his range, from a whisper to the crash of thunder; from the mighty waves to the gentle ripples; the multitudinous sound of voices, instruments, movements.

The wind in the trees, the falling rain, the cry of bird and of beast: Oh, what a plenitude of sound across so vast a range, beyond tongue to tell.

And this is not to mention the faculties in man to receive such phenomenal expressions of the Creator: the eye; the ear; the tongue; the fingers; the nose: priceless recipients of 'the things that are made' all declaring his eternal power and Godhead.

Nor is this to speak of man created in the image of God: of humanity; of birth; of life: what gifts, withal the senses, reason, intelligence, sensibility, and faculties, I say, what gifts to evoke constant and overwhelming thankfulness!

And will ungodly men ascribe all this to *chance*? Impossible: for all these, in the creation and in the things that are made, plainly declare 'his eternal power and Godhead'.

No other explanation is credible than that of a Creator of omniscience, omnipotence, and omnipresence, beyond all comprehension, yet evident in all his works past the least scintilla of doubt.

And what of space: if once one *could* reach beyond the blue to the limits of infinity, What lies beyond? Then, the infinite—since it *must* exist—lies utterly outside the grasp of man, but yet subsists within the creation of God.

Of time: what was before time? What is beyond time? Eternity: but this is beyond man; then, it pertains to the Godhead.

What of matter? From whence did it come, that is so bewildering in its unsearchable forms? God created it: this is so *obvious*; How else could it *be*?

He upholds all things by the word of his power; How else is it upheld? the earth in space, the orbit of the earth, its revolutions upon the axis, countless myriad of infinitely small particles all in incessant motion: What explanation exists save 'his eternal power and Godhead'?

What of movement? Of life itself in such superabundant variety, of living movements, of the movement of the universe, of heavenly bodies, of terrestrial, in land and of it; or celestial, in heaven and about it, in the sky and throughout it? Countless varied movements, each unique to its order.

Why, take just the tongue, and all the movement–bewildering!– involved in one's own speech, let alone that of all mankind, besides every creature, withal the movement in growth of every kind of vegetation. All this is astounding beyond measure, past comprehension, save for 'his eternal power and Godhead'.

What obligation this witness lays upon man to remember now his Creator in the days of his youth, that in old age he shall not depart from it.

But man chooses to forget; man *would* depart from it, as scripture testifies:

'They are without excuse: because that, when they knew God'– both by subjective witness and objective testimony–'they glorified him not as God, neither were thankful; but became vain in their imaginations, and their foolish heart was darkened.

'Professing themselves to be wise, they became fools, and changed the glory of the uncorruptible God into an image made like to corruptible man', Romans 1:20-23.

Of how many is this written? It is universal. Then what is the word of God in such a case? It is that man is without excuse, having failed utterly in his obligation, accountability, and liability. Now, *this* is to miss the mark with a witness, and to do so wholly, continuously, and voluntarily.

If so, the account remains to be rendered to and by such penurious debtors, constituting the whole of mankind, not only collectively, but, one by one, individually.

Vast debts have accumulated over a lifetime of failed obligations both to God and man, and these will and must be paid when man is called to account at the last judgment. This is called 'the day of wrath and revelation of the righteous judgment of God', Romans 2:5.

It is the day in which God 'will render to every man according to his deeds', Romans 2:6. The judgment of God is according to truth: in that day guilty men should and must be brought to account for all their ungodly living and unrighteous deeds which they had committed during their lifetime in this present world.

The eyes of the Judge, as a flame of fire, burn through all pretence and superfluous appearance, exposing the reality from which they had utterly shielded themselves throughout their existence on earth.

The sentence of the Judge will bring to light all hidden things 'in the day when God shall judge the secrets of men by Jesus Christ according to my gospel', Romans 2:16.

The sharp two-edged sword, which is in his hand, cuts and pierces through soul and spirit–for this sword is spiritual–joints and marrow, revealing the thoughts and intents of the heart. This is judgment that is according to truth with a witness.

The day of wrath and revelation of the righteous judgment of God is that tremendous day in which he will render to every man according to his deeds, Romans 2:5,6. It is called the day of the Lord; the last day; the day of judgment; the day of resurrection; the day of wrath; the day of vengeance; and the great day.

It is the day appointed in which God shall judge the world in righteousness by that man whom he hath ordained, whereof he hath given assurance unto all men, in that he hath raised him from the dead.

Then, this lies beyond the present life, after death, by resurrection, when the works and lives of men will be brought into judgment according to the righteousness of God, who will, as Judge, render unto men according to their deeds, Romans 2:6.

The word 'render' indicates that the judgment is not arbitrary. It is not a sentence that is beyond the sinner's comprehension. The Judge does not conjure up a judgment: sinners themselves will have provided the cause of that judgment by their own lives on earth.

The Judge assesses and weighs nothing other than that life against the rule of law and the work of the law written in the heart, dispassionately passing the sentence accordingly. This is the function of a judge. Not to have mercy, but to pass judgment.

As to appeal, the time for appeal will have passed. Agreeable to what was sown, the sentence will be pronounced on what is raised up: for whatsoever a man soweth, that shall he also reap.

The word 'render' means To give back, to requite; to repay a claim, to discharge an obligation. God gave to man his being: God maintains in man his breath. And shall man not requite him? Mankind would not own the knowledge of God, neither would render what was owed to him, nor yet requite him his due.

Neither yet did men fulfil their obligations to their fellows: and for this also they must give an account, and pay the price accordingly.

Now God is to judge in righteousness. Right, inherent in God's nature and attributes, requires that God should judge. His character obliges him to judge, and to judge in righteousness. 'Shall not the Judge of all the earth do right?'

Then, he will render to every man according to his deeds, without respect of persons. God shall requite them.

But what shall he requite? What shall he judge? Sins, yes, but what does this mean? Does it refer to base outward actions? Yes it does, but it refers to much, much more.

There are those outward actions which are obvious sins, so that they are called as much by the generality of mankind.

Hence Paul teaches, 'Know ye not that the unrighteous shall not inherit the kingdom of God? Be not deceived: neither fornicators, nor idolaters, nor adulterers, nor effeminate, nor abusers of themselves with mankind, nor thieves, nor covetous, nor drunkards, nor revilers, nor extortioners, shall inherit the kingdom of God', I Corinthians 6:9,10.

The apostle likewise declares in Ephesians 5:3-7: 'But fornication, and all uncleanness, or covetousness, let it not be once named among you, as becometh saints; neither filthiness, nor foolish talking, nor jesting, which are not convenient: but rather giving of thanks.

'For this ye know, that no whoremonger, nor unclean person, nor covetous man, who is an idolater, hath any inheritance in the kingdom of Christ and of God. Let no man deceive you with vain words: for because of these things cometh the wrath of God upon the children of disobedience.'

Yes, because these are sins. These outward actions are sins. They are lawless and disobedient, they are the outward actions of ungodly sinners: of the unholy, profane, murderers of fathers and mothers, menslayers, whoremongers, them that defile themselves with mankind, menstealers, liars, perjurers, and such like.

Now, these are obvious sins, of which the sober majority of men would disapprove.

But Paul goes further in Romans 1:29-31 concerning those outward actions which God shall judge: unrighteousness, fornication, wickedness, covetousness, maliciousness; envy, murder, debate, deceit, malignity, whispering, backbiting, hating God;

Spite, pride, boasting, inventing evil things; disobedience to parents, having no understanding, covenantbreaking, being without natural affection, implacable, and unmerciful.

These outward actions, and, indeed, all the hateful propensities mentioned, are manifest in the behaviour of the sinners concerned. That is, manifest in outward actions and exterior behaviour. For these the wrath of God comes upon sinners.

But from whence do such things arise? Jesus tells you: 'There is nothing from without a man, that entering into him can defile him: but the things which come out of him, those are they that defile the man', Mark 7:15.

Then, all those outward actions, and all that exterior behaviour, disapproved of men in sinners, come from *within* them.

And so Jesus teaches: 'For from within, out of the heart of men, proceed evil thoughts, adulteries, fornications, murders, thefts, covetousness, wickedness, deceit, lasciviousness, an evil eye, blasphemy, pride, foolishness: all these evil things come from within, and defile the man', Mark 7:21-23.

However, that heart from which all these things proceed, is common to all men, not just to those who without restraint allow what is within to break forth outwardly.

From fear of man, or constraint of religion, what moves *within* – that breaks forth outwardly in gross sinners – is no less existent in the interior for being externally checked and prevented.

But *it is that which is within that gives rise to the outward action.* Before God, it is the *interior motive and volition* that comes into judgment rather than the action itself.

For from the like evil heart other sins proceed that are even more obnoxious to the wrath of God. Yet, being deceitful in appearance, these blind the eyes so much that they are approved of and admired by men.

Then, neither the obvious worthlessness nor the apparent worthiness of outward actions gives to either their true character, but the interior spring of such actions – of each class – alone determines the assessment of the Judge.

In the judgment of God it is not the outward action but the inward intention – irrespective of exterior appearances – that gives to every word and deed, habit and trend, direction and course, the real character that is its due.

Because it is the inward determination of the will, the interior intention, that in fact generates every outward action, and therefore reveals the real character behind the appearance *even when ostensibly this seems to do and be good, or is approved of as religious before men.*

This is precisely what Jesus taught in the so-called 'Sermon on the Mount'. Of old time by the law murder brought the killer into judgment; 'but I say unto you, that whosoever is angry with his brother without a cause shall be in danger of the judgment.'

Why? Because, first, murder proceeds from anger, and, second, even when outwardly restrained and inhibited or when fear of the consequences prevents that inward anger and hatred from coming to fruition, *God still counts it as murder by judging the issue of the heart's intention.*

Again. Of old, adultery–the lying with another man's wife– was utterly condemned. But though the lust which begat that wickedness were denied or suppressed, still, *the intention is as condemned of God as the act.*

'But I say unto you, whosoever looketh on a wife'–Tyndale, Great Bible, and the Bishops' Bible were all correct: it should be *wife*, the *wife* of another–'to lust after her hath committed adultery with her already in his heart.'

The truth is, all that prevented either murder or adultery was the fear of man, the love of a good appearance, the dread of the consequences, or the shame of being found out afterwards. But these constraints do not count before God as less guilty than if one had broken through them and committed the deed itself.

Indeed, by intending it, but not executing it for mere selfish reasons, the guilt of the actual deed is not only imputed as if one *had* committed the sin, but it is actually increased by the hypocrisy of the restraint. For the inward state and desire was as vile as that of those outwardly culpable of the act itself.

Thus in the case of what is professed to be the worship of God, though it should appear to be genuine to all appearances, yet in reality this is very often motivated by nothing other than a desire to make a vain show before man.

Hence the Saviour gives several instances where apparently holy deeds are in fact really deceitful sins in the sight of God.

For example, 'take heed that ye do not your alms before men, to be seen of them: otherwise ye have no reward of your Father which is in heaven.' No, their reward is to be seen and admired of men on earth. As to heaven, the judgment went against them as hypocritical sinners in reality.

Why? Because such hypocrites merely use the name and worship of God to gratify their own inward lust for applause from men. And that is reckoned against them as a sin of the highest degree in the day of judgment, according to the Lord Jesus.

Likewise Jesus said, 'When thou prayest, thou shalt not be as the hypocrites: for they love to pray standing in the synagogues and in the corners of the streets, that they may be seen of men. Verily I say unto you, They have their reward.'

Yes, and their judgment also, for in them is fulfilled the petition of David, 'When he shall be judged, let him be condemned: and let his prayer become sin', Psalm 109:7. And the wise man concludes, 'even his prayer shall be abomination', Proverbs 28:9.

Again, as to fasting: 'Moreover when ye fast, be not, as the hypocrites, of a sad countenance: for they disfigure their faces, that they may appear unto men to fast. Verily I say unto you, They have their reward.'

Yes, in the satisfaction of having gained the praise of man.

But their reward from God is judgment upon their presumptuous and hypocritical sin in the last day. For, 'the hypocrite's hope shall perish', Job 8:13, and 'the joy of the hypocrite [is] but for a moment', Job 20:5, because 'the hypocrites in heart heap up wrath', Job 36:13.

Whence it follows that outward actions spring from immediate inward resolutions, which alone give the actions their true character, no matter what the appearances.

Moreover, just as outward actions are governed by immediate inward intentions, so those resolutions also take their rise from a deeper form of volition.

This deeper volition is the proximate intention which rules over every immediate issue of the will.

So that the sinning hypocrite does not sin *once* in his alms-giving, prayer, and fasting; nor does he sin *intermittently* in these things: a deeper underlying choice or voluntary intention ensures that he is both *constant and consistent* in all that he does in his lifetime to gratify his desire for the applause of man.

This is the voluntary choice of the required means to an end.

Here is a deep-rooted intention always to gratify self by the means of religion, and, indeed, in effect attempting to bring in God and man to serve the gratification of self as the end and purpose of one's being. It is *this* that is the whole of sin, properly so-called.

This deepest intention of the will—therefore of wilfulness—is abundantly illustrated, though by no means confined to, the example of the Pharisees, and is clearly exemplified by Jesus in his doctrine, which finds its application in all those professing religion till the end of the world.

'Woe unto you, scribes and Pharisees, hypocrites! for ye are as graves which appear not, and the men that walk over them are not aware of them', Luke 11:44. Here the outward appearance is nothing. Nor, even, comparatively, the immediate intention of the will which gives rise to it.

But—like the hidden grave—buried deep down within, lies death. Nothing but death. Inwardly, the man is nothing but a rotten and rotting corpse, in the all-penetrating sight of the just judgment of God.

Again, 'Woe unto you, scribes and Pharisees, hypocrites! for ye make clean the outside of the cup and of the platter, but within they are full of extortion and excess', Matthew 23:25. Yes, outwardly, concerning the righteousness which is in the law, these hypocrites are blameless, washed clean and sparkling white.

By this men are utterly deceived. Because they do not see within. But God does, and judges their using his name and worship to live for their own gratification as a ruling intention, to be not only sinful and filthy, but utterly abominable in his sight.

Once more, 'Woe unto you, scribes and Pharisees, hypocrites! for ye are like unto whited sepulchres, which indeed appear beautiful outward, but are within full of dead men's bones, and of all uncleanness. Even so ye also outwardly appear righteous unto men, but within ye are full of hypocrisy and iniquity', Matthew 23:27,28.

This exposure points not merely to the immediate intention, but to the proximate resolution: they are *resolved* to make God and religion the means by which they gratify their lust for the applause of men *as a ruling principle.*

It underlies their *choice of career.* Self-gratification is their voluntarily *chosen lifestyle.* And Jesus calls this inward volition *hypocrisy and iniquity*, for all the fair appearance to the contrary.

Yet for all the foregoing, neither the immediate intention nor the proximate resolution lie at the very heart of the wilful sinning to which man gives himself, judged aright in the inward parts.

The former reveal that man is given up to both the ways and the means of self-gratification: that form of selfishness which is the whole of sin.

Nevertheless, the voluntary intention to *live as the end of one's existence* for selfish gratification manifests the ultimate intention of both nature and being.

That is, the resolution of the heart and will to exist for self-gratification as the end for which one exists, God and man being used as the subservient means to that supreme purpose to which the life is yielded.

This is utter selfishness, the antithesis of which is love. The one is the *essence* of sinning; the other is the *heart* of benevolence.

Nowhere is this made more clear than in I John 3:4-6 once this is translated correctly: 'Every one that practises sin also practises lawlessness, and sin is lawlessness. And ye know that he was manifested, that he might take away our sins, and in him sin is not.

'Anyone that abides in him sins not. Anyone that sins has not seen him, nor known him.'

This accurate translation is taken from Bagster's Englishman's Greek New Testament, 1877.

It is unquestionable that John refers to the *will* when he refers to sin in I John 3:4-6. But it is the will at a depth beyond that even remotely considered by the vast majority.

It is not the immediate motive and volition which gives rise to outward actions to which the apostle points. Nor is it the underlying proximate resolution which generates and gives rise to every such motive and immediate volition.

I John 3:4-6 refers to the ultimate intention, the hidden man of the heart, that determination of the innermost will and deepest volition, profound and constant, governing the course and end of the life, *and giving character to every other class of action of the will.*

This direction of the life—as the flight of an arrow or javelin—determines the aim, course, and end of existence.

It is *this* that is God's measure of sin: one either *does* sin, or else one *does* righteousness, *as an end of being, of existence, of the interior course and inward direction of the life.*

There are no alternatives; and there can be no mixture.

Nothing is clearer from I John 3:4-10 than that *one cannot do two things at once.*

Either one *does* sin, or else one *does* righteousness. Then, it is a matter of the will. And if so, at its very source and heart. It is the *ultimate* aim and intention of existence.

To summarize: The *doing* of sin clearly indicates the action of the will: it is wilful; lawless; and voluntary: one *wills* it. There are three classes of wilful or voluntary action. First, that which precipitates outward action; next, that which determines interior resolution; finally, that which governs the ultimate intention.

These three classes of the action of the will are harmonized and united respectively, taking rise from the deepest, most inward spring, namely, the ultimate intention. This gives character and direction to *everything* else.

In the judgment of God sin is not measured by outward appearances and actions, whether base or–apparently–virtuous. Ultimately, it is the innermost *intention* of the will that gives rise to outward actions.

Then *that* is what the judgment will discern. No matter what the appearances of exterior deeds and works, the actions of the will, each springing in turn from the interior resolution, where still deeper lies the ultimate intention of the life.This gives to *everything* its real and determined character.

And that character is one. There is no question of some good and some bad in the ultimate intention of the same person: 'he that practises righteousness is righteous, even as he is righteous. He that practises sin is of the devil', I John 3:7,8. It is black and white: no mixture is possible. It is all one or all the other.

The sin in this place, though voluntary, does not refer to gross outward actions, 'a' sin or 'some' sins. It is, by definition, 'missing the mark'. *Because of the determined ultimate intention of the heart.* That is 'practising sin'. It is *this* that God judges.

And his judgment finds it *always and in every case* to be continuous and constant, without intermission, irrespective of appearances or feelings to the contrary. It is both the aim and the direction to which the life is dedicated.

'Doth a fountain send forth at the same place sweet water and bitter?' No: that is impossible. If the spring is sweet at source, all is sweet in the flowing forth of its waters. If the source is bitter, of necessity all the water that issues from it must be tainted with bitterness.

'Can the fig tree, my brethren, bear olive berries? either a vine, figs? so can no fountain both yield salt water and fresh', James 3:11,12.

Wherefore observe that I John 3:7,8 presents *two entirely separate, distinct, and diametrically opposed practices, or doings, of two radically different persons*. One practises, does, or commits righteousness, and is represented *as doing so consistently and perpetually*. The other practises, does, or commits sin, and is represented *as doing so consistently and perpetually*.

There are no other classes of persons than these two, respectively. None other exists, or has ever existed, since the foundation of the world, nor will till its dissolution.

This is precisely what Jesus taught in his doctrine. 'The people were astonished at his doctrine: for he taught them as one having authority, and not as the scribes.'

At the heart of his doctrine Jesus taught 'The light of the body is the eye: if therefore thine eye be single, thy whole body shall be full of light. But if thine eye be evil, thy whole body shall be full of darkness', Matthew 6:22.

And again, 'A good tree cannot bring forth evil fruit, neither can a corrupt tree bring forth good fruit', Matthew 7:18.

Nothing could be more clear. On the one hand – say, the right hand – man is given exclusively to the practice of righteousness, judged by the ultimate intention of the heart. Here are Christ's sheep.

On the other hand – the left hand – the entire remainder of mankind is given wholly to the practice of sin, judged by the ultimate, most interior, and fixed resolution of the will. These are called the goats.

The one lives in and for interior and pure benevolence; the other exists in total inward selfishness.

So that mankind *either* gives himself entirely to the practice of righteousness, *or* to the practice of self-gratification, that is, to the practice of sin, *as the end of being.* Consistently and continually.

This has nothing to do with outward actions; or with the processes of the will leading to those actions; or with the choice of ways and means by which the end of one's existence is realized; *it has to do wholly with the ultimate intention.*

Of necessity this is either wholly benevolent, fixed upon the love of God and the good of man as the end of being; or it is wholly selfish, given to self-gratification as the reason for existence, no matter by what means – religious or otherwise – that this gratification is fulfilled.

There are no, but no, absolutely no alternatives. Moreover the two – the practice of righteousness or the practice of sin – cannot, but cannot, absolutely cannot subsist together in the same person.

It must be one or the other. Sheep or goats; just or unjust; saints or sinners; righteous or unrighteous; elect or reprobate; good or bad.

Call them what you will. But, in the judgment of God, *character* determines the one or the other of the only two classes of humanity that exist in the eyes of him that is appointed to judge the quick and the dead.

The one character is formed by faith, so that 'as he is, so are we in this world'. This is to eat the flesh of the Son of man, and to drink his blood, just as it is to be possessed of eternal life. It is to abide in Christ, in the law of the Spirit of life which is in Christ Jesus.

It is to hear the voice of the Son continually say of the Father: 'I have declared unto them thy name, and will declare it: that the love wherewith thou hast loved me may be in them, and I in them.' And how could *this* ever issue in *less* than the practice of righteousness 'even as he is righteous', I John 3:7?

But he that practises sin is of the devil. If so, this is the bad tree, which cannot *but* bring forth bad fruit, and nothing other than bad fruit, and that continuously. This is the corrupt fountain, that can issue in nothing save bitter water, in one continuous flow. This is the evil eye, whose light is darkness, that fills the whole body full of darkness.

Here the heart, the ultimate intention of the being, the end resolution of the life, is set upon self-gratification by whatever means. Selfishness is the reason for the existence of this class of person.

This is the whole of sin, and such persons do nothing but sin. It is to sin indeed. This is sin in its essence. It is sin from the very heart. This is 'to miss the mark' as widely as the mark can be missed.

In the pursuit of the ultimate intention of the heart, the unrighteous may often confess Christ; but they never possess him.

To fulfil that gratification upon which their heart is set, it may well please them to seek him; but they shall not find him. 'Ye shall seek me, and shall not find me: and where I am, thither ye cannot come', John 7:34.

'For he is not a Jew'–nor a Christian–'which is one outwardly; neither is that circumcision'–nor baptism; nor breaking of bread– 'which is outward in the flesh: but he is a Jew'–or a Christian– 'which is one inwardly; and circumcision'–or baptism; or communion–'is that of the heart, in the spirit, and not in the letter; whose praise is not of men, but of God', Romans 2:28,29.

But those who are outward Christians, whose trust is in the form of godliness without the power, in outward performances without inward regeneration, these hide among the sheep, but the end of their existence, that for which they live, declares them to be goats.

They profess to believe, but it is not 'like precious faith', or 'the faith of God's elect', it is the faith of devils: 'the devils also believe, and tremble', James 2:19.

These never tremble. There is no fear of God before their eyes, Romans 3:18. But the sheep always tremble. They 'work out' their 'own salvation with fear and trembling', Philippians 2:12.

Outward-form 'Christians' think that they have their conjured 'eternal security of the believer', as they call it and themselves, but Christ says of their believing, 'Ye believe *not*'. And why not? He tells them why not: 'Ye believe not, because ye are not of my sheep', John 10:26.

Of this kind of hypocrite Jesus declares, 'Verily I say unto you, That the publicans and the harlots go into the kingdom of God before you', Matthew 21:31. Of the religious–of whatever sort– God says 'he which is filthy, let him be filthy still'.

That is, in the unchanged self-gratification of the heart. Such cannot cease from sin. They are dogs who return to their vomit. Sows who revert to their wallowing in the mire.

So that whether by means of religion, or by the gospel of Christ; or whether by means of profligacy, or by atheism, it makes no difference. Not to the unchanged, unregenerate, inner heart: namely, to the *ultimate* intention.

Only *that* change within, by the divinely wrought interior power of God, makes the difference. All the difference.

As to the end of all others, no matter *how* religious their appearance, the fixed resolution of their hearts declares by the innermost aim, intention, and direction of their lives, that they *practise sin*. And if so, nothing but sin.

Given that the entire moral worth lies in the intention of the heart – interior, ultimate, single, and continuous – then it is from *this*, not in the outward appearance, that every resolution of the will, each single exterior action, throughout the entire pathway of the whole lifetime, gains its character.

Then what mountains of guilt already lie to the account of the unforgiven sinner, awaiting the judgment of that last and great day of the Lord?

II
The Remission of Sins

THESE things being so, one might well reiterate 'Who then can be saved?' With man this is impossible, but with God all things are possible. And, more than possible, the remission of sins has become a reality through the blood of Jesus Christ, God's Son.

It is this that is preached in the evangel. There is *no other way* in which the sinner may be forgiven, and his sins blotted out.

'Neither is there salvation in any other: for there is none other name under heaven given among men, whereby we must be saved', Acts 4:12.

'But those things, which God before had showed by the mouth of all his prophets, that Christ should suffer, he hath so fulfilled. Repent ye therefore, and be converted, that your sins may be blotted out', Acts 3:18,19.

'To him give all the prophets witness, that through his name whosoever believeth in him shall receive remission of sins', Acts 10:43.

And how shall sins be remitted, and the sinner forgiven? By taking heed to his word: 'For this is my blood of the new testament, which is shed for many for the remission of sins', Matthew 26:28.

'If we confess our sins, he is faithful and just to forgive us our sins, and to cleanse us from all unrighteousness', I John 1:9. 'If we walk in the light, as he is in the light, we have fellowship one with another, and the blood of Jesus Christ his Son cleanseth us from all sin', I John 1:7.

'This is a faithful saying, and worthy of all acceptation, that Christ Jesus came into the world to save sinners', I Timothy 1:15.

This 'coming into the world' was testified to the shepherds by the angel of the Lord at the beginning: 'And, lo, the angel of the Lord came upon them, and the glory of the Lord shone round about them: and they were sore afraid. And the angel said unto them, Fear not:

'For, behold, I bring you good tidings of great joy, which shall be to all people. For unto you is born this day in the city of David a Saviour, which is Christ the Lord', Luke 2:9-11.

Likewise witness was borne by the ancient Simeon, to whom it was revealed by the Holy Ghost that he should not see death till he had seen the Lord's Christ. He came by the Spirit into the temple, just as the child Jesus was brought into its precincts:

'Then took he him up in his arms, and blessed God, and said, Lord, now lettest thou thy servant depart in peace, according to thy word: for mine eyes have seen thy salvation, which thou hast prepared before the face of all people; a light to lighten the Gentiles, and the glory of thy people Israel', Luke 2:26-32.

Again, John the Baptist bore witness, declaring, 'Behold the Lamb of God'. And, if so, sacrifice was in view from the beginning.

How perfect was the sacrifice offered upon the cross at Golgotha: as of a lamb without blemish and without spot.

How suited to bear away sins was that sinless humanity: a humanity indissolubly united with deity in the one divine person of the Son. Jesus Christ, the Righteous One, the spotless Lamb of God, the sinless Surety: without fault throughout his life, both in the eyes of his Father, and before the judgment of the law.

He was led as a lamb to the slaughter, and as a sheep before his shearers is dumb, so he opened not his mouth.

At Golgotha, in spirit, he stood on the brink of the abyss opened by the Fall, truly man, yet really possessed of the divine nature, spotless in the eyes of the law, and agreeable to the righteousness of God.

This is the Lamb of God, able to bridge the abyss, the only one capable of meeting the incalculable distance between heaven and earth, God and man, so as to bring both together in himself.

For salvation called for a *sacrifice* capable of bridging the vast gulf between God and sinners, a gulf stretching away into the uttermost reaches of infinity, above the bottomless depths of the abyss, that is, the gulf and the abyss between a holy God, and sinful man.

In his sufferings as the substitutionary sacrifice in the place of sinners, the Saviour would travel untold spiritual distances, past all imagination, beyond the mind of man to conceive.

Not only would he ascend the weary steps of mount Sinai, but he would climb the infinite steeps of heaven, the immeasurable heights to the glory, to tread out the fierceness of the wrath of Almighty God.

During those hours upon the cross, in an inward, spiritual way that never could and never shall be seen by natural vision, or understood by the carnal mind, the Son of man was submerged beneath the seas of God's wrath.

All God's waves and billows passed over his head. Spiritually, the waters came into his soul, he sank in deep mire, where there was no standing, as, in the place of sinners, the roaring of the great deep assailed him, and the proud waters went over his soul.

In that darkness, if a stone could have been dropped into the well of his silent sufferings for sinners, neither in time nor eternity would ever be heard the sound of its striking bottom. Here are infinite sufferings, whilst about him raged the powers of darkness in their hour.

All the strength of Satan in his fury, principalities, and powers in their hatred; the dominion of spiritual wickedness in the heavenlies in their hostility; the rulers of the darkness of this world in their relentless malice, combined to vent their implacable enmity against the sufferer on the cross, shrouded in darkness, outcast by men, and forsaken of God.

'My God, my God, why hast thou forsaken me?' The sorrows of death compassed him about, the sorrows of hell compassed him about: the snares of death prevented him.

He felt the pangs of death and of hell. He sensed the great, the outer darkness. He experienced the burning wrath to come. He anguished alone bearing the wrath due to sinners, rejected of men and forsaken of God.

Eternity was in a mystery compressed in the hours on the cross. The endless reaches of infinity bowed themselves together, converging upon the man on the tree.

An incalculable multitude, as the sand on the sea-shore in-numerable, was joined to the soul of the suffering Saviour, so that their sin became his sin; their iniquities, his iniquities; in a mystical union so intimate that he could cry in spirit, 'Mine iniquities are gone over mine head.'

'Who his own self bare our sins in his own body on the tree': yes, and, having been laid upon him, thereupon the great deep of the vengeance, indignation and wrath of Almighty God against sinners broke out, issued forth, and drained through the agonizing substitute on the cross.

With what effect? 'My God, my God, why hast thou forsaken me?'

'My God', saith he, 'My God'. God is smiting him as his people, for his people, in the place of his people. 'For the transgression of my people was he stricken.' 'It pleased the LORD to bruise him; he hath put him to grief.'

In the place of the sinner under judgment he was forsaken. God had forsaken him, in that he had put him to grief, bruised him, stricken him: for 'the LORD hath laid on him the iniquity of us all.'

In no other way could sin be covered, atonement made, and God be just in forgiving sinners. For this to happen, God must be glorified in the place of sin, and, if so, in righteous judgment upon the sin-bearer of his people. 'That he might be just, and the justifier of him which believeth in Jesus.'

He gave his back to the smiters, his cheeks to them that plucked out the hair; he was stricken, smitten of God, and afflicted: for the rod, the legal rod, was not spared, neither was the wrath of God in righteousness withheld.

The fire was kindled below, and the curse sounded above. Vengeance rose from beneath, and out of the throne proceeded lightnings, and thunders, and voices.

Christ in his death in the place of sinners met all the legal penalties incurred by the guilty, at once discharging transgressors from all debt for ever, and the Judge from all vengeance world without end.

In his vicarious death he finished the transgression, made an end of sins, made reconciliation for iniquity, and brought in everlasting righteousness, even the righteousness of God by faith of Jesus Christ.

He blotted out the handwriting of ordinances that was against us, which was contrary to us, and took it out of the way, nailing it to his cross. The ashes of cancelled sins fell away as dust through the grating of God's altar of everlasting judgment in righteousness, drifting pale into the great void of eternity to be remembered no more for ever.

Jesus in his substitutionary death for sinners justified the Judge in discharging the ungodly. He magnified the law and made it honourable. Therefore God could say, 'As for thee also, by the blood of thy covenant I have sent forth thy prisoners out of the pit wherein is no water.'

The seven vials full of the wrath of God which liveth for ever and ever had been poured out without mixture upon the substitute and Saviour of sinners, till all was utterly exhausted for ever.

Then, the sinner has been saved from wrath through him. His sins and their just deserts having been borne by the perfect and only substitute acceptable to God.

Though infinity be searched out to the uttermost; though eternity be opened to its remotest reaches, not one sin of those for whom Christ died shall ever be found, world without end. Amen.

Only he could, but he did, free his people from their sins for ever. In his humiliation he was taken from prison and from judgment. In his suffering he was ground between the upper and nether millstone of the judgment and justice of God, that he might deliver the guilty from the wrath to come.

Their iniquity was laid upon him, and, being laid, the due punishment was exacted from him who willingly stood in the place of sinners. To this end he received the wrath of God against all that and all those with which and with whom he was identified.

Worse than the flood, the terrible waters of wrath roared down upon the vicarious sacrifice of the Saviour of sinners. Worse than the yawning pit, the dark depths gaped beneath the suffering soul of the Substitute of the ungodly.

Worse than the searing fire and brimstone that rained upon Sodom and Gomorrah, the wrathful vengeance of Almighty God issued as a deluge from heaven.

He passed through fire and flood, poured out in judgment to engulf the lonely sin-bearer, hung between heaven and earth in the midst of time at the end of the world.

The equivalent of unquenchable fire, the undying worm, the bottomless pit, and the endless torment, for the equal of eternity compressed into time in the hours on the cross, seized upon his unique humanity borne up in the arms of his everlasting deity.

But at the last, with the uttermost curse of the law exhausted, the last bolt of retributive justice shot, and the final sentence of punitive judgment exacted, when the law could say no more, and the curse find no further cause of vengeance, when the sounding trumpet had ceased to utter, then nothing but satisfaction remained.

Following the cry 'It is finished', his dead body hung upon the cross. But there was a great and everlasting calm, and from heaven swelled the echoing sound, 'On earth peace, good will toward men'.

Sins were covered. Nothing offended. The Almighty looked down from heaven, but there was no offence, nothing. Not one spot, not one blemish. Not in all those countless souls mysteriously united with the sin-bearer hanging dead upon the tree.

There was nothing against them: nothing in time, nothing in eternity, nothing in heaven, nothing on earth. Nothing at all.

The sacrifice on behalf of sinners was consumed in the flames of the wrath of God, and in the fires of everlasting justice.

The sin offering was burned to ashes without the camp, and with it, all that had been taken away in the substitutionary sacrifice. The blood bore witness to the remission of sins borne away in death.

Nothing but ashes; nothing but the blood of sprinkling. He had finished the work that God gave him to do, and finished it to perfection.

Now, here is the basis, the solid, sound, and only foundation for the preaching of the remission of sins. Here is the ground once laid for the forgiveness of sinners. Here is that preceding work which alone provides the price for the ransom of souls.

Other foundation can no man lay. But on this foundation, and this alone, with certain assurance, with ringing conviction, with joy unspeakable and full of glory, remission of sins is preached in the name of the Saviour, Jesus Christ.

Hence, upon so firm a basis, it follows that repentance and remission of sins should be preached in his name among all nations, beginning at Jerusalem.

The Holy Ghost having been given, the disciples endued with power from on high, the apostle Peter declared the evangel on the day of Pentecost, 'Repent, and be baptized every one of you in the name of Jesus Christ for the remission of sins, and ye shall receive the gift of the Holy Ghost'.

On so sound a foundation as the blood of Christ, shed for many, it follows of course that the remission of sins should be preached in his name. Being proclaimed 'to the Jew first': 'Him hath God exalted with his right hand to be a Prince and a Saviour, for to give repentance to Israel, and remission of sins.'

But the evangel was to the Gentiles also, hence Peter testifies to them, 'To him give all the prophets witness, that through his name whosoever believeth in him shall receive remission of sins.'

Hence Paul bears record in the synagogue at Antioch before both Jews and Gentiles, 'Be it known unto you therefore, men and brethren, that through this man is preached unto you the remission'–as it should be: not forgiveness–'of sins.'

At this point observe that *sins* are not forgiven: there is nothing to forgive them: *they* have not done anything; they were committed by the sinner. If they are to be cleared and discharged, they must be *remitted*. It is the sinner–who has committed the sins–that is forgiven: not the sins themselves!

Whence observe the inaccuracy of the translation, both in respect of the Greek, which means, Send away; dismiss; or *remit*; and also of the meaning of the plain English: *Sinners* are *forgiven*, on the basis of their *sins* having been *remitted*.

When the Lord shone upon and spake to Saul–thereafter called Paul–he was sent to the Gentiles 'to open their eyes, to turn them from darkness to light, and from the authority'–it is not Power–'of Satan unto God, *that they may receive remission of sins*'.

Here notice what an inward work of God *precedes* the sinner being brought to the place of receiving remission–'and inheritance among them which are sanctified by faith that is in me.'

How wonderfully the blood of Jesus Christ brought in the remission of sins to such an increasingly great multitude, widening from the Jews to the Gentiles. For to the Corinthians Paul declares the evangel which he preached unto them, affirming with the words, 'Christ died for our sins according to the scriptures.'

This preaching began with the descent of the Holy Ghost, as saith the epistle to the Hebrews: When he had by himself purged our sins. That was the foundation. Upon that, the preaching of remission of sins was declared in the evangel.

Again, Hebrews tells us that Christ made propitiation–or appeasement: it is certainly not reconciliation–'for the sins of his people'.

So effective was the foundation of the shedding of the blood of Jesus Christ in vicarious substitution for sinners, that upon such a basis God declares with triumph of those brought to faith in Christ for the remission of sins, 'Their sins and iniquities will I remember no more'. No, never. Neither for time nor eternity.

For 'Christ was once offered to bear the sins of many', and, on such a stable ground, the many shall certainly be brought to faith, and to the assured knowledge that they are forgiven through the remission of their sins.

This is settled and absolute with God, having this solid foundation: 'This man, after he had offered one sacrifice for sins for ever, sat down on the right hand of God.'

So Peter assures us: 'Who his own self bare our sins in his own body on the tree.' Then, they were there borne *away*. If so, they are remitted. Then what can hinder the forgiveness of the sinner brought to faith?

For, 'If we confess our sins, he is faithful and just to forgive us'–that is, forgive our persons–'our sins'–because they are remitted–'and to cleanse us from all unrighteousness.'

Because 'the blood of Jesus Christ, God's Son cleanseth us from all sin.' This is the blood that was shed for the remission of sins.

What remains? Why, that we love him so much that we are lost in wonder, love, and praise at the love of Christ which passeth knowledge. We love him because he first loved us.

That is, he loved us from eternity; he loved us in his coming; and he loved us in his dying in our place, that he might bear our sins in his own body.

'Whom having not seen, ye love; in whom, though now ye see him not, yet believing, ye rejoice with joy unspeakable and full of glory: receiving the end of your faith, even the salvation of your souls.'

Nor is salvation only from the guilt of all our sins. For in that Christ Jesus came into the world to save sinners, and, Thou shalt call his name Jesus, for he shall save his people from their sins, it follows not from the guilt of sins only, but from the commission of those sins likewise.

Yea, and in the resurrection of the body, in the last day, from the presence of sin also.

Consider that even now, for every one whose sins are remitted, they that are of faith are both saved from sinning, and–despite all the lawyers advocating sin in Christendom and evangelicalism giving the lie to the apostle–saved from the power of sin.

For the apostle Paul testified of Christ in his substitutionary death, 'Who gave himself for us, that he might redeem us from all iniquity'.

Now, 'iniquity' in this place is *anomias*, which properly rendered, should read 'lawlessness'. And John assures us that 'sin'—that is, in the doing of it; committing sin; the will, in whatever class of it, but especially the ultimate intention of the heart—'sin is lawlessness'.

But Paul had taught, Christ shed his blood not only for the guilt of sin but 'to redeem us from all'—mark that: *all*—'lawlessness'.

And so John confirms, to the fury of every hypocrite in Zion to this latest day—*especially* in this latest day—sounding forth the immutable truth following on from the death of Christ for the remission of sins, 'Whosoever abideth in him sinneth not'.

So that Christ's blood was shed for the remission of sins, and, thereafter, his risen and ascended life delivers all those that are of faith from the commission of sins.

What could be plainer? What could be more incontrovertible? 'Whosoever abideth in him sinneth not: whosoever sinneth hath not seen him, neither known him.

'Little children, let no man deceive you: he that doeth righteousness is righteous, even as he is righteous. He that committeth sin is of the devil; for the devil sinneth from the beginning.

'For this purpose the Son of God was manifested, that he might destroy the works of the devil. Whosoever is born of God doth not commit sin; for his seed remaineth in him: and he cannot sin, because he is born of God.'

Who can contend against this? Who will contend against such plainness of speech? Why, every hypocrite; all the hirelings for reward; each one of the lawyers who plead the cause of sinning, at once contending against the Holy Ghost, the word of God, and the apostles of Jesus Christ.

And why? Because these servants of men plead for the flesh, and hire themselves to please man. Not so the apostles: 'Being then made free from sin, ye became the servants of righteousness', and, 'he that doeth righteousness is righteous, even as he is righteous.'

Of course we *were* sinners: some of us of the most dreadful kind. 'And such were some of you: but ye are washed, but ye are sanctified, but ye are justified in the name of the Lord Jesus, and by the Spirit of our God.' And how shall these do less than answer to I John 3:3-10?

Likewise the Hebrews. They were to leave the–old testament– principles of the doctrine of Christ–in type and prophecy–and 'go on unto perfection'. And what less than perfection ought we to expect from him who is able to save them *to the uttermost* that come unto God by him?

The more so, when, having changed our *hearts*, he puts his laws into our minds, writes them on our hearts, proves to be our God, and imparts the inward and spiritual knowledge of himself to us by experience? What then would you expect? Failure and imperfection?

The blood of Christ having purged the consciences of once guilty sinners from dead works, they are saved from the power of sin to 'serve the living and true God'.

For by one offering he hath perfected for ever them that are sanctified, whereof the Holy Ghost also is a witness to us: for after that he had said before, This is the covenant that I will make with them after those days, saith the Lord, I will put my laws into their hearts, and in their minds will I write them; and their sins and their iniquities will I remember no more.

If so, those who are saved by the blood of Christ from the guilt of sins, are saved by him from the power of them also.

Wherefore he saith, 'Now the God of peace, that brought again from the dead our Lord Jesus, that great shepherd of the sheep, through the blood of the everlasting covenant, make you perfect in every good work to do his will, working in you that which is wellpleasing in his sight, through Jesus Christ.'

'Wherefore come out from among them, and be ye separate, saith the Lord, and touch not the unclean thing; and I will receive you, and will be a Father unto you, and ye shall be my sons and daughters, saith the Lord Almighty.

'Having therefore these promises, dearly beloved, let us cleanse ourselves from all'–mark that: all–'filthiness of the flesh and spirit, perfecting holiness in the fear of God.'

'And the very God of peace sanctify you wholly; and I pray God your whole spirit and soul and body be preserved blameless'– note that: blameless–'unto the coming of our Lord Jesus Christ.' Observe '*unto* the coming': not *after* it.

Those saved from guilt by the blood of Christ, whose sins have been remitted, 'walk'–mark that: walk; it is continuous progress– 'not after the flesh, but after the Spirit.'

'For they that are after the flesh do mind the things of the flesh; but they that are after the Spirit the things of the Spirit. For to be carnally minded is death; but to be spiritually minded is life and peace.'

Here those who have been saved walk after the Spirit, and mind the things of the Spirit, consistently and constantly.

'So then they that are in the flesh cannot please God. But ye'–whose sins have been remitted–'are not in the flesh'–no, ye are saved from the power of sin by the life and Spirit of Christ– 'but in the Spirit, if so be that the Spirit of God dwell in you. Now if any man have not the Spirit of Christ, he is none of his.'

'For if ye live after the flesh, ye shall die: but if ye through the Spirit do mortify the deeds of the body, ye shall live. For as many as are led by the Spirit of God, they are the sons of God.

'For ye have not received the spirit of bondage again to fear; but ye have received the Spirit of sonship, whereby we cry, Abba, Father.' This is the heritage of all whose sins are remitted.

Indwelt by Christ, filled with the Spirit, having received the Spirit of sonship, the law of the Spirit of life, of liberty, of love, and of Christ, being written of God in their hearts and minds, these press forward to the mark of the heavenly calling of God in Christ Jesus.

Then let as many as be perfect be thus minded. This is the obedience of faith for the life of faith with a witness.

And this life of faith, as you read in the eleventh chapter of Hebrews, is a like common faith to that of all the saints in the old testament from the very beginning.

It began, as it must, with the remission of sins through the blood of the Lamb. This was set forth in figure, type, and prophecy from the first, until the coming of Christ.

That is why he is described as 'the Lamb slain from the foundation of the world'. But all these, who were of faith, having their sins remitted, became pilgrims and strangers in the earth, sanctified in their very character.

Nothing can ever change the character of the sojourner, to whom the remission of sins has been assured. It is a settled character of other-worldliness; a constancy of righteousness; and a continuance in holiness.

It is this that makes the sheep to be seen as sheep in the Judgment. As to false claimants in the letter, they will appear to be what they are in fact: nothing but goats.

They would, but they cannot change the immutable verity and sworn truth of God that the Judgment is according to the character, made manifest over a lifetime on earth. This word is unalterable from him who will render to every man according to his works.

'To them who by patient continuance in well doing seek for glory and honour and immortality, eternal life:

'But unto them that are contentious'—especially those rebels who contend against these very words—'and do not obey the truth'—which they never fail to profess—'but obey unrighteousness'—professing one thing, and obeying another—'indignation and wrath,

'Tribulation and anguish, upon every soul of man that doeth evil, of the Jew first, and also of the Gentile;

'But glory, honour, and peace, to every man that worketh good, to the Jew first, and also to the Gentile: for there is no respect of persons with God.'

Then, since 'all have sinned, and come short of the glory of God', and 'there is none that doeth good, no, not one', it is high time to awake out of sleep, and repent towards God, believing in Jesus Christ for the remission of sins, receiving the Holy Ghost.

For the righteousness of believing in and conforming to the letter of scripture will not do. This is no more than the righteousness of the scribes and Pharisees. To this Saul of Tarsus attained: 'touching the righteousness which is in the law, blameless.'

Yes, Saul, but Jesus saith, 'Except your righteousness shall exceed the righteousness of the scribes and Pharisees, ye shall in no case enter into the kingdom of heaven.'

But Saul—later Paul—found that. Found that all his previous righteousness, in which he trusted, was as filthy rags. Found that the light that was in him was darkness. But, apprehended by Jesus Christ, he was brought to cry for the remission of sins through faith in his blood.

This he received, scales falling from his eyes as he heard the words 'that thou mightest receive thy sight, and be filled with the Holy Ghost.

'And immediately there fell from his eyes as it had been scales: and he received sight forthwith, and arose, and was baptized.'

Paul was baptized for the remission of his sins, and went on to perfect holiness in the fear of God, under great tribulation. For, saith the Lord, I will show him how great things he must suffer for my name's sake.

And all those whose sins are remitted, who receive the Holy Ghost, and are delivered from the power of sins, abiding in Christ and walking in the Spirit as pilgrims and strangers, must suffer great tribulation.

'For', saith Paul to the Philippians, writing from prison, 'unto you it is given in the behalf of Christ, not only to believe on him, but also to suffer for his sake; having the same conflict which ye saw in me, and now hear to be in me.'

Likewise to the Thessalonians, 'That no man should be moved by these afflictions: for yourselves know that we are appointed thereunto.'

Wherefore Paul glories in these fellow-sufferers, 'for your patience and faith in all your persecutions and tribulations that ye endure: which is a manifest token of the righteous judgment of God, that ye may be counted worthy of the kingdom of God, for which ye also suffer.'

Whence it is clear that all those brought to receive the remission of sins through the blood of Jesus Christ are found in him, and are filled with the Spirit, and walk in the Spirit, minding the Spirit.

Through the Spirit they mortify the deeds of the body, seeking for glory and honour and immortality as pilgrims, strangers, and sojourners upon the earth.

This brings them into persecution and affliction. But the light of the glory is before them, and these who before had been forgiven, and their sins washed away, are now going on unto perfection.

And what short of this could please the Father? Nothing short of this. For, saith Jesus, 'Be ye therefore perfect, even as your Father which is in heaven is perfect', Matthew 5:48.

III
Inbred Sin

HITHERTO the word 'sin' has been regarded as the voluntary intention of the will, ranging from that which genders outward action – rather than the exterior appearance itself – through to the settled resolution of the choice of whatever means give rise to inward self-gratification, religious or otherwise.

All this has been shown to be rooted and grounded in the ultimate intention of the heart, governing the aim and direction of the life and being as an entity.

This is the proper use of the verb 'to sin'. It is what is wilfully intended: it is what is purposed to be done. In man this is to be given up to self-gratification as an end, irrespective of the means or appearances.

For it is the inward, ultimate intention that is the whole of sin, and this is to sin wholly and without intermission. It is selfishness in its essence, using God and man as a means of self-gratification, providing the reason for existence.

But – apart from innumerable allusions in the Evangelists and Acts – in the new testament Romans 3:9 introduces a deeper meaning, declaring not that all sinned, but that all are 'under sin'.

Here 'sin', as such, occurs for the first time in Romans. It is the noun form of the word. This does not denote action or intention, what is done, but rather the thing itself, the state of being.

The noun *can* refer to 'a' sin, but, generally, the word has a much more profound significance. This refers to 'sin' as a condition.

Romans 3:9 denotes neither the deed, nor the intention, but *the inbred state from conception*.

However the apostle – having shown the inexcusable and continual action of sinning of all mankind, whether without the law or under the law – certainly does not introduce this revelation of the *state* of mankind to mitigate the guilty outrage of sinful intention on the part of all born of woman.

Rather, he increases the exposure of the sinfulness of each individual by pointing to a far deeper and more serious interior *state* common to the entirety of humanity as such.

The action 'sinned' came before the state 'sin' in the revelation. Romans chapters one to three sets forth God's charge against a sinning humanity. Romans 3:9, for the first time, distinctly sets forth the interior state of that guilty humanity, as it stands by birth.

Romans 3:9 introduces the truth of the state of fallen man. However it does so only after having first charged home individually the guilty state of man's sinning disposition.

The words 'under sin' in the conclusion 'We have before proved both Jews and Gentiles, that they are all under sin', therefore indicate not only proven wilful rebellion in the individual, but a deeper inbred condition in the whole of humanity.

But this neither affects nor mitigates the sheer culpable wilfulness laid to the charge of each deliberately sinning individual at the bar of the just judgment of God.

Nevertheless, that given, 'They are all under sin' commences another and more profound exposure, albeit that it comes to light from the determined conduct of mankind individually.

In the case of Romans 3:9, 'Under', in context, makes clear the precise bearing of the noun form of *hamartia*, sin, regarding the interior *state* of mankind.

The pronoun 'they'–in 'they are all under sin'–refers to the whole human race, Jew and Gentile, religious or irreligious.

Humanity's wilful, inexcusable sinning shows that in every nation, all generations, each circumstance, mankind is 'under' sin from the Fall, but in such a way that this *manifests* the corporate will of mankind without in the least diminishing individual responsibility and wilfulness during any given lifetime.

However, the important truth of mankind corporately being 'under sin'–first mentioned in passing under Romans 3:9–is yet to be taken up and thoroughly revealed in the chapters following on from this passage.

For example, after chapter 3:9 'sin' is mentioned again in Romans 3:20. Then the noun occurs again in chapters 4:8; 5:12, 13,20,21; after this a further seventeen times in chapter 6; then twelve times in chapter 7; and so on.

These references all point to the *state* of man *in the fall*, at first revealed – chapters 1 to 3 – by his deliberate sinning from the heart and in life, the one in no way diminishing the enormity of the other, but both alike meriting the just judgment of the righteousness of God in the day of wrath.

It is this that the apostle had 'before proved', Romans 3:9.

'By the law is the knowledge of sin', Romans 3:20, and of nothing else. But this knowledge is experimental, not intellectual. He saith not, of sins, as of many, but as of one, of sin, the thing itself.

That is, the inward state. For the scripture hath concluded all under sin, the commandment finding out the carnal mind, which is not subject to the law of God, neither indeed can be.

Under the sentence of death the law commanded 'This do and thou shalt live'. And the Jew set to with a will. But how to perform that which he willed he found not, it was not present with him: what he discovered was the power, the inwardness, and the origin of sin in the flesh.

This discovery to those under the law showed the interior state of man to be one of enmity against God.

It was not the law that was at fault. The law was holy, and just, and good. But man was carnal, sold under sin.

The law, once inwrought, discovered the interior state of man's heart to be thoroughly obnoxious to the wrath of God. Man was discovered to be full of unrighteousness, under sin, and with the sentence of death already passed upon his mortal body.

Then, if the wilful intention of the individual does not reflect this, What does? It was the will of mankind as a whole, corporately, and, if so, from the very beginning in the fall of Adam, as it is written, 'by one man sin entered into the world, and death by sin', Romans 5:12.

In context, by the use of the noun form 'sin', the apostle refers to the *state* of inbred corruption–leading to the death of the body–into which Adam fell beneath the judgment and curse of God under the condemnation of man in the transgression.

That *state*, of necessity and by nature, passed through conception and birth to Adam's entire posterity by carnal or fleshly generation. It must be so. It was an inbred corruption inherent in the life, soul, and body of mankind ever since 'by one man sin entered into the world'.

Corruption, in the form of inbred sin, rots, decays, and, in time, inevitably overcomes body and soul by mortality and death. And 'death passed upon all men.' But the beginning was 'by *one man* sin'–the *state* caused by God's judgment to condemnation upon mankind in Adam–'entered into the world.'

Then, inbred sin is not a question of what man *does*. It is a matter of what man *is*. It is not man's *acts*. It is his *state*. It is not what the individual *wills*. It follows from what Adam resolved on behalf of his entire posterity.

The result of this is the constitutional state of corruption, dishonour, weakness, and carnality.

It is the deadly condition of inbred sin inherent in the conception and birth of all humanity, man, woman, and child, in the fall of Adam. This must–because inbred sin must–shortly end in death. From this, mankind cannot escape.

'As by one man sin'–mark that, *sin*–'entered into the world': this is not a question of what was *done*; it is a question of *what man became*. What he *became* is said to have *entered*. This *state* of inbred sin is *innate*. It is in the *seed* of both man and woman. Therefore, both ways, it is *inherent in conception, let alone birth.*

However man may rage against this truth revealed by the Holy Ghost, testified by the Lord Jesus and his holy apostles, verified by the word of God, and *obvious in life, death, history, and consciousness*, such a rage is futile. As well beat one's fists in frustration against an impregnable and towering wall of granite.

'Sin entered into the world' with the fall of Adam. Then, 'the judgment was by *one man* to condemnation.' Hence 'through the offence of *one* many be dead.' Again, 'by *one man's* offence death reigned by one.'

Once more, 'by *one man's* disobedience many were made sinners.' See Romans 5:12-21. 'By the offence of one judgment came upon all men to condemnation.'

One man: one offence; namely, the one offence of Adam. Not a succession of offences on the part of each man in turn; nor by any successive offences at all: by *one* offence. Of *one* man.

Then, probation stood in Adam for his posterity; not that his posterity stands under probation. The issue was all settled in the beginning by that unique man in whom was the life of all humanity, through whom humanity was tried in the beginning.

With this consequence: *one* man; *one* fall. In that and of it the whole of Adam's posterity was conceived and born.

By one offence? Yes, by one fall, all fell. All fell in that one fall of him who represented *mankind*, in whose loins *the whole of humanity* stood. Or fell.

But if *he*, directly created of God, perfect in innocence, the very epitome and exemplar of all that man *should* have been: I say, if *he* fell, where would *we* have been? But in truth, we *were* in the loins and in the life of that one man, the man who acted on behalf of us all.

If one faces reality, it is blindingly obvious that *nothing else answers to the facts of life and death*. David saw this: 'Behold, I was shapen in iniquity; and in sin did my mother conceive me', Psalm 51:5.

No birth is mentioned here: this was all *before* birth, in the womb; as it were from the loins of Adam, who stood in for his entire posterity.

Again, Psalm 58:3, 'The wicked are estranged from the womb.' If so, in conception, and before birth. Then, before moral action was possible. Therefore, this must refer to *one man, one offence*, and *unto all men*, preceding that conception.

Hence Jesus teaches 'that which is born of the flesh is flesh', John 3:6, adding, 'the flesh profiteth nothing', John 6:63. How could it? for, 'flesh and blood *cannot* inherit the kingdom of God; neither doth corruption inherit incorruption', I Corinthians 15:50.

How could the flesh profit anything? It springs from the 'one offence'–or 'one fall'–however many the subsequent generations. Hence John teaches 'the *whole* world lieth in wickedness'–or, rather, 'in the Wicked one'–I John 5:19.

Wherefore Satan is called 'the prince of this world', John 16:11, and 'the god of this world', II Corinthians 4:4. Because 'by *one* fall unto *all* men.' What else could that one fallen man beget? Nothing other than the inevitable consequences of the 'one fall', upon which the sentence of death had already been passed.

Thus, death reigned. Why? Because sin had entered into the world, and death by sin. This was 'unto all men to condemnation.' That is, condemnation to death.

If so, the whole human race is fallen, 'sold under sin', and beneath the reign of death through that one man in whom the will of humanity gave expression once and for all.

This state is summed up by expressions such as 'the flesh' or 'the world'. Hence Paul teaches, 'They that are after the flesh do mind the things of the flesh', and, 'to be carnally'–fleshly– 'minded is death.'

For the reign of death is over all born after the flesh, which sums up the very nature of the incorrigibly disobedient will of man, expressed on behalf of all men by the first man Adam.

Paul continues: 'The carnal'–fleshly–'mind is enmity against God: for it is not subject to the law of God, neither indeed can be. So then they that are in the flesh cannot please God.' See Romans 8:5-8.

But, as to these things, man is blind from birth, spiritually blind, wilfully blind, and in total interior and spiritual darkness, in which 'the god of this world hath blinded the minds of them which believe not', II Corinthians 4:4. This is the vanity of man's mind.

'Having the understanding darkened'–as to the true nature of God, and as to the least vestige of what is spiritual–'being alienated from the life of God through the ignorance that is in them, because of the blindness of their heart', Ephesians 4:18.

And this state from Adam–by whom sin entered into the world–continues unabated, passing by natural generation from age to age till the world shall be no more. Nor was it man alone that was affected to such depths by the fall of Adam.

The world itself had been committed into the hand and under the dominion of Adam in innocence. What obligation then to his Maker, seeing that the earth is the Lord's, and the fulness thereof; the world also is his.

Nevertheless all this–with his entire posterity yet to spring from his loins–was given in charge to Adam.

Then as to such a dominion also probation stood in Adam for his posterity; not that his posterity stands under probation. It was all settled by *one* fall. In that, and of it, Adam's whole posterity subsisted.

O, What has Adam brought to pass? Not only the entrance of sin, and death, but the will of all humanity, inherent in him whose disobedience expressed that of the posterity of which he was the head and representative.

Moreover, cursed was the ground for his sake, so that the very creation itself became subject to vanity at the fall of man.

Man had done this with things not his own, things entrusted to him. As to the state of sin, and the reign of death, into which he had brought himself and his posterity, what prospect now was there for a Creator who had before delighted in a creation pronounced 'very good'?

What offence; what indignation; what wrath must have been gendered? How greatly—by *so great* a transgression, having such cosmic repercussions—I say, how greatly was the glory of God despoiled; his holiness violated; his righteousness outraged; and his justice offended.

He himself was of purer eyes than to behold iniquity, and, the very heavens—let alone the earth, and man upon it—now not being clean in his sight, at what distance henceforth should God stand from fallen man? At infinite distance.

Sin had been conceived; death had begun its unbroken reign; the curse had sounded over all the earth; and man was cast out from the presence of God.

From henceforth the race must be conceived in sin, shapen in iniquity, and estranged from the womb: the nature of man had become irrevocably altered from the original.

The farther mankind removed in time from the beginning the more it became him to stand back from his generation. Would that men might trace from the utmost branches of humanity to the deepest root, to find meaning in the first man Adam at the genesis of all things.

Hence it is that the apostle refers to all born of Adam, mankind as an entity, as 'sons of disobedience', Ephesians 2:2; and 'by nature children of wrath', Ephesians 2:3, for so the original reads.

Where, in the first quotation, it does not say that men were disobedient in turn, but that disobedience *begat* mankind as such: they were *sons* of disobedience. And in the second case, the phrase does not assert that each one in sequence gendered wrath: wrath had gendered *them*. They were *children* of it: wrath *begat* them.

There can be no doubt of the sum of the matter revealed by the word of God: The whole race fell in the fall of the one–the first–man, and inbred sin and corruption unto death from his seed thereafter infused that one man's posterity in its entirety, because by that one act on their behalf, they were constituted sinners.

Then, this is the case of and with inbred sin: It is incorrigible. There is no question of forgiveness: the one hope of mankind lies in God accomplishing a *deliverance* from it. Because it *must* be condemned.

But how can *it* be condemned, without *man* perishing in the condemnation? Only if God should send a Saviour, and the condemnation fall upon him in our place.

But that is exactly what has taken place. That is precisely what happened: our Saviour Jesus Christ *has* borne the condemnation of sin. Moreover the Saviour delivers his own from the power of sin. And, at the end, finally, the Saviour shall save his people from the presence of sin.

First, deliverance. Consider this. 'Behold the Lamb of God, which taketh away the sin of the world', John 1:29. How great is the love of God, over against the incorrigible enmity of the flesh, that–instead of a Judge–he should send a Saviour. And– instead of judgment–he should bestow deliverance.

But that is exactly what he has done: he *has* sent a Saviour; he *has* sent deliverance. And that over a state so vile, so foul, so alien, that words fail to convey the descent of man. Yet, withal, send deliverance he did, and that as of a free gift springing from the love of God for the world, John 3:16.

Are many dead through the fall of one? Then much more the grace of God, and the gift by grace, which is by one man,

Jesus Christ, abounds unto many! Was the judgment by one man's offence unto condemnation? Then the free gift is after many offences unto justification! Romans 5:15,16.

Was it by one man's disobedience that many were constituted sinners? Then by the obedience of one shall many be constituted righteous! Romans 5:19. Did sin abound in the man of sin and death? Then grace shall much more abound in the man of righteousness and life! Romans 5:20.

'That as sin hath reigned unto death, even so might grace reign through righteousness unto eternal life by Jesus Christ our Lord', Romans 5:21. 'For the wages of sin is death; but the gift of God is eternal life through Jesus Christ our Lord', Romans 6:23.

So great is the deliverance from sin wrought of God through the Saviour, that the apostle, transported, cries out with joy at the blessing, declaring, 'Blessed is the man to whom the Lord will not impute sin', Romans 4:8.

And why not shout for joy? For 'the sting of death is sin; and the strength of sin is the law', I Corinthians 15:56. Then what, alas, can we do? Nothing. God has done everything. 'Thanks be to God, which giveth us the victory through our Lord Jesus Christ', I Corinthians 15:57.

For though the scripture hath concluded all under sin—for Paul had before proved, Romans 3:9, both Jews and Gentiles, that they are all under sin—yet what was it, but that 'the promise by faith of Jesus Christ might be given to them that believe', Galatians 3:22. What promise? Why, of the blessing, Romans 4:8.

Hence it is written, I John 1:7, 'But if we walk in the light'—this light, which lightens the nature of inbred sin, the Saviour from it, and the deliverance wrought by him—'we have fellowship one with another, and the blood of Jesus Christ his Son cleanseth us from all sin.' This is at once the promise and the blessing.

For, 'if Christ be in you, the body is dead'–counted as dead; reckoned in the sight of God to be dead–'because of sin'–for, on our behalf, God condemned sin in the body of Jesus on the cross: it is this that is reckoned to us; hence–'the Spirit is life because of righteousness', Romans 8:10.

Blessing indeed, for, helplessly enslaved, inextricably bound, wholly ensnared in the body of sin: how could we be saved?

The wisdom of God in Christ, moved by everlasting love, found the way. Inbred sin could never be forgiven: it was impossible in time, much less eternity, that the holiness of God could abide such abomination in his sight, much less presence.

Then how could we, bound to it and by it, sold under it, ever be free of it, that we might come unto God?

Only by its being judged in another, a Saviour, who, having been *made sin for us* at the cross–O the breadth, length, depth, and height of the love of Christ, which passes knowledge–inbred sin *then* being condemned in *his* body, we should be free from sin.

Hence, 'Once in the end of the world hath he appeared to put away sin by the sacrifice of himself', Hebrews 9:26.

So momentous was his coming, that it is counted before God as 'the end of the world'. The whole world is–as it were–brought to a conclusion in the sight of God by the finality of his sacrificing himself for us in the place of judgment for sin.

That is, judgment at the hand of God, who, first, in a mystery, made him to *be* sin, so that, last, it should *be condemned* in his own body on the tree.

'For *he* hath made him to *be* sin for us, who knew no sin; that we might become the righteousness of God in him', II Corinthians 5:21.

And this was prefigured from the ancient ages of Israel, in the sin offering. 'The bodies'–mark that, *bodies*–'of those beasts, whose blood'–observe carefully, whose *blood*–'is brought into the sanctuary by the high priest for sin, are burned'–again, note this: *burned; annihilated:* not *forgiven*–'without the camp', Hebrews 13:11.

This is that of which the Holy Ghost speaks, saying, 'For he'–that is, God–'hath made *him*'–that is, the Son, *in his manhood*–'to be sin for us, who knew no sin.'

He was without sin; he did no sin; he knew no sin: no *inbred* sin, common to all mankind in Adam. Thus, he was the only, the perfect, the impeccable substitute.

Inbred sin, as has been shown, passed by conception and natural generation from Adam to all his posterity. But it did *not* pass to the unique humanity of Jesus, born of Mary. For *his* peerless humanity was 'without sin'. He 'knew no sin.'

Then he, and he alone, could be found acceptable, in the union of his deity with the perfection of his humanity, to offer himself a sacrifice acceptable to God in the place of sin. Because he knew no sin. Whereas all mankind without exception was born in sin, sold under sin, and condemned for sin.

As has been shown, the word 'sin' refers to the *state* by birth common to all mankind. It is the condition by natural genera-tion of all humanity from the Fall. Now, it was *that*–declares II Corinthians 5:21–which Christ was *made*, and, if so, on the cross.

Being 'made'–from the Greek *poieō, to make, produce, create, cause*–clearly does not refer to a *reckoning* objectively. The Greek indicates a *state* subjectively.

Did that state–which, as the sacrifice for sin at Golgotha–he was *made, created, formed to be* by the mysterious work of God, in order that he should put away sin by the sacrifice of himself; I repeat, Did that state cause his death?

It caused him untold anguish at Gethsemane even at the contemplation of so unspeakable a prospect of the *price* he must pay if ever men were to be saved and delivered from the body of sin.

There was but one way. The divine substitution of the sinless one in place of those born in sin, *so as really and actually to exchange places with them.* Then, in a mystery, *to be 'created',* 'made' in that state, that it might be condemned in judgment once and for all.

If but the prospect brought him to such strong crying and tears, to fall prostrate on the ground in an agony of prayer those three times, to sweat as it were great drops of blood: Then, submitting to his Father's will, what of the untold, unimaginable anguish of the experience itself?

Unbearable; yet borne. Intolerable; yet suffered.

Suffered: since he had been *made* sin. Made sin, till it was finished. Till the wrath of a holy God, and the judgment of that purest divine righteousness subsisting in unapproachable light, utterly consumed the sacrifice, *condemned it* till neither sin nor condemnation remained for time or eternity.

Thus our sin was borne away. And *thus* 'he gave up the ghost'.

'He was made sin.' By exchanging places—in context, *katallassō, to exchange; katallagē, the exchange*—where *kata* indicates 'from top to bottom', or, in context, '*thoroughly*'.

And if of sin *inwardly. Allassō* signifying *to exchange*; but if from 'without sin' to being 'made sin', the divine, spiritual, *inward* exchange. Now, the added preposition *kata*, indicates from top to bottom. The *thorough* exchange.

Utterly, from top to bottom, thoroughly, not just to take our place under the judgment we deserved but—*exchanging places*

thoroughly, from the uttermost to the innermost, first and last–
that this might be so, *made* in our state.

Otherwise, why does the Holy Ghost use the word *poieō, to create, make*? because that word, and nothing less than that word, is chosen of God to convey the truth.

Of God he was *made, created* in our state, in a mystery, at the cross: 'For *he*'–God–'hath made *him*'–Christ–'to be sin for us.' *Made* to *be* sin. So that he might bear justly the condemnation for what God had made him to be for us, and for our deliverance.

'Made sin': Incorrigible, unforgivable, irredeemable as it was, that he might thus be in justice–being made actually in our state–brought under the judgment of both the law and the righteousness of God against that state.

To what end? That sin might be *'condemned'*–not *forgiven; condemned*–'in the flesh'– *his flesh*–'that we might become the righteousness of God in him.'

This is the thorough exchange of places. As it was with the carcase of the sin offering, the blood having been brought by the high priest into the holiest, the body was carried outside the camp to be burned by fire utterly to destruction, till all that was left was a cone of ashes.

Equal in his spotless humanity, unblemished substance, and impeccable soul to take the place of any one of his people, in the mystery of his divinity, the infinity of his being, and the absoluteness of his ability undergirding that humanity, at Golgotha he took the place of countless myriads in one substitutionary sacrifice, offered up for sin, to bear its judgment once and for all.

Notwithstanding, through sickening pseudo-religious and sanctimonious 'piety', hypocritical theological philosophers, supplanting the mystery of Christ, and revelation of the Spirit of God, have shunned the truth that Christ was *made* sin, and that he *bore* sin.

Oh, no: to these whited sepulchres, he must be shielded from such a death, even the death of the cross. It was not for *their* 'Christ' to suffer such humiliation and degradation. Then how do they hope to be saved?

For as plain as plain words can be, the Holy Ghost declares what we have repeated from the mystery of Christ in the apostolic doctrine.

But these latter-day Pharisees, like their forbears, invent a tradition that is altogether without a basis in the evangel of Christ, being void of the witness of the Holy Ghost, in which they make the word of God of none effect by their traditions, and rob lost sinners of their salvation.

Such whitewashed deceivers—making their blinded followers twofold more the children of hell than themselves, Matthew 23:15—put on a 'pious' show, as if their refined souls cannot stand so much as the thought that the Saviour was made sin, or that he bore sin within his own body.

Then they have no Saviour. There is nothing to save their followers. And they know nothing of salvation. Neither do their adherents have any hope of being saved.

These false prophets and be-gowned priests, throwing up fairy-snow washed hands, cannot stand the thought of Christ's bearing sin, or of his being made sin, allowing only that the Saviour bore the judgment for sin.

Oh? Judgment for what was not there?

Do they think God to be as unjust as themselves, to judge what was not there? In that day, they shall find that their invented

'Saviour', together with their tradition-devised 'salvation', is not there either.

Ah, but, they say, Sin was 'imputed' to him. Oh? Then, why did Christ and his apostles not say so?

The fact that righteousness is imputed to us is utterly beside the point. Such wording *in relation to Christ's bearing sin* does not exist, nor is their notion of 'imputation' regarding sin-bearing so much as mentioned, no, not in the entire bible.

They contradict God, Christ himself, the Holy Ghost, the word of truth, the holy apostles, and the faith once delivered to the saints. 'Imputed'?

Then why the deafening silence? And why do they think it actually says *made*? That is, *poieō, created*?

They are so fond of their titles, collars, gowns, and the like trappings of their acting before men, that reality clean escapes them. 'Imputed'? Christ only suffered the judgment? Judgment for *what*? Whatever, it *must* be for what he actually *became* on the cross in reality, not theory.

If, unquestionably impeccable as when he was first crucified, he was then brought under judgment, judgment for what? Being impeccable? Judgment for a maths calculation, an algebraic equation, a paper imputation, in which he himself remained quite unaltered? Is that 'thorough substitution'?

Made unaltered, is it? Or *made* sin? Judgment on impeccability—even if some such objective mathematical calculation existed—could have imputed nothing but injustice to the Judge.

Christ was judged for what *he had become* for his people's salvation. Not for his impeccable qualification to become it. Having become sin, by the mysterious work of God, in thorough exchange in the place of the sinful, being of God *made sin*, then it was that *reality* which was justly judged.

In no other way *could* sin have been judged and put away with justice.

Otherwise, no *real* condition existed in him to be judged. But God *made, created* that real condition in him—for us—that it *might* be judged, and we delivered.

If not, if—contrary to the scripture—no *actual* condition existed in him—of course by the work of God—demanding of condemnation, such a condemnation would be utterly unjust, and void of saving consequences.

For it would have been impossible justly and in righteousness for him to suffer the punishment for deliverance from what—they say—did not exist in him at the cross.

The 'Christ' of these sanctimonious hypocrites being thought by them to be too 'holy' to submit to all that to which from the hand of God he did submit, then, God could not have been glorified, Christ could not have been a Saviour, and we could never have been saved.

Not by their scheme. No, by their imputation we are yet in our sins, like unto them.

But to the contrary, we have not so learned Christ. We witness that he was without sin. We confess that God *made* him to be sin for us. We *do* confess the Saviour. We *do* believe in his salvation. We *are* delivered from sin. And we *are* become the righteousness of God in him.

Withal—unlike these long-faced, pseudo-righteous, miserable religious academics—we are set at liberty in Christ, rejoicing with joy unspeakable and full of glory.

The apostle teaches precisely the same doctrine in Romans 8:3; 'God sending his own Son in the likeness of sinful flesh'–the Greek reads literally: *in likeness of flesh of sin*–'and for sin'–mark that: *and for sin*–'condemned sin in the flesh.' Ask: *Whose* flesh?

The expression 'God sending his own Son' shows that the Son was with God beforehand, in order to be sent. Contrary to heretics, who would say, God sent him to *be* Son, the word of God declares that he *sent* his Son.

Then, he *was* Son before being sent, without which verity he could not have been *sent* in that name and relationship.

From whom and whence was he sent? From God. With whom he was Son. From above all heavens, where he abode in the glory which he had with the Father before the world was. If, then, with the *Father*, it follows, *as Son*. If as Son with the Father before the world was, then, from eternity. If so, *eternally* Son.

This agrees with the parable: 'Having yet therefore one son'– not yet sent, though many servants had been sent; but the Son abode with the Father–'his wellbeloved, he sent him also last unto them, saying, They will reverence my son', Mark 12:6.

But they did not reverence him, they slew him. Spiritually, so do the Taylor Brethren, the so-called 'Vessel' Baptists, and many other self-deluded Brethren, besides countless that have crept in unawares throughout evangelicalism, Christendom, and the sects.

They do not reverence him: they destroy the truth about him. What truth? That eternally he was Son with the Father and with the Spirit in deity: one God in three persons; three persons in one God.

Take that away, and you take the Saviour away. Take the Saviour away, and you destroy your own salvation.

The one mediator, to be mediator between God and man, must be possessed of both divine nature and human nature in his one person.

Thus the Saviour in his person at once reaches to God, descends to man, and provides the substitutionary sacrifice. Nothing less could answer to salvation.

Hence it is written of the Son whom God sent, 'Who, being in the form of God, thought it not robbery to be equal with God: but made himself of no reputation, and took upon him the form of a servant, and was made in the likeness of men:

'And being found in fashion as a man, he humbled himself, and became obedient unto death, even the death of the cross', Philippians 2:6-8.

The humiliation of this sevenfold descent from the mystery of deity, from the Godhead into manhood, from eternity into time, from the heavenly glory into this present evil world, to take upon himself the likeness of sinful flesh, also appears in Hebrews 10:5.

'Wherefore when he cometh into the world, he saith, Sacrifice and offering thou wouldest not, but a body hast thou prepared me.' Cometh into the world? From whom, from whence? From God the Father, who, Romans 8:3, *sent* his Son, that is, *into the world*, Hebrews 10:5.

If into the world, then from heaven's glory. If the Father sent the Son, then from the highest heavens, inscrutably as Son with the Father and the Spirit, eternally one God in three persons. This is a great mystery, and beyond all understanding; but not beyond faith. By revelation we believe the mystery.

Why was he sent? Because 'Sacrifice and offering thou wouldest not', Hebrews 10:5. The Son uttered these words, Hebrews 10:5, *before* he came into the world, knowing that the carnal and hopelessly inadequate offerings which preceded could *never* take away sin or save sinners.

But he could. And, willingly, he came as the Saviour, who was sent into the world to save sinners, without whom and without which there could be no salvation.

If so, 'in the likeness of sinful flesh.' That is, to take to himself human nature, the chosen and prepared seed of the virgin Mary, into union with his divine nature in his own person.

This was 'the body prepared' of God, for, 'when he cometh into the world, he saith, A body hast thou prepared me', Hebrews 10:5. That is, 'Made in the likeness of men: and being found in fashion as a man', Philippians 2:7,8.

This answers to 'in the likeness of sinful flesh', or, *'in likeness of flesh of sin'*, Romans 8:3. The *likeness* mind. It was of the same liking as other men, but it was not of the same birth and substance as other men. It was *only* in their *likeness*, outwardly. For his birth was unique; and his flesh impeccable.

His flesh—his manhood—was without sin: that is, inbred sin. Therefore it was called by the angel Gabriel, 'that holy thing'. Utterly sinless: absolutely holy: peerless both in conception and substance, born of the virgin Mary, the Saviour, Jesus.

'And the angel said unto her, Fear not, Mary: for thou hast found favour with God. And, behold, thou shalt conceive in thy womb, and bring forth a son, and shalt call his name JESUS', Luke 1:30,31.

'Then said Mary unto the angel, How shall this be, seeing I know not a man? And the angel answered and said unto her, The Holy Ghost shall come upon thee, and the power of the Highest shall overshadow thee: therefore also that holy thing which shall be born of thee shall be called the Son of God', Luke 1:34,35.

Then, as to the conception, substance, and humanity of the Son of God, sent of the Father, it was 'that holy thing'. But, as to exterior appearances, this was like unto men: in the *likeness*, the external *likeness*, of sinful flesh.

But from conception in the womb of the virgin uniquely sinless and impeccable. This is the only Saviour, Jesus Christ.

Next observe the reason for God's sending his Son in the likeness of sinful flesh: it was 'for sin'. That was why he sent him. Then what love is this, both in God for the sending, and in the Son for his coming?

For *sin*, mark. The sin, the inbred sin, that passed from Adam to the entire fallen–yet deceived–human race. To deliver man from *that*, God sent his Son, and his Son came. 'For sin.'

To do what, concerning sin? Condemn it. Sin is a state forever abhorrent to God's holiness: it cannot be forgiven; it can only be destroyed: condemned.

But how to do *that*, without destroying mankind with it, and thereby condemning likewise a humanity born in sin, John 3:6, sold under sin, Romans 7:14, and dying in sin, I Corinthians 15:22?

How? By God's sending another man, a unique man, a sinless man, a perfect substitute, one who could justly exchange places with those born in sin, sold under sin, and dying in sin, so as perfectly–acceptably both to God's holy law, and to his immutable justice–to stand in the stead of the sinful.

Then? Then, God himself having wrought the exchange, to condemn the inbred sin of mankind in the one man who was without sin, that in the place of judgment he–*he!*–should be made sin for us. There is no love like this. All other love pales into insignificance beside this. Singularly, *God* is love.

'God sending his own Son in the likeness of sinful flesh, and for sin, *condemned sin in the flesh.*' This was in the thorough exchange of places. At Golgotha. There, sin was condemned in the flesh. *His* flesh. For us.

Observe that upon the cross, the exchange of places having been wrought of God in a divine mystery, Christ was *made* sin. To condemn sin in the flesh, first, sin must *be* in that flesh; it was: he was *made* sin. *That* is the very essence of the thorough exchange of places at Golgotha.

Condemn sin, notice, Romans 8:3. Not, firstly, receive our condemnation. Or if so, for what? impeccability? sinlessness? No, first, he who was without sin of necessity must be made sin.

Not, firstly take away condemnation. But, firstly, God created, made–*poieō*–those conditions in him on the cross *that were in us*, so that *then*, in him, all might justly and righteously be condemned.

Thereafter, at the cross, God could and did *condemn* sin in the flesh. *His* flesh. *That* took sin away for ever, and with it, all condemnation. So that 'There is therefore now no condemnation to them which are in Christ Jesus', Romans 8:1.

Then it follows, 'But now once in the end of the world hath he appeared to put away sin by the sacrifice of himself', Hebrews 9:26.

Hence, 'Unto them that look for him shall he appear the second time'–at the second coming–'without sin'–*that* having been put away for ever at his first coming–'unto salvation', Hebrews 9:28.

These things being so for all those brought to faith in him for salvation from the condemnation of sin, What of *now*? Sin, however cancelled, is *still* inbred, and still *within*. Then, what of the *power* of that sin?

'Shall we'–having been saved from the condemnation of sin– 'continue in sin'–that is, inbred sin, so as to be in subjection to it–'that grace might abound? God forbid. How shall we, that are dead to sin'–again, this refers to inbred sin–'live any longer therein?', Romans 6:1.

We have not come to the knowledge of the truth that Christ thoroughly exchanged places with us, being made sin in order to take away the terrible condemnation under which we stood, in order to continue under the dominion of sin as if nothing had changed. Or been exchanged. God forbid.

For if he took our place so thoroughly, carrying it down into death to pay the price of our condemnation, now that this *is* paid, and we *are* delivered, the union that was entailed in his having been in our place *is not dissolved*. It remains.

Only, from henceforth, it remains with sin put away and condemnation ceased in the death of the cross.

The union remains; but now 'we are'–in him–'justified from sin', Romans 6:7. In a word, if he exchanged his place for ours under condemnation, he exchanges our place for his in justification. That is, having set us free, taking our place in the crucifixion, freely he gives us his place in the ascension.

Then how shall we continue living under the dominion of inbred sin–however it is still *present* whilst we are in this vile body–when, through Christ having united us with himself in death, we are reckoned to be dead to it?

'Knowing this, that our old man'–from top to bottom–'was crucified with him, that the body of sin might be annulled, *that we no longer be subservient to'*—inbred—*'sin'*, Romans 6:6, literally rendered. Paul continues, 'For he that died has been justified from sin.'

So you see that faith in what Christ has done for us in the exchange of places, and in justification, though all took place in him for us, is no mere objective theory to the faithful, but resounds with tremendous repercussions in the issues of life. And death.

That is, we believe that if he was united with us, *then we are united with him*. A union fully—thoroughly—embracing his death, which faith receives as 'our old man' having been 'crucified with him'. Well, it was. Now how will you live, who believe?

'Now if we *died* with Christ, we believe that we shall also live with him: knowing that Christ having been raised from the death dies no more; death no more rules over him.' So the Greek reads, Romans 6:8,9.

Then, the thorough exchange of places being given, and it is given; union being sustained, and it is sustained: What shall be the reckoning of faith despite the *presence* of inbred sin still in our mortal bodies?

Why, the reckoning of faith looks up, and, like David, says, 'I foresaw the Lord always before my face.' Yes, but looking down, what of the inbred sin he bore away under condemnation, still in the body till the resurrection? But *why* look down, when everything worth seeing is up?

Rather, 'Reckon ye also yourselves to be dead indeed unto sin'—whether *it* is dead to *you*, or not: Christ died to it, and, in spirit, you are united to him—'but alive unto God through Jesus Christ our Lord.

'Let not sin therefore reign'—not *be*; only the resurrection will change *that*: but *be* or not, let it not *reign*—'in your mortal body'–because Christ took it upon himself, carrying it down into death, under judgment from condemnation, on your behalf– 'to obey it in its desires.

'Neither yield ye your members as instruments of unright-eousness unto'–inbred–'sin: but yield yourselves unto God, *as those that are alive from the dead*, and your members as instruments of righteousness unto God', Romans 6:11-13.

Then, if brought to faith in Christ; if believing that Christ exchanged himself in our place in death, and gives his place in exchange for us in life; if always beholding the Lord; if ever looking up into heaven: 'sin'–inbred sin–'shall not have dominion over you.' You can reckon on that.

What could be more clear, more transparent, or more lucid, than the light that shines from heaven upon this glorious truth of the evangel of Christ, laid up, treasured, credited, in the heart of the believer?

Nothing could be clearer to faith, because 'the true light now shineth', and, to all that are of faith, it shines upon this same evangel of Christ, radiating salvation from the Saviour in the glory.

But someone will object, All this is true, but why have you not mentioned the Holy Spirit?

Because the apostles' doctrine, revealing the evangel of Christ, focuses precisely upon deliverance from inbred sin in the sixth chapter of the epistle to the Romans. This point of focus has been reached by systematic exposition, commencing at Romans 1:18.

In Romans 1:18 to 5:10 the apostle had been opening the truth of salvation from sins.

However, from chapter 5:11 to 8:30 the doctrine reveals the root and nature of inbred sin, and sets forth in order the deliverance of the faithful from, first, the condemnation, next the power, and finally the presence of that sin.

Therefore in showing how God by Jesus Christ delivers from the power of inbred sin – the matter presently occupying the attention – no more appropriate place could be afforded us than Romans 6:1-14.

It is the word of God on this very question. It is where the apostle himself, having discovered to us the nature of inbred sin, goes on to show our deliverance.

Why do I say this? Because certain persons, deviating from the apostles' doctrine, object that nothing has been said – yet – about the Holy Spirit.

The answer to these simple-minded and erroneous persons is provided by this very epistle: *where nothing about the Holy Spirit has been mentioned as to experimental deliverance from sin up to and including Romans 6:14.*

Why not? Because the Spirit does not speak of himself: he takes the things of *Christ*, and shows *them* unto us. Nowhere is this better illustrated than in this context leading up to and including Romans 6:1-14.

'When he, the Spirit of truth, is come, he will guide you into all truth: *for he shall not speak of himself*; but whatsoever he shall hear, that shall he speak: and he will show you things to come.

'He shall *glorify me*: for he shall *take of mine*, and show *it* unto you. All things that the Father hath are mine: therefore said I, *he shall take of mine*, and shall show *it* unto you', John 16:13-15.

Once Christ's salvation and his deliverance have been set forth *to his glory alone* in the evangel, and every objection answered, *then*, and only then, truth as to the work of the Spirit himself – for that is another matter – is made clear in its place, as Romans chapter 8 demonstrates.

First consider all the references to the Holy Spirit, and, indeed, to the word 'spirit', from the very beginning of the epistle up to Romans 6:14, by which time both salvation from sins, and deliverance from sin, had been opened fully, to the glory of Christ.

At the commencement of this epistle, in which Paul proposes by the Holy Ghost to reveal the salvation of God in the work of Jesus Christ, his first words point to the *person* of Christ. Why? Because the value of the work depends upon the worth of the person.

Hence the opening reference, in the brief summary of the person of Christ in Romans 1:2-4, speaks of the person of the incarnate Son, risen from the dead, thence declared to be 'the Son of God with power, according to the spirit of holiness, by the resurrection from the dead', Romans 1:4.

But this—note the lower case 's' in the English—refers to *his* spirit, rather than the person of the Holy Spirit, a point no serious exponent would dispute.

The next reference occurs in Romans 2:29, where the apostle contrasts the outward with the inward Jew. It is the inward Jew whose praise is of God. What distinguishes him? Circumcision of the heart, in the spirit, and not in the letter. That is, in the interior spirit of him whose praise is not of man, but of God.

Clearly this does not refer to the Holy Ghost, but to the spirit of the man himself, however the work within that man may have been wrought by the Spirit of God.

The point made by Paul is that the man's religion does not stand in the mere profession and outward claim of text and letter of scripture.

No; it stands in both heart circumcision and the devoutness of the man's interior spirit to the glory of God, irrespective of pleasing man, or seeking honour from men, or of appearances in the world.

Here again, this second occurrence does not point to the Holy Spirit. As yet in this epistle, he has not been mentioned.

The first and only mention of the Holy Spirit in the entire text of the epistle to the Romans up to Romans 6:14 occurs in chapter 5:5, 'And hope maketh not ashamed; because the love of God is shed abroad in our hearts by the Holy Ghost which is given unto us.'

In context, these words conclude a series of expressions, one leading to another, concerning the experiences of those who, having been justified by faith, have been brought into peace with God.

Romans 5:5 is the final statement. It is not directly about our experience of the love of God, or of the Holy Ghost, it is directly to do with our experience of hope.

As to this hope, not only is the love of God shed abroad in our hearts, but we have an inward witness to its validity which makes its fulfilment certain.

That witness is the Holy Ghost, witnessing within–together with the love of God–to the certainty of the realization of all that upon which our hope is set.

Our hope is assured *because* the love of God is shed abroad in our hearts by the Holy Ghost. That tells us our hope is of God, that *his* love is set upon our receiving all that we hope for, and as to this, it has the divine testimony of the Spirit in our hearts.

But this is not directly to do with expounding our having been delivered from sin. Although Romans 5:1-5 certainly shows the consequence of deliverance, directly the passage has to do with our experience as being justified by faith, neither more nor less.

The context moves on completely from this cumulative expression—Romans 5:1-5—and leaves it behind as the apostle proceeds with the revelation of deliverance from sin, in particular, the *katallagē*, the exchange of places.

As to this brief mention of the Holy Ghost in Romans 5:5— the *only* mention in six chapters—note that it is in connection with the witness of the love of God being shed abroad in our hearts—observe, 'our' is plural; this is a *corporate* witness—the Holy Ghost is said to have been 'given to us'.

But when given—in the preceding chapters—if not mentioned before? And how given—in all the teaching from Romans 1:1 up to this point— if not one word about him has been written, no, not throughout some six chapters of evangelical doctrine?

And consider this also: there is mention in abundance and reference after reference to the Holy Ghost once the apostle reaches Romans chapter 8. *But not before.*

I repeat, *consider* this, and carefully follow the truth of our salvation proceeding from the mouth of the Lord, mind of the Spirit, and pen of the apostle.

Remember that before Romans chapter 8 the Holy Ghost has been mentioned only once, and at that, in what amounts to an aside. Yet, suddenly the references to the Spirit in chapter 8 are abundant.

Then, how did the saints receive that Spirit so manifestly apparent in the eighth chapter of Romans? From whence came he? And at what point?

This is not answered. It is not even remotely discussed. In chapter 8 he is simply *there*. It is just assumed that, believing, on arriving at that chapter, *one already has the Spirit*, thereafter to be referred to so frequently. Yet, before, he is virtually unmentioned.

But what *has* been mentioned – expounded in detail – is the wonderful salvation of God in the evangel concerning his Son, Jesus Christ our Lord, radiating in light from the central verity of his work on the cross.

The conclusion is inescapable: *embrace that, and the Spirit follows of course. Believe that, and the Spirit is received inevitably.*

Notice therefore with the greatest carefulness that *although there is no mention of the Spirit pertinent to the unfolding revelation of the evangel throughout Romans 1 to 7 inclusive, when it comes to chapter 8 reference after reference occurs, as if the Spirit were taken for granted as already having been outpoured.*

The Spirit is referred to in Romans 8 in verses 1,2,4,5,5,9,9,9, 10,11,11,13,14,15,15,16,23,26,26, and 27. And no mention before?

No. Nothing but *the truth* before. Yet in chapter 8 evidently the Spirit has *already been outpoured.* How is this? Because he is the Spirit *of truth*, who has come *not to speak of himself, but to glorify Christ.*

Testifying of Christ and his work in the truth, *the Spirit is the inspiration behind every word given by the apostle, from the very beginning of the revelation of the evangel to the end of it.*

Now, that salvation having been set forth from first to last, the faithful filled with the Holy Ghost in consequence, the issues of the Spirit follow in chapter 8.

Wherefore it is evident that the twenty references to the Spirit compacted together in this remarkable chapter – after seven chapters with no reference whatever, save one in passing, not germane to the teaching itself – follow *after the doctrine, and after the mind and heart of the saints has been settled in the word of truth, the evangel of their salvation.*

As if to say, once *that* is established in the faith of the saints, the Spirit is taken for granted as having *caused* the faith of all who believe thus to glorify Christ in his person, death, and risen life.

Moreover, at the last, so to reckon oneself as having died with Christ, and, accordingly, to be risen with him in newness of life: that is, life *in the Spirit*.

But to the Spirit, *Christ and his work are first and foremost*, and it is *of him and his things* that he came to speak: not of himself. Christ above all, the doctrine of Christ first, so that of all who believe it is said, 'Ye have obeyed from the heart that form of doctrine which was delivered you', Romans 6:17.

By this wonderful truth – for 'ye shall know the truth, and *the truth* shall make you free' – filling heart and mind in and with the Saviour and that salvation wrought by him, the Son of God is glorified in the midst of the *ecclesia*.

In this way the Spirit of truth – not speaking of himself – bears witness throughout the company of the saints.

That being given, chapter 8 opens up just how glorious is the inspiration and testimony of the Spirit, and precisely *how* the saints answer to such a divine witness.

If so, it is hardly surprising in such a case – the occasion now having arrived – to find no less than twenty references to his divine person and work in glorifying Christ to and within the saints.

Whereas the primary work of the Spirit in those brought to faith is – in a manner – one in which he effaces himself, because it is *the faith of Christ to which they are brought* that fills the vision of the heart, as is so evident in Romans chapters 1 to 7. This agrees entirely with the prophecy of Jesus.

'Howbeit when he, the Spirit of truth, is come, he will guide you into all truth.'

Then, it is *the truth of which he is the Spirit* that is primarily apparent. Just as it is *all the truth into which the saints are guided* that is at first more conspicuous than the Spirit who guides them into that truth.

This agrees entirely with the unfolding of Romans chapters 1 to 7, in which–save for one aside–*the Spirit is not mentioned.*

'For he shall not speak of himself.' Nor does he, *though, by the apostle, and by the resonance in the saints of the apostles' doctrine, it is abundantly clear that it is he who speaks.*

Then, speaks of whom? 'He shall glorify me: for he shall take of mine, and shall show it unto you.' If so, his speech is of *Christ.* This is exactly what has been demonstrably manifested in Romans chapters 1 to 7.

But now, chapter 8, Christ, and the salvation which is in him, having been set forth in the unfolding of the evangel; truth having been opened; Christ having been glorified: the Spirit declares of himself the things which pertain to the pathway of all who believe, and exhorts them in their response to his indwelling witness.

Romans chapter 8 falls into three parts, the first of which is pertinent to the present opening of salvation or deliverance from the power of sin, so wonderfully revealed in the doctrine which preceded in the previous chapters.

Hence it is to Romans 8:1-14–the first part of chapter 8–that attention is now drawn.

There is absolutely no question but that the Spirit witnesses that the saints still dwell in the body of inbred sin, though it is equally clear that they are reckoned, and reckon themselves, crucified to it as being dead with Christ.

Nevertheless this is the reckoning of faith: the fact is that though they are dead to the body of sin, it is neither removed from nor is it dead to them.

This creates an irreconcilable antipathy between what is theirs in Christ, with the indwelling Spirit testifying of all the grace wherein they stand, and the reality of what the apostle calls 'the flesh'. The flesh being the inbred sin which Paul calls elsewhere 'this vile body'.

It is the inward warfare and affliction that the presence of these two opposites create within the saints that constitutes the matter of Romans chapter 8.

There is no escaping the sufferings of this present time, or the inward groanings, afflictions, and tribulation caused by the presence of inbred sin – however crucified this has been on their behalf in Christ; and no matter to what degree this is reckoned to be the position of the saints – it is a warfare that is without quarter or cessation till the day of resurrection.

It is this warfare that occupies the apostolic revelation in the first part of Romans 8 – indeed, in the second part also: the third, however, shows the certain triumph assured to the saints in all their calling, sojourning, and overcoming.

Then it is no surprise to find in the first part of the chapter – Romans 8:1-14 – a series of contrasts, in which opposites are set the one over against the other, with the saints being exhorted appropriately by the Spirit through the apostle in each instance.

This is illustrated by the eightfold use of the word 'but', indicating contrariety: 'not this' *but* 'that'.

It is a question of *acting and of moving* by faith. Hence verbs are used.

The first verb is in verses 1-4, and concerns *walking*. Now, that is acting and moving in reality. The second occurs in verses 5-7 and pertains to *minding*. This is acting and moving mentally.

The third, verses 8-11, refers to *dwelling*. Here it is a question of constant habitation. And the fourth, in verses 12-13, concerns *living*. Which is the act or movement of life itself.

However, these four movements of faith are in the Spirit, despite the presence of inbred sin in the body, over which they have the ascendancy: 'for sin shall not have dominion over you.' In walking; minding; dwelling; and living in the Spirit, the saints have dominion over sin.

Nevertheless it is a warfare, and war is costly. Hence in respect of the four verbs there is a 'but'. Not walking *so*, but *thus*. Not minding *this* but *that*. Not dwelling in *the one*, but in *the other*. Not living *in this manner* but *in that manner*.

A contrast, you see: not merely intellectual, but for life. In fact there are *eight* 'buts'.

In a word, not after the flesh *but* after the Spirit. This follows of course, from the Spirit having previously glorified Christ and his work for and in the saints. Thus those that are of faith are given the victory, and embody the truth of salvation from the power of inbred sin.

But what of the *presence* of inbred sin? Well, that we must suffer, but not so as it should have dominion over us. That cannot be. The denial of self, and the daily cross, are the rule of faith. But, as said, this warfare is costly.

'For we that are in this tabernacle do groan, being burdened.' But we faint not, 'though our outward man perish, yet the inward man is renewed day by day', II Corinthians 4:16; 5:4.

The apostle reckons that 'the sufferings of this present time are not worthy to be compared with the glory which shall be revealed in us.'

Maybe. But sufferings, throughout the conflict, for the duration of the warfare, necessarily follow because of the contrast. And sufferings they surely are. But, behold, look up! For these sufferings 'are not worthy to be compared with the glory which shall be revealed in us', Romans 8:18.

We long to be delivered, groan to be saved, travail to be delivered from inbred sin in the body. But this cannot be; no, not till the resurrection. Nor do we groan alone: creation itself groans. 'For we know that the whole creation groaneth and travaileth in pain together until now.

'And not only the creation'—groans and travails in pain— 'but ourselves also, which have the firstfruits of the Spirit.'

We also groan and travail in pain, waiting for the manifestation of the sons of God in the resurrection, for the coming inheritance of glory.

Oh! we do groan; it is hard labour; pain abides our earthly pilgrimage, so long as we are in this vile body.

'Even we ourselves groan within ourselves, waiting for'— the translators give the utterly erroneous 'adoption', the very opposite of the Spirit's use of the Greek—'the place of sonship, to wit, the redemption of our body', Romans 8:22,23.

The redemption of our body—which body was the purchased possession when Christ put away sin by the offering up of himself— shall appear in the resurrection from the dead. This is to be saved from the presence of sin.

Because in the resurrection what was reckoned in the crucifixion, and imparted in sanctification, shall be realized in 'a body like unto his glorious body'.

Then, we shall have been 'delivered from the bondage of corruption into the glorious liberty of the children of God.'

Now, we groan; we travail; we suffer; we are in pain. But 'the Spirit also helpeth our infirmities: for we know not what we should pray for as we ought: but the Spirit himself maketh intercession for us with groanings which cannot be uttered.'

This is that of which Paul speaks, and for which he strove; travailed; pained; and groaned.

'That'–despite this vile body, and its inbred sin–'I may know him, and the power of his resurrection, and the fellowship of his sufferings, being made conformable unto his death; if by any means I might attain unto the resurrection of the dead', Philippians 3:10,11.

But, looking up, rejoicing in the victorious triumph of Christ on our behalf, 'our conversation is in heaven; from whence also we look for the Saviour, the Lord Jesus Christ:

'Who shall change our vile body, that it may be fashioned like unto his glorious body, according to the working whereby he is able even to subdue all things unto himself', Philippians 3:20,21.

Now, *this* is deliverance from the presence of inbred sin. That is, the presence of inbred sin in the body, whereby, in the ignominy of death, it is sown in corruption; it is sown in dishonour; it is sown in weakness; and it is sown a natural body.

Yes, but it is raised in incorruption; it is raised in glory; it is raised in power; it is raised a spiritual body. For the resurrection is in the likeness of his glorious body, in which death is swallowed up in victory.

Behold, for we, who groaned in travail below, shall cry in triumph above, O death, where is thy sting? O grave, where is thy victory? Thanks be to God, which giveth us the victory through our Lord Jesus Christ.

Now, this is salvation from the presence of inbred sin, and completes the work of God in Christ of Salvation from Sin. That is, from inbred sin, whether it be the guilt of sin; the power of sin; or the presence of sin. In all, the victory of faith speaketh on this wise: 'If God be for us, who can be against us?

'He that spared not his own Son, but delivered him up for us all, how shall he not with him also freely give us all things? Who shall lay anything to the charge of God's elect? It is God that justifieth.

'Who is he that condemneth? It is Christ that died, yea rather, that is risen again, who is even at the right hand of God, who also maketh intercession for us.' 'Thanks be to God, which giveth us the victory through our Lord Jesus Christ.' Amen.

PART TWO

SALVATION FROM SATAN

SALVATION FROM SATAN

IV
The 'Satan'

BECAUSE no one will miss the meaning, I have used the title 'Satan'. This is clearly understood in common parlance. But the meaning is not.

In fact, thoroughly scrutinizing the general idea of 'Satan' brings two anomalies to light. First, the word means nothing in English. It is a Hebrew word. It means something in Hebrew. Then why not translate the Hebrew, instead of transliterating it? Because it *ought* to be translated.

The second irregularity follows: when translated from Hebrew into English—instead of carting the unintelligible Hebrew word over into the English tongue so as to give us a foreign word that means nothing—what comes into prominence is that 'Satan' *is not a name at all*. It is the description of an activity.

But English-speaking—and other—people suppose it to be a name. Not at all.

In fact the malevolent being, wrongly understood to be named in English 'Satan', is not so named at all. This has been effectively obscured by the unwarranted but long-standing transliteration of the Hebrew. But in truth one knows him *by what he does*. That, 'Satan', rightly translated, begins to make clear.

So also do some fifteen other such descriptive words concerning his activity. As to any *personal* name, it does not exist. He is never given a name.

In obscuring this, whether by unwarranted transliteration, or blundering mistranslation, to which might well be added, the unbelieving and dumb ignorance of the blind leaders of the blind, few have *the least idea* of what they are talking about. Or what they are hearing.

Then, let this be remedied forthwith, beginning with the truth concerning 'Salvation from Satan'.

The Hebrew description *satan* is the first unequivocal reference in the bible to that supernatural, spiritual, and invisible being who gives himself to the activity portrayed by this word.

I say unequivocal reference because of course an allegorical reference in Genesis precedes this intimation. The allegorical reference will be opened in its place.

Whilst the Hebrew *satan* connects with certain cognate words, including one differing only by the occurrence of vowel 'points'—old testament Hebrew virtually possesses only consonants: the Masoretic 'pointings' were added external to these by scribes—it is quite sufficient to take the word in question by itself: little or nothing is to be gained by a more extended enquiry.

In the English bible the description *satan* occurs in this form some twenty-seven times, but not all refer to the activity of the same being: indeed on one occasion the descriptive Hebrew word *satan* is attributed to the work of the angel of the LORD.

Perhaps no more than seventeen old testament references—though more likely fifteen—point without question to the opposition and disposition of the supernatural being implacably at enmity against the work of God on earth.

These occurrences are found first in the book of Job, and last in that of the prophet Zechariah. Here without question appear indisputable allusions to the relentless enmity of a vastly superior, supernatural, and heavenly opponent of the people of God.

Then why transliterate, and not translate? As to the translation, nothing serves to render the Hebrew *satan* in English better than the word *adversary*. Indeed, the translators themselves have rendered the word 'satan' as *adversary* seven times, then failed to translate it at all—simply transliterating *satan*—nineteen times.

I suppose it *is* possible to be more confounded, and likewise further to sow the seeds of confusion by this ridiculous partiality in picking and choosing whether to translate or transliterate.

The reason for this is of course the conjecture that in the Hebrew 'adversary' can *also* refer to a *virtuous* opponent, as, for example, Numbers 22:22 'the angel of the LORD stood in the way for an adversary'—a *satan*—'against him.'

But the translators intended to substitute their intellectual musings concerning the Hebrew word *satan*—in place of the wisdom of God by the Holy Ghost—by picking and choosing what they should translate and what they should transliterate.

This arrogance caused them to insert the Hebrew *satan* into an otherwise entirely English text, wherever they thought the

Hebrew referred to the malevolent spiritual being in question. But they were neither consistent nor right.

This naturally led to the assumption on the part of the English reader that *satan* was a proper name. It is not. It is the description of an activity that may be applied to *any* opponent, good or bad.

The fact that the opponent was malevolent in Job and Zechariah is beside the point: translation was their duty, not meddling with words which the Holy Ghost gave. The Hebrew *satan* should have been translated by the English *adversary* consistently.

The book of Job properly introduces the supernatural and heavenly being described under his activity *satan*, the adversarial pursuit to which he was given from the beginning.

The adversary appears twice in the opening chapters of this scripture, but these two appearances are not on earth: they are in heaven. They are not before mankind: they are before God.

To all intents and purposes this is the first unquestionable appearance of the dread and malevolent supernatural being who assumes the character of an adversary—*the* adversary—or, to give the equivalent Hebrew, a *satan*—*the* satan—implacably devoted to the fall and destruction of the true worshipper.

The two appearances of the adversary in the book of Job are remarkable, not least because both are before the LORD in the highest heavens.

Nevertheless, these appearances have disastrous consequences for Job so far distant on the earth below, utterly oblivious of what had just taken place infinitely far in heaven above.

Having first drawn attention to Job's character, that he was perfect and upright, and one that feared God and eschewed evil, that the blessing of the LORD was upon him, his household, and his substance, is very evident.

There was none like him in all the earth. Yes, but immediately the narrative ascends to the utmost heights of heaven's glory, even into the presence of the LORD.

In these glorious heights 'the sons of God'–that is, 'offspring'; angelic beings so called to distinguish them from the children of men–assemble before the LORD. The *satan*–namely, and rightly in English, the *adversary*–came *also* among them. If so, already distinguished from them.

This is the first of two such heavenly assemblies, in each of which the *description* 'satan', the 'adversary', refers to him who came *also* among the 'sons of God' to present himself with them.

On both such occasions the LORD addresses Satan, drawing the adversary's attention to the unwitting Job, so far below.

The first of these incidents appears in Job 1:6-12. The second in chapter 2:1-7. Each time the description *satan*, properly translated *adversary*, occurs seven times: the number of perfection. If so, he is shown to be an adversary to perfection, as appears thereafter.

These assemblies are the only two visions into the heavens throughout the book. All else occurs on the earth. None upon earth had any idea that such things had taken place in heaven, least of all Job.

Nevertheless the two heavenly assemblies were the cause of all that happened in the forty-two long chapters which follow. The reader is privileged to witness a revelation in heaven utterly hidden from the contemporary earthly participants on earth.

In the first revelation of heavenly things the LORD questions the adversary, 'Whence comest thou?'. Then the adversary answered the LORD, 'From going to and fro in the earth, and from walking up and down in it', Job 1:7.

This indicates searching: restlessly questing for something below, as if it were lost. Searching for what? For true worshippers.

In which search, evidently, the adversary was hard put to find success in his to-ing and fro-ing and walking up and down in the earth.

But the LORD assists him in his restive seeking: 'Hast thou considered my servant Job, that there is none like him in the earth, a perfect and an upright man, one that feareth God, and escheweth evil?'

Thus the LORD defines the true worshipper: he is the LORD's servant; he is unique; he is perfect; he is upright; he is a man; he fears God; and he eschews evil. Sevenfold. Perfect.

And *had* the adversary considered him, in all his agitated wanderings, looking here and there over all the earth? Oh, yes: he had considered him. But sullenly he implies, What was the use?

For God had put a hedge about Job, and the adversary could not walk through it, go beyond it, but must retreat from it. However, now he has a suggestion, provoked and encouraged by the LORD's deliberate question.

For the LORD had a purpose unknown to Satan. Hence the question, provoking precisely the desired response, and leading to exactly the ultimate realization of the will of God.

But the adversary, frustrated by the hedge, provoked by the question, complains. He asserts that Job serves the LORD from no motive save gain: for selfish reasons. But this is to judge Job by his own nature. He can do no other: he cannot believe in any good, nor that such a thing as unselfishness exists. Therefore, to him, Job cannot be other than himself.

Hence the suggestion: 'Put forth thine hand now, and touch all that he hath, and he will curse thee to thy face.' The adversary really believed that. He could not, and he cannot, believe in goodness, or selfless love. Cynical to the core, he supposes everything to be according to his own disposition.

And, on earth, this might well be so. With an exception. The true worshipper. But he does not believe in true worshippers. He believes they have a selfish motive. Then, saith the LORD, Take away his motive. Satan did. He descended, and, the hedge removed, went in and took away all that Job had. All that was left, was his person.

But Job did not react as the adversary predicted. He did not at all curse God to his face. He did precisely the opposite. Because in fact he *was* a true worshipper. Far from the adversary's prediction, Job worshipped, saying, 'The LORD gave, and the LORD hath taken away; blessed be the name of the LORD.'

Frustrated, the adversary ascended, attending the second and last assembly in heaven recorded in the book of Job. The LORD asked, and he answered, as before. But again the LORD replied, 'Hast thou considered my servant Job, that there is none like him in the earth?

'A perfect and an upright man, one that feareth God, and escheweth evil? and still'–after such terrible destruction–'he holdeth fast his integrity, although thou movedst me against him, to destroy him without cause', Job 2:3.

That was it: for all the adversary had presumed, and all the havoc he had wrought, Job held fast his integrity. The adversary would not accept it. This did not fall within his comprehension. To him, there must be a hidden reason. Then, it must be because Job *himself* was untouched.

Therefore the adversary answered the LORD, 'Skin for skin, yea, all that a man hath will he give for his life. But put forth

111

thine hand now, and touch his bone and his flesh, and he will curse thee to thy face. And the LORD said unto the adversary, Behold, he is in thine hand; but save his life.'

So the adversary went forth from the presence of the LORD, and smote Job with sore boils from the sole of his foot unto his crown. And Job took him a potsherd to scrape himself with, and he sat down among the ashes.

'Then said his wife unto him, Dost thou still retain thine integrity? curse God, and die. But he said unto her, Thou speakest as one of the foolish women speaketh. What? shall we receive good at the hand of God, and shall we not receive evil? In all this did not Job sin with his lips', Job 2:9,10.

So much for Job's wife. As to his friends, these come to Job as false comforters, tormenting him beyond measure even while beholding his appalling bodily affliction and anguish of spirit, finding the reason for his calamities in what Job knew within himself was not true.

But what was true? Job agonized over this question throughout his long affliction. He knew what was untrue: then what was the cause? Without vision into heaven, and revelation from the LORD, Job remained in perplexity. So much so that the expression became legendary: 'Ye have heard of the patience of Job.'

For some forty-two long chapters Job's three false comforters–and Job himself–searched for a reason for his affliction.

But none either mentioned or so much as envisaged the existence of the adversary; or of the two assemblies in heaven; or of the LORD's praise of Job before the adversary; or yet of the adversary's challenge and contention, or, finally, of the twofold permission granted to him.

However neither Job nor his three 'friends' had the reader's advantage of the heavenly visions declaring the true cause of all

that followed thereafter, written and revealed at the commencement of the book.

Nevertheless, to all intents and purposes, this is the first
time that so malevolent, supernatural, invisible, and heavenly
a spiritual being appears under the description 'adversary'–
Hebrew, *satan*.

And the character of that appearance is one of unmitigated
and relentless malice against the true worshipper. Which was
the more aggravated by his inability to vent that hatred without
the express permission from the LORD in heaven.

The granting of this permission was the real cause of Job's
affliction: if it was anything in Job himself–as his three 'friends'
laboured so long and hard to prove to Job's condemnation–it
was in fact that the LORD in heaven asserted him to be unique,
a worshipper, a perfect man, both upright and God-fearing.

But for it all, the end of the LORD–whatever permission was
granted the adversary at the beginning–resulted in so much the
more experimental knowledge of God to Job, that this quite
eclipsed the light he had at the beginning of his long, long trial.

In that, the adversary, unwittingly, brought the greatest blessing
to Job, and the most glory to God.

And if this is not salvation, What is? 'So the LORD blessed
the latter end of Job more than his beginning', Job 42:12. This
is called 'Salvation from Satan'.

The second and last incontestable reference in the old testament to the adversary, that is, *the* 'satan'–with the article,
and under that description–occurs in the book of the prophet
Zechariah.

'And he showed me Joshua the high priest standing before the
angel of the LORD, and the adversary standing at his right hand
to be his adversary'–for so the Hebrew should be translated.

'And the LORD said unto the adversary, The LORD rebuke thee, O adversary; even the LORD that hath chosen Jerusalem rebuke thee: is not this a brand plucked out of the fire? Now Joshua was clothed with filthy garments, and stood before the angel.

'And he answered and spake unto those that stood before him, saying, Take away the filthy garments from him. And unto him he said, Behold, I have caused thine iniquity to pass from thee, and I will clothe thee with change of raiment.

'And I said, Let them set a fair mitre upon his head. So they set a fair mitre upon his head, and clothed him with garments. And the angel of the LORD stood by.

'And the angel of the LORD protested unto Joshua, saying, Thus saith the LORD of hosts; If thou wilt walk in my ways, and if thou wilt keep my charge, then thou shalt also judge my house, and shalt also keep my courts, and I will give thee places to walk among these that stand by', Zechariah 3:1-7.

This is the fourth of eight visions revealed to the prophet Zechariah at what was left of Jerusalem.

For seventy years Jerusalem had been razed to the ground, the temple destroyed, and the people carried away into Babylon. Now at last the decree had gone forth from Cyrus, king of Persia, and well over forty thousand Jews returned to Judah and Benjamin from the captivity in Babylon, to rebuild the house of God.

At length the altar was set up and the foundations of the temple were laid. But this was amidst the blackened ruins of what had once been the glorious and holy city of Jerusalem.

And when the adversaries of Judah and Benjamin heard of the setting up of the altar and laying of the foundations, their offered 'help' being rejected, they hired counsellors against the Jews, and by guile and envious hatred caused the work to cease.

For some years the adversaries prevailed, and the work languished. There was no further progress. Nothing was added to the existence of the altar or of the foundations.

Then God raised up and sent the prophets Haggai and Zechariah, whose prophesying in the name of the God of Israel stirred up the Jews to continue the rebuilding, despite the enmity of their adversaries, whose opposition, rekindled, came to nothing.

For this thing was from the LORD. The matter was heavenly and spiritual. It was not of man at all. This was what the visions of Zechariah the prophet depict so vividly, and none more so than the fourth of these openings.

Zechariah, whose eyes were lifted up and opened to behold the true and ultimate cause of the matter, was not disobedient to the heavenly vision revealed to him by the God of Israel: 'And he showed me Joshua the high priest standing before the angel of the LORD, and the adversary–*the satan*–standing at his right hand to be an adversary to him.'

Over all the rolling ages of time since first the adversary appeared in the opening of the book of Job, this second appearance in the book of the prophet Zechariah shows that the implacable malice of the supernatural and invisible being in heaven was unabated, and his opposition unrelenting. Though nothing had been openly revealed since Job, nothing had changed.

The adversary–invisible and unaltered–was stirred to activity by the return of the captivity to rebuild the house of God. To his consternation, the altar had been set up, and the foundations laid.

Agitating both the enemies of the Jews, besides false brethren, the adversary played upon the fear and unbelief of the people, so that in the visions it becomes evident that *he* was the one who had caused the work to cease.

For, as in Job, the malevolence of the adversary was set against the true worshipper. But the very cause for which the LORD had brought back the captivity was the rebuilding of God's chosen place of worship, the temple of God, God's house.

This was at the centre of the recovery of the worship of God, of the service and priesthood; of God's ways, God's charge, and God's courts. Thus, to rebuild the house was to bring in the true worshippers and place of worship, and against it the adversary set himself.

It was evident to the adversary that the time was critical. Having so long succeeded in ruining the testimony of God, and advancing the Babel of confusion, he was aroused to prevent the recovery of worship by the priestly remnant now returned from Babylon to Jerusalem.

All that he had cast down was in jeopardy, and, given the sending of the prophet, in imminent danger of being wholly undone.

Hence *the satan* contests the right of the recovery because of the unfit state of the worshipper, embodied and represented by Joshua the high priest.

In this contest stand four parties: Joshua; the angel of the LORD; the adversary standing at his right hand; and those that stood before the angel of the LORD, Zechariah 3:1,4.

The contest was legal. Hence the adversary's stance on the right hand.

What was contested? The dreadful and filthy state of Joshua the high priest, and therefore the rightness and lawfulness of so unsuited a person to bring in recovery or to order the rebuilding of the house: 'Now Joshua was clothed with filthy garments', Zechariah 3:3.

The mute witness of that defiled figure should have ended any contest. Joshua could say nothing. He remained speechless.

But he had an advocate in the angel of the LORD, who, whilst admitting the case put by the adversary, nevertheless pointed to an antidote which nullified every argument against the suitability of Joshua the high priest ministering in a recovered testimony.

An high priest to whom iniquity is imputed, and, at that, clothed in filthy rags? Then how can *he* minister in God's house?

How can he himself worship, let alone lead the worshippers? How could the house be rebuilt for such a polluted service? Iniquity is the barrier. Dirt prevents; filthy rags exclude. The adversary is right.

It is not the ungodliness of the uncircumcised, of a man in the world, nor is it a question of the justification of a sinner. It is a matter of a defiled condition in the priesthood, then, in the worshippers represented by Joshua.

This—given the right pleaded by the adversary—*must* prevent the rebuilding of the original testimony of God, which had been broken down and ruined by the Babylonians so long before.

Yet the LORD has an answer. The angel of the LORD puts the accuser to shame. 'I Jesus have sent mine angel', Revelation 22:16. Not to accuse, but to acquit. Not to condemn, but to justify. Not to exclude, but to include.

For there is a 'Lamb slain from the foundation of the world', Revelation 13:8, and, if so, *provision in the mind of God to apply salvation through his blood in view of all those under the old testament who trusted in a coming Saviour, the sacrifice of whom in the event would be counted in their stead.*

This propitiation, through faith in his blood, is more than sufficient for God to impute righteousness, not iniquity, to all the old testament saints who died in faith.

As saith the apostle Paul, 'to declare his'–God's–'righteousness for the remission of sins that are past'–that is, past in the old testament–'through the forbearance of God', Romans 3:25.

Where, evidently, the apostle refers to remission applying to those of faith in times long gone by.

For example, to Joshua in Zechariah's time past. In time long gone by even unto Joshua the high priest. Yea, to the patriarchs from the foundation of the world. To Abraham, who believed God, and it was accounted to him for righteousness. And, pray, what can the adversary say to that?

No wonder *the satan* could answer not a word when the angel of the LORD showed forth the salvation of God in the teeth of the adversary's otherwise just accusation, commencing with–not the filthy garments, but what preceded them–Joshua's iniquity.

'And unto him he said, Behold, I have caused thine iniquity to pass from thee', Zechariah 3:4.

As said the prophet Isaiah of the coming Saviour so long before, 'He was wounded for our transgressions, he was bruised for our iniquities: the chastisement of our peace was upon him; and with his stripes we are healed.'

And again, 'the LORD hath laid on him the iniquity of us all.'

And if so, then of Joshua the high priest. And if laid on the Saviour before the time yet to come, no less effectual in the time then present.

As saith David, long before Isaiah: 'Blessed is the man unto whom the LORD imputeth not iniquity.' And again, 'Who forgiveth all thine iniquities.' Once more, 'He shall redeem Israel from all his iniquities.'

Wherefore the LORD saith to Joshua the high priest so much later, 'Behold, I have caused thine iniquity to pass from thee'.

But what of the filthy garments? This of the filthy garments: 'And he answered and spake unto those that stood before him'– that is, those ministering spirits, sent forth to minister for them who shall be heirs of salvation, Hebrews 1:14–'saying, Take away the filthy garments from him.'

'And unto him he said, I will clothe thee with change of raiment.'

Priestly raiment. The raiment of Aaron his father, and of his sons.

Concerning which it was said to Moses, 'And thou shalt take of the blood that is upon the altar, and of the anointing oil, and sprinkle it upon Aaron, *and upon his garments*, and upon his sons'–such as Joshua the high priest–'*and upon the garments of his sons with him*:

'And *he* shall be hallowed, *and his garments*, and *his sons*, and *his sons' garments with him*', Exodus 29:21.

This is to wash one's robes, and make them white in the blood of the Lamb, with a witness, Revelation 7:14. This is to pluck a brand out of the fire. This is to silence the adversary by the salvation of the LORD.

Joshua never said a word. Not a word. Not once, throughout the vision. The LORD spoke, and alone brought his salvation to pass. Now, *this* is salvation from the adversary.

But the saved are intelligent about it: 'Let them set a fair mitre upon his head', Zechariah 3:5. The head being the seat of the intelligence, *there* they set the fair mitre. If so, of spiritual intelligence.

Such *know* what the Lord has done, and why he has done it, *because he did it to them, and that it is theirs by experience.*

Nevertheless there is a cause to being plucked out of the fire; there is purpose in iniquity being taken away; there is a reason for the change of raiment. In reality–of which this was the foreshadowing–it is to be set up in priestly dignity in the house of God as worshippers of the Father in spirit and in truth.

For if the Lord brings in his saving power, and shows forth his salvation from the adversary, it is to this end:

'If thou wilt walk in my ways, and if thou wilt keep my charge, then thou shalt also judge my house, and shalt also keep my courts, and I will give thee places to walk among these that stand by', Zechariah 3:7.

In the new testament this is called 'That thou mayest know how thou oughtest to behave thyself in the house of God, which is the *ecclesia* of the living God, the pillar and ground of the truth.

'And without controversy great is the mystery of godliness: God was manifest in the flesh, justified in the Spirit, seen of angels, preached unto the Gentiles, believed on in the world, received up into glory', I Timothy 3:15,16.

Before leaving this second and last revelation of the adversary in the old testament–to which the Hebrew *satan* properly belongs–it is well to rehearse in context precisely what reduced every accusation–however justified it appeared at the time–to silence.

To show forth precisely what it was that had brought to pass the salvation of the Lord from the authority of the adversary.

The case in law brought forth by the adversary against the rebuilding of the house and the recovery of worship rested upon the iniquity of the shamefaced and silent Joshua on the one hand,

and upon his unsuitability to minister in the service because of his having defiled the priesthood on the other.

Then, by what right should the house of God be rebuilt, and the worship of God in such a remnant recovered?

Take the first case: Joshua's iniquity. It is not denied: it is confirmed. 'Behold, I have caused thine iniquity to pass from thee', verse 4. Yes, But why and how? Because, saith the LORD, 'Is not this a brand plucked out of the fire?'

That was it: if the brand had been plucked out of the fire by the LORD, who was the adversary to tempt the LORD to thrust him back into it?

But what was this burning, and if the brand was in it, on what ground was it plucked out from such a fiery consumption, that this should stop the mouth of the adversary? There is no question of this being the salvation of a sinner from the wrath to come.

It is the case of the high priest of Israel, the son of Aaron, having been plucked from the burning indignation of the LORD against the iniquity of the priesthood.

It was their iniquity, and that of the rulers, embraced with such abandon, that—after so great patience, longsuffering, and warning from the prophets of the LORD—had brought about the destruction of Jerusalem, the razing of the walls, and the burning of the temple, seventy years before.

As saith the psalmist, 'They have cast fire into thy sanctuary', Psalm 74:7. Yes, and Joshua and the priesthood were the brands that gave kindling to it.

Why should the LORD have mercy, when they had ruined his testimony? Especially now, when the fire of his indignation had burned these seventy years? Why have mercy, and pluck this iniquitous brand from the burning? He deserved it for ever.

'How long, LORD? wilt thou be angry for ever? shall thy jealousy burn like fire?', Psalm 79:5.

No, not for ever. For he will have mercy on whom he will have mercy. And he would have mercy upon Joshua, and pluck him out of the burning. On what ground of justice? cries the adversary.

On this ground of justice, and of mercy: 'My sheep hear my voice, and I know them, and they follow me:

'And I give unto them eternal life; and they shall never perish, neither shall any pluck them out of my hand. My Father, which gave them me, is greater than all; and none is able to pluck them out of my Father's hand', John 10:27-29.

Then, this was a brand plucked from the burning, and the adversary can say not one word against it. How could he?

But there was a higher cause. This is not a question of a sinner being saved, it is a question of what a sinner is saved for. It is not a question of individual salvation. It is a question—in the old testament type—of sons in God's house. And that speaks to us today.

For as to God's house, God's service, and God's worship, and the simplicity which was in Christ Jesus in the beginning, and that which was in the Holy Ghost, and that which was in the apostles' doctrine and fellowship in the beginning, it is as if it had all been burned up by fire.

But is there not a brand plucked from the burning to begin again? to rebuild again?

Then shall he not pluck us—who are sons—from the fire to recover the testimony today for his glory, for the honour of his Son, for the obedience to the Holy Ghost, and for the magnifying of his word in the house of God, that it should be thronged with worshippers? Not if the adversary had his way!

But we are plucked from the fire. Sheep cannot be plucked from his hand. 'All that the Father giveth me shall come to me.' 'Of them which thou gavest me have I lost none.' 'Other sheep I have, which are not of this fold: them also I must bring.'

Yes, bring from the fire, to be built into the house of God in a recovery from our long captivity.

Neither can the adversary say a word against it. We have been iniquitous, and our fathers before us. We have polluted our sanctification and defiled our sonship. But 'Is not this a brand plucked out of the fire?'

And what? Why, to be set up in priestly dignity, in unity, in the house of God—which is thus rebuilt—which is the *ecclesia* of the living God, the pillar and ground of the truth. Now, this is salvation from—*the satan*—the adversary.

Finally observe the second case of the adversary against the recovery of the testimony.

This rested upon the evidence of filthy rags demonstrating the unsuitability of the high priest Joshua to minister in the service, and, by implication, of the defilement of the priesthood rendering them unfit for the holy ministrations of the sanctuary.

Then, this was a case for the abandonment of Jerusalem in perpetuity, or the leaving the razed city and walls a perpetual monument to the failure of the testimony. In a word, here appeared an apparently invincible case for *not* rebuilding the house.

Once the adversary's implications were granted, By what right should the house be rebuilt, and the worship of God in the remnant recovered and revived?

However, to all this the LORD has an answer. It is this: 'The LORD rebuke thee, O adversary; even the LORD that hath chosen Jerusalem rebuke thee', Zechariah 3:2.

Yes, but a rebuke is not an answer. No, *but election is*. Observe the words: The LORD *that hath chosen Jerusalem* rebuke thee. Then, the rebuke is grounded upon the answer.

None knew better than the adversary 'that the purpose of God according to election might stand, not of works, but of him that calleth', Romans 9:11. And the purpose of God according to election *had* stood; and it *would* stand; and the purpose of God according to election *must* stand.

If so, that *the LORD* hath *chosen* Jerusalem, dismisses the adversary and his case even as the chaff is blown before the wind.

Nothing can overturn the election of God. 'It is not of him that willeth, nor of him that runneth, but of God that showeth mercy.' 'Therefore hath he mercy on whom he will have mercy, and whom he will he hardeneth.' 'For who hath resisted his will?', Romans 9:16,18,19.

Who hath resisted his will? Certainly not the adversary. And at the words 'The LORD rebuke thee, O adversary; even the LORD that hath chosen Jerusalem rebuke thee', he knew immediately that his malevolent cause was lost. Neither does he open his mouth, nor once appear again throughout the old testament.

But what is this Jerusalem that the LORD hath chosen by an everlasting election? Not the figure, but the true. Not the type, but the antitype. Not the shadow, but the substance. What substance? The apostle tells you: 'But Jerusalem which is above is free, which is the mother of us all', Galatians 4:26.

Now here is a mystery in an allegory, but blessed are those eyes that see, those ears that hear, and those hearts that understand the truth of it, for to them the old testament prophecies are opened.

They see immediately the spiritual meaning of the Jerusalem which the LORD hath chosen, that it is from above and not below, and that it is free and not in bondage with her children.

Hence what is in view in the new testament is depicted as an old testament figure.

The substance of the matter is that of saints worshipping in the Spirit of sonship, united in the spiritual house of God, now recovered by the election of God, who hath chosen heavenly Jerusalem, experimentally manifest in the restoration of new testament Christianity in its essential apostolic principles.

Such a recovery is of the LORD, 'The LORD that hath chosen'. The unsanctified, unbelieving, self-condemned, discouraged people did not choose. The LORD takes responsibility for those whom he has chosen.

Joshua stood there, but could not open his mouth. Nor can you and I open our mouths.

You expect the LORD to accuse you, but you suffer from a case of mistaken identity: the adversary does the accusing, not the LORD. The LORD chooses, and acquits. 'It is God that justifieth.'

But it is *you*, not *thee*. 'The LORD that hath chosen *Jerusalem*.' It is *his* glory, *his* worship, *his* service that is in view. Then, it is corporate. If so, a *city*, not an individual.

This is that Jerusalem—'the LORD that hath chosen Jerusalem'— that John saw: 'And I John saw the holy city, new Jerusalem, coming down from God out of heaven.' That is it: Jerusalem *above*.

It is this that fills our inward vision and entire aspiration: 'But ye are come unto mount Sion, and unto the city of the living God, the heavenly Jerusalem.'

Not, Ye are going to come, but, Ye *are* come.

The heavenly vision, to which we are not disobedient, quickens our spirits, fills our gaze, moves our feet, and creates our unity. 'The LORD that hath chosen Jerusalem.'

'And I looked, and, behold, the temple of the tabernacle of the testimony in heaven was opened.' Such a looking in the Spirit, such a beholding of the revelation, this rebuilds the house in a heavenly people set for the testimony on earth.

This is Jerusalem that is compactly built together. These are the lively stones being built up into a spiritual house.

'In whom all the building fitly framed together groweth unto an holy temple in the Lord: in whom ye also are builded together for an habitation of God through the Spirit.'

This is the LORD rebuking the adversary. This utterly undoes the ruin of the testimony brought in by the adversary through our iniquity and filthy rags. What undoes it? The election of God.

It is the LORD that builds up Jerusalem. And he does it because he hath chosen Jerusalem.

What we do is destroy and raze Jerusalem by our iniquity, then sit in the dust and rubble full of self pity, unbelief, and a peeved spirit of resentment and despair.

We have not chosen Jerusalem. Rather, we have rejected Jerusalem.

But what of that, when the set time for Zion is come? What of that when the LORD chooses Jerusalem? What of that when the LORD builds Jerusalem?

It is to fill us with wonder that mercy should find us out, that pity should lift us up, and that love should build us in. Glorious things are spoken of thee, O city of God.

This rebukes the adversary. This dismisses him in shame: 'The LORD rebuke thee, O adversary; even the LORD that hath chosen Jerusalem rebuke thee.'

And so it comes to pass, when the LORD awakens as one out of sleep, and like a mighty man that shouteth by reason of wine, smiting his fleeing enemies–and the adversary–in the hinder parts.

'The LORD that hath *chosen* Jerusalem rebuke thee.' 'Ye have not chosen me, but I have chosen you.' Yea, be confounded for your own sakes. But whatever you are, or have done, *it is his election that prevails.* 'And of Zion it shall be said, This and that man was born in her: and the Highest himself shall establish her.

'The LORD shall count, when he writeth up the people, that this man was born there. Selah.' Yea, 'Every one of them in Zion appeareth before God.'

And not appear in filthy garments either: that was *their* doing. But in a glorious change of raiment, and a fair mitre: that is *his* doing. 'The LORD that hath chosen Jerusalem rebuke thee, O adversary.'

Even now, as it was even then. Though then *reflective* of what was to come, that reflection was of a *present testimony.* And in the figure under the old testament the house *was* rebuilt.

And in the reality in the new testament what is of God, of the city from heaven, is manifested by the Holy Ghost in a testimony *here and now. That* rebukes the adversary.

Above all the adversary was and is against *that.* The recovery and rebuilding of what has been lost and has lain in ruins for so long. *But he cannot resist God's election.*

And as it was in the days of Zechariah, not for our sakes–be ashamed and confounded for your own sakes–but for his glory it shall come to pass, 'Thou shalt arise, and have mercy upon Zion: for the time to favour her, yea, the set time, is come.'

And when? What saith he? 'I have heard thee in a time accepted, and in the day of salvation have I succoured thee: behold, now is the accepted time; behold, now is the day of salvation', II Corinthians 6:2. And what? Why, *this* sets forth salvation from–*satan*–the adversary.

Above all, the adversary is against the rebuilding of the house of God, which is the *ecclesia* of the living God, the pillar and ground of the truth, upon and into which is let down from God out of heaven all the glory of Jerusalem above, which is free, which is the mother of us all.

This spiritual house is to be thronged with worshippers: 'We will go into his tabernacles: we will worship at his footstool. Arise, O LORD, into thy rest; thou, and the ark of thy strength. Let thy priests be clothed with righteousness; and let thy saints shout for joy.'

'For we have not an high priest which cannot be touched with the feeling of our infirmities; but was in all points tempted like as we are, yet without sin.' 'And his face did shine as the sun, and his raiment was white as the light.'

'It is God that justifieth. Who is he that condemneth? It is Christ that died, yea rather, that is risen again, who is even at the right hand of God, who also maketh intercession for us.' If so, discerning the times, What hinders? 'Arise and build.'

'The God of heaven, he will prosper us; therefore we his servants will arise and build'–but as to all the hypocrites in Zion, the false brethren, the smooth-tongued deceivers, the corrupters of the faith–'ye have no portion, nor right, nor memorial, in Jerusalem', Nehemiah 2:20.

No, for we can show our genealogy, which is what none of these bastard Calvinists, misshapen Arminians, Taylor Brethren Sabellians, loose modernist 'evangelicals', and base-born un-circumcised can ever do.

We can say with the witness of the Spirit and in the truth, 'This man was born there'. 'Which were born, not of blood, nor of the will of the flesh, nor of the will of man, but of God', John 1:13.

If so, Jerusalem above is our mother, 'the mother of us all', whom God has begotten by the Spirit of Christ. We are of the city.

A city is a people. It is not individuals obsessed with themselves and their so-called 'witness' and self-deceiving 'ministry'. It is not even a family. It is a people compactly built together, built upon foundations, and surrounded by walls.

This is Jerusalem above, seen in an assembly below: one assembly, the *ecclesia*. For 'there is one body, and one Spirit, even as ye are called in one hope of your calling; one Lord, one faith, one baptism, one God and Father of all, who is above all, and through all, and in you all.'

That is, in you all that are builded into the city. One city. Jerusalem above. One house. The house of God. Now, over and above everything else, the adversary resists the recovery and rebuilding of this. But the LORD arises for the restoration and building of it. And who, think you, will prevail?

The Hebrew word *satan* occurs thirty-seven times in the new testament. This is a transference of the old testament description and language into the Greek.

Such a transliteration – well understood by the Jewish Evangelists, the writers of the epistles, and those whom they instructed – teaches that already the Holy Ghost had revealed fully what was to be disclosed about the activity of the supernatural being described under that precise Hebrew wording.

Therefore I do not intend to draw out unduly what appears in the new testament under this old testament characterization: everything needful – in essence – had been made manifest in the books of Job and Zechariah.

By the transliteration of the original language – in which the new testament writers had been brought up – the Holy Ghost teaches that the further thirty-seven references constitute no more than a contemporary unveiling of what had long been revealed in essence.

Since the Hebrew *satan* is not a proper name, but a descriptive characterization, the English translators are at fault in the Greek transliteration – as well as the Hebrew original – by the use of the upper-case – capital – 'S'. No authority exists in the Greek text for this presumption.

Bearing in mind the lesson from the Spirit in the Hebrew transliteration into the Greek, let the reader substitute the English word *adversary* to gain the true meaning intended by the scripture.

Almost always the Greek prepositive article – answering to a considerable extent to the English definite article *the* – precedes the word 'satan' – *adversary* – in the original new testament text. But there are exceptions: for example Mark 3:23; Luke 22:3; and II Corinthians 12:7.

Again – another confirmation that the Hebrew *satan* is a description of an attitude or characteristic – there is no article when Jesus calls Peter *satan*, or *adversary*, Matthew 16:23; Mark 8:33. Although, of course, it is perfectly true that the article has no vocative.

However, little is to be gained by these passing observations concerning the article. The real value of the last example lies in the obvious truth that Peter was *not* that malevolent supernatural being, but on that occasion momentarily in ignorance shared with him the disposition of an adversary.

'Get thee hence, σατανᾶ – *satan*, or *adversary*', Matthew 4:10. Here the descriptive term – note the absence of the capital 'S' –

is applied by Jesus in the Temptation. But it is not the first descriptive name given to that malevolent and supernatural being in the narrative of Jesus' Temptation in the wilderness.

But it is the first time that this particular delineation σατανᾶ, *satana–adversary–*occurs in the Temptation narrative; also it is the first time that this word appears in Matthew; and, of course, it follows that this is the first occurrence in the new testament.

Having used other characterizations previously in the Temptation, here Jesus quotes the ancient Hebrew description finally to dismiss the adversary.

Thus the Holy Ghost by the word of the Lord casts the adversary–not to say the Jewish and other saints–back into the bible. For the old testament scripture–recording a vast period actually known and lived through by the adversary–*was* the bible of the new testament disciples and saints.

And *satan* is very strictly an old testament concept. If so, by the use of the Hebrew, Jesus pin-pointed the original adversary for and from time immemorial.

Hence the Lord takes and applies the descriptive title from across the centuries immediately to the present circumstances.

The one so described may have been invisible, but the Lord saw him, and saw through him, instantly.

This intangible and spiritual being, untouched by the ravages of time, was as alive and active at that time as he had been from the day of his creation. He had neither slumbered nor slept throughout the rolling ages of time.

If he went to and fro upon the earth until the ascension, equally he might and did appear in the highest heavens.

Mark states precisely that Jesus was 'in the wilderness forty days tempted of the adversary'–*satan*–Mark 1:13. To take the ultimate concept, there were but three occasions for the adversary's temptation. This is to speak of temptation in the absolute sense.

First, the whole world and age in Adam at the garden: the adversary's temptation was completely successful. Second, the Lord Jesus in the wilderness: the adversary's temptation was entirely defeated.

Thirdly, the apostolic *ecclesia* in the unity of one body: before the scriptures closed, the adversary's triumph was both astounding and devastating.

By the Holy Ghost's transliteration of the Hebrew *satan* – English, *adversary*–in the Greek of the new testament, the apostles drew attention to the truth unveiled in the Hebrew root of revelation.

What the adversary was, had been fully revealed: all that remained was repetition of the same activity, however contemporary the application.

Then, these are things which must be recalled and held in remembrance: 'To write the same things to you, to me indeed is not grievous, but for you it is safe', Philippians 3:1. Commencing with the book of Job we are given a remarkable and mysterious insight into realms infinitely beyond the visible and apparent.

In metaphysical and symbolic terms heavenly dimensions otherwise incomprehensible to man are portrayed so as to convey the idea of that supernatural sphere eternal in the highest.

Two interviews with the LORD are described when the adversary comes also to present himself with those figuratively described as 'the sons of God'.

In the first, the adversary requests permission to take away that in which he supposed Job's piety to rest.

Secondly, foiled by a love for the LORD in Job quite beyond his comprehension, the adversary requires that he might sift Job in his sieve, as wheat is sifted. The matter of the book of Job then immediately drops to the earth, and there the long process is enacted.

But the entire cause lay in the two visions of the glory revealed in the first two chapters. Yet nearly the entire book unfolds on earth without the least revelation from heaven to those attempting to puzzle out the real cause of Job's affliction.

But these reasoners had seen nothing: it is the reader who sees everything that preceded in the heavens.

As to the adversary, he is never mentioned again in the whole book, nor once seen or envisaged again throughout the ensuing chapters. Regarding men, he hides behind events, at once unseen and unknown.

The adversary does not appear again in the scriptures until virtually the end of the old testament. Where had he been? What had he been doing? The spiritual knew, and do know.

Zechariah, in the dark of the night, by visions into the heavenlies, finds as it were a door open in heaven, and, ascending in the spirit, beholds the courts of the Most High.

In the fourth vision of Zechariah Joshua the high priest stands in filthy rags, being persecuted with all the rigour of the law by the adversary before the LORD. The malevolent spirit stands at the right hand 'to be an adversary'. He is undiminished in years. He is unwearied in function. He is undeterred in purpose.

This is the last mention of *satan*–the adversary–in the old testament. Why have I repeated these things? Because precisely these things filled the mind of Jesus, and were forced upon the mind of the adversary, when the Lord Jesus said at the Temptation, 'Get thee behind me, *satan*'–adversary.

These old testament visions had revealed everything about the adversary under that character. They tell all that there is to be known of him in this activity. It is from such a revelation that the new testament writers expounded.

Hence the necessity of thoroughly assimilating what had been written in Job and Zechariah. And thus the reason–nay: *necessity*– for repetition.

'Get thee behind me, *adversary*.' In the recognition of the Hebrew *satan*, Jesus spans the past centuries as if they were no more than days.

The adversary, invisible in himself and concealed in his nature, had once more come down from the heavens, narrowly tracing the descent of the Son of God.

Doubtless observing the incarnation with a mixture of fear and wrath, pondering the beginnings, marking the flight into Egypt, brooding over the events at Nazareth, although not for one moment neglecting the significance of the ministry of John the Baptist.

And, if so, at once shocked and alarmed at the momentous events unfolding during Jesus' baptism.

Now, freed to do his worst in the wilderness, still hiding his ultimate identity, this invisible spirit–appearing if possible as no more than some subjective impression or sensation–makes manifest three forms of influence, each disguised in its true character.

But Jesus' use of the ancient Hebrew title shows that the adversary had hidden nothing, but rather, that everything was perfectly open and clear before the spiritual perception of the Saviour.

The use of the Hebrew '*satan*' lays bare the real personality of the adversary, known these centuries past. By the old Hebrew description this heavenly adversary was exposed, rebuked, and dismissed by Jesus at the close of the Temptation.

Regarding the difference between the account of the Temptation in Matthew and Mark–and of course the transliteration *satan*–besides the exposition of the momentous event in Mark, I see no need to repeat what has been expounded fully in 'The Messiah' and 'Mark' respectively.

That the adversary had deceived the whole world in Adam, and that the entire posterity of mankind lies in the Wicked One, oblivious of his existence or of the nature of man's blindness– not to say bondage–is evident from the words of Jesus:

'If *satan* also be divided against himself, how shall his kingdom stand?', Luke 11:18.

What kingdom? That of humanity in the Fall. First blinded by the adversary, as if that adversary did not exist; and last, as if this world were at once both harmless and permanent.

But the adversary does exist; and this world is judged already– John 12:31–just as was the old world in the days of Noah.

But this is an idle dream to mankind and the present world, as was the warning of the fiery deluge about to fall upon Sodom and the cities of the plain *within hours of that warning being given*.

This had no effect whatever. 'But the same day'–*day*–'that Lot went out of Sodom it rained fire and brimstone from heaven, and destroyed them all', Luke 17:29.

135

Then if Sodom and Gomorrah were not totally deluded by the adversary, what is delusion? And if the world, by such things warned of a worse destruction to come, laughs the warning to scorn, convinced to the contrary, then of whose kingdom are these the subjects?

What? When Jude calls Sodom and Gomorrah *an example*, 'suffering the vengeance of eternal fire', Jude 7? And if that were but an example, What shall be the like of the thing exemplified?

That Jesus came to save from *satan* – the adversary – is evident, just as it is crystal clear that all mankind stands in just such a need of salvation.

First, to see the character of the one who deludes the whole world in the Fall; second, to open the eyes of those blinded to so catastrophic a judgment; and third, to shine within the heart to give both the true light and a certain deliverance from the delusions of the *satan*.

Hence Jesus says of the adversary, 'Or else how can one enter into a strong man's house, and spoil his goods, except he first bind the strong man? and then he will spoil his house.'

Where the context of Matthew 12:29, Mark 3:27, and Luke 11:21,22 show beyond question, First, that *satan*, the adversary, is the strong man; Second, that this world is his 'house' or 'palace'; Third, that the strong man's 'goods' refer to all humanity.

And, Fourth, that 'the stronger than he' who 'enters his house' and 'binds him' so as to 'spoil his goods', refers to and exalts the Saviour in bringing to man 'Salvation from Satan'.

Woe to those who know nothing of such a salvation. But a worse woe betides those who know in the letter and in theory of him concerning whom in unexperimental ignorance, empty prattling in the dark, they called 'Satan', knowing nothing whatsoever of the spiritual reality of his power.

Their end will be little different from him of whom it is written, 'Then entered *satan* into'–mark that: *entered into* 'Judas'. 'After the sop *satan* entered into him.' And again, 'Ananias, why hath *satan* filled *thine heart* to lie to the Holy Ghost?'

As it is written, 'the god of this world hath blinded the minds of them which believe not, lest the light of the glorious gospel of Christ, who is the image of God, should shine unto them.'

What then of Job? He was–up to his very life–'delivered unto the adversary'. Yes, but not for destruction, but for salvation, so that 'the LORD blessed the latter end of Job more than his beginning', Job 42:12.

And so it was with that daughter of Abraham whom *satan*– the adversary–had bound, lo, these eighteen years. She was saved with a mighty salvation, and her latter end also was more blessed than her beginning.

Job foreshadows another, though different, case, when the apostle, by the Holy Ghost, in the word of the Lord, is moved to 'deliver such an one'–who sinned so blatantly, defiling the entire assembly of God–'unto *satan* for the destruction of the flesh'.

Was that the end? Not in such a case: 'that the spirit may be saved in the day of the Lord Jesus', I Corinthians 5:5.

For the Saviour preserves his saints from Satan, lest they bring shame on the testimony: 'that *satan* tempt you not for your incontinency', I Corinthians 7:5. 'Lest the adversary should get an advantage of us', II Corinthians 2:11.

Again, the true congregation of the Lord would be vindi-cated by the abject humiliation of 'the synagogue of *satan*', Revelation 3:9.

Hence, apart from the faithful remnant, in the true unity, there were apostates, in a false unity, called by themselves 'the church', but called by the Lord, 'the synagogue of *satan*', Revelation 2:9.

But long before this the apostle laments, 'for some are already'– mark that: *already*–'turned aside after *satan*', I Timothy 5:15.

For it all, the adversary can do no more than is permitted. And some permission is extraordinary indeed, such as the apostle Paul having to suffer 'the messenger of *satan* to buffet me', II Corinthians 12:7. But, as Job exemplified, this served the man of God well in the issue.

And in hindrances also, which turned out rather to the furtherance of the gospel, as when '*Satan* hindered us', I Thessalonians 2:18.

But more terrible yet the case of Peter: but the Saviour had commanded, Thus far, and no further; his prayers prevailing with God: '*Satan* hath desired to have you, that he may sift you as wheat: but I have prayed for thee', Luke 22:31,32.

Then, though they be tried, the elect will and must overcome: 'The God of peace shall bruise *satan*'–the adversary–'under your feet shortly', Romans 16:20. The term 'God of peace' occurs seven times in the new testament, and the peace which he brought in by Jesus Christ is perfect.

Christ brought peace on earth; Christ made peace; Christ is our peace; Christ preaches peace; and three times over he declares to his own, 'Peace be unto you'. This is from the God of peace. On such a basis he shall certainly bruise *the satan* under our feet shortly.

But the cost to the Saviour was great, and if he bruised the adversary's head, giving him a deadly wound, it is true that this bruised the Saviour's heel, as he stamped upon the head of *the satan*.

This cost the Saviour his life, but his total victory in death, on behalf of his people, ensured that God should raise him – and those in him – from the dead, unto justification of life.

'The God of peace, that brought again from the dead our Lord Jesus, that great shepherd of the sheep, through the blood of the everlasting covenant,

'Make you perfect in every good work to do his will, working in you that which is wellpleasing in his sight, through Jesus Christ; to whom be glory for ever and ever. Amen', Hebrews 13:20,21.

Now, *that* is to bruise *the satan* under our feet shortly, after that we have suffered a while: even suffered at the hands of the adversary by the permission of God, for this brings in a broken and a contrite spirit, without which none shall overcome.

But overcome we shall, though our sifting – and being bruised – be terrible in the process.

Terrible: even to 'bruising him hardly departeth from him', Luke 9:39. But depart he must at the Saviour's word, and depart he will.

And as for us, by such things alone we learn the truth experimentally. But at the last, we are clothed and in our right minds, *the satan* lying bruised under our feet by the grace of the God of peace.

However the ultimate triumph – when the victory of Christ in death, in the descent, in the resurrection, and in the ascension shall have been fully applied, body, soul, and spirit – will be seen in the resurrection from the dead.

When this vile body shall be put off, and the body of glory – like unto his glorious body – shall have been put on, world without end. Amen.

For whom? For all those for whom Christ was bruised, whom he purchased with his own blood, the blood of the everlasting covenant. These he calls 'my sheep', who is 'that great shepherd of the sheep'.

These shall be in everlasting peace. To them, God is the God of peace. But to none other. All others are of the adversary, and, too late, they shall find out the God of vengeance, Psalm 94; II Thessalonians 1:8.

The last new testament references where the descriptive Hebrew translation *satan* occurs—Revelation 20:2,7—have been opened exhaustively in my book 'The Revelation of Jesus Christ', to which the reader is referred.

I cannot add more to that which then I received of the Lord, nor add to the vital contextual opening.

But there is one further enlargement from the visions in the book of Job to which reference ought to be made. 'Now there was a day when the sons of God came to present themselves before the LORD, and the adversary'—Hebrew, *satan*—'came also among them', Job 1:6; 2:1.

Such descriptive language is expressed allegorically, the terminology condescending to the impossibility of man's reason to take in dimensions surpassing all human capacity.

For example, there are no 'days' in the highest heavens of glory. There is no night there. Again 'sons of God'—referring to the elect angels—is in contrast with 'children of men'.

As to the adversary, he was not of them, albeit he came with them. 'And *the satan* came also among them.'

Till he obtained permission first to tear Job's life apart with bereavement, destitution, and desolation, then to ruin his health under pain beyond measure, so that he was often but a hair's breadth from death.

Given that permission from the glory of the highest, the adversary could not wait to exert his malice to the lowest. Could not wait. He 'fell as lightning from heaven' in hatred against the true worshipper, who wrought the works of God, to be an adversary to the very death.

Neither did he change, nor will he change, as saith the Lord, when the seventy, having been appointed and sent two by two before his face into every city and place whither he would come, returned again with joy, saying, Lord, even the devils are subject unto us through thy name.

This alarmed the adversary, to see such servants of the Lord going forth everywhere in such numbers with power unprecedented: so that Jesus answered them, 'I beheld *the satan* as lightning fall from heaven.'

Thus, permitted, so had he fallen upon Job so long before, unable to stand the sight of the true worshipper. How much more worshipping servants in the power of the Lord in the new testament, Jesus' feet following in their pathway.

As lightning he struck downwards: so quick; so bright; so set on destruction; yet, impaled upon the LORD's hedge about his serving worshippers, his descent availed him nothing at all.

Lightning? Literally, what is brighter? What is quicker? What is so devastating? And, as it is literally, so is the case spiritually, as the adversary's descent in the book of Job foreshadowed.

'Whose coming is after the working of *the satan*, with all power and signs and lying wonders', II Thessalonians 2:9, 'and with all deceivableness of unrighteousness in them that perish; because they received not the love of the truth, that they might be saved.'

Who has been struck by lightning and been saved? What tree, what building, can survive this devastating brilliance, so shocking a strike, such awesome power?

And do self-conceited Brethren think themselves inviolate–cocooned in dead complacency–simply because they can recite the dead letter of the text, whilst knowing nothing of the power of which it speaks?

Useless, without the experimental inworking of the Holy Ghost to bring within the power of God unto salvation.

For there is not one Jesus, but also 'another Jesus'; not one Spirit, but likewise 'another spirit'; not one gospel, but 'another gospel'.

And do dead old men, and light chaffy youths, think that to profess texts will save them whilst they remain strangers to the power of God in Christ unto salvation?

As well hope to return lightning with equal brilliance and power back into heaven from their own fingertips. It is *the Holy Ghost* they want. It is *salvation* from *the satan* that they need.

None but the Saviour, by the infallible witness of his interior anointing, by the inward working of the Spirit, can open the eyes of the blind, turn men from darkness to light, and from the power of *the satan* unto God: that–*then*–that they might receive forgiveness of sins.

Nor can any appoint himself to this ministry: it is of an apostolic kind of sending, Acts 26:17,18.

Then shall the eyes of the blind be opened. Not till then. Till then the minds of the hypocrites are closed, and closed to the reality of the scripture by the working of *the satan*. 'For such are false apostles, deceitful workers, transforming themselves into the apostles of Christ.

'And no marvel; for *the satan* himself is transformed into an angel of light.' You should have known that: 'The *sons of God* came to present themselves before the LORD, and *the satan* came *also among them.*' But who could tell the difference, bright as lightning?

'Therefore it is no great thing if his'–the adversary's–'ministers also be transformed as the ministers of righteousness; whose end shall be according to their works', II Corinthians 11:4,13-15.

Then *how much* we need 'Salvation from Satan', ever praying, ever watching, ever lowly, ever contrite, ever vigilant, ever led by the anointing, even to the very end.

One further passage remains to show that Christ is our Saviour from the adversary. However, two things cause me to hesitate in coming to this place.

First, it is in Revelation, therefore couched in the allegorical and symbolic language and vision distinctive of this book. Hence I would prefer to direct the reader to the full contextual exposition in 'The Revelation of Jesus Christ'.

Secondly, the passage concerned, Revelation 12:9–depicted in highly mystical form–does not concern the description *the satan* alone, or even primarily, but conveys several other characterizations of that malevolent being.

Now, to divide–mark that: *divide*–the word of God rightly, it is essential to focus precisely on one thing at a time.

However, I will drop some remarks on the passage, though, of course, only as it relates to the description *the satan*. 'Satan, which deceiveth the whole world: was cast out into the earth, and his angels were cast out with him', Revelation 12:9.

The law being the strength of sin, it was this that provided the armoury and fortress of the adversary. But Christ took away all his armour wherein he trusted, binding him irrevocably. The Saviour obtained the victory, nailing the law of commandments contained in ordinances to his cross, freely delivering his people.

Satan fell. He was cast out of heaven. From then on, all access was denied to him. The propitiatory hid the law from view; the blood was sprinkled upon the propitiatory; and five scars before the throne of God in heaven proclaimed eternal salvation for all the children of God in the Saviour.

Hence the adversary could not prevail. He was cast out of heaven into the earth. When Christ went up, he fell down. When Christ ascended in victory, he was cast down into defeat.

Christ's sheep 'overcame him by the blood of the Lamb', for this silenced the curse of the law by the shedding of blood; and hid the body of the law under the blood-sprinkled propitiatory.

And not only so: 'they overcame him' also 'by the word of their testimony'–to the truth of the evangel of the grace of Christ by which they were called; in which they stood; and to which they witnessed–'and they loved not their lives unto the death', Revelation 12:11.

Now, *this* is 'Salvation from Satan', that is, *the satan*, or, *the adversary*, with a witness.

'Therefore rejoice, ye heavens, and ye that dwell in them', for the Lord is gone up with a shout, with the sound of a trumpet, and with the cry of triumph, assured of the victory for all his people, in that day when 'all his foes shall be made his footstool'.

V
The 'Devil'

THE new testament Greek 'translated' as *the 'devil'*, reads ὁ διάβολος, *ho diabolos*. However the English is as meaningless as it is irrelevant, translating nothing whatsoever. To the contrary, the English not only sows perplexity, it reaps confusion worse confounded.

To open up and clarify the meaning of the original Greek—for *ho diabolos* is an entirely new testament concept: the Hebrew of the old does not come into it—therefore requires the preliminary work of clearing up a thoroughly chaotic shambles left untouched for ages and generations to the general reader.

Nevertheless, this must be done first if ever the word of truth and of revelation is to be cleared, explained with lucidity, and realized in its true meaning. A meaning, I may add, that signals dreadful danger; yet at the same time brings to light the wonderful salvation of God in Christ our Saviour.

The original absurdity lies in the fallacious word 'devil'. This means nothing in English and translates less from the Greek. Quite apart from the fact that the *English* is a nonsense word in itself, the translators have not so much as attempted to convey an accurate English equivalent to the meaning of the original *Greek*.

Over and above this travesty, the resultant obfuscation has been compounded by the extended use of the meaningless word 'devil' to convey another Greek word altogether, namely, that used to render δαίμων, *demon*.

Whatever the precise grammatical form of *daimōn* in the Greek, this outrageous blunder of the translators occurs some seventy-eight times.

As with the fabled Hercules confronted with the task of cleaning out the Augean stables, a veritable river of clean water must be diverted to flow through and clean out the ordure deposited by these prodigious manufacturers, directed first at the very base. That base is the word 'devil'.

It will have been noticed that I have put the word 'devil' in inverted commas. Why? Because it is a word foisted by the translators upon the scriptures, bearing absolutely no resemblance to the Greek *ho diabolos*, which it makes not the remotest attempt to translate.

Instead, this *Old English nonsense word* has been imposed upon the original, wilfully perpetuated by Lexicographers, Commentators, Translators, Theologians, and, of course, the entirety of the general trade of the clergy and their imitators, down to the most presumptuous 'gospel' hall demagogue.

For this reason I have put such a hopelessly misleading and totally incomprehensible insertion by the translators in inverted commas. Because it means nothing whatever, least of all that which the original Greek conveys.

In fact the ridiculous and unintelligible expression 'devil' is a mutation of a very Old English word, namely, *deofol*. Observe, *that* is its origin. Not the Greek. Old English superstition.

The translators blotted out the Greek, supplanting it with a superstitious word rooted in Old English medieval ignorance.

And, by now, this folly has flooded not merely the bible, but the entire English language.

Deofol is nothing other than one of the imaginary nightmare figures of mythology, now thankfully obsolete. Except that the translators – and the clergy – have perpetuated this nonsense word *through the English bible*.

They might as well have used another expression of equal ignorance, such as 'troll', or 'elf', or 'hobgoblin'. All – together with 'deofol' – representing nothing other than the dark fears of a benighted peasantry, played upon by what called itself the 'Church', so that this potent weapon of superstition might be employed to the full.

Here is the frightening unknown evil that lurks in the shadows of the child's bedroom, or in the dank undergrowth of the peasant's wildwood. It is the *idea* behind the figure conjured up to personify all the suppressed phobia latent in the terrified child, or the simple and uneducated villager.

Expressed by other names in fairy-tales, in the English bible – *of all places* – the same *idea, by just such a stupid, meaningless name,* was foisted upon the word of God by the clergy, utterly obliterating the original Greek, thereby obscuring the most precise, essential, and intelligible revelation.

And this is perpetuated to this very day, save in the godlessness of an age the unbelief of which lies squarely at the door of the 'Church' – evangelicals and all – everything divine has been dismissed with barely concealed contempt as little more than irrelevant.

But in a previous day, when 'religion' was more effectual, then the equivalent of the chief priests, elders, scribes, Pharisees, Sadducees, doctors, and lawyers, played without scruple upon the common people's terror of the unknown.

Why? Because this served their self-interest far greater than unveiling the clear light and intelligible truth of the Saviour through the grace of God.

Above and beyond this mischievous folly, however, there remains the incredibly gross error of using the word 'devil' also to distort the plain meaning of another–and wholly distinct– Greek word–expressed in a variety of grammatical forms–namely *daimōn*, 'demon'.

By what diabolical perversity have they called the original *daimōn*, 'devil'? not just once, but–in all its grammatical forms– seventy-eight times?

Such an inexcusable tampering with the plain and clear scripture, blinding the eyes of the simple to the truth, shall surely require an answer in the day of recompense of Almighty God.

Nevertheless, despite this revolting deposit overlaying the word of God, let it be clearly understood that *daimōn* means 'demon', and that 'devil' means nothing either in Greek or English.

For the present this brief intimation is at least sufficient to clear away the accumulated matter beneath which lies the pure truth revealed in the scriptures.

Later, under the general division of 'Salvation from Satan', a separate heading–'prince of demons'–will open and enlarge the meaning of the Greek new testament word *daimōn*, as revealed by the Lord Jesus and his apostles through the Holy Ghost.

This is not–but that will be–the appropriate place to con- vey the revelation of the word of God concerning 'demons'.

However, let it suffice the reader that at least the muck is washed away, leaving for the future a clean approach to the word of truth, the gospel of our salvation. Thus cries a voice in the wilderness: 'Prepare ye the way of the Lord, make his paths straight', Mark 1:3.

The Greek–which the Authorized Version translators perversely rendered *the devil*–reads ὁ διάβολος, *ho diabolos*, a noun which occurs with the article some thirty-four times in the new testament.

The devil is not merely a mistranslation; nor is it only an aberration: it is a grievous and blinding iniquity, at once hiding the truth of the original from the people, then heaping upon that hidden truth a vile deposit of refuse.

The word *diabolos* – with or without the article – appears thirty-nine times in the original Greek. It is the article that makes the difference: '*ho* diabolos' is specific. In all, the word 'diabolos' occurs five times without the equivalent of our definite article 'the', thus leaving the thirty-four references to *ho diabolos*.

This is an entirely new testament concept. *Ho diabolos* is not a proper name. The adversary *has* no proper name. All his names are descriptive, *ho diabolos* being no exception.

Each descriptive title afforded to the adversary– *the satan*; itself a transliterated word from the Hebrew–actually signifies an activity. The sum of these descriptions therefore reveals the full scope of his activities. There are some fifteen such significations.

One of these–and a major one–is *ho diabolos*, effectively obscured in meaning from the English reader. Nor are the Lexicons much use: in fact most are both misleading and inaccurate.

As to this, 'receiving honour one of another' is indicated by the syndrome of constipated and unmoving stasis endemic to the tradition of the elders from of old, up to this very day.

Diabolos is a Greek compound, derived from the conjunction of the preposition *dia* and the verb *ballō*.

First the preposition: as always precision is difficult, because grammatical use varies the emphasis. However it is safe to say that the primary sense of *dia* in this compound stresses the concept of *through*.

The verb *ballō* basically means *to cast; to throw;* or *to thrust*.

From the conjunction of these two words, the compound *diaballō* is formed. Then, the fundamental sense *must* be 'to cast through; to throw through'; or, 'to thrust through'. This concept holds good, verb or noun, no matter what further form, meaning, or particular application may have evolved subsequently.

In the new testament, particularly with the use of the definite article, ὁ – *the* – διάβολος – *diabolos*, the resultant development and particular application is specific. The meaning in such cases is more precise than the general '*one who throws or casts through or across*'.

The Lexicons make such unwarranted assumptions from lackeying to traditional 'scholarship' – some scholarship! – typically, for example, 'a calumniator, slanderer, treacherous informer, traitor'.

But why always the implication of malice? The compound describes an *action*, neither a malicious nor a virtuous intent in performing that action.

Of course, with the noun, given the definite article, the translators and the Lexicons uniformly cast Greek to the winds, and, fools and blind, render ὁ διάβολος, with diabolical inaccuracy, *the 'devil'*.

Moulton and Milligan are more balanced, commenting that 'malice need not be assumed ... any more than falsehood.' Precisely. Neither the verb nor the noun – *per se* – predicate anything other than an action, or the one characterized by that action.

However Lexicographers in general stress '*a slanderer; false accuser*'. Of course the word in a given place *could* mean 'what is cast across or through' in slander, but there is no necessity for such an assumption from a compound *describing no more than the action*.

Any intention of the actor is mere presumption, at best from context, at worst from prejudice.

But I have neither the desire nor the inclination – nor is this the place – further to draw out what I consider sufficiently exposed: the blind follow-my-leader assumptions of the academics in religion concerning that which uniformly they have failed to translate.

The fact that they impose 'the devil' so as to obliterate the Greek speaks for itself.

The compound *diabolos* – as in *ho diabolos* – indicates *one who casts or throws through or across*. That meaning is indisputable. So is the fact that this descriptive term in the new testament applies to *the* '*satan*', acting in a capacity not characterized hitherto.

Then the question is, What does he cast or throw? And again, Through or across what does this activity take place? Answer these questions and the development and application of the description in the new testament becomes transparently clear.

Apply that clarity to the English equivalent, and, at last, the Greek will have been properly *translated*.

The simplest and safest answer to the first question – What does he cast or throw? – clearly suggests *accusations*. But these need not be slanderous. In fact, they are rarely – if ever – slanderous. The accusations appear perfectly true, just, and, above all, legal. Otherwise, where were their weight?

151

Again, with the second question—through or across what or where does this activity take place?—though the answer may vary according to circumstances, in the ultimate sense, given that the accusations being cast are *legal*, the place for this kind of activity is before the judge in court.

And, given such a contestant, before the Judge in the highest court of all.

There 'the accuser of our brethren' casts or throws his accusations through or across the courtroom, before the Judge, and against the accused at the bar of judgment.

That the new testament usage of *ho diabolos* is redolent of the atmosphere surrounding an opponent in law, and of legal implications, appears strongly in certain passages, and is never quite without hint to this effect in others.

Likewise it is clear from contemporary Greek references that here is *one* of the shades of meaning associated with the use of this compound.

This 'thrower across', the 'casting through' does not appear in haphazard circumstances, nor are his activities general.

Hence 'accuser' alone carries far too broad a range of application to satisfy the parameters of new testament usage. These constraints lay down a formidable basis demonstrating that *the accuser* is insufficiently adequate to pin-point the new testament meaning of *ho diabolos*.

Of course malicious and unfounded slander can be found in the mouth of an accuser, but such scurrilous untruth will carry no weight with a just judge, even should it so much as reach the courtroom.

Ho diabolos is no inventor of accusations, nor does he creep about with tittle-tattle to backbite in secret. The character portrayed in the new testament is much more suited to appear in judicial robes in the solemn environment of the lawcourts.

His activities show him to be counsel for the prosecution; he presents the legal case against the accused. He stands before the Judge in view of the great assize. He is prosecutor at law; his cause is valid; his case is legal; the hearing is before God.

This is the kind of brief, from that elevation of prosecution, with accusation after accusation hurled across the courtroom of heaven, indicated by the essence of the new testament term *ho diabolos*.

That is the highest, ultimate meaning. However, it is not to say that lesser applications never occur, nor that in such cases 'accuser' sufficiently indicates the Greek.

The first occurrence of the descriptive title *ho diabolos* – a characterization unique to the new testament – occurs in the account of Jesus' temptation in the Evangel according to Matthew. Four times the term *ho diabolos* is mentioned in this case; once the delineation 'satan' appears; once 'the tempter'.

Mark's account of the Temptation is brief to the point of curtness, the only descriptive title being that of 'the satan'.

Luke equals Matthew in length, but differs in order of narration as to the last two temptations. Five times Luke refers to *ho diabolos*, and once to 'satan'.

The use of alternative titles in the three different accounts of the Temptation indicates a sudden switch of function and suggestion – *ho diabolos*; 'the tempter'; 'satan' – in which the adversary seeks to confuse the issue.

This makes it difficult to extricate the use of *ho diabolos* from that which pertains to the other descriptive terms.

Indeed, it is difficult for the spiritually unlearned so much as to see, first, What *was* the temptation in each case; and, second, Just *how* the description *ho diabolos* – the prosecutor or accuser – was applicable in any case at all.

But such perplexity actually reveals a lack of spirituality in the reader, not a lack of subtlety on the part of the tempter.

The Temptation is unique to Christ. There can be no reducing of this to petty 'lessons' degrading so elevated an occurrence to ordinary human circumstances. There is no comparison between Jesus' Temptation and ours. Indeed, it is difficult enough to discern where and in what the temptations lay.

Christ's temptations are altogether above us, they are too high for us. Where is the 'accusation'? What is being 'prosecuted'? Here are things peculiar to the Son of God. The Temptation proper is solely to do with the Saviour, Jesus Christ the righteous.

To perceive the significance of the Temptation, one must soar above in time and space and view history stretching back to the Creation, imagine it reaching forward to the end of time.

Among all the countless teeming millions of mankind emerging and submerging by birth and death generation after generation of rising and falling civilizations throughout the rolling ages of destiny there is but one other parallel.

There is but one other who may be compared with the man led up of the Spirit to be tempted by *ho diabolos*. I repeat, there can be but one comparison. It is between the first man Adam in the garden, and the second man Christ in the wilderness.

Such a view shows that the long dark night had reigned supreme over the world. Thick darkness covered the people.

Fallen in Adam, conceived in sin, shapen in iniquity, born under the sentence of death, the time of mankind's temptation in the light was long, long, past. Since then it was all groping in the darkness like the blind.

But now at last came the Lord from heaven, the unique man, conceived of the Holy Ghost and born of the virgin Mary. The second man and true Messiah, this spotless Saviour appears as the Light of the world, the only one since the fall of Adam to be without sin.

Therefore it follows that his person, his position, and his Temptation are all unique. So is his challenge to the god of this world, the adversary, the prince of darkness, *ho diabolos*, namely, To destroy him and all his works, and to redeem his own people from under that ancient and universal sway.

The three temptations constitute The Temptation because singly and together they are ultimate. There is nothing that could be added to any one, and there cannot be more than three.

Nothing could be added to any one temptation because each represented the diabolical ultimate within its sphere. Beneath it, myriad forms of that temptation may appear: but above it nothing exists because it is the absolute quintessence of diabolical subtlety within that realm.

There cannot be more than three temptations to warrant the name 'The Temptation'—encompassing the whole—because there are no realms of existence common to man other than body; soul; and spirit. Correspondingly there are no spheres of human obligation beyond the personal; the social; and the religious.

Try these to the limit, and nothing is left. But in Matthew and Luke it is evident that, respectively, they *were* tried to the limit. And, in each case, defeated to the uttermost.

The order of the last two temptations in Matthew and Luke is reversed—for doctrinal reasons—because each of these respective groups of three belongs properly to that aspect of Christ and his work peculiar to the Gospel concerned.

The first is the only one of the three temptations in which Matthew – alone – uses the characterization *the tempter*. This is to apply that title absolutely: considering whom he comes to tempt as pure and unfallen manhood from the hand of God.

Originally, it was the whole Creation and purpose for the age tried in Adam in the garden. The tempter's success was complete.

The dispensations ran unbroken till this, the second possible occasion. The sinless, impeccable, perfect Lord Jesus in the wilderness. The tempter's defeat was total.

Still, the questions remain, Where was the *temptation* in the three instances making up The Temptation itself?

And why was the predominance of the name *ho diabolos* so conspicuous? Where was the *accusation*; where the *prosecution*?

The answer is all encompassing. Everything has to do with the baptismal message from the Father in heaven.

The voice from the opened heavens at Jesus' baptism – immediately preceding the Temptation – had spoken out of the Hebrew scriptures.

The first part was from the Psalms; the second out of the prophet Isaiah.

Firstly the divine relationship and kingly destiny of the Son of God was extolled. But secondly the path of lowly humiliation and intense suffering by which that predestined crown should be attained was heralded by the prophet.

'Thou art my beloved Son.' He shall be exalted to reign for ever as God's King upon mount Zion. His enemies shall be trodden down and perpetually overthrown. Of his kingdom and of his dominion there shall be no end. That is his sure destiny, proclaimed in the second psalm.

But to this is added, 'In whom I am well pleased.' Taken from Isaiah 42, the passage is part of a series of prophecies concerning the suffering servant of Jehovah.

The expression appears in a context which culminates in the most terrible anguish: he is to be bruised and struck down to death by none other than the very Jehovah whom he had served so faithfully. Yet this was the only way to save his people from their sins. By his suffering in their place.

The baptismal message sets before us One who, being in the form of God, thought it not robbery to be equal with God. But for all that, it was in his mind to become the suffering servant for the Father's good pleasure.

He made himself of no reputation. He took upon him the form of a servant. He was made in the likeness of men.

And thus he was found in the wilderness by *ho diabolos* at the Temptation, who then received his first, universal, and total defeat since the beginning of the world, departing crushed and vanquished.

As to the Saviour, he went on to victory in all the suffering tribulation of his prophesied pathway: 'and being found in fashion as a man, he humbled himself, and became obedient unto death, even the death of the cross.'

Though he were a Son, yet learned he obedience by the things which he suffered. And suffer he did, even unto death. Therefore it is said 'In whom I am well pleased.'

The accusation implied by *ho diabolos, the prosecutor*, in these temptations is that failure to draw on the authority signified in the *first* part of the baptismal message to avoid the suffering marked out by the *second* would amount to unbelief.

Indeed it was proposed that the power and authority acknowledged in 'Thou art my Son' was the *very reason* for avoiding the path of the suffering servant in whom—and in which—God was 'well pleased'.

Hence the inference '*If* thou be the Son of God'.

Then surely—the tempter insinuated—the consequence must be to demonstrate this Sonship so that by it humiliation and indignity should be seen as dismissed and divinely averted.

The tempter proposes that the glorious and omnipotent authority by which the kingdom will be established—'Thou art my Son'—should in fact be used *now* to circumvent the bitter affliction and suffering unto death inherent in the words 'In whom I am well pleased'.

He submits promises pertaining to the glory *beyond* the resurrection, in order to obviate the prophecies belonging to Jesus' suffering and death *before* it.

In fact *ho diabolos*, the accuser, the wily counsel for the prosecution, *never even mentions* the second part of the baptismal message. On the two occasions he quotes only the first part, relating to the glory of the Son of God and the establishment of the Kingdom.

Consistently he ignores the latter half of the message as if it had never been spoken.

The accuser and tempter proposed action—'If thou be ... then'—on the basis of the divine, glorious, and exalted statement in the primary part of the message alone.

He wholly takes away the second that he may altogether establish the first: a temptation suggesting that the will of God could only be fulfilled by avoiding suffering altogether.

The third temptation is the last: overcome, at the end it is written '*then* the 'devil' leaveth him'. There is no subtlety about the third temptation. No 'If thou be the Son', or sly craftiness with the baptismal oracle. It is a blatant all-or-nothing offer which in the making shoots *diabolos*' last bolt.

Having seen that subtlety and deception avail him nothing, he piles all that he possessed upon the counter to trade in exchange for Jesus' spiritual virtue.

'All the kingdoms of this world, and the glory of them.' 'All the kingdoms of the world in a moment of time.' The Greek for 'world' differs in Matthew and Luke, and for such refinements—as, indeed, for all the detail fulfilled in The Temptation–the reader is referred to the enlarged account in 'The Messiah'.

'All the kingdoms of *this* world, and the glory of them; and saith unto him, All these things will I give thee, if thou wilt fall down and worship me.' But *is* it his to give? Yes: 'to whomsoever I will I give it.'

Here is the god of this world, the ruler of the darkness of this world, the prince of the power of the air, governing 'the course of this world'. Oh, it is his to give. If not, Where were the temptation?

Jesus did not *contest* this temptation. He *despised* it.

Though 'the *diabolos* deceiveth the whole world', so that it is written, 'All the world may become guilty before God', and thus it is concluded 'the whole world lieth in the Wicked One', Jesus' contempt for this last temptation of *ho diabolos* is total.

'Get thee hence, *satan*.' Occurring for the first time in the Temptation, the first time in Matthew, and the first time in the new testament, the ancient Hebrew title used by Jesus finally to dismiss *ho diabolos* opens up the entire wealth of accumulated revelation from the old testament.

Hitherto the narrative had employed the descriptive forms 'the tempter' and 'the accuser'—or 'prosecutor'—from the common Greek tongue.

At last however the old testament Hebrew is quoted giving the title revealed from of old time 'the satan'— the adversary— as if to emphasize the final identification of this wicked being now exposed at the last in the wilderness beyond all shadow of doubt.

The new testament *tempter* and *diabolos* was none other than the old testament *satan*.

All prior descriptions were of a spiritual being whose character remained to be exposed till the fulness lay open and revealed— with an unfolding *consistently brought to light by the salvation of God through the Saviour who vanquished and destroyed his power at every unfolding.*

Appearing in differing characterizations in the Temptation, at the last Jesus dismisses him under the title by which he had been revealed in Job and Zechariah: *the satan; the adversary.*

From so long ago! Indeed, from the beginning. Invisible; spiritual; not subject to the ravages of time, as alive and alert in the Temptation in the wilderness, as he was in the garden of Eden at the Creation.

He neither slumbers nor sleeps; he 'walks' to and fro on earth, inhabits the heavenlies, and with his hosts rules the world and its celestial environs. He is the god of this world, the prince of the power of the air, the spirit that now worketh in the children of disobedience. But he is discerned and overcome by the Saviour.

But not identified till the third temptation. Tempter, *diabolos*, yes. But now, 'Get thee hence, *satan.*'

Then, entering the new testament, *he* was the prosecutor, *he* the tempter. He had come down from the heavens, narrowly tracing the descent of the Son of God.

Alarmed at the incarnation, he fell as lightning from heaven. Marking the virgin birth, considering the beginnings, pondering the flight into Egypt, brooding over the events at Nazareth.

Alerted over John the Baptist, alarmed at Jesus' baptism, astounded at the opened heavens, the voice from heaven, the descent of the Spirit. And incredulous that *then* — straightway — Jesus was 'led up of the Spirit into the wilderness to be tempted of *ho diabolos*'.

As if to say, *Now* do your worst. And he did. But at the last, everything exhausted, he retired defeated. Here is the strength of the Saviour.

A number of passages referring to *ho diabolos*, the *accuser*, or *prosecutor*, follow in the new testament.

However for the sake of brevity — sufficient having been indicated — I intend only to touch on those places which add to the revelation, or, in particular instances, to open up whatever remains of singular importance.

Although the parable of the Sower is recorded in Matthew and Mark, the reference to *ho diabolos* is singular to Luke.

'Now the parable is this: The seed is the word of God. Those by the wayside are they that hear; then cometh *ho diabolos*, and taketh away the word out of their hearts, lest they should believe and be saved', Luke 8:11,12.

The parable of the tares — together with its exposition — is exclusive to Matthew. This parable likewise mentions *ho diabolos*.

'He that soweth the good seed is the Son of man; the field is the world; the good seed are the children of the kingdom; but the tares are the children of the wicked one; the enemy that sowed them is *ho diabolos*; the harvest is the end of the world; and the reapers are the angels', Matthew 13:37-39.

The same is true of the parable of the sheep and the goats, in which each profess to love and serve the Lord with equal fervour. But Jesus, speaking of the dismissive contempt shown to the sheep by the goats, in fact identifies *himself* with his elect, whereas he equates the persecutors with *ho diabolos*.

'Then shall he say also unto them on the left hand, Depart from me, ye cursed, into everlasting fire, prepared for *ho diabolos* and his angels.' And again, 'These shall go away into everlasting punishment', Matthew 25:41,46.

With inexorable certainty this judgment must follow upon all whose deluded profession of Christ was as palpable as their outward show of religion, and of their real conviction of the virtue of their charitable disposition.

What exposed the falsity of both profession and charity in this passing life was their treatment of the sheep, Christ's elect.

What follows in eternity to come is their commensurate punishment, precisely equal to that of *ho diabolos*, from whom, it follows, their deluded form of Christianity and universal charity in this world proceeded.

Observe that punishment; First, its maximum intensity: fire. What causes pain so searing, or over so great an area as the whole body? Second, its maximum duration: everlasting; then, it is beyond the possibility of cessation under any and all circumstances.

Third, its maximum involvement: 'ye *cursed*'; this is the precise opposite of 'ye *blessed*', where that is brought to bear upon each

class respectively which envelops them to the maximum involvement. Hence, cursing equal to that of *ho diabolos* and his angels.
Indeed, 'prepared' for them.

The accuser, *ho diabolos*, wrought through superficial, hypocritical, and carnal 'believers', full of 'good works' for the needy
of this world, together with a kind of neglect and contempt for
the like needy condition in the true, elect, chosen sheep of Christ,
whom they were inspired to regard with detestation.

'Because ye are not of the world, but I have chosen you out
of the world, therefore the world hateth you', John 15:19. But
the carnal, in their worldly religion, professed to love Christ.
It was just that they hated *these*.

But *these* shall enter the kingdom. They are blessed. However
those shall enter everlasting fire prepared for *ho diabolos* and his
angels. They are the cursed.

Luke 8:12 tells us *ho diabolos* takes the word of God out of
the hearts of certain hearers. Not out of their sentiments, mind,
much less out of their heads. It is the *heart* at which he aims.
Hence 'the 'devil' having now put into the *heart* of Judas Iscariot,
Simon's son, to betray him', John 13:2.

This is heart to heart work. If so, Jesus tells those who have
such a heart, 'Ye are of your father the 'devil', and the lusts of
your father ye will do.

'He was a murderer from the beginning, and abode not in the
truth, because there is no truth in him. When he speaketh a
lie, he speaketh of his own: for he is a liar, and the father of it',
John 8:44.

What lusts lie in such a heart? Jesus tells you: Murder. 'For
from within, out of the heart of men, proceed ... murders',
Mark 7:21. And who put those murders there? Why, their father
the 'devil'.

Into whose heart? Why, an apostle, for example: the 'devil' having now put it into his heart. Why, the most scrupulously religious men on earth, who, concerning the righteousness which is in the law, were blameless. The Pharisees. It was these whom Jesus addressed.

But they never committed murder. No, but they brought those accusations which engineered the murder of Christ, and the blasphemy against the Holy Ghost. Out of their hearts they brought them.

'Whosoever hateth his brother is a murderer', I John 3:15. Then, the father of such brethren is *ho diabolos*, the 'devil', no matter *what* their mouth professes: their *hearts* speak louder.

The other lust mentioned is that of a liar: 'When he speaketh a lie, he speaketh of his own: for he is a liar, and the father of it.' What lie is this, that fathered all lies and all liars?

Why, the *original* lie. What was that? 'Ye shall *not* surely die', Genesis 3:4. But they did surely die, the liar. And all mankind died in them: 'As in Adam *all* die', I Corinthians 15:22.

'Death passed upon all men', Romans 5:12. Because Adam— and Eve—believed the lie for mankind. What lie? That sinning does not bring judgment. But it does bring judgment. And it will bring judgment. And it must bring judgment. Even to the resurrection of the dead, and the undying second death.

Then, here are the characteristics of *ho diabolos*. He puts murder in the heart. Cain's heart, for example. Saul of Tarsus, for example. Lies also. Slanderers, whisperers, backbiters, deceivers, for example. These are of their father the 'devil'.

They murder reputations. And they are liars. They think 'Thou shalt not bear false witness' brings no punitive judgment. So they lie against their neighbour.

But their father the 'devil' has been judged already: because of Jesus it is written that 'through death he might destroy him that had the power of death, that is, *ho diabolos*', Hebrews 2:14.

He *had* the power, yes, but through the death of Christ he lost it utterly, and was 'abolished' as to all the power that he had. And that power was in the law.

For in death Christ blotted out 'the handwriting of ordinances that was against us, which was contrary to us, and took it out of the way, nailing it to his cross; and having spoiled principalities and powers'–that is, *ho diabolos*' principalities and powers–'he made a show of them openly, triumphing over them in it'– namely, in *the cross*, Colossians 2:14,15.

But then this mighty, final, absolute, and everlasting victory over *ho diabolos* at the cross was reflected and foreshadowed throughout the ministry of Jesus on earth, leading up to the ultimate triumph of the cross.

So teaches the apostle Peter, 'God anointed Jesus of Nazareth with the Holy Ghost and with power: who went about doing good, and healing all that were oppressed of the 'devil'; for God was with him', Acts 10:38.

Ultimately the authority of *ho diabolos* lay in the law of God, because of sinners' inability and condemnation under it: 'The strength of sin is the law', I Corinthians 15:56.

This Peter confirms by the expression 'your adversary the 'devil'', I Peter 5:8. Where the term *adversary*, ἀντίδικος, refers to '*an opponent at law*'. In other words, *counsel for the prosecution*.

And, in the last analysis, that is the heart of the meaning *ho diabolos*. Since 'by the deeds of the law there shall no flesh be justified in his sight', Romans 3:20, and, 'no man is justified by the law in the sight of God', Galatians 3:11.

Evidently, by prosecuting mankind in general—and the saints in particular—for their transgressions under *that law which God is bound to uphold*, there lies the strength of the case of the prosecutor, *ho diabolos*.

Save for one thing: the work of the Son of God by which—having become incarnate—'through death he might destroy him'—render his power, his legal case, his forensic authority *null and void*—'that had'—but, after the death of Christ, had no longer—'the power of death, that is, *ho diabolos*', Hebrews 2:14.

And again, 'For this purpose the Son of God was manifested, that he might destroy the works of *ho diabolos*', I John 3:8. And what terrible and diverse works were these!

Ho diabolos is no inventor of accusations, nor does he creep about with tittle-tattle to backbite in secret. Such work is for the dregs of men. Counsel for the prosecution is much more aptly depicted in judicial robes in the solemn environment of the lawcourts.

His works and activity—the more climactic they appear—show him to be counsel for the prosecution: he presents the legal case against the accused. He stands in view of the great assize.

He is prosecutor at law; his cause is valid; his case is legal; the hearing is before the Judge in the ultimate tribunal at the end of the world.

But for one thing: 'For this'—yes, *this*—'the Son of God was manifested, that he might unloose'—undo—'the works of τοῦ διαβόλου', I John 3:8. And, indeed, the manifestation of the Son of God brought about the undoing of *ho diabolos* and all his works, with a witness.

How? 'And I heard a loud voice saying in heaven, Now is come salvation, and strength, and the kingdom of our God, and the power of his Christ: *for the accuser of our brethren is cast down, which accused them before our God day and night.'*

Yes, this is the kind of brief, from that height in elevation of prosecution, with such sort of accusation after accusation hurled across the courtroom of heaven, indicated by the term *ho diabolos.*

But for it all, 'For this cause the Son of God was manifested, that he might unloose'–undo–'the works of τοῦ διαβόλου', I John 3:8.

'And they overcame him'–*they overcame him*–'by the blood of the Lamb, and by the word of their testimony; and they loved not their lives unto the death', Revelation 12:11.

What is this but 'And you, being dead in your sins and the uncircumcision of your flesh, hath he quickened together with him, having forgiven you all trespasses;

'Blotting out the handwriting of ordinances that was against us, which was contrary to us, and took it out of the way, nailing it to his cross; and having spoiled principalities and powers, he made a show of them openly, triumphing over them in it'–namely, in the cross, Colossians 2:13-15.

That is–watched helplessly–he took the brief out of the prosecutor's hand; he destroyed all the strength of the prosecutor's case; because, spotless and unimpeachable, to the astonishment of the court, *he exchanged places with the accused in the dock.*

And what? bearing in his own body the rigorous penalty of the law to the extreme, he satisfied every forensic requirement, and the strictest judgment of the righteous Judge, whilst magnifying the law and making it honourable.

Then what is the cry from the court concerning the accused? What is the witness of the blood that speaketh better things than that of Abel? What is the testimony of the handwriting of ordinances, so requited that it cannot move further than that to which it—the whole of it—had been nailed, namely, his cross?

What? It is this: 'loose him, and let him go.' And that is the word which reaches to the deliverance of every last one of Christ's sheep.

What of the prosecutor, after this? His brief in tatters, his legal arguments annulled, his case dismissed, he who once cast accusations across the courtroom of heaven must be expelled from that realm of jurisdiction, together with his entire legal panoply.

Thereafter the heavenly glory resounds with the cry for ever-more: 'And prevailed not; neither was their place found any more in heaven', Revelation 12:8.

Meanwhile *ho diabolos*, the accuser at law, has been made a laughing-stock.

Shamed, degraded, made redundant, dismissed and cast out of court, he has been for ever banished, silenced world without end from uttering so much as one word against all those freely justified by God's grace through the redemption that is in Christ Jesus.

The word translated 'destroy'—as in 'destroy' the works of the 'devil', I John 3:8 – appears—despite Young's error—some forty-three times in the new testament.

The translators have distributed the occurrences of this single Greek verb between eight English alternatives.

Most of these arbitrary allocations vary between one to three times per English word, though they have allotted as many as six of the occasions to the word 'break', which, of course, the Greek λύω, *luō*, does not mean.

The vast majority of these references—despite Young's error—have been rendered 'loose', which is precisely what the Greek *does* mean.

Then why so many alternatives, a number of which are downright inaccurate?

Should the reader consult a Young's Concordance, note that the Lexicon section erroneously indicates that *luō* has been translated 'loose' twice. Actually, it has been translated 'loose' twenty-seven times.

Neither 'unloose' nor 'undo' is inaccurate, although in most cases I favour the majority translation 'loose', not least because *luō* is the root verb from which all the family of words belonging to 'redeem', 'Redeemer', 'ransom', and 'redemption' spring.

So that the basis from which redemption takes its rise may be discovered in the Greek of I John 3:8, so badly translated 'destroy'.

Let the reader substitute 'loose', 'unloose', or 'undo'—in my judgment, in this context, 'unloose'—and the result gives the most accurate reading: 'For this the Son of God was manifested, that he might *unloose* the works of the 'devil'', I John 3:8.

The vital question that remains to be answered follows of course: What are the works of the 'devil' that were 'unloosed' by the manifestation of the Son of God, and how was this accomplished?

Already it has been made clear from the opening of the term *ho diabolos*, that, at the cross, all the arduous work and hard labour of the accuser to bring in by lawful prosecution the condemnation of the children of God, was utterly 'undone'.

They were 'loosed' and he was disgraced. They were brought in but he was cast out.

Whence it follows, that, without a brief in law, his case was dismissed, his person banished, and he was excluded from practice. Expelled from court, disqualified from office, he was laughed out of court and for ever disgraced. That is called 'undoing' the works of the 'devil'.

It is certain that *ho diabolos* was rendered impotent at the cross. The death of Christ brought all those for whom he died beyond the reach of the law in perpetuity. See my book 'Deliverance from the Law: the Westminster Confession Exploded.' But is *that* the context of I John 3:8?

For it is not upon the death of Christ, but upon the *consequences* of that death that the verse in question lays emphasis.

The context refers to what the 'devil' *does*–and has done from the beginning–namely, he *sins*, and has *always* sinned, I John 3:8. This is precisely what the context declares that the unrighteous do, and have done from *their* beginning.

Now, it is what the Son of God was manifested to do about *this* that is being stressed in the passage and context in question.

Of course, before anything could be done to bring about such a deliverance, the death of Christ must *precede* all. But then, equally, the consequences of that death must *follow* all.

This is precisely the truth which the apostle Paul declares to Titus concerning the death of Christ: 'Who gave himself for us.' Unequivocally that refers to his sacrificial and substitutionary offering up of himself on our behalf and in our place.

Yes, but observe what follows immediately after the words 'Who gave himself for us'–'*That he might*'–here follows the necessary consequence–'redeem us from all iniquity, and purify unto himself a peculiar people, zealous of good works', Titus 2:14.

Although it is much more developed, the word 'redeem' in Titus 2:14 is derived directly from the verb *luō* used by John in I John 3:8.

Of equal significance is the fact that our being 'loosed' from all 'iniquity', refers to *lawlessness*. The Greek of Titus 2:14 is *anomias*, the *anomia* of I John 3:4. Hence being loosed from lawlessness *now*—as a *result* of his death *then*—is the common factor in these two passages.

Paul is saying to Titus, Christ's death *had this in view*. And that is exactly what John sets before the reader as to the manifestation of the Son of God. His death is *implied*—though not *stated*—in I John 3:8. What *is* stated is the *consequences* of that death: the *present consequences*.

Precisely the same is said by Peter: 'Who his own self bare our sins in his own body on the tree, *that we*'—and here are the consequences—'*being dead to sins, should live unto righteousness: by whose stripes ye were healed*', I Peter 2:24.

The context of I John 3:8 clearly indicates that the works of the 'devil'—'the 'devil' sinneth from the beginning'—and the works of him that 'committeth'—practiseth—sin are identical, and, in proportion, amount to the same thing.

Then, in context, 'He that committeth sin is of the 'devil'', I John 3:8. These are, and were, his works. They are what he, and his, actually *do*, and do voluntarily and continually.

It is in respect to *these* works that the Son of God was manifested. To 'undo' *them*. 'For this the Son of God was manifested, that he might undo the works of the 'devil'', I John 3:8.

This must mean his works *in us*. It is impossible that it should signify, To stop *him* sinning. He always sinned; he always does sin; and he always will sin.

Then in whom are the works of the 'devil'–that is, the constant doing or practice of sin–*undone*? Who is *unloosed* from living in self-gratification as the end of his existence? In whom is a selfish ultimate intention *undone*?

In the righteous. This 'unloosing' is so to change the inmost heart; so to make the tree good; so to purify the fountain-head.

So to cause the direction of the life to *hit* the mark; so to change the ultimate end of the being of the life, that all that went before, which was of the 'devil', is 'undone', *and undone in the will itself at the heart of its innermost determination of existence*.

Thus there is a *loosing* from that bondage of practising unrighteousness–like the 'devil'–transforming and freeing the inner man to practising righteousness–like the Son.

This 'unloosing' from the works of the 'devil', *in context*, without doubt means *our* being unloosed *experimentally*. It is to stop *us* committing–doing; practising–sin, and, if so, by definition, in and from the ultimate and innermost resolution of the volition and existence.

That undoes it; that unlooses it. Certainly the penalty was paid at the cross. But with equal assurance the power of sin in every realm of the volition has been broken, through our having been begotten of God in experience.

If so, the word of the LORD, as fire and a hammer, has broken the rock in pieces: then the stony heart was removed, and an heart of flesh bestowed within the inward man.

'A new heart also will I give you, and a new spirit will I put within you: and I will take away the stony heart out of your flesh, and I will give you an heart of flesh.

'And I will put my spirit within you, and cause you to walk in my statutes, and ye shall keep my judgments, and do them', Ezekiel 36:26,27.

This is called 'a new creation'. 'Therefore if any man be in Christ, he is a new creature: old things are passed away; behold, all things are become new', II Corinthians 5:17.

The ego has been utterly broken up; it has been mortified by the mighty regenerating work of God, so that what is of God in Christ *takes the place* of that from which both heart and life have now been 'unloosed'. 'Being then made free from sin, ye became the servants of righteousness', Romans 6:18.

'Little children, let no man deceive you: he that doeth righteousness *is* righteous, *even as he is righteous*', I John 3:7.

And again, 'If ye know that he is righteous, ye know that every one that doeth righteousness is born of him', I John 2:29. In these, the power of the 'devil' over them, his works in them, are wholly broken up in pieces.

The children of God are thus 'loosed' from the works of the 'devil'. 'He that committeth'–doeth; practiseth–'sin is of the 'devil'', I John 3:8. Hence, 'Whosoever is born of God doth *not*'–do; practise–'commit sin', I John 3:9. 'In this the children of God are manifest, and the children of the 'devil'', I John 3:10.

For the Son of God is manifest *in* the children of God, so as to unloose and undo the works of the 'devil', in the innermost parts of their heart, spirit, life, will, and being. For this the Son of God was manifest, and by this the children of God are made manifest.

But how is such an interior experimental victory achieved? O no. That question is incorrect: it is not, How *is* it achieved?

The question is, How *was* it achieved? For it *has been* achieved. And it is by fastening the eye of faith upon *that*, that effects the immediate, interior, experimental, and present inward overcoming *now*.

To overcome within, faith looks up to heaven now, yes, and keeps her eyes fastened upon Christ, steadfastly beholding the Lamb as it had been slain.

And what is the voice of faith? Why, by the Spirit, it is the word of God in the evangel of Christ: 'For thou wast slain, and hast redeemed us to God by thy blood out of every kindred, and tongue, and people, and nation', Revelation 5:9.

And again, 'Unto him that loved us, and washed us from our sins in his own blood', Revelation 1:5.

This is the voice of triumph in heaven, and of woe upon earth.

'And I heard a loud voice saying in heaven, Now is come salvation, and strength, and the kingdom of our God, and the power of his Christ: for the accuser of our brethren'—that is, once, lawfully, by the law—'is cast down, which accused them before our God day and night.'

'And they overcame him by the blood of the Lamb'—which silenced the curse of the law by the shedding of blood, and hid the body of the law within the ark under the blood-sprinkled propitiatory.

Once *ho diabolos* had access to the court of heaven, to hurl accusation after accusation against us, the courtroom ringing with his just case of prosecution: but no more.

The blood of the Lamb silenced all, answered all, and, in consequence, voided of his brief, cast him out of court.

Hence, testifying to the blood of the Lamb, 'For ye were not redeemed with corruptible things, as silver and gold, from your vain conversation received by tradition from your fathers; but with the precious blood of Christ, as of a lamb without blemish and without spot:

'Who verily was foreordained before the foundation of the world, but was manifest in these last times for you, who by him do believe in God, that raised him up from the dead, and gave him glory; that your faith and hope might be in God', I Peter 1:18-21.

The accusing prosecutor, once in the court of heaven, has been cast out for this cause: the blood of the Lamb answers every accusation, thus robbing him of any further activity, and expelling him from any right of place.

When Christ ascended, he descended. When heaven embraced the Son, the Judge expelled the prosecutor: 'the accuser of our brethren is cast down.'

The blood of Christ, shed on earth, sprinkled in glory, answers every legal prosecution. 'Having therefore, brethren, boldness to enter into the holiest by the blood of Jesus', Hebrews 10:19.

'If we walk in the light, as he is in the light, we have fellowship one with another, and the blood of Jesus Christ his Son cleanseth us from all sin', I John 1:7.

If so, 'He that spared not his own Son, but delivered him up for us all, how shall he not with him also freely give us all things? Who shall lay any thing to the charge of God's elect? It is God that justifieth. Who is he that condemneth?' He is clean gone that condemneth: banished out of court.

Will he, the banished prosecutor, accuse us on earth, hurling his accusations against lack of sanctification? But God in Christ has answered for our sanctification: 'Wherefore Jesus also, that he might sanctify the people with his own blood, suffered without the gate', Hebrews 13:12.

Then, holding fast the confidence of their faith steadfast unto the end, this is the Spirit's testimony of the saved: 'These are they which came out of great tribulation, and have washed their robes, and made them white in the blood of the Lamb', Revelation 7:14.

Then of what can *ho diabolos* accuse these? Of absolutely nothing.

'And they overcame him by the blood of the Lamb, and by the word of their testimony.' Their testimony agrees with his testimony: 'the testimony of Jesus is the spirit of prophecy.'

Their testimony agrees with God's testimony: 'For there are three that bear testimony, the Spirit, and the water, and the blood: and these three agree in one.' 'This is the witness of God which he hath testified of his Son.'

This is their testimony, the testimony of Christ, and they loved not their lives unto the death. 'Whosoever will come after me, let him deny himself, and take up his cross, and follow me. For whosoever will save his life shall lose it; but whosoever shall lose his life for my sake and the gospel's, the same shall save it.

'For what shall it profit a man, if he shall gain the whole world, and lose his own soul? Or what shall a man give in exchange for his soul?

'Whosoever therefore shall be ashamed of me and of my words in this adulterous and sinful generation; of him also shall the Son of man be ashamed, when he cometh in the glory of his Father with the holy angels', Mark 8:34-38.

That is it: that is to overcome *ho diabolos* in *the experience of Christ's victory, who defeated and abolished him at the cross*: 'For the accuser of our brethren is cast down, which accused them before our God day and night.

'And they overcame him by the blood of the Lamb, and by the word of their testimony; and they loved not their lives unto the death.' Amen and amen.

VI
The 'Prince'

IN the new testament the adversary is referred to as 'prince' in terms of presiding over four distinct but interrelated realms. The revelation of this is exclusive to the evangel.

But before proceeding with the teaching, it is necessary to determine the meaning of the word *archōn*, prince, in the Greek of the new testament.

To accomplish that, however, it is first required to understand the root, *archē*, from which the Greek *archōn*, prince, is derived.

The Greek root, *archē*, appears fifty-six times in the new testament, and has been translated *beginning*, forty times; *principality*, eight times; *corner*, twice; and, once only—in each case—*first*; *first estate*; *magistrate*; *power*; *rule*; and, again, *first*. Evidently the translators favoured 'beginning' most of all, and 'principality' next.

The concept of the word *archē* ranges from *eminence, pre-eminence*, or *principality* to *beginning, extremity*, '*from the first*; *originally*'. It is easy to grasp the idea connecting these applications.

This word is that from which we get the English 'archaeology' or 'archaic'. Indeed, the word forms the first part of our word 'archangel' or the Anglican—*sic*—'archbishop'.

What is most significant in the root *archē* as bearing on its derivative *archōn, prince,* lies in the translation 'principality'. Because *this* is the underlying force beneath the concept 'prince'.

Hence before examining the word 'prince' it is well to see the usage of the root as it pertains to 'principality'.

For example, proclaiming the victory of the Saviour, ascended on high over all that stands against his people, Paul declares, 'For I am persuaded, that neither death, nor life, nor angels, *nor principalities,* nor powers, nor things present, nor things to come, nor height, nor depth, nor any other creature, shall be able to separate us from the love of God, which is in Christ Jesus our Lord', Romans 8:38,39.

Where – with all else – *principalities* lie broken beneath the feet of the Saviour.

Again, not only did God raise Christ from the dead, but he set him in the ascension 'at his own right hand in the heavenlies, far' – mark that: *far* – 'above all *principality,* and power, and might, and dominion, and every name that is named, not only in this world, but also in that which is to come', Ephesians 1:21.

Where the use of the *root* of the Greek for 'prince' shows just how total was the triumph of Christ over him and all his realm and dominion.

Indeed, the apostle assures the saints, 'We wrestle not against flesh and blood, but against *principalities,* against powers, against the rulers of the darkness of this world, against spiritual wicked-ness in heavenly places', Ephesians 6:12.

This is true, and is a continuous spiritual, heavenly, and experimental exercise in prayer day and night, albeit the victory is assured. But *not on paper.* It must be experienced in application. And where and how often does one find *that* in reality. For it *is* a reality.

And so Colossians 2:15 assures us: Christ blotted out the handwriting of ordinances that was against us, which was contrary to us, and took it out of the way, nailing it to his cross; 'having spoiled *principalities* and powers', making a show of them openly, triumphing over them in the cross.

This root, *archē, principality*, underlies and gives basis to the meaning of the derived branch *archōn, prince*, helping us to understand the concept on which the latter is based.

The word *archōn, prince*, itself, occurs thirty-seven times in the new testament. Again, one finds a conceptual word, the idea of which may be spread over a variety of applications. This is evident from the translation: twice *archōn* has been rendered *chief*; once *chief ruler*; once *magistrate*; eleven times *prince*; and twenty-two times *ruler*.

The concept or idea of *archōn* therefore implies *one invested with power and authority; chief, ruler, prince, magistrate.*

Evidently this may be, and is, applied to the authorities among and over men, even to the highest ruler.

But equally it may be, and is, used of unseen and heavenly authorities, even those who are hostile, reaching so far as to the 'prince' over them all.

It is in this sense that the adversary is viewed in four different realms of authority and government, unseen, spiritual, and even ascending to heavenly places. In each and all of these instances he is the 'prince' the 'ruler' the 'chief'.

Over all this authority Christ has triumphed and broken his power, bringing him beneath his feet. Thus he is the Saviour, and hence this is the salvation, which God has given and the Lord has wrought for his people.

It follows that the descriptive title and respective realm in each case should be considered in order.

First, *The prince of demons*

The fact is, however, that the term 'prince of *demons*' is not that used in the Authorized Version. What appears there is 'prince of *devils*'.

Apart from the fact that the word 'devil'—as has been shown—is an appalling aberration, nevertheless *the Greek ho diabolos is always in the singular*. The plural 'demons' is a different Greek word entirely.

The new testament Greek *daimōn* or *daimonion* occurs in four different grammatical forms, the first appearing five times, the second once, the third sixty times, and the fourth and last, thirteen times.

That is, in one way or another 'demon' or 'demons' appears seventy-nine times in all, mainly in Matthew, Mark, Luke, and John. Hence it is the presence of Jesus that brings these to light.

Demons are disembodied evil spirits, which seek to indwell men, women, children, and even animals, such as pigs.

The in-dwelling of demons may be in the singular or plural, and can be multiple.

Demons are moral beings, albeit invisible, but, through their host, may hear, see, speak, feel, and will. They may be cast out, but detest this: embodiment is their goal.

They are not individualistic or disorganized: they have a *prince*, and constitute a kingdom.

Demons knew Jesus as the 'Holy One', but he refused and despised their testimony. Likewise they knew the apostles, witness 'Paul I know'.

However they overcome those who have not the authority and anointing of the Lord. As to the Lord, they are perforce utterly subservient. Jesus cast out demons by his word, and through 'the Spirit of God', thus despoiling the kingdom of their 'prince'.

The 'Prince of demons' rules over them absolutely, and that with a purpose of malice. Setting himself against the Son of God, who indwells his people by the Holy Ghost, the prince of demons envies not only the authority but emulates the place of the Son.

Then, he seeks to rule over men—especially religious men—and indwell mankind—particularly those professing the scriptures.

Albeit, such is the malice of the prince of demons, he ravages the weak and helpless of mankind at will with wanton and savage malevolence and often ferocity.

Demons then, properly so-called, are invisible, malicious, and unclean spirits which, whilst brought to light by the presence of Jesus on earth, since then more often than not hide their presence whilst seductively and insidiously influencing the direction of men and mankind.

These spiritual beings are sent forth of their prince, and are in communion with him, who seeks by them to indwell mankind or at the least so to influence men as to assert possession of the whole of humanity.

The 'prince of the demons'—atrociously rendered 'prince of *devils*' in the Authorized Version—is called *archonti tōn daimoniōn*, *prince of the demons*, Matthew 9:34, 12:24. The same is the case in Mark 3:22. Precisely the same Greek wording is used in Luke 11:15.

The gross imposition 'devils' for the plural *daimonion* mangles the scripture, just as 'devil' mistranslates *ho diabolos*, which is, of course, in the singular. It is *he* that is the prince of the *daimonion*, the *demons*, a different word entirely in the Greek.

Both the prince and the demons, individually and collectively, were wholly beneath the authority of Jesus on earth, and likewise now of the Son in heaven.

The demons knew Jesus, who he was, feared him greatly, trembled, and were perforce cast out at his word, whether singly or in great numbers.

The Lord gave authority to his apostles, and, later, to his chosen ministers, to cast out demons in his name, so that salvation from them is assured when and where authority is exercised by the Saviour.

The prince of the demons has a name. This occurs seven times in the new testament, three times in Matthew, once in Mark, and three times in Luke. However on each occasion the wording has been bungled.

Uniformly the Greek has *Beelzebul*. But with monotonous consistency this has been unlawfully rendered *Beelzebub* by the translators. There is no authority for this presumption, no excuse for such audacity, and there should be no toleration of such an outrage.

This preposterous conjuring trick began with the Roman Catholic Jerome—as did so much else!—who turned the plain Greek *Beelzebul* into what did not exist in the new testament, namely, *Beelzebub*.

He was followed blindly by Tyndale, the Great Bible, the Geneva Bible, the Bishop's Bible, the Rheims Version, the King James Bible—with the notable exception of the single and best publication of this version, the 1873, which, whilst having Beelzebub in the main text, at least had a footnote, '+[Gr. *Beelzebul*]'.

The Revised Version likewise followed Jerome's *Beelzebub*, although, strangely, the Revised Standard has *Beelzebul*. Strange for that version, because it happens to be the correct wording.

Then, virtually from the year 400 until 1960–save for the footnote in one publication of the King James Version–1873– Jerome's *Beelzebub* prevailed over the new testament Greek *Beelzebul*. Why? Blind tradition.

Whence? because Jerome could find no reason for the name *Beelzebul*. The *fact* that it was 'Beelzebul' in the new testament Greek was as irrelevant to him as it became to the train which followed blindly after him in his folly.

However Jerome had observed that the name *Beelzebub*–or Hebrew, *Baalzebub*–occurred in the old testament four times, II Kings 1:2,3,6,16. This records the name of a Philistine idol in Ekron, meaning '*Lord of the flies*'.

On no basis other than the superficial similarity of names, this papist 'scholar' jumped to the conclusion that the *Hebrew* 'Baalzebub' was what was actually meant by the Greek *Beelzebul*.

From such a wild guess–not to say gross stupidity–based on nothing more solid than a fanciful association of ideas–or sounds– *Jerome changed the Greek*.

And this they did, papist and Protestant, for over a millennium and a half in edition after edition through the following centuries.

That *Baalzebub*, god of Ekron, means 'Lord of flies' if not 'of dung' is not in question. Indeed, the latter seems quite suitable.

Notwithstanding, what is required first of all is faithfulness to the *Greek text* in the new testament, from which Jerome and company's wild fancy disgracefully departed. The *Greek* is '*Beelzebul*'.

Now, since the new testament Greek scripture reveals the name of the prince of demons, the question that demands the strictest attention and accuracy is this: *What* does '*Beelzebul*' mean?

First, there is no doubt about the meaning of *Beel*, or as the old testament has it, *Baal*. Baal was the heathen idol – or 'lord' – who was implacably set against Israel.

He corrupted the Israelites at Baal-peor. He corrupted the ten tribes and was utterly opposed by Elijah the prophet.

His idol figure represented the supernatural being whose whole energies were directed against Israel occupying the land for the pure worship of God. To this end, he appeared in various ways and places, as Baal; Baalim; Baal Berith; Baal Peor; Baal Zebub. But *never* as Baal Zebul! Anywhere, or at any time.

Then where is honesty? The truth is, plain honesty is the quality conspicuous by its absence. Yet it is essential to the receiving of the Holy Ghost. But what is foisted upon us? Dishonesty.

Rather than admit ignorance, these 'scholars' change the Greek word into a different Hebrew word, making a nonsense because 'lord of the flies' means absolutely nothing in the context of Matthew 10:25; 12:24,27, or any other such passage.

So why not be honest, rather than wrest the scriptures to avoid the humble admission of ignorance?

Then, given that *Beel* answers in the Greek to the Hebrew *Baal*, lord, What of Zebul? There is no Baal-*zebul* in the old testament. Only Baal-*zebub*. Just as there is no Beel-*zebub* in the new testament. Only Beel-*zebul*.

But just as 'Baal'–of which the Greek is Beel–appears on its own as a single word in the old testament, *so does Zebul* stand singularly as a word on its own account in the same scriptures.

The Hebrew *Zebul*, meaning *habitation*, is recorded in the words of Solomon at the dedication of the temple, the house of God: 'I have surely built thee an house *to dwell in*', I Kings 8:13.

Likewise II Chronicles 6:2, 'I have built an house of *habitation* for thee, and a place for thy dwelling for ever.' The word indicated in both texts is the Hebrew *Zebul*.

Again, among other places, observe Isaiah 63:15, 'Look down from heaven, and behold from the *habitation* of thy holiness and of thy glory.'

From which it is apparent in these texts that *Zebul, habitation,* refers to *the habitation of the LORD. His* dwelling.

It is *this* that is both contested and imitated by the adversary under the name 'Beel-*zebul*'– transliterated into the Greek from *two separate Hebrew words*.

To the contrary, however, *Zebub*–which never appears in the new testament, either by itself or as part of a compound word– is the Hebrew word for *fly*–Ecclesiastes 10:1; Isaiah 7:18–and occurs in the old testament compound Baal-*zebub, lord of the fly,* II Kings 1:2,3,6,16, and nowhere else in the original tongues throughout the bible.

The occurrence of the name *Beelzebul* is unique to the new testament, meaning *'lord of habitation'* or *'dwelling'*.

That is, of *'indwelling'* which is precisely the objective of *the prince of demons*, an objective reached by his indwelling mankind, and filling the world, with myriads of these evil spirits, even reaching to animals, Mark 5:12,13.

An extraordinary feature in the four evangelists, recording the life of Jesus on earth, unique to that period, appears in the vast number of demons that swarm everywhere, excited and activated by their prince at the presence of the Saviour.

The prince–or lord–of habitation–or *indwelling*–lays ferocious claim and hold upon his spoils, knowing that neither he nor they can challenge or resist the power and authority of Jesus.

It is the hearts, minds, and souls of the people that is the scene of the battle, but a battle won already by the very nature, anointing, authority, and power of the Son of God. Neither prince nor demon dare challenge or resist him. They cannot.

But just as the redeemed are indwelt by the Holy Ghost, so the prince of demons would indwell all whom he can. But he can do *nothing* before the power and presence of the Saviour.

Jesus cast out demons by his word without exception. All were subject to his authority. And so was Beelzebul, their prince. These demons, inhabiting the souls of men, Jesus cast out by the Spirit, that the saved should be filled by the Holy Ghost.

Beelzebul with his vast hosts of demons was likened by Jesus to a strong man armed that keepeth his palace, in which his 'goods'–the souls of men–are at peace.

For it is his genius not only to ravage many by violent fits, but to influence more by unseen and unfelt persuasions.

Of such were the Pharisees and scribes. But the one was not the less 'inhabited' than the other. All were 'his goods'.

Yes, the strong man armed 'keepeth his palace', but 'when a stronger than he shall come upon him, and overcome him, he taketh from him all his armour wherein he trusted, and divideth his spoils', Luke 11:21,22. That 'stronger than he' was the Saviour, the Saviour from Beelzebul, the prince of the demons.

Jesus–Jehovah saves; or, Salvation of Jehovah–utterly overcame the whole realm of Beelzebul, breaking down his palace,
overcoming all the panoply of his power, disintegrating his
kingdom, and wholly demolishing all his armour wherein he
trusted, spoiling his goods.

Moreover, not one individual demon existed that was not
utterly vanquished at the same time by the Saviour–the Saviour
from the prince of demons, and demons themselves.

He is King of kings, the Prince of peace, the Prince of the
kings of the earth, the mighty victor, the triumphant deliverer–
the *only* deliverer! the sole Saviour.

And, to this day, neither Beelzebul–with what is left of his
broken domain–nor any single demon, whether violent and
physically apparent or subtle and wholly unnoticed, none, no,
no one, can resist the Saviour's power nor fail to come out at
his word at once resounding from the heights of heaven. Thus
far, the 'prince of demons'.

Second, *The prince of spiritual darkness*

This is indicated in the epistle to the saints at Ephesus, and
to the faithful in Christ Jesus: 'For we wrestle not against flesh
and blood, but against principalities, against powers, against the
rulers of the darkness of this world, against spiritual wickedness
in heavenly places', Ephesians 6:12.

Although this passage does not mention the precise word
'prince', by referring to the entirety of the system by which his
realm is governed, of necessity the prince whose domain it is
must be implied. If so, it is as the head of a realm of spiritual
darkness reaching to the heavenlies.

How terrible is the extent and authority of this fearful domain
of the prince: how distinctly each one of the fourfold powers
must be met by the saints, and engaged in spiritual warfare.

The apostle does not say we wrestle against all four at once; he uses the word 'against' in each case: 'against principalities' then again, separately '*against* powers'.

Each towering over all the world, the heavens and the earth, as far as the north, south, east, and west, terrestrial and celestial, each *one* must be recognized, engaged, and wrestled *distinctly*.

'Against' applies to each agent of the prince: '*against* the rulers of the darkness of this world, *against* spiritual wickedness in the heavenlies.'

This is not individual combat as such: it is *all* saints; in the unity of *one* body; in the indwelling of *one* Spirit: not 'I' wrestle, but 'we' wrestle.

Against each of the four under their prince distinctly. They cover and keep in subjection the whole earth; all the world. *Except* the wrestlers! And these? These are those who abide in the unity of one body, the unity of the faith.

For 'there is one body'–that is visible; a visible unity of the saints in any given congregation, and of all the saints united as one in *all* the congregations as one body. 'And one Spirit'–that is invisible; it is the divine person sent from the Father by the Son to indwell the saints so as to glorify Christ, inwardly, spiritually, and experimentally.

'Even as ye are called in one hope of your calling.' No denominationalism, no sectarianism, no independency here: just the return of the Lord, the hope of the resurrection, and the glory of the world to come, whereunto all are called.

'One Lord, one faith, one baptism.' The faith is the common faith, the faith once delivered to the saints, that received in the apostles' doctrine: there is *absolutely no diversity*. Then there can correspond but *one* baptism. *This* answers to 'One Lord'.

'One God and Father of all'–saints, and faithful in Christ Jesus, begotten of God, drawn by the Father, into that one unity–'who is above all, and through all, and in you all', Ephesians 4:4-6.

Now, *that*, indwelt as one in the unity of the Spirit; glorifying the Lord *in experience*; holding the unity under the Head, indwelt by Father, Son, and Holy Ghost *in one visible body*, I say *that* is what is contested by the prince.

And *that* is what we wrestle *for*, and *they* are those against whom we wrestle with all prayer, according to the one faith, and by one Spirit.

Against principalities, against powers, against the rulers of the darkness of this world, against spiritual wickedness in the heavenlies.

All these bear down from high above, with all their pressure and force, power and dominion, unseen hosts, to assault *the only assembly, the sole ecclesia, the one body*, that is not subject to their power and influence.

These powers of the prince cannot undo the work of grace, but they can and do labour continually and fight without ceasing to darken and mar the clarity of such a testimony.

And *unless wrestled against, they will succeed*. But the wrestling of all prayer; the triumphing of all faith; the rising up of continual praise and thanksgiving, worship and glory, as all in one abide as one in the unity of one body *defeats them*.

And do you expect to get by without being in the unity, going forth without the camp, bearing his reproach? And given that unity, do you expect to get by without wrestling, continual wrestling, and wrestling till the end? What? Against such powers as *these*?

Of course the Lord has overcome them, ascending far over their entire realm, the prince beneath his feet. Of course the Father has given the Spirit on our behalf to our victorious Saviour. Of course the Son has sent down the Holy Ghost to constitute and indwell the one body, and maintain the testimony of Christ.

And of course, spiritually, inwardly, experimentally, in unity, consciously, continually, that is what we wrestle to maintain in a divine witness on earth.

These powers of the prince tower up to the very heavenly places: these are *his* principalities, immediately under *his* dominion; and beneath them are *his* authorities. And subordinate yet are the prince's rulers of the darkness of this world.

Yet more: pervading all from heaven above to earth beneath there is borne down upon the world the spiritual wickedness conceived in heavenly places.

If spiritual, it is unseen. Spirits are invisible. But they choke the very air. Except that about the wrestling saints, praying in the Holy Ghost, overcoming by faith.

The world, dead religion, and worldly evangelicalism are all blinded as to the reality of what is actually taking place.

They cannot see it: so to them it is not there. They cannot feel it: so to them it does not exist.

But the things they cannot see are *the* reality. And the beings of which they are unconscious are the *actual* powers by which they are unwittingly governed.

'Rulers of the darkness of this world'? 'Spiritual wickedness in heavenly places'? What darkness? The world thinks night-time is the darkness of this world. But that is because the world is blinded. The darkness of this world *from the prince*, is not *outward* darkness.

It is *inward* darkness. And mankind is in *inward* darkness from principalities and authorities they *cannot see*. But if they cannot see them, it is equivalent to their being in darkness.

Darkness in the heavenlies? Then, to obscure God, his throne, the Lamb, and the glory above all. Between that and the world lies a thick obscuring darkness, and none can see through it.

This darkness, irrespective of day or night, blinds men to all knowledge of God, or of the truth. And it descends to *within* men, to blind, veil, and obscure them to any true knowledge of themselves or their state before God. They just cannot see it.

It ascends to the heavenlies, this obscuring darkness, and it descends to the inward consciousness of the world. Because it is *spiritual* wickedness in the heavenlies that brings it down.

Then it is *spiritual* darkness. Moreover it is not *inanimate* spiritual darkness: 'the *rulers* of the darkness of this world.'

Then it is *ruled* darkness. There is no escape from that, or, rather, from *them*. Them? Yes, those that inhabit it to rule in and over the world.

Darkness? Spiritual darkness? Ruled spiritual darkness? Darkness in mankind? Yes: 'having the understanding darkened'; and 'because of the blindness of their heart', Ephesians 4:18. Or, spiritually, 'And the light shineth in darkness; and the darkness comprehended it not', John 1:5.

That is the ruled, spiritual, darkness of this world. Blind to the origin of things. Blind to the Fall. Blind to the law. Blind to the Saviour. Yes, and blind to the 'prince'.

But the salvation of God has overcome all, and is over all. The Saviour has defeated and vanquished all, he has risen over all, and is ascended over all.

191

Hear the word of the Lord: 'And what is the exceeding greatness of his power to usward who believe, according to the working of his mighty power, which he wrought in Christ, when he raised him from the dead, and set him at his own right hand in the heavenlies,

'Far above all principality, and power, and might, and dominion, and every name that is named, not only in this world, but also in that which is to come: and hath put all things under his feet, and gave him to be the head over all things to the church, which is his body, the fulness of him that filleth all in all', Ephesians 1:19-23.

The principalities – under their 'prince' – the powers, the might and dominion, all overcome and vanquished by Christ *for his ecclesia, the one body, for the world to come*. As to the world that now exists, these are unseen, spiritual, and heavenly powers.

That is why Christ's ascension must be so high, in order to bring 'all things' under his feet. Then, his victory is as total as it is eternal.

The 'prince', and the dominion exercised by him, are neither seen nor comprehended as possibly existent by the world. Scoffers mock for no other reason than that these titanic authorities of spiritual darkness are neither visible nor tangible.

Yet, invisibly and intangibly, there *exists* a vast panoply of power, in a huge complex of a greater spiritual society far over and above the rulers of the earth, and wholly in control of their machinations. Notwithstanding, far beneath the feet of the ascended and glorified Lord Jesus Christ.

What the apostle reveals by this passage is that the economy of the world and age is not just a matter of human society on earth, nor of uncomplicated direct divine government.

The entire structure soars unseen above where earth's visible authority ceases, ascending into realms spiritual and heavenly, even unto the throne of God.

Moreover beneath the throne but within the heavenly economy of this present world there subsists the fallen system, the 'present evil age', with 'rulers of the darkness of this world' and 'spiritual wickedness in heavenly places'.

But, even so, as to outward authority and order, God upholds all for his purpose in the present age.

None may overstep the bounds with impunity in heaven or on earth, for law, order, and the decrees of God's counsel in an outward manner – from an interior power and source – shall be observed, whilst heavenly and interior things, whether known or unknown to men, run their course to the end of the age.

These principalities, powers, might and dominion – the invisible realms and order of the economy – are upheld by God for the maintenance of the cosmic structure throughout the present age, first and last.

God requires from his throne that all powers must yield to the Almighty.

Even the heavenly powers that were the origin of the Fall must themselves perforce exercise a certain restraint upon lawlessness and destruction. This curb, however, will be lifted at the very end for a little season.

Thus, although the world is fallen, the age evil, and the heavenly powers ruling this age are those of darkness, still God is over all and requires restraint to be exercised for the fulfilment of his will and purpose in history, and among the rising and falling of the nations.

To all these things the world is oblivious, and in total spiritual darkness.

Such discipline upon the principalities and powers is necessitated by the almighty power and authority of the Highest.

This, all powers are obliged to maintain: so that the Fall with its lawless rebellion–both before and after the Flood–can be exercised only within these permitted limits according to the will of God in the unfolding of time to the end of the age.

It is over this economy of principalities, powers, might, and dominion, the realm of the prince of spiritual darkness, that Christ rose and ascended far on high and above all.

And, though all is permitted in this present world to remain in place, nevertheless by the Holy Ghost in his chosen servants through the evangel he calls a people as *one* in Christ, illuminated and drawn by his Father, and their Father.

This *wrestling congregation* he keeps by his power from on high, moment by moment, experimentally and inwardly.

Moreover at the last he will judge, dismiss, and supplant all the present authorities in heaven and on earth, and, in the world to come whereof we speak, establish a suited order from the throne, according to godliness, in the 'new heavens and a new earth' wherein dwelleth righteousness.

'But now we see not yet all things put under him.' No, not by sight, but our hope is both assured and certain by faith.

What is to come cannot now be seen in the heavens, nor discerned upon earth. As to this world, we see not yet all rule and authority put down.

The old powers are still in place, albeit beneath his feet. The economy arrayed beneath him, albeit perforce subject to him, is alien to him. His enemies—and ours, who wrestle against them—occupy the seats of authority, and they are not yet put down out of their place in this present evil age.

Yet a little while he permits the alien powers their authority in the heavens and on the earth, withal under his feet. And so it shall be to the end of the age. Till then he reigns over them, but does not put them down.

But in the end of the world he shall rise, and tread underfoot all his enemies, and overthrow from their places all principalities and powers, lordships and dominions, and every foe.

And in the world to come, and the new economy of the glorious inheritance, he shall establish righteousness in his holy angels. 'All things in Christ.' Then, all things in Christ shall have come to pass.

However even now the spiritually discerning and exercised saints know Christ Jesus exalted as Lord, who once descended and through death delivered his own out of the world. 'I pray not for the world, but for them which thou hast given me; for they are thine.'

It is for these, having been redeemed by his blood, that he rose from the dead, to whom the righteousness of faith is imputed, and on whose behalf he now reigns in heaven, making intercession for them.

He loves them; yes, and they love him. As head over all things, he reigns in them by the Holy Ghost, whilst they are united as and in one body below.

The LORD reigns over his new creation and will deliver it, and this reign is absolute and almighty, with all things fulfilling his merest inclination and will even now, and that for and in behalf of the poor little flock of his redeemed people below.

However, it is true that on account of the suffering way that he brings his own out of this present evil world as pilgrims and strangers, due to the chastenings and afflictions that in love he often lays upon them, this reign is frequently difficult to perceive.

And this is the more so because of the confusion sown by the prince of spiritual darkness, governing the realm of principalities, powers, the rulers of the darkness of this world, and spiritual wickedness in heavenly places.

But faith looks up, love abides within, and hope shines ahead, as all is seen beneath the soon-coming feet of the Lord: the cry of triumph sounds out even now from the midst of the fire: THE LORD GOD OMNIPOTENT REIGNETH!

Third, The prince of this world

This is a description exclusive to the evangel according to John. The term 'prince of this world' is uttered by Jesus when speaking to his disciples. The expression occurs three times over. The first occasion appears in John 12:31, 'Now is the judgment of this world: now shall *the prince of this world* be cast out.'

First, What is meant by 'world'? Nothing more nor less than what is generally understood by it: the cosmos. It is that which came into existence at the creation, and will cease to exist at the dissolution.

In terms of the succeeding generations of mankind and the nations, the world is that which—having been entrusted to Adam in behalf of humanity—from the Fall is subjected to the power of the adversary. Hence the term 'prince of this world'.

But in truth 'the earth is the LORD's, and the fulness thereof; the world, and they that dwell therein', Psalm 24:1.

Whatever mankind has done, humanity perpetuates, or the prince of this world has usurped, nothing can alter the verity of the Creator's rights. Rights which are absolute: over the cosmos; over humanity; and over every individual.

Nevertheless it is the fact of the matter that throughout this present evil age, by definition the world is under the dominion of the prince, the god of this world – II Corinthians 4:4 – who hath deceived the whole world, Revelation 12:9, which 'lieth in the Wicked One', I John 5:19.

So that 'If any man love the world, the love of the Father is not in him.

'For all that is in the world, the lust of the flesh, and the lust of the eyes, and the pride of life, is not of the Father, but is of the world', I John 2:15,16.

Hence, 'The friendship of the world is enmity with God: whosoever therefore will be a friend of the world is the enemy of God', James 4:4. Of course: Look who is its prince.

Therefore saith Jesus of the world, 'me it hateth', John 7:7. Why? Because 'I am not of this world', John 8:23.

Whence he calls upon the Father, 'I pray not for the world, but for them which thou hast given me.' And again, 'The world hath hated them, because they are not of the world, even as I am not of the world', John 17:9,14.

No surprise then, that when he cometh into the world, it is written, 'He was in the world, and the world was made by him, and the world knew him not', John 1:10. Nevertheless, he still came.

But why? To judge, to destroy the world? No, for 'God so loved the world, that he gave his only begotten Son, that whosoever believeth in him should not perish, but have everlasting life.

'For God sent not his Son into the world to condemn the world; but that the world through him might be saved', John 3:16,17.

And again, 'Behold the Lamb of God, which taketh away the sin of the world', John 1:29. Once more, 'The bread that I will give is my flesh, which I will give for the life of the world', John 6:51.

If so, how is it that Jesus saith, John 12:31, 'Now is the *judgment* of this world'? In answer, first enquire, when was the 'Now' to which Jesus refers?

It was a coming hour, when he spake it, witness the context, '*Now* is my soul troubled; and what shall I say? Father, save me from this hour: but for this cause came I unto this hour. Father, glorify thy name', John 12:27,28.

'Then came there a voice from heaven, I have both glorified it, and will glorify it again', John 12:28. Glorified it? Glorified what? Glorified God's name as *Father*. In the name of the Father God *had* been glorified, uniquely by the *Son*.

That, every chapter, every verse, up to this very point in John had demonstrated abundantly and beyond all precedent and controversy.

The Son *had* glorified the *Father*, by the works which the Father had given him to do, and the words which he had given him to speak. Till 'now'.

But now in and through the Son the Father would glorify his name again.

In a way that was unique to 'now', to 'this hour', that is, to the imminent crucifixion, resurrection, and ascension of the Son. 'This he said, signifying what death he should die', John 12:33. *That* would glorify the Father, in an unprecedented manner.

How? By *then* and *there* judging the world, and *thus* casting out the prince of this world in consequence, John 12:31.

Judging this world? But of that we read at the end of the age in the terrible conflagration, II Peter 3, or in the dreadful recurrent descriptions of the last judgment in the book of the Revelation. That is true.

But it is *also* true of the *transferred consummation of that same judgment* which was *then* to fall upon Jesus at Golgotha. Hence, '*now* is the judgment of this world.'

Then, Jesus speaks of *the judgment of the world falling upon the crucified Saviour*. In that sense, Jesus spake, saying, 'For the bread of God is he which cometh down from heaven, and giveth life unto the world', John 6:33.

Thus 'he was made sin for us', II Corinthians 5:21. It is a question of sin, not of sins. As to sin, *it is common to all mankind*. Whereas sins are individual. But to save sinners, apart from bearing *their* sins, the *sin of mankind* as such must *also* be judged.

Hence it is written, 'He is the propitiation for our'—God's children's—'sins: and not for our's only, but'—he is the propitiation—'for the whole world', I John 2:2.

He is the appeasement for the sins of his people, but not only so, he is the appeasement for sin—itself: as such; of all mankind—for the whole world.

Else the world had been destroyed *then*. But it was not: instead, the sin of the world was judged in the Saviour then.

Hence the apostles could testify, 'And we have seen and do testify that the Father sent the Son to be the Saviour of the world.' Every issue of the judgment of the *sin* of man fell upon the Saviour: 'Now is the judgment of this world.'

This saved the world *from its immediate deserved destruction and dissolution.*

This caused God to suffer time to run on, till the judgment that was transferred, and thus deferred, should be consummated at the end of the world.

But if the sin of this world was judged, it must follow, the prince of this world was dispossessed. *That on which he relied, his whole armour wherein he trusted, the very gates of his house, the power of his kingdom, was utterly taken from him.*

If so, *he* fell. As it is written, 'Now shall the prince of this world be cast out', John 12:31.

Whence it is obvious that when Jesus 'now' was 'made sin' and 'took away the sin of the world', all that gave the prince of this world his legitimate power *was lawfully answered and legally dismissed.*

Then '*now* shall the prince of this world be cast out.' Thus, Jesus is our Saviour from the adversary under this title and description.

Next, Jesus spoke of '*the prince of this world*' as follows: 'Hereafter I will not talk much with you: for the prince of this world cometh, and hath nothing in me', John 14:30.

This follows the words 'And now I have told you before it come to pass, that, when it is come to pass, ye might believe', John 14:29.

And now he should speak little more; in truth there was hardly time left in which he could speak more.

Unseen to the disciples, outside in the darkness of the night, Judas had gone to and fro; rulers and priests had consulted hither and thither; groups of shrouded figures had moved from one place to another: all poised, awaiting his exit from the temporary seclusion of the upper room.

Beyond, in the shadows, positions had been taken. Decisions had been reached. Everything but awaited implementation. As it were, heaven and earth held its breath in anticipation of that which would be unleashed once Jesus opened the door and departed from the temporary sanctuary of those four walls.

Beyond, outside, the massive array of spiritual darkness restlessly waited in the night. Titanic forces of satanic wickedness uncoiled their hidden springs from all about the world, throughout all the heavens, to concentrate their energies upon the opening of the door of the upper room.

The Lord Jesus knew this. He discerned in the Spirit what lay outside. He knew that soon he must put forth his hand to the lock. Then, hardly any time would elapse before the full force of the enemy, whether spiritual or temporal, should fall upon him.

Hence he turned to his disciples, saying, 'Hereafter I will not talk much with you'.

It was not that he had no wish to do so. It was that all opportunity would cease. Because even then he sensed that of which they were unaware: 'The prince of this world cometh.'

And if the prince of this world, the world being ruled by him, all its strength was concentrated in the devices of the prince, and all its might was gathered up in array against the Saviour.

The prince of this world 'cometh'.

All the vigour mustered in heavenly places, all the efficacy of principalities and powers, the energy of the rulers of the darkness of this world, yea, *ho diabolos* himself, the *satan*, the adversary in person, in the form of the prince of this world, unseen and spiritual, all focussed upon the door, waiting for Jesus to turn the lock, thereupon to make his exit.

'The prince of this world cometh.' Cometh where? To the door. To await the emergence of Jesus, the Saviour.

And if the prince, then, spiritually, in every moral issue, the world came with him, so that essentially he came with the world, the world being in him, and he in the world. The 'beasts' arose, and mankind, secular and religious, arose in them, waiting.

'And hath nothing in me.' He had all things in every man born since Adam, even in those in whom God had wrought. Nature had first wrought, and in the holiest of saints, much of nature remained. He had, even in the disciples, all the eleven and each of the eleven. And what of the twelfth?

Even the preceding questions of the eleven showed how much *darkness* was in them, how much of the *visible world*, and of *worldly outlook* remained. Oh, much in them: how *little* was spiritual.

Yes, the prince of this world had so much: but he had absolutely *nothing* in Jesus. There was no darkness: he was the light. The prince could not enter that. He could not stand that spiritual light. He was the prince of spiritual *darkness*.

The Lord was not only full of light, he was nothing but light. He *was* the light.

'This is the message which we have heard of him, and declare unto you, that God is light, and in him is *no darkness at all*', I John 1:5.

This is the true light. Not outward; but inward. Not carnal; but spiritual. Not visible; but invisible. Not earthly; but heavenly. 'Because the darkness is past, and the true light now shineth', I John 2:8.

Then the prince of this world had nothing in him. No worldliness: he was altogether heavenly. Nothing of the flesh: he was consistently spiritual.

The prince had no covetousness to which to appeal: it was not in him. There was no self-interest; no self-indulgence; no vitiating sentiment; no ambition for power or glory; no desire for applause. Nothing in him.

Nothing at all; no earthly or worldly aspect at all: *he had nothing in him*.

Jesus was without sin; he knew no sin; he did no sin. He was impeccable. No inbred sin passed from that natural to his mother. His body prepared was so prepared as 'that holy thing', from the power of the Highest overshadowing, and the Holy Ghost coming upon Mary in the impeccable preparation of that spotless seed.

Not a vestige, not a trace of the Fall was in him, though it was in everyone else. The world was utterly full of the Fall, and under it, in body and soul, in sensibility, mentality, volition, in the very life itself.

But not in him. Nothing of all this was in him: 'he hath *nothing* in me.'

No guilt was or could be found in the Holy One, the just and the true. Everyone else, without exception, was guilty, but he was guiltless. The religious were secretly guilty. They had their secrets.

But he had no secrets: he was all light. He *was* the light. The secrets of men should be discovered by the law, and in the judgment. But the law found him faultless, transcendent, and he was the one that should execute the judgment.

Men had their secrets, and, beyond them, in terrifying areas undreamed of, the law cursed and damned the secrets of men.

Voices, thunderings, lightnings roared forth from the law, condemning a thousand commissions, ten thousand heedless, thoughtless, unknown omissions.

Outraged, the offended law sounded forth its flaming penal sanctions without partiality, remission, intermission, or mercy.

The law thundered against the inward states, the habitual pride, the empty vanity, the voluntary condition, the heedless ignorance, the means and end of wasted life, the missing the mark. And all this filled the world. And by it the prince of this world ruled legally.

Yes, but *there was nothing in Jesus*. 'He hath nothing in me.' He was the one exception. Only him. None other: 'hath nothing in'—O, mark it, *in, in*—'nothing in me.'

Behold the man! Here is your Saviour. Here the peerless, the unique, the impeccable Lord Jesus. 'The prince of this world cometh, and hath nothing in me.' No, nothing in him, but everything in the world he deluded through Eve and brought down in Adam.

Gladly man received his rewards, gratefully embraced his advices, living utterly in devotion to the prince of whom they were oblivious, hidden behind the lust of the flesh, the lust of the eyes, and the pride of life.

And hidden within the heart of humanity, infusing the life, permeating the soul of a world wholly subject to the prince of this world, the god of this world, the satan, *ho diabolos*.

And the world, which had believed his lie from the beginning, in practice and experience believed his lie now: That they had neither the need of salvation from this mythical 'prince', nor had they the least necessity of some 'Saviour' from that which presented no danger.

Then why did he die? Let the world answer *that*. If God did not pity the penurious, enslaved, blinded, and dead world, *Why did he send and deliver up his only begotten Son on their behalf?*

If he were not the Saviour of the world, your Saviour, *then why did he die to save you from the prince of this world?*

And had he not overcome the prince of this world, and destroyed all that wherein he trusted, leaving him broken and vanquished, cast out and powerless beneath his feet, *and all that through his death*, Say: had he not died for the life of the world in victory, How was it that the Father raised his Son in love?

How was it that God in the resurrection brought him back from death in love unspeakable, love beyond measure, love that could not suffer him to see corruption? *For he did so raise him.*

And that, the prince of this world, the father of lies, cannot obscure, so that no lie against it can stand even in *his* world, deceived by him as it is, even the world of which he is the prince: for no lie can stand against the truth.

The Saviour *did* die. And so effective was that death, the prince was abolished, and the Saviour was raised from the dead by the glory of the Father to reign for ever and ever, KING OF KINGS, AND LORD OF LORDS.

Finally, the Lord refers to the prince of this world when speaking of the coming of the Holy Ghost.

'And when he is come, he will reprove the world of sin, and of righteousness, and of judgment: of sin, because they believe not on me; of righteousness, because I go to my Father, and ye see me no more; of judgment, because the prince of this world is judged', John 16:8-11.

Consider the comfortable doctrine taught by Jesus to his disciples in view of his imminent departure: 'If I go not away, the Comforter will not come unto you; but if I depart, I will send him unto you', John 16:7.

And not comfortable doctrine in this only, for here the Son sending the Spirit determines the 'you' to whom he is sent.

It is that body of disciples who, later, would be gathered together with one accord in one place, on the day of Pentecost.

That was when 'he sent him unto them'. 'And they were all filled with the Holy Ghost.' Here was the fulness of God, filling the whole, dwelling together in love. One fellowship.

Here were days of heaven upon earth; though the world–and the prince of it–raged about them. But God, in Father, Son, and Holy Ghost, descended to dwell within that separated body.

This was the one unity, not one outside, all within the true *ecclesia*, the one body of Christ. Then, as thus viewed, and so recorded in Acts and the epistles, here is the fulfilment of 'I will send him unto you'.

And when he came, the word that the Lord had prophesied in John 16:11 was fulfilled.

Three distinct causes and effects take place according to that word.

This was not the ministry of the apostles or any gift or person in the assembly or congregation.

It was the result of the Spirit coming and indwelling the *whole* as an entity irrespective of the apostles, ministers, or any gifts: it was the effect of the Spirit himself upon the world, in his coming in life, light, and love in the *ecclesia*.

This was nothing to do with how the Spirit witnesses with the preaching of Christ's apostles or individual ministers. It was altogether to do with the descent of the Spirit into the disciples as an entity.

It was the effect of *the Spirit in person indwelling the whole ecclesia,* or assembly. *That* had its own effect upon the world–yes, and withal the *religious* world–the world and its religion being the only other body that existed on earth according to the judgment of God.

By the Spirit filling the one separated body, *that was this effect* of the saints dwelling together in unity upon the outside world in consequence.

Moreover, besides this, the Spirit, exercising his manifest presence and power, convinced the whole world–religious or otherwise–by his total absence from *them.*

Immediately there existed this glaring difference between the manifestation of him who indwelt the body as opposed to the emptiness and destitution of all that was in the world.

Thus the very coming of the Spirit within the *ecclesia,* the one body, reproves the world by its very exclusion from that wonderful spiritual baptism which constituted the *ecclesia.*

In three ways: ways that can only take place when there *is* one body. And when the world *sees* what takes place in that one body.

When the world sees this *stark contrast,* and sees that it, itself– religious or otherwise–is *utterly void,* dark, empty, and dead, the Spirit absolutely absent from them, being *solely* in the body of Christ separated from them, *then* these three consequences come to pass of a truth.

The Spirit reproves the world by his manifest presence, power, and glory, in the midst of that *ecclesia* distinctly separated from the world, sojourning on its pathway to glory through the very midst of all that is destined for perdition.

The world holds three distinct and highly offensive lies against the truth, which the faithful utterly repudiate, renouncing the world, its darkness, and its prince.

From the midst of the body of Christ, the *ecclesia*, filled with the glory of God, the Spirit of truth does not *passively* contemplate the three distinct and offensive lies held by the world: he *actively* repudiates them. 'He will *reprove* the world.'

By the very presence, light, life, and love of the Holy Ghost, so manifestly indwelling the united company of all who hold the truth, the darkness, deadness, and enmity in which the whole world abides is convinced and reproved by a threefold conviction.

It is the coming of the Spirit *in person*, so as to *fill the disciples as one body*, and in no way the effects of that coming on the apostles or of any individual gifts – but, solely, *the coming itself* – to which the Lord draws attention.

The presence of the Spirit in the *ecclesia*, and the absence of the Spirit from the world, *is that which in and of itself convinces the world – in its dead, dark, and deceived bondage – of the sin of believing a lie against the Son of God; of believing a lie against divine righteousness; and of believing a lie about the coming judgment.*

Consider these three things of which no more than the presence of the Spirit in the congregation, the *ecclesia*, and his total absence from all the world besides, convinces the world:

First, 'He will reprove the world of sin', 'because they believe not on me', John 16:8,9. If so, it is sin not to believe on the Son.

Not to believe on him is to be a liar. As if God's testimony to his Son were not true; as if the signs and miracles were not true; as if his discourses were not true. But if these things *are* true, Why are they not disciples?

Why? Because they love the world. And to make that love more comfortable whilst they are here in their lifetime, they compound their lie against the Son, *by pretending that he is other than he is*. That is, they fabricate a false Jesus.

And if *this* is not lying in the dark, what is? But the Spirit is not in the dark: he is in the light. Then, by *this* the world is reproved.

Second, 'He will reprove the world of righteousness', 'because I go to my Father, and ye see me no more', John 16:8,10. But how shall the coming of the Holy Ghost to the one body, the *ecclesia*, convince the world of righteousness?

By his coming to 'you', the united, gathered disciples, in the one fellowship in Christ, as he came to them at Pentecost, when 'they were *all* filled with the Holy Ghost'.

But, so coming, he utterly abjured, reproved, and treated as unsuited to the presence of God all outside that company. *This* reproved the world of righteousness. Is that not convincing enough?

Yes. But why 'of righteousness'? Take the context: 'of righteousness, because I go to my Father, and ye see me no more', verse 10.

By his–Jesus–going to the Father, and thereupon sending the Spirit, the disciples *do*–in inward experience–'see him'.

That is, see him at the right hand of the Father, and by the Spirit, indwelling the body, *spiritually*. Albeit invisibly, they see him *spiritually*.

As to such interior enlightenment, revelation, and experience, the world, the whole world, the world in every generation, finds itself utterly blinded, because it can see nothing but what is tangible and externally visible. Hence, as to the world, 'ye see me no more'.

But, as to the spiritually enlightened body of Christ, 'Ye shall see me, because I go to the Father', verse 16. Then, this *must* be because from his ascension to the Father thence *he sends the Spirit*.

If so, his united disciples thenceforth see him *inwardly and spiritually*.

No more *visibly and tangibly*, because he is no longer in the world, but 'because I go to the Father', *invisibly and spiritually*, the disciples see him, because the Spirit has come, and the Spirit indwells the congregation of his gathered people.

But not the world. The world sees he has gone. And sees that it is destitute of his spiritual presence *so obviously indwelling his people*. This convinces them.

Convinces them? Reproves them? 'Reproves the world' of what? Of righteousness. But why does the coming of the Holy Ghost to indwell the united, assembled disciples convince the world of righteousness?

Because the Holy Ghost came only after Christ had departed. 'Of righteousness, because I go to my Father, and ye see me no more', John 16:10.

That is, *righteousness* is the reason the Son of God left the world. A world which, in its entirety, together with the worldly religious as an entity, finds so congenial. Of whose *own* righteousness they are content, sure that it will certainly satisfy a God of love and mercy.

But it does not. Because his love and mercy *can never deny his righteousness and justice*.

The 'righteousness' that satisfies the world is an abomination to God. The false righteousness; legal righteousness; self-righteousness to which the world lays claim is an abomination to the LORD.

All the world's claims to righteousness amount to no more than what the prophet calls 'filthy rags', and the apostle designates 'dung and dross'.

But the Son answers to the righteousness of God. So, he left the world, and went to his Father.

Thence to receive and send the Spirit of God to indwell those *separated from the world*, who, as a distinct and united company in Christ, for whom his blood was shed, and to whom the righteousness of God was imputed, were *thenceforth filled with the Spirit.*

Of which the whole world was destitute. That convinced them. That reproves the world.

The departure of the ascended Son from the world. The coming of the descended Spirit into the body of Christ. The sharpness of the distinction between the two: Where does that leave the world? Reproved. Convicted.

That body in which the Spirit dwells exclusively *trusts in the blood of Christ for righteousness before God, and of God.*

And the Spirit manifestly bears witness to that faith by his indwelling the whole body, and none other.

The disciples repudiate what the world asserts. They hate what the world loves. They confess what the world denies.

They do not deny their sins, sinfulness, depravity, but, as self-confessed sinners, they fall at the feet of the Lord for mercy through faith in his blood *to impute to them a righteousness equal to that of the Father.* To this, the coming of the Spirit bears witness.

And by his dwelling in the one body of Christ, believing to be justified by faith through the body and blood of their crucified

Saviour, they are all baptized in one Spirit into one body, and all drink into that one Spirit.

What a witness to a world in darkness and destitution, death and deception, governed by its prince!

On high in light unapproachable, accepted of his Father in divine righteousness, God having received the Saviour's work on behalf of his people in death, imputes divine righteousness to them by faith in his blood, the Spirit being outpoured to fill the believing, joyful disciples.

Thus those justified—reckoned righteous before God by faith—are indwelt by the Spirit of God, of which the entire world is utterly empty, void of the least vestige or the slightest hint of divine approval.

Rather, reproved and convinced, the world is left destitute of the Father, the Son, and the Holy Ghost, abhorrent to God in its self-justification, namely, that of ungodly men who hold the truth in unrighteousness.

For the Son has *left* that world so congenial to itself, but utterly uncongenial to him, and totally unsuited to *his* measure of righteousness, that is, the righteousness of God, thence to ascend to his Father in glory, to sit upon that throne whose habitation is justice and judgment.

Hence the world is reproved of righteousness, because the Son has gone, he has left it for ever, to ascend to his Father, so that the world sees him no more.

But the saints see him spiritually, because, as in a pool of light surrounded wholly by thick darkness, the Holy Ghost, radiant with glory, dwells within that one body and congregation for evermore.

Finally, When the Spirit comes, whom the ascended Son will send unto *you*, 'he will reprove the world' of 'judgment', John 16:8. Namely, 'of judgment, because the prince of this world is judged', verse 11.

First of all, the world is reproved of the sin of unbelief, because the world believed a lie, that Jesus was not the Son of God, nor would they believe the signs that he was. They changed the truth of God into a lie.

But the evident and abundant witness of the Spirit of truth in those—as one—that held the truth convicted them to the depth of their desolate and empty hearts.

Next, in sequence, came the astounding truth that, though he was raised from the dead, *he departed from this world*. He would not, and he could not remain in a realm and scene of such unrighteousness as existed in the character and nature of this world.

The outward show of legal and self-righteousness that filled the world—let alone the unrighteous abominations of the Gentiles—was such that 'I go to my Father, and ye see me no more'.

There remains the third and last of the reproofs and convictions following the descent—in and of itself—of the Spirit to indwell the one body, consequent upon the ascension of the Son.

This concerns judgment: 'of judgment, because the prince of this world is judged', John 16:11.

'The prince of this world' is the descriptive term of a usurper. It is the adversary in his function of ruling over the darkness of this world *since the Fall*. Not before it. God created the world: whence it must follow, 'The world is *mine*, and the fulness thereof', Psalm 50:12. And again, 'he hath established the world by his wisdom', Jeremiah 51:15.

Yes, and it was entrusted to Adam. But he fell, and brought down the curse upon the earth, and darkness, sin, and death upon all humanity. That was when the adversary came into his title, by the exercise of the principality which is described as 'the prince of this world'.

Through him 'all the world wondered after the beast', Revelation 13:3, and that from the beginning, hence by him 'the whole world lieth in wickedness'.

Of him a thick veil and imperceptible spiritual darkness comes down upon the entire human race, and inward blindness with it, in which the prince rules over the entirety of the human race; hence, 'the prince of this world'.

This insensate state of mankind is called 'the vanity of their mind, having the understanding darkened, being alienated from the life of God through the ignorance that is in them, because of the blindness of their heart', Ephesians 4:17,18.

And again, 'In whom the god of this world hath blinded the minds of them which believe not', II Corinthians 4:4. Once more, they 'became vain in their imaginations, and their foolish heart was darkened', Romans 1:21. And this, from the Fall, when 'sin entered into the world, and death by sin', Romans 5:12.

In Adam, humanity believed the lie: 'Thou shalt not surely die.' Forthwith man died in his soul; received the sentence of death in his body, and was shut up to the second death world without end at the judgment in the last day.

Against this reality, the prince of this world blinds the heart and understanding of mankind.

To deliver from this fearful dominion, the Prince of life died for the blind and dead, held in gross darkness and in the shadow of death, sending his ministers 'To open their eyes, to turn them from darkness to light, and from the power of Satan unto God, that they may receive forgiveness of sins', Acts 26:18.

But within his domain, the prince of this world blinds the minds of them that believe not, denying despite the evidence before their blinded eyes that death has passed upon all men, leading the whole world on in a united and common denial of any judgment falling upon mankind.

What? Can man not see that the Flood came, 'and took them all away', and that 'the old world perished'? No. Humanity has 'educated' itself out of such incontrovertible evidence, preferring rather to believe and perpetuate a lie, under the guise of 'science'.

Thus the world has willingly followed its prince, who, having become established when sin entered into the world, and death by sin, lied in the very inward parts of man against the judgment.

Forthwith he drew the heart of mankind after the desires of the flesh and of the mind, setting before humanity the glittering prospects of the lust of the flesh, the lust of the eyes, and the pride of life.

This is called 'the course of this world', and the world blindly stumbles on, hands outstretched, after these vanities, as if this life were the whole of existence.

Yea, as if humanity's true origins never existed, and eternity did not yawn before the very feet of passing and fleeting generations of mankind. Thus the prince of this world rules in his dominion.

But he was defeated, cast out, and judged at the cross. There, his dominion was taken, and all his armour wherein he trusted was utterly destroyed.

All was brought under the feet of Christ in death.

For he hath broken the gates of brass, and cut the bars of iron in sunder. The old yoke has been shattered in pieces, and the ancient shackles cut off for ever.

At the cross we see God's estimation of the sin of the world, which the world itself so glibly sets aside as non-existent. But so existent is it before God that the apostles could write, 'And we have seen and do testify that the Father sent the Son to be the Saviour of the world', I John 4:14.

How? 'Behold the Lamb of God, which taketh away the sin of the world', John 1:29.

Where? In his own body, on the cross: 'the bread that I will give is my flesh, which I will give for the life of the world', John 6:51.

Giving himself, he was delivered up to be crucified: he was made sin; his soul was made an offering for sin. Sin was *judged* in him.

Then how can the world make light of sin? Easily; because it ignorantly follows its invisible, intangible, imperceptible prince, who puts it into the carnal mind of humanity 'there *is* no judgment', and as to sin, 'it is naught, it is naught'.

Naught? It is so massively consequential that to save sinners God spared not his own Son, but judged – utterly condemned – sin at the cross in the body of Jesus.

Now sin having been judged in the body of Jesus shows up the lie by which the prince of this world deceiveth the whole world.

The cross makes manifest that not only *is* there a judgment, but so dreadful is that judgment, that God rather gave up his only begotten Son, to bear its punishment, than that the whole world should perish because of the offensiveness of sin.

And would God, would Christ, have done so for a lying fiction? Behold the suffering Son of man! Christ *suffered* for sin, namely, for that which the prince of this world assures mankind does not exist.

But the righteous judgment of God in justice not only recoiled at the offensiveness of sin, but in love God gave his Son a ransom for all, to save men from it, and its consequences.

Then the rather let judgment be formed from the Lamb as it had been slain, from the suffering, dying, bleeding, substitute for sinners, hanging upon the tree. Now lay thy hand upon thy heart, and tell me, for all the lies of the prince of this world, Is there not a judgment?

That Jesus suffered at Golgotha, accursed and forsaken, dead and bleeding, shows of a certainty that there is a judgment.

That Jesus hung there, and that for the sin of the world, declares the love of God, who so loved the world, that he gave his only begotten Son, that whosoever believeth on him should not perish, but have everlasting life.

That rather than the judgment falling upon the whole world, God condemned sin in the substitutionary Saviour, so exceeding terrible was it in the light of eternity.

These things being so, the spectacle of Jesus hanging dead, crucified upon the tree, blood and water having come out of his pierced side, he having been slain for sin, the sin of the world, Where now is the prince of this world?

Where is he in the presence of this dreadful judgment—vicarious judgment—of sin, whose whole realm and reign depended on *sin not being judged*?

Where? And yet he had filled humanity in its fallen darkness with the lie that sin being a mere trifle, there would be no judgment. 'Thou shalt not surely die'? Then why had the only begotten Son of God died, judged in the place of sin, and for sin?

I will say where the prince of this world is: he is hiding for shame.

He is shown up for what he is: a liar who abode not in the truth, because there is no truth in him. When he speaketh a lie, he speaketh of his own, for he is a liar, and the father of it, John 8:44.

Faced with the evidence that God in love, who is love, gave his only begotten Son as the Lamb of God that taketh away the sin of the world, on the cross to judge sin in his own Son, Where is the prince of this world? He is judged.

He is judged for having lied about God; he is judged in that he deceived the world about sin; and he is judged because sin was condemned for us in the Saviour.

The prince of this world is judged for his imperceptibly having deceived the whole world that sin was a thing of no consequence; that the love of God was such that we should be indifferent to it; and that hence no judgment would follow.

To all this the crucified Saviour–and, that crucifixion being accepted in heaven in the ascension–utterly gave the lie to the prince of this world.

But the motive of the prince of this world was shown up also, and judged in itself before the whole world. For what motive could possibly have possessed the prince of this world?

He gains nothing. The world loses everything. For eternity. The prince is neither enriched nor impoverished. But the world is deliberately deceived and wilfully led in blindness to ever-lasting destruction.

Why did, why does, the prince of this world do it? Sheer malice. And now, from Golgotha, the whole world is reproved for its submission to the lies of its prince, for ever exposed and judged in his nature.

At the cross of Jesus, and in the descent of the Holy Ghost on the day of Pentecost, the world can see for itself, saith the Spirit, that the prince of this world is judged.

He is judged at Golgotha, and by the cross upon Golgotha, because of the sufferings of the Son of man, slain for sin *by the judgment of God*. If this be not love divine, What is love divine?

The prince of this world is judged by the revelation of the love of God, that God is love, and the nature of that love revealed and unveiled by the cross of Christ at Golgotha.

Thereupon the prince of this world is judged in his lie that there is no judgment.

Judged in his lie distorting the love of God. Judged in his lie concerning the Son of God. Judged in his lie over the cross of Christ.

How? Because the Spirit of God fell upon, filled, and indwelt the entire company that received the truth, but left destitute and in darkness all who believed his lie.

When he, the Spirit of truth, is come, 'he will reprove the world', that is, 'of judgment'. 'Of judgment, because the prince of this world is judged.'

And that is how he is judged: by the coming and witness of the Spirit of truth, baptizing and indwelling all who believe the truth, but leaving void and destitute the whole world, which loves and believes the lie of the prince of this world, dwelling in a deceived world of sin, darkness, and death.

219

The world is deluded by the lie of the prince of this world. But the disciples are convinced of the truth of the crucified Lamb of God.

The first, the Spirit utterly excludes. The second, the Spirit fills with his manifest presence, filling the separated company with joy unspeakable and full of glory. 'And of the rest durst no man join himself to them', Acts 5:13.

Now this reproves the world. Because the Spirit bears witness by his interior indwelling of the entire assembly of those who believe and receive the truth, that the prince of this world – with all his lies – is judged.

And the world lost in the darkness – reproved – can but look on at the wonderful divine attestation of the Spirit in those dwelling in the true light.

Wherefore the world – since the cross, the resurrection, the ascension, and the descent of the Spirit to fill the entire company of the united believers, and none other – *must* be convinced of judgment, whatever its prior delusions.

Its being reproved is inevitable, because before all peoples, all nations, every tongue, 'the prince of this world is judged'.

And by *what* a judgment the world is reproved! The disciples being delivered from this present evil age, set free from the love of this world, filled with the Spirit of truth, the whole assembly exults in the love of God, spiritually in union and communion with Christ in glory.

Eagerly they await his coming and their resurrection to everlasting glory in the world to come.

The Spirit in the body of Christ, the true *ecclesia*, the house of God made without hands, appears as the very opposite to the spirit that is in the world. The Spirit of God is the Spirit *of the world to come*, the earnest of our inheritance, till the redemption of the purchased possession.

The Spirit testifies in the assembly, Come out from among them, and be ye separate. Come out of her, my people. Up, Get ye out! He makes us to be strangers and pilgrims, looking for a better resurrection.

He hurries us out before the fire falls. He fills us with the hope of glory in the unity of one body, awaiting the coming of Christ, with the cry 'O death, where is thy sting? O grave, where is thy victory?'

'Death is swallowed up in victory.' How utterly then, 'the prince of this world is judged', world without end. Amen.

Fourth, *The prince of the power of the air*

Here is yet another entirely distinct realm of activity, not so much as mentioned hitherto under the works of the adversary, yet warranting so distinctive a description under his authority as prince.

Then, for how much have we to bless the Lord, and to give thanks unto the Saviour, for having saved us from realms and spheres of helpless captivity, to which we had been so utterly oblivious?

For all this, as is the case with a number of the some fifteen descriptive terms of the adversary, the title 'prince of the power of the air' occurs once only.

However the significance and situation of the occurrence, besides the proper completion of the definition 'prince', demand its inclusion in this exposition.

221

The translation 'prince of the power of the air', Ephesians 2:2, could be bettered. 'Power' is more suited to convey the Greek *dunamis*–from which we derive 'dynamite'–rather than *exousia*, which really refers to 'authority'.

Where *exousia* occurs, the translators have often given preference to the power exercised by the authority, rather than to the authority exercising that power, despite the clear use in the Greek of *exousia*. And that is the case in Ephesians 2:2.

So that the translation would be better served if rendered 'prince of the *authority* of the air'. But that said, it remains a fact that this is a mystifying expression on face value.

'Of the *air*'? 'Authority of the *air*'? In what sense? There are references to 'air' in the original, and in the other six instances 'air' as we know it is clearly the meaning. Indeed, it is almost a transliteration: ἀήρ, *aēr*, or, as we say, 'air'.

It is of the utmost importance that the context must be observed. The apostle declares of the Gentile nations of mankind, without exception or distinction, 'You who were dead in trespasses and sins', Ephesians 2:1. This is the condition on which he is about to elaborate.

But this does not exclude the Jews, for he says later 'among whom we all'–all we Jews–'had our conversation in times past in the lusts of our flesh, fulfilling the desires of the flesh and of the mind; and were by nature the children of wrath, even as others', that is, the rest of mankind, namely, the Gentile nations, Ephesians 2:3.

All, all were 'children of wrath'. Then, wrath begat them. Man was not only born under it, he was begotten by it, wrath begat them. It was their nature. If not, What does the wording mean?

Consider the kind of nature such a birth generates: 'dead in trespasses and sins', Ephesians 2:1.

Dead? Then this refers to the *inability* of the nature of man: he is without life before God. Therefore without ability in God's sight. As are those in the graves to living men, so are both the quick and the dead before God.

But this death is not without accountability individually, any more than was the wrath which generated their humanity. It is a death 'in trespasses and sins', whether alive on earth or dead in the grave.

Then, whether living or departed, a culpable death. And, since neither trespasses nor sins have been blotted out, an *accountable* death.

Nevertheless, for those called of God, for those appointed to obtain salvation, for those who have Jesus Christ as their risen, living Saviour, *the account has been paid*. He paid it at the cross. He paid the ransom price.

The saved are 'bought with a price': that of the body and blood of the Saviour; hence the text reads as it concerns the saved—note the tense; the *past* tense—'ye *were* dead in trespasses and sins.' But no more. Now, 'you *hath* he quickened.'

But—dead within or not—in those trespasses and sins mankind 'walked': but only as men walked, they were utterly dead before God; entirely dead to any awareness of their condition; wholly dead to their being begotten of wrath; and absolutely dead to the mountains of guilt they accrued as they walked on to the grave.

How can this be? Because of powers and forces malignant to them but outside of themselves, and beyond their remotest comprehension.

What powers and forces were these? Those that, unknown to them *governed their walk*.

'Ye walked according to the course of this world, according to the prince of the authority of the air'–namely–'the spirit that now worketh in the sons'–it is not *children*; it is υἱοῖς, *sons*–'of disobedience', Ephesians 2:2.

Humanity, children of wrath, though dead within whilst active without in the multiplicity of their trespasses and sins, nevertheless moved in a uniform direction, namely 'the course of this world'.

The word 'course' is *aiōn*. To this corresponds the English *aeon*, according to the dictionary, *an age of the universe*.

It is the flow of time, like a river, from the Fall to the end of the age. It all flows in one direction, and all humanity is carried upon its tide.

It is the flow, the tide of time, that sweeps the whole world, the cosmos, all humanity, Jew or Gentile, it makes no difference to this remorseless river, mankind as a whole, as an entity, as a cosmos, is swept by this ever flowing river, to empty into the sea of eternity.

And in time past 'ye walked according to the course of this world.' But no more. When *will* the saved realize as they ought just how much the Saviour has wrought for them? Is not this complacent ignorance a sin?

'According to the prince of the authority of the air.' Of the *air*? Why 'air'? Obviously this is a metaphorical use of the term, but why is it used?

What is the *air* literally? It is the atmosphere. The layers of gas which envelop and surround the earth. These are divided into several concentric spheres the outermost shell of which, from which light gases can escape, being some two hundred and fifty miles at the extremity above the sphere.

The concentric layers reaching up to this differ radically in content, the most significant changes being at roughly ten, twenty-five, fifty, and one hundred and fifty miles respectively.

As a result of the composition of the atmosphere, or air, a pressure is exerted upon the earth.

At sea level the average pressure of the earth's atmosphere is equal to about fifteen pounds per square inch. This varies considerably according to location, circumstance, and environment.

These are bare facts. The metaphorical use of them, by adapting the physical reality to a spiritual figure in the term 'prince of the authority of the air', is another thing.

But, since based on the known reality, the question is, What is meant by the transference of things physical to things metaphysical; of things material to things spiritual?

To answer, the word 'air' must be viewed in the sense of *atmosphere*. At times the atmospheric pressure can be *felt* as a weight bearing down consciously upon those beneath its oppressive heaviness.

Or else if beyond the consciousness, yet still a reality, imperceptible and undiscerned; nevertheless making *all* the difference. Yet it is this weight of the atmosphere – of the air – to which men of necessity accustom themselves as if it were not there.

And yet there are times and locations in which the sheer pressure of the atmosphere forces itself upon the attention of men, as in the intrusion of oppressive conditions, or in the foreboding sense before an oncoming storm, as it were making the very air to be 'electric'.

In such atmospheric conditions *then* men take account of power in the air, and, restless, cannot but fear.

From the analogy of the oppressive weight of the atmosphere, given those ominous conditions known to all, the Spirit of God by the apostle adopts the description 'prince of the power of the air'.

That is, of the air, or atmosphere, alluding to the word atmosphere *spiritually*, as a kind of pressure under which man is helpless; an oppression which he is powerless to control. But this *spiritual* atmosphere is *inward*. Moreover, it is *governed*. It has an *authority*.

Thus the 'prince of the power of the air' rules over the whole world, pressing down with a force against which no man can stand; nor, willingly submissive, has mankind the least desire to raise himself above this atmosphere, so as to fear God and work righteousness.

That kind of uprightness, inward, spiritual, heavenly righteousness comes not by nature, but by the Saviour, and the Saviour alone.

However, so startling and unexpected is the revelation that the adversary is described as 'the prince of the power of the air', that a clause is added immediately to describe the analogy intended.

Likewise the figure refers to *spiritual* air by the breathing of which men sustain their *interior* existence and walk; it points to *inward* 'atmospheric' pressure to which humanity is subjected of necessity.

It is indicative of man's compliance in bowed obeisance to the *authority* that brings all perforce into submission beneath the sheer inward pressure and weight of such power, albeit as unfeelingly as to the weight of the atmosphere itself.

The clause describing the 'prince of the power of the air' follows: 'the spirit that now worketh in the children'—it should be *sons*—'of disobedience', Ephesians 2:2.

Albeit this is supernatural, since it is 'according to the course of this world', because it is universal, and as a result of its being from generation to generation, it is taken as a perfectly natural state of affairs.

But it is not. However, as to spiritual reality, the Spirit of God, by the word of truth, awakens the saved.

Consider that 'the prince of the authority of the air' is a spirit: he is 'the spirit that now worketh in the sons of disobedience.' If a spirit, then invisible, intangible, and imperceptible. Never willingly does he make himself felt, nor give away his presence or advertise his existence.

Humanity is oblivious of this spirit, though possessed by it. This is nothing to do with that number possessed by demons. It is to do with *humanity as such*, all mankind throughout the age, being governed by a spirit commonly indwelling the human race.

And if a spirit, indwelling at the deepest and most inward level of being. Human being. In which the spirit of the prince of the authority of the air cannot be discerned by humanity.

Mankind is oblivious of the indwelling of this one vast and universal spirit inhabiting and governing as an authoritative prince all humanity alike.

So deeply does he indwell that it is as if he is on the other side of the consciousness of mankind, unseen and unfelt behind a curtain of oblivion.

But subtly moving and activating mind, heart, consciousness, and will—which *themselves* are felt, but *not* what moves them— this mighty authority, this unseen spirit, reigning as if from high above the atmosphere, imperceptibly pressed down upon all mankind.

For, observe, this spirit, the prince of the authority of the air, not only—unlike the physical pressure of the atmosphere—*indwells* within and behind the deepest spirit in humanity, he does so in order to *work*.

'The spirit that now'—*now*, mark it—'now *worketh in*'—*in*, observe—'in the sons of disobedience', Ephesians 2:2.

The word 'worketh' is really inadequate. The Greek reads ἐνεργέω although the grammatical form of this word is accommodated to the context.

The word is a compound, the first part of which is the preposition ἐν, meaning *in*, and the second, ἔργον, *work*. That is, *to work in; to inwork; inworking*. The English *energy* is derived from this compound.

Then, not just an indwelling spirit, but an inworking one.

He indwells to *effect a work within oblivious mankind, throughout the age, from birth to death, creation to dissolution.*

So deep within, so spiritually subtle, the inworking so profound, man is unaware of it? Yes, unaware of it; and yet the inworking is even deeper: *energia* in the text is *followed* by yet another *en*, in, so as literally to read, *inworking in*.

The prince of the authority of the air, or atmosphere—used metaphorically—in fact presses down upon the entirety of humanity throughout the course of this world, in a manner as imperceptible as the physical and outward weight of the atmosphere.

But yet far, far exceeding all perception in a way that is spiritual and interior, so that he is described as 'the spirit that now *inworketh in* the sons of disobedience'.

Then what a Saviour, to deliver his people from such a subtle, imperceptible, yet fearsome enemy! What a salvation, that we should be saved from so interior, universal, and entrenched a power, from so great dominion as that of the prince of the authority of the air!

But that is the nature of the Saviour, and the character of that salvation, received by us through grace.

'But God, who is rich in mercy, for his great love wherewith he loved us, even when we were dead in sins, hath quickened us together with Christ.' 'For by grace are ye saved through faith; and that not of yourselves: it is the gift of God.' 'For we are *his* workmanship', Ephesians 2.

And again, 'That he would grant you to be strengthened with might by his Spirit in the inner man; that Christ may dwell in your hearts by faith.

'That ye, being rooted and grounded in love, may be able to comprehend with all saints what is the breadth, and length, and depth, and height; and to know the love of Christ, which passeth knowledge, that ye might be filled with all the fulness of God', Ephesians 3:16-19.

For this is the Saviour, and that is the salvation, not only from the prince of the authority of the air, but also from the adversary in all his fourfold activities as prince.

Yea, and abundantly more, saved from the very adversary himself, through Christ Jesus our Saviour, to the praise of the riches of God's grace. World without end. Amen.

VII
The 'Serpent'

T HE 'serpent' is introduced in Genesis chapter 3. 'Now the serpent was more subtil than any beast of the field which the LORD God had made. And he said unto the woman, Yea, hath God said, Ye shall not eat of every tree of the garden?

'And the woman said unto the serpent, We may eat of the fruit of the trees of the garden:

'But of the fruit of the tree which is in the midst of the garden, God hath said, Ye shall not eat of it, neither shall ye touch it, lest ye die.

'And the serpent said unto the woman, Ye shall not surely die: for God doth know that in the day ye eat thereof, then your eyes shall be opened, and ye shall be as gods, knowing good and evil', Genesis 3:1-5.

Once again, 'And the LORD God said unto the woman, What is this that thou hast done? And the woman said, The serpent beguiled me, and I did eat.

'And the LORD God said unto the serpent, Because thou hast done this, thou art cursed above all cattle, and above every beast of the field; upon thy belly shalt thou go, and dust shalt thou eat all the days of thy life:

'And I will put enmity between thee and the woman, and between thy seed and her seed; it shall bruise thy head, and thou shalt bruise his heel', Genesis 3:13-15.

There can be no doubt about the difficulty in interpreting Genesis 3:1-5 and 13-15.

That is, of the meaning of the 'serpent' and all that he is said to have spoken, done, and that which was pronounced upon him in consequence.

But then there is the like difficulty in the interpretation of the tree of life and the tree of the knowledge of good and evil.

But God shall give us an answer of truth, as may be seen in the latter case in the book 'Creation'. As to the 'serpent' there is far less on which to base interpretation, and the passages in Genesis 3 are inherently more difficult.

Nevertheless, I will offer what I believe, having the witness that I have received it of the Lord and by the Spirit; but let the reader judge for himself.

However I cannot put my own inward witness as affirmatively as I would wish, since so little proof – or material with which to provide proof – exists in either the Hebrew or Greek languages, or in the text itself.

What I believe to be the true, sound, and spiritual interpretation will be opposed on two different fronts.

One, 'safe', but stolid – I could say, stupid – and immovable, and, I add, wholly unspiritual. This is Pharisaical.

Two, unsafe, but fully admissive of Hebrew, Greek, and textual evidence, but moveable, modernistic, and in a different way, just as unspiritual; perhaps even more so. That is Sadducean.

In such a rare case as the interpretation of the 'serpent' I accept this, and am obliged to assent to the right of either opposing party to question on the respective basis of each what I set forth as my belief from my own devotion, meditation, study, and decades of waiting upon the LORD.

If I should say, I know that what I have received is of God, I must put my hand upon my mouth: for you should and must answer, Then prove it from the original tongues and from the scripture itself.

From the available slender evidences and sources I will do my best, presenting these and my conclusions to the judgment of the reader.

Immediately let me say that I believe Genesis 3 should be interpreted *spiritually* and therefore *figuratively*, on the basis that is granted on all hands, that the latter passage, Genesis 3:13-15, is one which is undoubtedly spiritual and figurative, referring to Christ and to the adversary.

But if the adversary is *there* called 'serpent', and *that* use of 'serpent' is obviously figurative and spiritual, then surely the rule must hold good in Genesis 3:14. And if so, then in Genesis 3:1-5 also.

For, in Genesis 3:14, *it is the same figurative adversary*, given as representative and symbolical in the figure in Genesis 3:15.

Likewise no one doubts that the 'great red dragon'–in heaven?– is metaphorical, and that this is really a symbol of *ho diabolos* and *satanas*. But in the same breath the figure 'that old serpent' is uttered. If so, with equally definite a confirmation that the term is figurative, Revelation 12:9.

'Serpent' is the first description by which the adversary is made known. Then, that 'old' serpent suitably equates the metaphor in the last book of the new testament with the figure in the first book of the old.

However 'the serpent' is introduced in the very beginning of the bible, when not so much as angels have been mentioned, and all is concentrated on what pertains to *man*, his creation, fall, and destiny–not to what excites the curiosity of 'religious' speculators.

Rather, here are the origins of the desperate, agonizing verities of life and death; time and eternity; God and man–and in which *already* highly allegorical inferences have been presumed.

Why two accounts of Creation? Why two names for God respectively? Why the obvious, proven allegories–read 'Creation'– of 'the tree of life' and 'the tree of the knowledge of good and evil'?

Why the highly poetic language from which nothing but spiritual inferences may draw deductions to give sound interpretation? All these things surround–no more than surround– the creation of Adam, and the 'building' of Eve. And in such a context is the 'serpent' an exception?

And since when does a 'serpent' speak? Over the most vital matter ever to affect the whole human race?

A *serpent* speaking, to cause the fall of mankind? And would God speak to a *serpent*, v.14?

No; in neither case: it is ridiculous to literalize–I could say, trivialize–such momentous calamities. Besides, the serpent *already* went on his belly in 3:1, well before 3:14.

And it is just the *one* serpent, by the way. Cursed above *every* beast of the field? Cursed above *all* cattle? All *cattle*? Oh? Do *they* speak too, like this 'serpent' apparently just deprived of legs?

Then there can be no other rational explanation than that the figure and passage must be regarded as allegorically and spiritually. The alternative is simply inane. It is not merely irrational: it is wholly unspiritual, damaging, and superstitious at the outset.

That presents one with the question, Is 'serpent' really a correct translation of the Hebrew?

And, whatever the correct translation, Why was the adversary so called at the very beginning, *and hardly at all since,* certainly never in the Hebrew, so as unequivocally to refer to this passage?

Moreover, in the new testament Greek *only one place* refers to this most vital occurrence in the entire history of mankind, *save for a few clearly and undoubtedly spiritualized references in Revelation.*

The Hebrew letters that comprise the word translated 'Serpent'– thirty-one times–are written in English transliteration as NACHASH. But it is not as simple as that.

NACHASH appears as a separate word in two other instances.

In the first, it has been translated *divine,* twice; *learn by experience,* once; *observe diligently,* once; *use enchantment,* thrice; *enchantment,* once; *enchanter,* once; and on two further occasions, the translation is too dubious to mention.

The second occurrence of the transliteration NACHASH appears twice only. On each occasion it has been translated *enchantment.*

Then again, finally, *exactly the same Hebrew characters* form a third variation–as has been said–NACHASH, *serpent,* so translated thirty-one times. Then why the three variations, and why the variety of meanings?

The answer to this does *not* stand in the ancient Hebrew text. In that, there are *no* variations of the word originally written in characters that should be rendered uniformly NCHSH. The reason for this is that, in the sense in which we know them, in practice there are no vowels in the original Hebrew.

To quote—if I must—Sir Frederic Kenyon, 'the special peculiarity of it'—i.e. of biblical Hebrew—'is that in its original state *only the consonants were written*, the vowels being left to be filled in by the reader's mind', Kenyon, Ancient Manuscripts, Eyre and Spottiswoode, 1958.

If so, How did *three* variations of NCHSH occur?

This was due to the gradual introduction—and very late at that—of the Massoretic 'points', small signs inserted outside of the original Hebrew letters, to give 'direction' to the reader as to *how* the series of consonants comprising any one word were to be pronounced: basically, *vowel* or punctuation points.

This system was evolved by the Massoretes, a name given to the Scribes and Rabbis devoted to resolving such difficulties and anomalies in the pronunciation of the original Hebrew—from the accumulation of a number of varying schools of thought—into a uniform and acceptable mode of reading around the year A.D. 500.

It was *this* Rabbinical system that gave rise to three forms of the original NCHSH, now pronounced NACHASH, but, *external to the original Hebrew*, governed by three *different* sets of 'pointings'.

Nevertheless, *originally*, it was the same word, whether translated *enchanter, enchantment,* or *serpent.*

From which it follows that *the name of the reptile* never appeared in the original.

What appeared was *a descriptive characteristic or activity applicable to whatever or whoever fitted the definition.* Man or beast. Largely the lexicographers miss the point entirely.

Gesenius – one of the most respected and oldest of the lexicographers – differs. He states 'an onomatop. word, i.q. *to hiss, to whisper*, specially used of the whispering of soothsayers. PIEL – (1) *to practise enchantment, to use sorcery.* (2) *to augur, to forbode, to divine.*' Again, 'A second root is given in Thes. probably signifying *to shine.*'

Of the variations from the Massoretic points Gesenius states '*enchantment, omen, augury.*' Then, '*a serpent*, so called from its hissing'– NB: '*see the root.*' Exactly. '*So-called*' and '*See the root.*'

If *that* be observed, then the word 'serpent' is ridiculous. It is what is *done.* Not *what does it*, however Genesis 3 mystically adapts the figure.

I ought to mention that the lexicographers associate this Hebrew word with 'brass', but for no good reason – apart from two distinct words in sequence – from little more basis than the association of ideas in connection with Moses' 'brazen' serpent.

Chaldee or not, I find no profit to lead the reader into this so-called 'second root' of *nachash.*

What has been stated is grounded upon the indisputable basis of fact, well illustrated by the range given by the English translation of the word.

The word – in itself purely indicative, as with all the descriptions given of the adversary – means 'to enchant'.

So that one given to this activity is an 'enchanter', as has been shown clearly by the favoured translation in the English, with the exception of the rendering 'serpent'.

But the latter is wrong. The fact that a serpent 'enchants' its prey, no more makes the word *nachash* mean 'serpent', than it makes a diviner who uses enchantments to be a serpent. The Hebrew describes the *activity.* It does *not* describe who or what *acts* in that manner.

It is clear that this, the first name given to—and the introduction of—the adversary in the scriptures, has a double meaning: it is used *allegorically*. It is a *figure*.

The Spirit by Moses without doubt surrounds the record of Adam with spiritual figures, as the two distinct accounts of the creation, 'the tree of life'; likewise 'the tree of the knowledge of good and evil'—again, see my book 'Creation'—these things being no less true than is the case with the *figure* of the 'enchanter', or—misleadingly—so-called 'serpent'.

The fact that allegory surrounds the creation and the record of Adam in no way presumes that either Adam or Eve are *themselves* allegorical: that conclusion would be farcical, were it not a blasphemy against the constant references to the actual and real persons by the Holy Ghost throughout the scripture.

Jesus himself points to Adam and Eve as distinct persons. So do the apostles, Paul in fact building an entire—and pre-eminent—thesis upon the literal reality of Adam being 'the figure of him that was to come', Romans 5:14.

And why should this seem surprising? The apostle takes the case of Abraham's two sons, one born of a bondwoman, Hagar, the other of the freewoman, Sarah, and states specifically that these circumstances constitute an allegory: first of two covenants; next of two mountains; then of two cities; and finally of two births.

But the fact of the surrounding allegories in no way whatsoever calls into question the real existence of the actual persons of Ishmael or Isaac.

As with the tree of the knowledge of good and evil, Genesis chapters 2 and 3 provide the *only* occurrence of one of the most important factors in the history of mankind.

A history, in the bible, stretching from the creation to the conflagration, encompassing all time and the whole of humanity.

Then, a figure may be used in the appropriate place, but not appear again other than as the thing prefigured.

So with the so-called 'serpent'.

Genesis 3:1-15 is the *only* place in the whole old testament where this word has a double—or allegorical—meaning.

Yet everyone knows that it refers to the adversary. Does that figure make this his only form? Obviously not. Then the very fact that the term is not used elsewhere in the old testament scriptures is overwhelming proof that *nachash*, properly *enchanter*, was a figure for the time then present.

Apart from an allusion in II Corinthians 11:3—to be explained in its place—the only other references in the whole bible are to be found in the highly allegorical book of the Revelation.

For example, in a chapter envisaging a woman in heaven clothed with the sun, and the moon under her feet, her travail watched by a great red dragon set upon devouring her man child, who is caught up unto the throne of God, the great dragon then being characterized as 'that old serpent, called the Devil and Satan', Revelation 12:9.

This undoubtedly places all the references in the realm of allegory.

Then, so is the 'old serpent' in Genesis 3:1-15, for it is he to whom that designation refers, John being the last writer in the new testament, and Moses the first in the old, and the Genesis passage being one of the most ancient, the description 'old' puts the identity beyond question.

But that which puts it beyond question is entirely allegorical. Then 'serpent' in Genesis 3:1-15 must of necessity be a figure, an allegory of the adversary.

Besides, however vulnerable Eve might have been in her innocence, no one can suppose her to have been so gullible as to be taken in by a talking reptile!

What? A talking 'serpent' that afterwards is supposed to have lost its legs, being forced to crawl on its belly? How utterly juvenile to literalize such an allegory.

But a reptile *thus created originally*, to whom the term *enchanter* applied so naturally, provided the perfect figure, and, as such, it was used. Used, that is, as a pictorial metaphor of the invisible, intangible, and inaudible adversary.

'Now the 'serpent' was more subtil than any beast of the field which the LORD God had made. And he said unto the woman, Yea, hath God said, Ye shall not eat of every tree of the garden?', Genesis 3:1.

Ignoring for this present purpose the lies and blasphemy inherent in this speech, 'hissing' or not, it is obvious beyond all question that the heart of this matter is expressed in metaphor, figure, and symbolism.

No 'beast of the field' can speak, and none is remotely capable of the subtlety that lay behind the temptation.

'And out of the ground the LORD God formed every beast of the field.' Further, 'and brought them unto Adam to see what he would call them: and whatsoever Adam called every living creature, that was the name thereof', Genesis 2:19.

Adam saw over them, but they could not see over him.

As was vegetation to the creature, so was the creature to Adam. Incapable of comprehension or communication. Then not only speech, but above all subtlety superior to man, are out of the question. But not the metaphor.

'And Adam gave names to all cattle, and to the fowl of the air, and to every beast of the field; *but for Adam there was not found an help meet for him*', Genesis 3:20.

No, Adam, made in the image of God, was altogether superior to dumb beasts, they were *utterly* beneath him, and *incapable* of reaching to the height and depth, the length and breadth, of his soul and spirit, let alone intelligent consciousness and consequent speech.

What? A serpent? A reptile? A snake? Equal with man? 'For what man knoweth the things of a man, save the spirit of man which is in him?'

The strata of life of the beasts of the field, of the creature, just as much as that relative to vegetation, having neither soul, spirit, light, consciousness, moral responsibility, or intelligent capability, lie an infinity of distance beneath the heights to which God made man in his own image.

Then, Genesis 3:1 is as allegorical regarding the speaking 'serpent' as it is in respect of the symbolical tree of the knowledge of good and evil. Which, incidentally, was *not* 'in the midst of the garden'.

These things being so, the *enchanter* or so-called 'serpent'–*sic*– was a *figure* of what was inaudibly 'whispered' or 'hissed' in enchantment into the mind of Eve by the adversary–not as yet mentioned in the Creation–under the most suitable possible figure itself, namely the silent, motionless, unblinking 'serpent', whose form of utterance was the almost inaudible 'hiss'.

Yet which could flash into action with the speed of lightning, injecting deadly poison into its entranced but helpless victim.

In the case of the metaphor, *mankind in Adam*, from whom the poison of inbred sin ran and passed in the lifeblood of all his posterity by natural generation, What better figure than the 'enchanter' when applied to that reptile?

Clearly the sort of subtlety implied in Genesis 3:1 could apply to no 'beast of the field', any more than could human speech.

No such creature, by definition, could speak, reason, possess light, have moral agency, could comprehend responsibility or obligation, nor reach in any degree to the morality, spirituality, intelligence, or speech of man.

And was Eve likely to be 'deceived' by a 'snake' speaking with man's voice? And speech concerning supposedly 'literal' fruit presumed capable of changing *moral and spiritual nature*?

This kind of mindless literalism might do for children entertained by the brothers Grimm or Hans Andersen. Or, come to think of it, simpletons hoodwinked by 'fundamentalist' hirelings and 'scriptural' upstarts: all worse than the scribes.

How utterly stupid the very idea. Taken literally such an astonishing manifestation would have been far more likely to make Eve run for her life at the incredible apparition, or else rather to laugh to the point of bursting at such a ridiculous spectacle.

Furthermore, the verse does *not* say that the 'enchanter' *was* a beast of the field. In fact the implication is to the contrary.

Carefully examined – it is even stronger in the Hebrew – the verse asserts that the 'enchanter' had reservoirs of subtlety way above *any* beast of the field.

Not that he *was* one; albeit, because of certain characteristics unique to that reptile, nothing could exemplify in a figure so suggestively the traits of the *real* 'enchanter' that beguiled Eve.

In the original the English word 'more' – as in *'more* subtil' – does not exist.

Literally the Hebrew reads, 'And the *enchanter* was crafty above every beast of the field.' Not *more* than them. *Apart* from them.

Albeit *one* of them is taken for a figure in the allegory. But he who was thus figured was subtle way and 'above'– now mark this–'*every*' beast of the field. Then how could the *real* enchanter have been one? He was above them all. 'Every' one of them.

At best, *theirs* was an *earthly* subtlety. *His* was heavenly. *They* were beasts of the field. *He* was above every beast of the field.

The wording does not imply affinity, but lofty superiority beyond the reach of *every* beast of the field.

Actually the translation 'beast of the field' is not satisfactory either. The Hebrew word is taken from that meaning 'life', not 'beast'. Strictly the translation should be 'living' as in 'a living creature'. So as to read 'every living creature of the field'.

But the 'enchanter' was above all these: then 'a living creature' of another order, as yet undisclosed. However the physical characteristics of the reptile as an 'enchanter' lent themselves to the figure.

The heavenly and spiritual being who was thus allegorized was 'that old serpent, called the Devil, and Satan', Revelation 12:9, and *he* was *above all* living creatures of the field, of an order and strata of supernatural existence yet to be revealed in subsequent enlightenment from the scriptures.

Hence the *figure* in Genesis 3:1-15. At this point in scripture, not so much as angels had been mentioned. Supernatural beings are not so much as hinted at, no, not until the mysterious Cherubims, Genesis 3:24.

As to subtlety, craftiness, or just plain prudence and intelligence, it was beyond all dispute that *man* was the one that utterly towered above all other 'living' of the field, though he had been made of the dust, as had they.

Still, he was immeasurably above *all* others, so that of them no help meet could be found for him, subtle 'enchanter' withal. No comparison. Nevertheless, *nachash* provided a suited figure – and descriptive name – for what was yet to be revealed.

The very fact that the descriptive Hebrew word – ineptly translated 'serpent' – does occur again throughout the old testament but yet *never again* in terms of Genesis 3:1-15, confirms beyond a peradventure the necessity of an allegorical interpretation of this passage.

The fact that the literal *nachash*, the so-called 'serpent' *always* – from its creation – went on its belly, is helpful to the figure, not destructive of it.

Besides what 'serpent' literally eats dust?

But once admit of the allegory and – dust thou art and unto dust shalt thou return – the symbol of the adversary whose wickedness brought in sin, and if sin, death, then that he 'feeds' on the dust of death could not be more appropriate, Genesis 3:14.

But it is both prophesied and predestinated that his head shall be crushed. Save only, that this shall 'bruise the heel' – in death – of him who is both prophesied, predestinated, and purposed to 'destroy the works of *ho diabolos*'.

All the works, under whichever of some fifteen characters, and, if so, first of the 'serpent'.

The Seed of the woman, Revelation 12, shall bruise the head of the 'serpent', but it shall bruise his heel. However, there is no doubt of the outcome: a crushed head abolishes and 'kills' the reptile. It is 'death' to him and all his works.

A 'bruised heel' neither abolishes nor kills. But – to ascend above the metaphor – it does mean, in the resurrection, five scars, glorified in the Saviour's body for evermore, witness of his triumph overall in victory, world without end. Amen.

This refers to the 'seed of the woman' of whom the LORD God declared to that 'old serpent', 'I will put enmity between thee and the woman, and between thy seed and her seed; it shall bruise thy head, and thou shalt bruise his heel', Genesis 3:15.

Then there are but two seeds. The seed of the 'old serpent' of whom it is said, 'Ye are of your father the devil'. He begets enmity against the seed of the woman, and is the father of lies. 'He that committeth sin is of the devil; for the devil sinneth from the beginning.' And, naturally, so does his seed.

But there is another seed, begotten of God through 'the Seed of the woman', Christ Jesus. These love one another, as they love the Saviour, and there is no hatred in them. They walk in the light, and no lie can abide the light. They are of the truth, and come to the light.

Of these it is said, 'Whosoever is born of God doth not commit sin; for his seed remaineth in him: and he cannot sin, because he is born of God', See I John 3:7-10. There are no seeds other than these. By this the victory of the Saviour over the 'enchanter' is made manifest.

In the Greek of the new testament the word 'serpent', ὄφις, *ophis*, occurs fourteen times, but, apart from the allegorical references in the book of the Revelation, whatever allusions may be presumed, only one passage *directly and unequivocally* points to Genesis 3:1-15.

The references concerned are as follows: 'As the serpent beguiled Eve through his subtilty', II Corinthians 11:3. 'And the great dragon was cast out, that old serpent, called the Devil, and Satan, which deceiveth the whole world', Revelation 12:9. 'From the face of the serpent', Revelation 12:14.

'And the serpent cast out of his mouth water as a flood', Revelation 12:15. 'And he laid hold on the dragon, that old serpent', Revelation 20:2.

Unquestionably these are all allegorical and metaphorical passages, save that II Corinthians 11:3 is not *directly* allegorical, as are those quoted from Revelation, but refers *back* to the allegorical and metaphorical original text from Moses in Genesis 3:1-15.

The question that hangs in the air, therefore, is that whilst the Hebrew *nachash* has been shown to be descriptive, What of the Greek equivalent?

It must be admitted that the new testament word ὄφις, *ophis*, translated 'serpent' appears to be precisely the same as the English. Contrary to the Hebrew, it is not a word descriptive of what the reptile *does*, but an arbitrary name given to distinguishing it from any other creature.

Then the Greek equivalent of this name used in II Cor. 11:3– since it refers directly to the 'serpent' who beguiled Eve–would appear to destroy all that had been said of the interpretation of the Hebrew *nachash* in Genesis 3:1-15.

Because, ostensibly, the Greek refers to as limited a species of reptile–as opposed to a description associated with its activities– as does the English 'serpent'.

It points to *that* creature, and nothing else. Almost universally this is the view of the lexicographers.

This would appear to destroy the metaphorical interpretation of *nachash* in Genesis 3.

If 'serpent' really meant 'enchanter' and actually refers to the adversary himself in that–invisible–character, How can it be that Paul uses the Greek word for the *species of reptile alone as such*, descriptive of no characteristic whatsoever? Just as in the English 'serpent'.

But is this really the case with the Greek after all? Is it really valid? I submit that it is invalid.

I admit that it is hard – if not virtually impossible – to *prove* the case with the Greek.

But without bias I affirm that by an association of ideas, Greek letters, comparative grammar, not to say conceptions, *with which I associate the strongest influence of all to me, the witness of the Spirit,* the Greek ὄφις, *ophis,* 'serpent' has almost hidden descriptive connotations after all.

But one renowned lexicographer, Professor Grimm of Jena, translated by J.H. Thayer, provides a depth of research into the ramifications of the Greek that provides at least hints – if not evidence – suggesting a definite connection between the Greek word for 'serpent', and that for 'sight' or 'looking'.

In which case the Greek ὄφις, *ophis,* 'serpent' *is in fact* – however that fact lies in obscurity – *a descriptive word after all.*

Hence Grimm/Thayer give the word ὄφις, 'serpent', in the lexicon, *and follow this immediately with the notice* '[perhaps named for its *sight*]'.

Now, this remark from perhaps the most meticulous and thorough of all the lexicons, by the most particular and precise of lexicographers, *must have a sound basis.* Otherwise it would not be added.

Then, *ophis is another descriptive name,* not just a mere designation of a species of reptile.

And does anyone suppose that the Greek ὀφρύς, *the eyebrow,* or *projection,* bears no relation *either* to ὄφις *or* to the Greek for 'sight'?

And what of ὀφθαλμός, *ophthalmos,* translated 'eye' one hundred times, and 'sight' (plural) once? Coincidence? I think not, and nor can one deny a spiritual witness to such association of ideas in a context of this sort.

But what is the Greek for 'sight'? Once again I refer to Grimm/Thayer: "ὁράω, *horaō, to see; to see with the eyes.*' As to the root, 'ὀπή, *opē, perhaps from* ὄψ [root ὀπ (see ὁράω *horaō, through which one can see*)].'

From ὁράω, *horaō* two grammatical forms are derived which have a direct influence on ὄφις, 'serpent', namely, 'ὤφθην, *ōphthēn* (pass. 1, Aor.) *I was seen, appeared, showed myself*', and 'ὀφθήςομαί (fut. pass.) *I will appear.*'

It can hardly be doubted that the latter are allied closely to ὄφις, 'serpent'. Indeed, Grimm/Thayer go further and announce that ὀπή, *opē*, [root ὀπ, *op* (see ὁράω *horaō, 'through which one can see')*] lies at the bottom of this complex system of interwoven words and grammatical intricacies.

And again, as to ὄφις, *serpent*, observe from the same authority the words: 'ὄπτω, see ὁράω, *horaō,* ὀπτάνω [ΟΠΤΩ] *to look at, behold.*'

Now, all this is directly connected with ὄφις, (so-called) 'serpent', by a coincidence beyond reasonable dispute.

And who can set aside the scholarship of Liddell and Scott, of all the lexicographers the most respected, when they give the secondary branch of the meaning of the Greek: 'ὀπτός (B), ή, ὀν, (ὁράω, ὄψομαι) *visible.*'? Where ὁράω, *horaō*, is the basic conception, *to see*, and ὄψομαι, *visible*, speaks for itself.

It is simply too much to disassociate this from some connection, however remote, with ὄφις, *serpent*.

To return to Professor Grimm, translated by Thayer, what is now discovered in such a connection? 'Ὄπτω, see ὁράω'. And then? 'ὀπτάνω (ΟΠΤΩ) *to look at, behold*'. But that is precisely that by which we are led back—by however devious a route—from ὄφις, *serpent*. Then, '*to look at, to transfix with the gaze.*'

247

It ill becomes me–and I detest it–to quote Bullinger, but for the confirmation of the weak with great distaste I give the transcript of his quotation: 'SERPENT, 1. ὄφις a serpent, lxx for *nchsh*, Gen. 3:15; Ex. 4:3. *Hence*, symbolically used of the devil.

'Ὄφις *is probably from* ὄπτομαι, to see, (as δράκων, a species of serpent, *is from* δέρκω, to behold, *and the Hebrew nchsh*, a serpent, *is* from *nchsh*, to eye, view acutely).

''A serpent's eye' *was a Greek and Roman proverb. (non. occ.).'* I really hate to quote this man, but it *does* give some support– of its kind–to all that I have been advocating.

And what is this? That the *enchanter* of Genesis 3:1-15 *transfixes by his immovability on the one hand and unblinking eye on the other*, the prey on which he is set, quite bewitching the helpless victim.

So immobile, so inert; so unblinking: yet when the moment comes, the strike is faster than the eye can follow.

Then, it is all over. But for long moments together, it was the basilisk stare that transfixed and hypnotized the victim.

I fully own and confess that the root of the Greek *ophis* is complicated, oblique, and *directly* obscured.

But it is true with equal certainty–and assuredly by inference from Grimm/Thayer above all, and others–that *ophis* is not a word merely indicative of a species.

The root lies in the description of an activity to do with sight, and the use of the eyes. In this case, *reptilian* sight. The *basilisk* gaze.

Ophis has as its origins the Greek *horaō*, to see. That in turn finds its root in ΟΠΤΩ, a word indicative of sight, the function of the eyes. Hence the English 'optician'; 'optic'; 'ophthalmic'; 'optical'; and so on.

Hence '*ophis*', by however remote the strands, connects with a web which is inextricable in both Greek and English derivatives from ὄπτω, the origin of the word ὀράω, which draws the intelligence by sheer force of circumstances to the central concept of the use of the eyes and the function of seeing.

Thus the 'serpent'–the *enchanter*–beguiled Eve. Bewitching by unblinking penetration the attention of the sensibility and imagination, whilst enchanting with the insertion of thoughts which, had she fled to her husband, would never have occurred.

Whence you may discern the *activity*–not the unspiritual and inadequate interpretation of traditionalism–of the 'enchanter' and with it, find the witness of the Spirit to the truth. Because the Spirit *is* truth, I John 5:6.

But if any choose to believe otherwise, let them believe otherwise. Then how will they explain the passages?

They cannot, unless they descend to the depths of modernistic unbelief and discount everything, or become blind to the unspirituality of literalism and make fools not only of themselves, but of the word of God itself. And if it be not so, pray: put forth a better alternative for me to receive.

In II Corinthians 11:3 the context recalls that as Eve had been espoused to Adam, so the *ecclesia*, as the bride, had been espoused to Christ. But 'the serpent'–ὁ ὄφις, *ho ophis*–beguiled Eve through his subtlety.

Hence, the apostle feared lest by any means their minds should be corrupted from the simplicity that is in Christ. Now, at very best, this is a reference to Genesis 3, not an exposition of it!

And, I believe, with sufficient allusion to be able to say, using a descriptive Greek word here translated not as such, but as 'serpent'. However, the original suggests what that reptile does, not the name of a species descriptive of nothing but itself.

In any event, Paul confirms the way the interpretation is to be received: Eve and the *ecclesia* are completely different things in this comparison, *but the 'serpent' is not different.* He remains the same in both cases, Genesis 3 and II Corinthians 11.

The apostle's fear was *lest the same 'serpent'* should do to the *ecclesia* these thousands of years later, what he did to Eve all those ages before: 'as'–in the same manner that–the 'serpent' *then* beguiled Eve, so he might *now* beguile the *ecclesia.*

Now, does anyone suppose that the adversary would beguile the *ecclesia*, the bride, *literally* as a 'serpent'? *Literally* with an audible voice in a physical form? Not unless they are religious maniacs.

Then, *if he would not beguile the ecclesia in such a ridiculous manner, it follows, neither did he so beguile Eve.* Likewise, if not thus to Eve, then neither in like manner to the *ecclesia.* Whatever he did to the one, it follows that in the same form of allegory, he would–if he could–do to the other.

In Revelation 12–an avowedly metaphorical passage, full of allegorical allusions–'Dragon' and 'Serpent' are used interchangeably. 'Dragon'–δράκων, *drakōn*–occurs thirteen times in the new testament.

This descriptive word is derived from δέρκω, *derkō, to behold,* answering to the derivative of ὄφις, *ophis,* namely, ὁράω, *horaō, to perceive with the eyes, sight.* In the case of the allegory, *hypnotic, fascinating sight,* transfixing the prey.

Nevertheless, he is doomed, he is to be bound, his goods are to be spoiled, his realm to be taken, and, his head crushed.

He shall be consigned to the flames of everlasting wrath, whilst the redeemed shall rejoice and triumph in the glories of the God of their salvation, singing praises with joy unspeakable at the deliverance of the lawful captives through Jesus Christ, the Saviour of sinners.

The birth of the Saviour brought down the glorious praise of heaven, and raised up the expectation of the hopeless captives that sat in the region and shadow of death.

God had sent his only begotten Son in love, that we might live through him, the appeasement for our sins. This crushed the 'serpent's', the 'dragon's' head, and salvation rang with joy throughout the whole earth.

The birth of Jesus Christ–do read the publication under this name–brought to light in the sequence of the narrative of the book of the Revelation–do read this title also–the great red dragon for the first time in holy scripture.

Elsewhere, even from the beginning, he had been manifest under other names–or, rather, descriptions: he is never given a name, always he is described in terms of his character or his activities.

But for the first time, in Revelation chapter 12, he is described–signified by the sign in heaven–under the allegorical figure of a great red dragon.

This is the second such significant sign and figure in Revelation 12: the first was that of the heavenly woman who brought forth the man child, immediately caught up to the throne of God in glory.

The figurative description of 'the great red dragon', the failed, defeated, and conquered adversary of the man child–Christ–occurs thirteen times in the new testament.

Alluding to 'Satan', the word 'dragon' does not appear outside the book of the Revelation of Jesus Christ in the new testament, the first reference being Revelation 12:3.

Of the thirteen occurrences of this descriptive title, no less than eight are in chapter 12. The remaining five follow after in subsequent chapters.

The symbol–or description–is qualified in the first appearance, Revelation 12:3, by the words 'great' on the one hand, and 'red' on the other. On one other occasion the qualification 'great' occurs, Revelation 12:9. Thereafter 'dragon' in and of itself provides the description.

Revelation chapter 12 is the most intense and concentrated chapter containing the descriptive titles of the adversary in the entire bible.

Fifteen times under eight different titles or symbols he appears in this chapter, of which three are qualified, with one of those qualifications having a significant addition. This concentration is unique, and so is the variety of descriptive titles.

The chief appearance is that of 'dragon' occurring eight times in all, but qualified twice, and in one of these two qualifications with a unique additional description, namely, 'great *red* dragon', Revelation 12:3. This is followed by the most frightening and lurid description. Nevertheless, it is a heavenly sign.

That the dragon is called 'great' indicates the titanic size of this monstrous apparition in heaven. That he is described as 'red' would suggest that he is inflamed with wrath, suffused with merciless rage, and bent upon total destruction: he is filled with murderous, fierce, and intense enmity.

That he is called a dragon indicates the epitome of implacable and stony malevolence.

As still as the grave, yet, his prey inadvertently wandering near, all his monstrous strength is released with lightning ferocity in the twinkling of an eye.

Then absolute, unblinking stillness. The dragon seems not to have moved. But the prey has disappeared, swallowed up in a flash faster than can be registered by sight. That is the dragon.

It is not that the adversary *is* a dragon: he is an invisible spirit; but, when once his sway over mankind, the world, and the nations is challenged – for the true heir, Christ, had come into the world not only to challenge, but to take up his rightful inheritance – the vehemence of the adversary exceeds all bounds.

Then, were he to be depicted in some visible form, were he to materialize, nothing would suffice to symbolize his raging ferocity at this point than the figure of some gigantic red dragon, a hideous figure stretching across the vault of heaven, so powerful that his tail sweeps the very stars from the firmament.

That he cannot be seen in fact, takes nothing from the symbolism.

This is the vision that comes to light at the birth of the one, Christ Jesus, appointed and anointed of God to rule the nations with a rod of iron.

At the nativity of the King of kings to whom the crown rights of all the nations properly pertain, the heir who is to rule the world, the adversary is galvanized into such rapacity that no figure could be more suited to portray him than a 'great red dragon'.

Never before. But at last, with the birth of the chosen and elect heir, the hitherto unbroken sway of the adversary, in contention for world dominion, not only is challenged, it is downright denied and contested root and branch. This brings out the dragon.

Fifteen times under one descriptive name or another – great red dragon; great dragon; dragon; serpent; old serpent; accuser; 'devil'; and 'satan' – the adversary appears, disappears, reappears, or changes his appearance, in Revelation chapter 12.

But first he is signified as 'great red dragon'. As 'dragon' the term is later interchangeable with 'serpent'.

The 'great red dragon'–a 'great dragon' or 'dragon': it is the same; simply a question of contextual emphasis–in an almost hideous metaphor is said to have seven heads.

But this is not to conjure monstrosity in itself, it is to use allegory to convey truth. This apparently grotesque feature of the vision indicates–seven being the number of perfection, and the head being the site of the brain–perfect intelligence.

The dragon appearing in the vision with ten horns–ten indicating the round number of completeness, and the horn being that through which the whole thrust of power is exerted–this concept is symbolical of complete power.

Seven crowns upon the heads of the dragon in turn signifies perfect rule. That is, over fallen man, the kingdoms of the nations, the whole world.

That the dragon is red is indicative of ferocity and suffused wrath, whereas 'great' indicates the titanic size of this monstrous apparition, coiled and unfolding across the vast expanse of the firmament.

Inflamed with wrath, overwhelming in proportions, engorged with merciless rage, and bent upon total destruction, he is filled with pitiless, fierce, and intense enmity.

From the heavens above, the dragon holds sway over the earth beneath: it is his realm. 'All the kingdoms of the world in a moment of time.' 'For that is delivered unto me.' As it is written, 'the whole world lieth in the Wicked One.' And again, he is called 'the god of this world'.

And for world dominion he contends, and in such contention his character is thus depicted.

But Christ is come to take it from him, for the adversary obtained it by rebellion, subtlety, and wickedness, but God had afore chosen his Anointed, appointing to him the crown rights of world dominion. I say, the advent of the Anointed brings out the 'dragon'.

'And his tail drew the third part of the stars of heaven, and did cast them to the earth', Revelation 12:4. When he fell— a matter over which a veil is drawn, and about which curiosity is inappropriate—he brought in his train a vast number of angels, 'the third part of the stars of heaven'.

Now the stars are symbolic of angels, as it is said, 'the seven stars are the angels of the seven churches', Revelation 1:20.

Again, that the 'third part of the stars' figuratively drawn by the tail of the dragon, indicates the fallen angels appears in Revelation 12:7, 'and the dragon fought *and his angels*'. Hence Peter speaks of 'the angels that sinned', II Peter 2:4.

Likewise Jude, 'the angels which kept not their first estate, but left their own habitation.' This was at the sweeping instigation of the dragon, who carried the third part with him in his rebellion, even from the foundation of the world.

In the imagery of the figure, the dragon is depicted as 'a sign in heaven'. In the allegorical vision, he stands before the heavenly woman, for to devour her child as soon as it was born, because in the purpose and will of God that child was born to rule all nations with a rod of iron.

But this rule the dragon had usurped, and for that usurped authority he would fight to the last.

He may fight, but the man child is caught up, and the dragon is cast down. As the one ascends, the other descends. The prince of this world is judged: *that* was when the dragon was cast down.

However, deliberately limiting the scope of the vivid imagery of the vision to the contest for world power—hence to the symbolic figure of 'dragon'– it is the ascension of the Son that testifies to the defeat of the adversary.

The 'man child'–Christ–having glorified God in the salvation of his people, glorifying God in every divine purpose, counsel, covenant, will, attribute, word, and testimony from and before the foundation of the world, by the blood of his cross, now ascended to the right hand of the Father, is set down on the throne at the right hand of the Majesty in the heavens.

That throne exceeds the throne of mere world dominion as high as the heavens are above the earth. From thence, it is just a question of time.

'And the great dragon was cast out, that old serpent, called the Devil, and Satan, which deceiveth the whole world: he was cast out into the earth, and his angels were cast out with him', Revelation 12:9.

And what does he do there, on the earth? Why, he seeks to bring back the body of Moses! Jude 9.

What for? What does this figure mean? It means that the adversary and the accuser seeks to *regain his lost armour*. What is that? The body of the law. 'For the strength of sin *is* the law.'

The body of Moses contended, Jude? What about the body of Moses? Why, to bring back the law. Because it embodies the law.

But Christ has taken the law wholly out of sight in the new testament, *and that is what caused the accuser of the brethren, the adversary, to be cast out and to fall down.*

Christ triumphs over all in his victory on the cross 'Blotting out the handwriting of ordinances that was against us, which was contrary to us, and took it out of the way, nailing it to his cross;

'And having spoiled principalities and powers'–casting them out of heaven, where in and by himself he has raised the faithful in his ascension–'he made a show of them openly'–that is, of principalities and powers, casting them down to the earth–'triumphing over them in it', that is, *in the cross*, Colossians 2:14,15.

Then, the accuser has neither place, occasion, or law, in, by, or through which *ever to accuse the brethren again, no, not for time or eternity.*

Therefore Christ and his holy apostles dispute–as did 'Michael'–any attempt to reintroduce the law, lacerating it, and perverting the evangel.

This was and is a constant battle on earth in the new testament, when at every opportunity the 'serpent' sought and seeks to beguile the *ecclesia* by subtly reintroducing the law, II Corinthians 11:1-5; the Corinthian epistles as a whole; Romans; Galatians; and the Acts, for example.

And what has the exploded Westminster Confession done? Read 'The Westminster Confession Exploded: Deliverance from the Law.' What has it done? It has reintroduced the law, lacerating it, whilst perverting the evangel.

Which is what many blind–I might say, deceitful–hypocrites attempt to this day, calling their 'law' their banner.

But they never keep the mutilated fragment they profess. They profane even that. Banner? The law is no banner, it is 'the strength of sin', I Corinthians 15:56. And they are false witnesses to a man that think that their intellectual pretensions in man's traditions do not bring down a curse.

Bring back the law, and you have served 'the Devil, and Satan, that old serpent' with a witness, and by it, perverted the profession of the doctrine of Christ, the faith once delivered to the saints, so causing the simple to fall from grace.

What then is the truth? 'But now we are delivered from the law, that being dead wherein we were held', Romans 7:6. 'Ye are become dead to the law by the body of Christ', Romans 7:4.

'Ye are not under the law, but under grace', Romans 6:14. 'For I through the law am dead to the law', Galatians 2:19. Tell me, is that dead enough for you? Dead is dead is dead.

And that is the position of the saints in Christ in relation to the law. Or to the body of Moses. Satan contends against this, but 'Michael' defends it in the LORD.

And if I, or an angel from heaven, preach any other gospel unto you than that which is preached unto you, let him be accursed, Galatians 1:6-10.

For this *is* the evangel – the gospel – of Christ. The law being the strength of sin, it provided the armoury and fortress of Satan. But Christ bound him, and took away all his armour wherein he trusted, breaking up his house.

The Saviour has obtained the victory once and for all, nailing the law of commandments contained in ordinances to his cross, freely delivering all his people.

Satan fell. The dragon was cast out of heaven. 'Michael' took to the fight in the light and power of such an evangel carried up and ascended in him, the Saviour, who had wrought it out to the uttermost.

The propitiatory hid the law from view; the blood was sprinkled on the propitiatory, and five scars glorified in the Saviour's body before God in heaven proclaimed everlasting salvation for all the children of God.

Hence the dragon could not prevail. He and his angels were cast out of heaven into the earth. When Christ went up, he fell down. When Christ obtained the victory, he was cast into defeat.

When Christ occupied the throne of God in heaven, every throne on earth tottered, swayed, and crumbled.

I say, it is only a matter of time. When time shall be no more, then shall you see the certainty of the salvation which is proclaimed in your ears this day.

'And they overcame him by the blood of the Lamb, and by the word of their testimony; and they loved not their lives unto the death', Revelation 12:11.

Other descriptive names besides the sum of the foregoing are given to the adversary, such as abaddon and apollyon for example.

But the victory of the Saviour, and the triumph of the salvation of God has been sufficiently set forth and established over the character of the Wicked One in what has preceded.

Further to this I see no point in enumerating more of this malevolent being's titles, when already the Saviour has been seen to a demonstration to have destroyed him, and all his works.

PART THREE

SALVATION FROM
THE WORLD

PART THREE

SALVATION FROM THE WORLD

ONCE again, the translators have served us ill, supposing to 'translate' *four* completely distinct and diverse Greek words by one and the same *single* English word 'world'. As if that could suffice in place of *four* words of entirely different meaning.

But since the salvation of God wrought by the Saviour was and is victorious in each of the four realms indicated in the original, and since each Greek word has a precise–unique–meaning separate from the others, How are we to know of this salvation unless faithfully served by accurate translation into the English?

The more so when Jesus taught 'Ye shall know the *truth*, and *the truth* shall make you free'; and again, '*Thy word* is truth'. Once more, 'Thou hast *the words* of eternal life.' Then *tell us the words*!

263

I say, Tell us the words, because salvation from 'the world' is essential if a people is to be brought to glory. For the meaning intended by the Lord and his apostles must be understood, believed, inwrought, and experienced by all those who are to be saved and sanctified through the grace of Christ.

But saved from *what*? The four words in the original, obscured to the confusion of the reader by the indiscriminate common use of the single English word 'world', must be distinguished and taken in turn, and opened up in order, so that in every instance and each case we may be saved by faith, for 'faith cometh by hearing, and hearing by the word of God'.

Therefore, that the Saviour may be glorified in his work, and that the Spirit of truth may bring home this salvation of God respectively to our hearts, to the praise of his glory, the four words in the Greek of the new testament are set forth in order forthwith:

VIII
Salvation from the World: 'Aiōn'

THE Greek αἰών, *aiōn*, used very often in conjunction with a preposition–and at that with different grammatical cases– not to mention the further form αἰώνιος, *aiōnios*, seems on face value to be exceedingly complicated.

But it is not inextricably so, nor should the translation and interpretation be made the subject of questions that bring into dispute the reality of eternity.

Yet how many uncalled and presumptuous upstarts, who would make something of themselves, rushing headlong into things which they know not, spout their fancies as if they were divinely given inspirations!

Before coming to the meaning therefore, it is our wisdom to know this first, that no prophecy of the scripture is of any private interpretation. For the prophecy came not in old time by the will of man, but *holy men of God* spake as they were *moved by the Holy Ghost.*

Then only by similarly called, holy men, through the spirit of prophecy alone, and that by the Holy Ghost solely, can the same prophetic word rightly be interpreted. It is nothing to do with *man*: it is *all of God*.

For there is a God in heaven that revealeth secrets, and maketh known what shall be in the latter days. To him be all the praise and the glory, for this is all his own work, and in it the hand and work of man can never appear save utterly to confound and confuse the issue.

The Greek word αἰών, *aiōn*, among other alternatives, has been translated 'world' some thirty-two times. This is grievously misleading to the English reader.

The Greek is a word which has to do with *time*, as is indicated by the English derivative. To quote the Oxford dictionary, '*aeon, eon*: an age of the universe, immeasurable period (Latin *aeon*, from Greek *aiōn*, age.)'.

From which it is obvious that the *age*, or *an age*, or *that which has to do with the ages*, must be at the root of the Greek new testament meaning.

Whatever grammatical–or merely theoretic–complications may unnecessarily be involved by the ingenious reasoning of some, *nothing* can obscure *the basic meaning*, and it is *this* that the reader should grasp and hold fast at the very beginning and to the very last.

The Greek *aiōn* refers to the age, or the ages. It may be used of the present age, of the age or ages past; or the age or ages to come. Context alone determines which. It is a duration: a vast period marked by a certain dispensation of God's dealings distinctive of that time.

Moreover such duration may be beyond distinguishable horizons, past or future. Out of sight: stretching even to infinity. In certain grammatical forms, For ever. Or, For ever and ever.

However it is the word *aiōnios* that has properly been translated 'eternal'. Now, this lies beyond all duration, every dispensation, it is outside of time.

Even though time in its entirety does constitute a diminutive – as it were bracketed – period within eternity, it is irrelevant to it: relatively, it is nothing; it makes no difference; no matter how many dispensations may be embraced within the brackets: What is that to *eternity*?

Strictly, I accept that *aiōnios*, closely related to *aiōn*, includes time. But on that account – there being no Greek word as such for 'eternity' – to deny the translation *eternity* is mere semantics; trifling with the obvious.

It is to time that reference is made when saying 'outside of time'; but what is that but 'timeless' or, 'eternal'? Just as much as the strictly accurate 'for ever' – timeless – and 'for ever and ever' – 'timelessly' – merely *utilize* a form.

Although the word is not strictly 'eternity' – not surprisingly: there being no word *other* than the development of *aiōn* and *aiōnios* – this is so phrased that it is impossible to make it mean anything other than *eternity* in fact.

In such a case and context 'eternity' must follow from such relevant and particular uses of the Greek.

So what was before time? Eternity. What will be after it? Eternity. Like 'space'. What is beyond space? When that ends, what is beyond it? Infinity.

Such absolutes exist. So who but a blind fool would quibble about words in the face of what utterly staggers all human understanding; absolutes that stun the mind?

But *nothing* will humble the conceit of these blind fools in religion.

267

As infinity to space; omnipotence to impotence; omnipresence to absence; omniscience to ignorance; absoluteness to relativity; immortality to mortality; incorruptibility to corruption; so is eternity to time, world without end. Amen.

Aiōnios is—quite rightly therefore—translated *eternity*. It reaches in its eternal duration to life; damnation; glory; salvation; judgment; redemption; inheritance; fire; things that are not seen; and weight that cannot be conceived.

And why? Because absolutes *are*. And why? Because God *is*. As *is* the eternal Spirit. They that worship in spirit and truth are conscious enough of all these things.

The 'world', rightly considered as an age, or rather, as time, had a beginning.

Of the Son it is said 'by whom also he made the worlds'—the recurring dispensations of time, in context, from the beginning to the end of it—and again, 'through faith we understand that the worlds'—the ages—'were framed by the word of God', Hebrews 1:2; 11:3.

But time itself, falling at the beginning under the authority of the prince of this world, the prince of the power of the air, with the rulers of the darkness of this age, is that from which we need a Saviour.

Time is *alien*. It is *deadly*. It is an environment from which men need to be saved. Souls need *salvation* from the age. All ages. And thereunto the Father sent the Son.

Then, under the responsibility of Adam, fallen on behalf of all humanity, since born in sin and conceived in iniquity, the age itself was corrupted under the responsibility of man, to fall beneath the authority of darkness.

If so, the present continuity *of the whole age* is evil in its nature, and dangerous in its unfolding.

Hence Jesus warns those who had received the word, believed, and inwardly continued in its power and growth, of *the deadly effects of time that still stood between them and the glory*. Namely, 'the care of this age, and the deceitfulness of riches, *choke the word*', Matthew 13:22.

Moreover, implacable vengeance can fall upon the careless—however lightly 'evangelical' in their course through this present age: 'whosoever speaketh against the Holy Ghost, it shall not be forgiven him, neither in this *age*, neither in *that to come*', Matthew 12:32.

Therefore the man of God, ordained of the Lord, must warn all who profess Christ, who are wealthy, 'Charge them that are rich in this *age*, that they be not highminded, nor trust in uncertain riches', I Timothy 6:17.

Witness Demas, who forsook the apostle—and if so, Christ— 'having loved this present *age*', II Timothy 4:10.

Then, *the age itself is deadly dangerous*. It is 'the god of this *age*' who has 'blinded the minds of them which believe not', II Corinthians 4:4.

Wherefore God has sent the Saviour, Jesus Christ, 'who gave himself for our sins, *that he might deliver us from this present evil age*', Galatians 1:4.

Without which deliverance all shall be found trusting in a lie, and be damned by their obstinate cleaving to this present evil age, despising the salvation of God.

No surprise then, that those whose sins are forgiven, who are delivered from this present evil age, continually—mark that, *continually*—'wrestle against the rulers of the darkness of this age', Ephesians 6:12.

And, by the grace of Christ, such saints must–and do–win the fight to be saved experimentally out of this age unto everlasting glory in the inheritance of the world to come.

Hence Jesus speaks of 'they which shall be *accounted worthy* to obtain *that age*, and the resurrection from the dead', Luke 20:35.

But self-conceited 'brethren' will dispute this, challenging even the Lord Jesus' words, and 'evangelicals', enraged that their easy-believism is nothing worth, will contend against the Holy Ghost, as did their fathers before them.

But 'Where is the wise? where is the scribe? where is the disputer'–against the truth of the evangel in the scriptures–'of this *age*?', I Corinthians 1:20.

'Hath not God made foolish the wisdom of this *age*'–by showing all that is in it, and of it, is evil, and that to be saved, the Saviour must apply his salvation inwardly to deliver us from it? But unto us which are saved–from this present evil *age*–the cross is the power of God unto salvation, I Corinthians 1:18.

For only *in times past* did we walk 'according to the *age* of this world', but now, saved by the Saviour through the salvation of God, no longer, Ephesians 2:2.

Now, it is all glory, and glory within and to come, passing through the tribulations of this passing age with the Son of God as did the three Israelites through the fiery furnace.

Still, if a fiery furnace, *time itself*, withal our own finite passage through it, from birth to grave, *it is a deadly danger*, from beginning to end.

For there is an end, and it is nearer than when we first believed. It is well for the soul therefore to ask loudly, clearly, and continually, the questions, 'What shall be the sign of thy coming, and of the end of the *age*?', Matthew 24:3.

'The harvest is the end of the *age*; and the reapers are the angels', Matthew 13:39.

'So shall it be at the end of the *age*: the angels shall come forth, and sever the wicked from among the just, and shall cast them into the furnace of fire: there shall be wailing and gnashing of teeth', Matthew 13:49.

But for those who look for his appearing, and by the Spirit are prepared for it, obeying the Lord in his evangel brought by his ordained and sent ministers, What is there to fear?

For he says to the apostles, and through them to those called and set apart to reiterate their doctrine, 'Lo, I am with you *alway*, even unto the *end of the age*', Matthew 28:20. Now, *this* is salvation from the *aiōn* indeed.

O, be sure of this: there is an age, an endless age, an eternity to come hereafter, following this present world, hence Jesus says, 'It shall not be forgiven him, neither in this *age*, neither in the *age* to come', Matthew 12:32.

And again the Lord speaks of 'they which shall be accounted worthy to obtain that *age*, and the resurrection from the dead', Luke 20:35.

But many, who were sure that they were accounted worthy, shall find it to be otherwise, for all that they experienced 'the powers of the *age* to come', yet, afterwards, they fell away and were lost, Hebrews 6:5,6.

Alas, 'the care of this *age*, and the deceitfulness of riches, choke the word', and it perishes together with him in whom, for so long, it all looked so fruitful, Matthew 13:22. For, to save us from it, our Lord Jesus Christ 'gave himself for our sins, that he might deliver us from this present evil *age*'.

That is why he gave himself for our sins: then, if no deliverance from this present evil age follows, any claim that he gave himself for our sins is spurious. There is a cause and an effect. No effect; no cause. No cause; no effect. Galatians 1:4.

Here is a false gospel with a witness: How can the very reason he gave himself for our sins conspicuously be absent from those who claim forgiveness, yet so obviously sit at ease, clearly *belonging* to this present age? Such a contradiction cannot stand.

These are they 'in whom the god of this *age* hath blinded the minds of them which believe not, lest the light of the glorious gospel of Christ, who is the image of God, should shine unto them', II Corinthians 4:4.

Hence the apostle exhorts the saints, 'be not conformed to this *age*', Romans 12:2.

And the grace of God that bringeth salvation teaches us to deny 'ungodliness and worldly lusts, that we should live soberly, righteously, and godly, in this present *age*; looking for that blessed hope, and the glorious appearing of the great God and our Saviour Jesus Christ', Titus 2:12,13.

Then, such a Saviour, and such a salvation, from the *aiōn*, unto the *aiōnios*, is salvation indeed, without which there can be no salvation whatsoever.

For there is salvation in none other—any more than salvation could ever include less—'Neither is there salvation is any other: for there is none other name under heaven given among men, whereby we must be saved', Acts 4:12.

IX
Salvation from the World: 'Gē'

ALTHOUGH this Greek new testament word has been translated 'world' but once, still, once is quite enough to be misleading. Otherwise, the translators give 'country', twice; 'earth', one hundred and eighty-eight times; 'ground', eighteen times; and 'land', forty-two times.

Nevertheless the word denotes a consistently sinister context for the saints, and, as such, indicates that from which the pilgrim people of God need a Saviour; should seek salvation; and earnestly desire to be saved.

From the Greek gē, the English derivations 'geography'; 'geology'; 'geographical'; besides other suchlike words have developed. This hardly sounds alien: more academic. It hardly rings as an enemy: more as educational.

But that just shows how much the Lord's people need to be 'transformed by the renewing of your mind', rather than so gullibly and easily 'conformed to this world', Romans 12:1,2. One should take *absolutely nothing* for granted.

As to the one place in which gē has been translated 'world', this is to be found in Revelation 13:3. But what caprice moved these men to use 'world' but once, when they forged full steam ahead in sublime confidence with 'earth' one hundred and eighty-eight times?

Why, they thought that they would improve on the Greek, teach the Holy Ghost what he ought to have said, and correct the apostle's inappropriate usage. That's what they are like. They? Yes. Clergymen, 'ministers', so-called pastors, and know-all Brethren.

'All the *world* wondered after the beast', Revelation 13:3. But according to their own rule – reiterated one hundred and eighty-eight times – it should have read, 'all the *earth* wondered after the beast'.

But 'earth' does not wonder; 'geology' is not amazed; and 'geography' is incapable – being a subject, not a person or persons – of being astonished.

So they 'improved' on the word of God, and put 'world' – once – to fit in with 'wonder'.

But this is the Book of Revelation. Everything is expressed in terms of mysticism; all the expressions are metaphysical. The concept is symbolic; figurative; typical. Imagery characterizes every context.

However this was all too spiritual for the translators, being unable to comprehend John's figurative and symbolic use of 'earth' throughout the whole of the Revelation.

Nevertheless, the rest they could swallow. Revelation 13:3 was *too* much. So they felt obliged – *in effect* – to change the Greek!

In the Book of Revelation, God's people are regarded as persecuted pilgrims and strangers passing through this world: sojourners upon the earth, which is destined to be 'burned up', and 'shaken'.

In this highly metaphorical book, 'earth' is used some seventy-five times. The saints are seen as pilgrims *on* the earth, but they are not *of* it.

That people–the only other people in existence–who *are* 'of' the earth are called 'dwellers'. They live here. The saints do not. They are redeemed from the earth. Inwardly they dwell in heaven. They are a heavenly people. They *seek* a country. They do not belong on earth.

In contrast the worldly are distinguished from the heavenly people of God by being called 'they that dwell on the earth'.

Thus the martyred saints are viewed as crying out for vengeance against their worldly, earthly, murderers: 'How long, O Lord, holy and true, dost thou not judge and avenge our blood *on them that dwell on the earth?*', Revelation 6:10.

Hence, 'Woe, woe, woe, *to the inhabiters of the earth*', yes, and *all* of them, the only other persons in existence being the heavenly saints persecuted by them.

Why 'woe'? Because of the 'trumpets' of vengeance that are yet to sound from heaven against the inhabiters of the earth, in view of the tribulation and persecution brought by them upon the pilgrims and strangers, the heavenly sojourners, that is, the citizens of a heavenly country in the world to come.

At the cross, the 'great dragon' being defeated and cast out of heaven, called the *diabolos*, and *satanas*, which deceiveth the whole world: 'he was cast out into the earth, and his angels were cast out with him', Revelation 12:9. But with what consequence?

'Therefore rejoice, ye heavens, and ye'–pilgrims, strangers, sojourners, saints who look for a heavenly country–'ye that dwell in them', that is, *inwardly*, in the heavens, *now*.

But 'Woe to the inhabiters of the earth and of the sea! for the *diabolos* is come down unto you, having great wrath, because he knoweth that he hath but a short time', Revelation 12:12.

Yes, but a short time, as time goes, from the cross till the Second Coming of Christ to judge the world, to judge the inhabiters of the earth in righteousness.

And what protection have they? For they despised the Saviour, perverted his salvation, and would have nothing to do with being saved experimentally. And those that would, they persecuted.

Next there is the dreadful appearance of 'the beast', a figurative representation of the power and authority of this world.

Power is given to him over all kindreds, and tongues, and nations. Indeed 'All'–*all*–'that dwell upon the earth shall worship him', Revelation 13:8. But not the heavenly pilgrims and sojourners.

They will *never* worship 'the beast'. Hence, 'It was given unto him to make war with the saints, and to overcome them', with persecutions, tribulations, torture, and worse, Revelation 13:7.

'The beast' doeth great wonders—such as those ascribed to the discoveries and attainments of modern science –'and *deceiveth them that dwell on the earth.*' But not those whose names are written in the book of life of the Lamb slain from the foundation of the world.

These are not deceived. They dwell in Christ in heaven in the Spirit, waiting for his return, whilst looking for a better country, that is, an heavenly. Revelation 13.

Indeed, as to mystical 'Babylon the whore'–likewise 'Babylon the city'–'the inhabitants of the earth have been made drunk with the wine of her fornication', Revelation 17:2.

No wonder the Saviour sounds with a voice from heaven, saying, 'Come out of her, my people, that ye be not partakers of her sins, and that ye receive not of her plagues', Revelation 18:4.

In all this, however symbolically depicted, it is clear that the earth is the place of the Fall, it is cursed for man's sake, and that it will pass away in fire with a great noise, the elements melting with fervent heat; that is, after the destruction of the enemies that attempted to rule over it, with all the inhabitants thereof.

The expression 'inhabiters of the earth' refers to fallen man, born of the flesh, and not redeemed. The spiritual powers of the adversary blind and deceive all those who 'dwell on the earth'.

This answers to the whole earth in the Fall, of the first man, of the earth, earthy, bound and destined for judgment, without distinction between nations or classes, save only for that heavenly people redeemed from the earth and bound for glory.

Although not the world as such, it is the ground of it, and cursed ground through fallen man at that: 'Cursed is the ground for thy sake', Genesis 3:17. It is destined to pass away in wrath. God does not dwell there: he departed after the Fall and before the Flood.

But man dwells there: he is the 'earth dweller', the nations being 'the inhabitants of the earth'. To man, the earth without God is his home, he desires to pass his day in it, it is all as it should be, the result of natural causes, its origins and destiny a mockery to him.

The inhabitants of the earth invent a system from what they can see, and think to prove it from cause and effect. That is, what *they* cause, and its effect. The entire system of 'education' is built upon such ungodly theorizing and repetitive practising.

Man settles in, by, and for what is temporal, what can be seen and 'proved'. Humanity lives for time, denying the origins of the earth, both Creator, Creation, and the meanwhile ignoring eternity and the judgment to come. The Fall is denied. The Flood is a myth. The Conflagration a fable.

Then, the light that is in the dwellers on the earth is darkness, and the nations stumble on in their blindness.

If so, salvation from such deluded materialism is essential, and hence the Saviour redeemed and does redeem a people out of every kindred, tribe, people, and nation, as separate from the world, hated by it, and being persecuted for the testimony of Jesus which they hold in the spirit of prophecy.

'These are they which came out of great tribulation, and have washed their robes, and made them white in the blood of the Lamb', Revelation 7:14.

Figuratively, they are the hundred and forty-four thousand which are redeemed from the earth, standing on mount Sion with the Lamb, Revelation 14:3.

Consider the father of the faithful, who set forth in a figure the reality of the heirs of faith being strangers and pilgrims on the earth, as Stephen recounts.

'The God of glory appeared unto our father Abraham, when he was in Mesopotamia, before he dwelt in Charran, and said unto him, Get thee out of thy country, and from thy kindred, and come into the land which I shall show thee', Acts 7:2,3.

And was some mere earthly land that inheritance? What inheritance, when 'he gave him none inheritance in it, no, not so much as to set his foot on: yet he promised that he would give it to him for a possession', Acts 7:5.

Yet, years later, still landless, he must needs buy a plot for a grave.

Nor had he land to build a single house. He dwelt in tents with his son and grandson. Then *that* land was not the inheritance. It was the *figure* of the inheritance.

And so the apostle Paul interprets, expounding this very promise of *the land* to Abraham, saying, 'For the promise, *that he should be the heir of the world*', Romans 4:13.

No such promise of the world exists in the record of Abraham. What exists is that of *the land* of promise, on this present earth, *gē*. But that is cursed. But the world to come is blessed.

Then, the promise of the *land* was a figure. It was what *symbolized* the promise, namely, *the everlasting inheritance of the world to come following the resurrection of the just.*

Abraham clearly understood this, as did – and do – all the heirs of faith. It is the perverted premillennialists and the deluded dispensationalists, whom Satan has blinded, that have the problem. Or, rather, the dark unbelief. Not Abraham. Not Abraham's believing seed. Not the heirs of faith.

Hearken: 'By faith Abraham, when he was called to go out into a place which he should after receive for an inheritance, obeyed; and he went out, not knowing whither he went.

'By faith he sojourned *in the land of promise, as in a strange country*, dwelling in tabernacles with Isaac and Jacob, *the heirs with him of the same promise:*

'For he looked for a city which hath foundations'*– not pegs: a *tent* has pegs: a *city* has foundations –'*whose builder and maker is God*', Hebrews 11:8-10.

If one receives a land for an inheritance, one builds a *city*. But Abraham, Isaac, and Jacob *looked* for a city. Not *built* one. As to the land, they put down not so much as a floorboard.

They pegged their moving tents, looking for a city in the world to come, whose builder and maker was God. That is, they *looked beyond this earth to the resurrection.*

So did all the heirs of faith: 'These all died in faith, *not having received the promises*, but having seen them *afar off*'–after the resurrection, and in the world to come–'and were persuaded of them, and embraced them, and confessed that they *were strangers and pilgrims on the earth.*

'For they that say such things declare plainly that they *seek* a country.' Not that they have *settled* on earth.

'And truly, if they had been mindful of that country from whence they came out'–but they must have come out *by faith*, spiritually and inwardly, as pilgrims and strangers, *because for the vast majority, the country from which they came out was the symbolic land of promise itself*–'they might have had opportunity to have returned.

'But now they desire a *better* country'–than this cursed *gē*–'that is, *an heavenly*: wherefore God is not ashamed to be called their God: for he hath prepared for them a city', Hebrews 11:13-16.

As to that country, that earth, that world to come: 'And I saw a new heaven and a new earth: for the first heaven and the first earth were passed away.'

And as to that city whose builder and maker is God: 'And I John saw the holy city, new Jerusalem, coming down from God out of heaven', Revelation 21:1,2.

The same figure is seen in Israel's departure from Egypt, which signified their bondage to the world as a system. But there was a vast stretch of *land*, *gē*, between the Red sea and the distant spiritual hope of the land of promise, depicting their glorious heavenly inheritance the other side of Jordan.

Beyond the land of their bondage, Egypt, lay a vast, howling, barren, dead wilderness, utterly hostile and alien to their life.

Yet through it they must pass, as strangers, sojourners, pilgrims. And pass with the figure of God's presence in their midst, the tabernacle. *But the tabernacle had no floor.* They passed, with the God of glory, *they passed through in tents.*

Then this wilderness, this earth, this *gē* is a place where the children of God have no continuing city. Figuratively they build no houses, they dwell in tents. They do not settle here.

But, seeing all the glory that lies beyond Jordan, looking for a city whose builder and maker is God, new Jerusalem in the world to come, they hurry through the wilderness as through a place of pilgrimage, in view of the glorious inheritance.

Hebrews assures us that he whose voice *then* shook the earth at Sinai, saith not in vain, 'Yet once more I shake not the earth only, but also heaven.

'And this word, Yet once more, signifieth the removing of those things that are shaken, as of things that are made, that those things which cannot be shaken may remain.

'Wherefore we receiving a kingdom which cannot be moved, let us have grace, whereby we may serve God acceptably with reverence and godly fear: for our God is a consuming fire', Hebrews 12:26-29.

That is, heaven and earth, as now constituted, will be shaken and removed. Then, *here* is a deadly danger to all that dwell on the earth, from which *nothing* can deliver men but the salvation of God through the Saviour, Jesus Christ.

However, the earth, the *gē*, in the blind acceptance of it, beguiles and lulls men to sleep concerning invisible realities, accepting the dreams of outward materialistic appearances as if *they* were real.

But all that can be seen, time itself, let alone the *gē*, is to be shaken, removed by a consuming fire, so that men need to be awakened by the Saviour to see the fearful dangers connected with *earthliness*.

Those who are of the earth, earthy, embrace it, cleave to it, love it, take from it their pleasures, shall perish and be buried beneath its surface.

But that is not the end. There is the judgment. Ultimately the earth is to be set aflame at and with the dissolution of its very elements.

So Peter assures us, that, as it was with the universal flood in the old world, so shall it be in the consummation of fire at the end of this world.

'The day of the Lord will come as a thief in the night; in the which the heavens shall pass away with a great noise, and the elements shall melt with fervent heat, the *earth* also *and the works that are therein* shall be burned up.

'Seeing then that all these things shall be dissolved, what manner of persons ought ye to be in all holy conversation and godliness, looking for and hasting unto the coming of the day of God, wherein the heavens being on fire shall be dissolved, and the elements shall melt with fervent heat', II Peter 3:10-12.

What manner of persons? Why, those redeemed by the Saviour from among men, those with the salvation of God, having been set apart from every kindred, and tongue, and nation, and people, who, having come out as pilgrims and strangers, have washed their robes, and made them white in the blood of the Lamb.

These, and these alone, know the Saviour, have experienced the salvation of God, and have been saved from the *gē*, the earth, the realm of the god of this world, wherein the worldly settle and have their 'city'.

But here the heavenly pilgrims have no continuing city.

Saved by the blood of the Lamb, the saints are pilgrims and strangers, looking for a better country, that is, an heavenly, and a city yet to come, that is, in the everlasting glory, whose builder and maker is God.

X
Salvation from the World: 'Oikoumenē'

T HE Greek οἰχουμένη, *oikoumenē*, has been translated 'earth', once; and 'world', fourteen times. In neither case is this a correct equivalent to the Greek of the new testament. In fact it is little better than careless, if not wild, guesswork, as the least enquiry into the source of this precise and particular word will show.

Nevertheless, it is that from which we need saving, and the Saviour has brought in the salvation of God to open the eyes, instruct the mind, move the heart, and deliver the soul from this dangerous and deceitful construction of the adversary, as will appear in due course.

But first, the word itself. *Oikoumenē* is derived from the Greek οἶχος, *oikos*, 'a house, dwelling, or place of abode'. *Oikos* is in fact the origin of a larger grouping which has developed from this root, one branch of which is the word *oikoumenē*, a particular refinement of and from this common stock.

The range of meaning of the entire family of words passes–for example–from 'home; house; household; dwelling'; to 'build; build up; edify; edification; steward; stewardship'; and then of course the obviously misplaced and wholly inconsistent rendering 'earth' and 'world' for the particular form *oikoumenē*.

What has 'earth' or 'world' to do with the root, 'house', 'home', or 'household', or any other derivatives which obviously and conspicuously bear a natural relationship to their origin? Nothing. Not the least connection. Then, once more, the clerical 'scholars' and their fellow-travellers, have quite misled us.

Just to take the number of occurrences of the two basic forms of the root of this family of Greek words – unquestioned in translation – in and of itself: οἰκία, *oikia*, 'home', once; 'house', ninety-three times – ninety-three times, take note – 'household', once.

Again, οἰκέω, *oikeō*, 'dwell', nine times.

Once more, οἶκος, *oikos*, 'home', four times; 'house', one hundred and two times – one hundred and two times, observe – 'household', three times; 'temple', once.

Now from two such common bases, how can anyone – *anyone* – possibly arrive at the translation of *oikoumenē*, as 'earth', once; 'world', fourteen times?

What! When every *other* branch of this multiple family points clean in a different direction, and is consistently in accord with the basic meaning of the common denominator?

The derivative οἰκουμένη, *oikoumenē*, (pr. fem. part. pass. of οἰκέω, *oikeō*) of course traces its source to the root, and branches out to a distinct area suited to the application of a meaning drawn from such an origin. To this the translators are not merely blind: they are downright perverse.

The root, *oikeō* – basically *'to inhabit'* – is generally associated with a well-ordered household. An economic household. However with the branch *oikoumenē* the meaning is extended far wider to embrace the well-ordered economy of the inhabited world. Observe: not that world *itself*. The *economy* of it.

This Greek sense is necessarily restricted by Greek or Roman parameters referring to their particular development of the inhabited world. For example, as opposed to the Barbarians.

To take in the breadth of the new testament revelation from the word used by the Holy Ghost – flatly refusing heathen 'sources' – the idea of *oikoumenē* might be conveyed – at a stretch – by 'humanity', and sometimes this is so, but not sufficiently to reach the breadth of use, or adequately to savour the essence of the proper meaning.

The English 'society' might be considered an alternative, but I think a weak and inadequate one, susceptible of being restricted to Anglican interpretation, restricting the meaning merely to a part of that intended by the Greek.

Certainly the English 'economy' – which actually originates from the Greek *oikoumenē*, as the pronunciation suggests – commends itself as a suited English translation.

To quote the Shorter Oxford English Dictionary: '1. Management of [(orig.) household] expenditure. 2. Political economy. The art of managing the resources of a people, and of its government. The laws of production and distribution of wealth.'

Yet still not *quite* broad enough to take in the full range used in the new testament, whilst *basically* underlying the whole concept.

Personally, I have no doubt that 'civilization' answers perfectly to the word in the Greek. That *does* take in the whole concept. First of government, not just national but international; then of law and order, together with and encompassing the power to enforce conformity to the 'common good' of mankind.

This must include the fiscal economy: the production, control, and management of money, not by printed deceit, but with the necessary resources of substantial wealth to support such a standard economically and internationally. Likewise the control of 'business' and 'labour'.

Health: the economy to oversee and safeguard the peoples from childbirth, a system for the care of the health of the young in particular, of all ages in general, and of the aged especially. The vast pharmaceutical complex. The cleanliness of food, water, and waste disposal to ensure the maintenance of hygiene.

Education: a system devised to incorporate a variety of subjects designed to grade 'students' by means of 'progress' according to a curriculum, organized as a means of delivery of classification of 'knowledge', ultimately arriving at a fixed status according to the ability and desired future occupation of the rising generation.

On the highest plane–in each area–this involves the establishment of institutions of research and development for the constant advancement, improvement, and application for the supposed benefit of society.

Of increasing importance to the vast task of organizing these various allied arrangements is that of entertainment and sport, the tentacles of which now reach out more and more to include a thriving and global industry without precedent.

But each scheme is dependent upon the other, and the whole utterly reliant upon the maintenance of the supply of power, derived ultimately– apart from oil, coal, and to much lesser extent wood–from electricity, however the latter is produced.

These parallel systems, welded together to organize and serve society, constitute civilization, national and international, local or global, increasingly dependent one upon another. If one falls, all fall.

That they may not fall, enormous energy and ingenuity is exercised by interrelating governments, more or less co-ordinating their systems. In the last analysis the name for this is *oikoumenē*.

Well, the saints need a Saviour, and cry out for salvation from that: there is nothing neutral or harmless about it. In fact it is described metaphorically as two beasts, a whore, and the city Babylon. It has a corporate mystical number: that number is 666.

From all that has been said it is evident that the overall government and systematic ordering of mankind collectively is at the heart of the understanding of *oikoumenē*, both nationally and internationally.

As a householder of a great house manages his household, and authorizes its economy, so the governments 'manage' humanity under them to their maximum efficiency, advantage, and satisfaction.

Evidently this is the ultimate concept of *oikoumenē*. That rationalization entails the full development of corporate mankind globally. In a word, what we call *civilization*.

If so, the question that will profoundly exercise the hearts and minds of the pilgrims and strangers, the sojourners and citizens of a heavenly country, the saints called and united by grace, is this:

Is the *oikoumenē* to be regarded as alien, and if so, in what way, and, given that it is so, How is the Saviour to be experienced in his salvation from that which otherwise stands between them and their glorious inheritance in the world to come?

Alien indeed, and a vast temptation from which the Saviour with the salvation of God is essential if we are to be saved, so that salvation is first wrought for us, then applied to us, and finally experienced by us, all the days of our life.

For example Luke 4:5, When ὁ διάβολος, *ho diabolos* leads Jesus up into an high mountain, and shows him all the kingdoms of the *oikoumenē* in a moment of time, tempting him *with them*, he says:

'To thee will *I* give all this authority and their glory, *for to me it has been delivered*, and to whomsoever *I will, I give it*': Then where is the temptation, if *ho diabolos'* words were not so?

Whence it follows, the *oikoumenē, the power and the glory of it*, is that temptation dismissed by the Saviour, and, for us, concerning which salvation is essential.

Once more, the apostles, by whose evangel alone men shall be saved by faith in Christ, are accused of turning upside down the *oikoumenē* by the truth of salvation.

If so, *civilization*, or the *oikoumenē*, was inverted in fact, so that to be saved from it, the Saviour must set the saved wholly the right side up, a truth surely essential to the evangel, the power of God unto salvation, Acts 17:6, Romans 1:16.

Again, the apostle declares in the evangel that God will judge *civilization*, the *oikoumenē*, in righteousness by that man whom he hath ordained, whereof he hath given assurance unto all men, in that he hath raised him from the dead, Acts 17:31.

Whence it appears that the whole of civilization by the justice and law of God must be brought into judgment; that the sentence is unto death: the second death; and from this there is no escape but by salvation in Christ.

Further, not only Ephesus, but the whole *civilized world*, the *oikoumenē*, is said to worship or at least admire the multiple and ample-breasted goddess Diana of the Ephesians. Now this may not be so in *name* or in *form* in subsequent civilizations, but it is certainly true in essence.

For nothing is more obviously displayed by this outward figure of man's inward imagination and lust than that in *any* civilization she appears as *the* sex-symbol *par excellence* of the concupiscence common to *any* period, Acts 19:26,35.

Which shows that whenever, wherever, or in whatsoever *oikoumenē* the gratification of the lusts of the populace – damning to the soul – must be that without which such systems can never be established so as to appease the people.

Where *oikoumenē* is regarded as an entity, spiritually, and in a metaphorical sense, in the mysticism of the Book of the Revelation, there is no doubt that it is alien and hostile to the saints, who of necessity must be saved and kept separate from its entire system.

'And the great dragon was cast out, that old serpent, called *diabolos*, and *the satan, which deceiveth the whole oikoumenē*', Revelation 12:9. He deceives – it is *continuous* – civilization in its *entirety*.

If so, we need the Saviour, who resisted the temptation, Luke 4:5, to save *us* from the universal and age-long deception.

That is, a deception universal except for the separated saints, delivered by the light of the glorious evangel shining in their hearts to give the light of the glory of God in the face of Jesus Christ. Now, *that* delivers from all delusion.

Of course the whole passage – as indeed the entire Book of Revelation – is mystical and spiritual in context, and each word of significance is used symbolically. All is allusion.

But no matter to what the allusion applies, there is no ambiguity about the *fact* that 'civilization' is completely deceived by 'the Devil' and 'Satan', that 'old serpent'.

As opposed to the illuminated, quickened, heavenly-minded saints, seen as *saved*. And if saved, then, in this context, saved from the blinding delusion that deceives global and age-long civilization.

Even more mysterious and metaphorical appears the place where the spirits of 'devils'–δαιμόνων, *demons*–working miracles–σημεῖα, *signs*–go forth to the kings of the 'earth'–γῆς, *gē(s)*–and of the 'whole world'–οἰχουμένης ὅλης, *oikoumenē(s) holes*.

That is, allegorically, to deceive all the civilization that ever existed, seen as an entity, to gather them to the battle of God Almighty.

Of course all is allegory, and everything is spiritualized–as also is 'Armageddon'–but, whatever, *civilization, the economy, the household of mankind on earth, ordered under its rulers, is anti-Christ.*

Hence, Revelation 16:14 reveals civilization, brought to a metaphorical climax, figuratively described as a battle–Armageddon–in which the global *oikoumenē* of all nations comes out in its true nature as hating Christ–once seen as he is in truth–and all the saints.

Not all the passages having the word *oikoumenē* are as hostile as these. Some simply refer to the system as such. Nevertheless, passing through as sojourners, citizens of a heavenly country, the saints sit loose to all that 'civilization' offers, educationally, diversionary, medically, politically, financially; *they are not of it.*

Their language is 'In the LORD put I my trust: how say ye to my soul, Flee as a bird to your mountain?', Psalm 11:1. That is, the mountain of corporate human dependence, scientific, medical, fashionable, fiscal, educational, or otherwise.

Certain of the systems comprising the entire *oikoumenē* are wholly out of the question for the saints: they are utterly separate.

This particularly applies to what is called 'entertainment'–such as 'sport', music, plays, films, and so on, as well as the means of projecting such things: and these include radio, television, personal computers, the web, the net, and even private e-mail.

In that day, what apostates now laugh to scorn, and think ridiculously exaggerated and extreme, will–too late–be the cause of these finding themselves inextricably caught in a web, snared in the net, and deluded by illusions, not to say stupefied by the opiate of the masses.

When God, who commanded the light to shine out of darkness, shines in our hearts to give the light of the knowledge of the glory of God in the face of Jesus Christ, then the saying is brought to pass spiritually, and thus this word is fulfilled: 'The world seeth me no more; *but ye see me.*'

But not outwardly. 'Whom having not seen, ye love; in whom, though now ye see him not, yet believing, ye rejoice with joy unspeakable and full of glory:

'Receiving the end of your faith'–for we walk by faith, and not by sight, no, not of this world, nor of the hearing of its enticing, exciting, or seductive sounds–'the end of your *faith*, even the salvation of your souls', I Peter 1:8,9.

Then shall those now scorned and derided pilgrims who receive these words be vindicated in having been saved by the Saviour from the *oikoumenē*.

Yea, even all those who look for his appearing, crying on their pilgrimage, 'While we look not at the things which are seen, *but at the things which are not seen*: for the things which are seen are temporal; *but the things which are not seen are eternal*', II Corinthians 4:18.

Thus, saved from the *oikoumenē* by grace, like Moses, they *endure*. But how? 'As seeing him who is invisible', Hebrews 11:27.

XI
Salvation from the World: 'Kosmos'

THE word *kosmos* occurs one hundred and eighty-eight times in the Greek new testament, being translated 'world' on one hundred and eighty-seven occasions, and 'adorning' once. From this source such English words as 'cosmic'; 'cosmopolitan'; 'cosmetic'; and others of similar type have their origin.

The definition 'world' as used in English is so nearly similar to the Greek *kosmos* that it must be considered as accurate a translation in new testament terms as is reasonably possible.

It refers to the visible global order or material arrangement either of men, substance, or both, from the whole to any particular part.

Mainly the new testament usage ranges from, first, the created world in its present visible appearance; second, to mankind in order and arrangement under the prince of this world; or, sometimes, the order and arrangement of some particular part.

'The world' is not always spoken of in an alien context, although of necessity it must always have an alien background.

Not every reference brings to light the essentially hostile or harmful nature inherent in the *kosmos*, but every reference implies it: context is the determining feature.

Matthew, Mark, and Luke have relatively few references. John presents by far the greater preponderance among the four evangelists.

One thing is certain from the synoptics: this evangel–inclusive of the doctrine from Matthew, Mark, and Luke–must be preached throughout the whole world.

Moreover in comparison to the loss of one's own soul, there is no profit whatsoever in gaining the whole world, since the balance falls out as that of the certainty of eternal perdition over against a fleeting dream of what is in fact a temporal impossibility.

Between the nine references to *kosmos* in Matthew, and three each in Mark and Luke, as opposed to seventy-seven in John, the contrast is both remarkable and instructive.

Apart from the one 'adorning' the remaining ninety-five occurrences of *kosmos* follow on from Acts to Revelation.

Proportionately, the balance of references lies in favour of First John, although in a far larger book, First Corinthians, there are almost as many occurrences as in the five short chapters of John's first epistle.

Whereas in the synoptics the context is more with an emphasis on the 'arrangement' of the creation as now constituted, in the Evangel according to John the emphasis is virtually always on the 'arrangement' of mankind, of humanity as existent in the Fall.

John glorifies the Son four times over as the Light of the world– a world which morally, spiritually, and towards God, lay in pitch darkness–this is the world into which the Light came in all his effulgent brightness, but the darkness comprehended it not.

The Light came into the world, and the world was made by him, and the world knew him not. His shining was inward; his glory was spiritual; his brightness was interior. But the world was outward; its light was carnal; its brightness exterior: 'and the world knew him not.'

'And this is the condemnation, that light is come into the world, and men loved darkness rather than light, because their deeds were evil', John 3:19.

That is, evil inwardly, where the light shone; evil spiritually, where the glory lightened; evil in heart, where the brightness illuminated; evil in the interior, where the true light gave forth its effulgence.

Men hated that radiance; they loved darkness. *There.* Because *there* their deeds were evil: at the source within.

The world was in spiritual darkness, and the world was in sin inwardly. But he who made the world came into the world as the Light of the world, and into the sinful world as the Lamb of God that taketh away the sin of the world.

'And the world knew him not', John 1:10. Especially the orthodox religious world. The detested, outcast, and execrable Samaritans, to the contrary, declared 'This is indeed the Christ, the Saviour of the world'. They embraced the light with joy, rejoicing therein for a season.

However, the *kosmos*–Jew, Samaritan, Gentile, the whole–hated Christ, but loved itself. Said Jesus unto them, The world cannot hate you; but me it hateth, because I testify of it, that the works thereof are evil.

'Ye are from beneath; I am from above: ye are of this world; I am not of this world.' Thus, 'For judgment I am come into this world, that they which see not might see; and they which see might be made blind.'

Hence, 'He that loveth his life shall lose it; and he that hateth his life in this world shall keep it unto life eternal.'

Then, behold, in the midst of time, whilst yet a little while longer in the world, in view of his imminent departure from it, Jesus declared, 'Now'– *now* –'is the judgment of this world: now shall the prince of this world be cast out.'

And so it came to pass upon the entire *kosmos* from that time henceforth, its effect hanging trembling till the great awakening, realization, and consummation at the final day of vengeance.

From John chapter 13 there is a certain mark of definition and distinction between Jesus' disciples, as opposed to the *kosmos*, that is sharper than that which preceded in the previous twelve chapters.

The *kosmos* could not receive the Holy Ghost, and never would. But the disciples would receive the Holy Ghost, and would for ever.

A little while–between then and the burial–and the world seeth Jesus no more. But the disciples–inwardly by the Holy Ghost–would see him again, and, spiritually, would be with him for ever.

He would manifest himself to the disciples, who would love him, keep his words, and whose Father would love them, and with the Son make his abode with them. But he would never, ever, no, not once again, manifest himself to the *kosmos*, for all they ever saw–and misconstrued–was outward and carnal.

The Lord would never give to the disciples as the *kosmos* gave to its own: he would give the disciples what was divine, heavenly, mysterious, spiritual, inward, free, and everlasting. Which is that of which, in any one part thereof, the world knew nothing, and could give nothing.

To the *kosmos*, the prince of this world came, yea, and came also to the Lord, and to his disciples. But, as to the world, it was his, and he had everything in it; but, as to the Lord, and his disciples, he had *nothing* in the Lord, and therefore *nothing* in the disciples. What a difference!

The *kosmos* would hate the disciples. But what of that? It was to be expected. 'Ye know that it hated me before it hated you.' This marks the difference between the *kosmos* and the disciples.

If the disciples were of the *kosmos* the world would love its own. But since the disciples were not of the *kosmos*, but of the Lord who had chosen them out of the *kosmos*, therefore the world hateth them.

Then, there is a *total, utter, irrevocable, and perpetual separation between Christ's disciples and the kosmos.*

If *that* is not apparent, then, no matter what the claims or protestations, the *facts* declare that they are none of his.

Thus humanity falls into but two classes. There is the *kosmos*, and there are 'the men which thou gavest me out of the world.' Of the latter, given by the Father to the Son, Jesus says, 'I pray not for the world, but for them which thou hast given me; for they are thine.'

These are to be separate and kept from the *kosmos*, though they must suffer the tribulation of being pilgrims and strangers, in their sojourn through this present world.

'And now I am no more in the world, but these are in the world, and I come to thee. Holy Father, keep through thine own name'–that is, keep them as the Father's, separate and distinct from the *kosmos*–'those whom thou hast given me, that they may be one, as we are.'

Then there is the world's unity, the *kosmos*, of which all hate the elect; and, over against the world, there are those given of the Father to the Son, dwelling in the unity of the Father, the Son, and the Holy Ghost: one, '*even as we are*'.

Saith the Son of these, 'I have given them thy word'. Not, they have bought bibles; or have read the scriptures themselves: but, *I* have *given* them *thy* word. This gift is of living, divine, experimental, spiritual, glorious, and interior revelation, and surely sounds and shines from the Son out of heaven.

'And the world'–the *kosmos*, religious, 'evangelical', or otherwise, it is all the same–'hath hated them.'

Why? Because for all their bibles, the Son never gave them anything by the Spirit from the Father into their own hearts. And they resent and hate those to whom he has. Why? Because the glory of the *kosmos* lies in what *man* can do, in or out of religion.

But the glory of the Son is what *the Father* does, inwardly by the Spirit: 'because they are not of the world, even as I am not of the world.'

No, they are not of the world, which lives for itself, for what can be seen, for that which is of time, for the gratification of worldly desires, for the praise of man.

But those chosen out of the world, given by the Father to the Son, do not. They live by the Son, they live for the Father, and they live in the Spirit, separate from the *kosmos*.

'O righteous Father, the world hath not known thee: but I have known thee, and these have known that thou hast sent me. And I have declared unto them thy name, and will declare it: *that the love wherewith thou hast loved me may be in them, and I in them.*' And *that* is the incalculable difference.

The world–*kosmos*–is in as stark a contrast to the disciples, as is darkness to light, the flesh to the Spirit, or hell to heaven.

In the epistle to the Romans the very *kosmos* of creation, by the arrangement of the heavens and the earth, condemns the *kosmos* of mankind.

'For the invisible things of him'–God–'from the creation of the world are clearly seen, being understood by the things that are made, even his eternal power and Godhead; so that they are without excuse.'

Above and beyond this the law of God, whether in its works written in the heart, or its revelation written upon tables of stone, or recorded in the books of the law, one way or another, calls down its curses upon the whole world.

It speaks on this wise, saying, 'Cursed is every one that continueth not in all things which are written in the book of the law to do them.'

If so, not only is the *kosmos* of the earth cursed for Adam's sake, but the *kosmos* of all mankind is cursed, each for the cause of his own continuous rebellion, but cursed above all are those with the greatest revelation, namely, the book of the law.

Romans 3:6-19 assures all mankind that God *shall* judge the world, and that by a standard the world mocks and repudiates to its own destruction. For the entire *kosmos*, without exception, is found guilty without law, under law, and by the law.

For 'by the deeds of the law there shall no flesh be justified in his sight': 'that *every* mouth may be stopped, and *all the world* may become guilty before God.' Now, should there not arise a cry for a Saviour, and for the salvation of God?

For 'by one man sin entered into the *kosmos*, and death by sin; and so death passed upon all men, for that all have sinned.'

Then shall the cry of those that know themselves to be lost be unanswered?

The cry is answered: 'That as sin hath reigned unto death, even so might grace reign through righteousness unto eternal life by Jesus Christ our Lord.'

For since the Saviour took the place of sinners, and bore away sin in righteousness, God is appeased in his wrath, satisfied in his judgment, and appears by grace in the salvation of God, 'A just God *and* a Saviour'.

In the Corinthian epistles the wisdom of this world is foolishness with God; and the wisdom of God is foolishness to this world.

The spirit of this world is in contrast to the Spirit of God: utterly incompatible and totally in contrast. Those who have the Spirit are therefore of necessity chosen out of and wholly separated from this world.

By wisdom—educational; academic; scientific; artistic; religious; philosophical; mystical—the world knew not God. Those to whom God reveals himself freely receive of his Spirit by grace: such will not be condemned with this *kosmos*. They are destined—predestinated—for the world to come, whereof we speak.

Thus, Galatians 6:14, Paul proclaims of Christ on our behalf, 'by whom the world is crucified unto me, and I unto the world'.

Before being saved by the Saviour with the salvation of God, precisely opposite conditions prevailed, both doctrinally and experimentally. Then what a massive, total change must be wrought in the heart by true salvation! And, with such a Saviour, what less would one expect?

For, 'in time past'—*past*, mark it: before being saved. And this addresses *all* who call themselves Christians; more accurately, all saints–'ye walked according to the course of this world, according to the prince of the power of the air, the spirit that now worketh in the children of disobedience', Ephesians 2:2.

All who have been saved, or ever shall be saved, *before* being saved 'walked according to the *aiōn* of the *kosmos*'. In context, *aiōn, age,* likely refers to *fashion.*

Where precedent and experience are overturned as 'old-fashioned' and new generations walk on in what is 'in fashion', successively loosening themselves from whatever restraints the work of God in times past had curbed previous ages.

Thus the *kosmos* passes over, cycle by cycle, through time into eternity.

Instantly forgetful, desperate to relegate the restrictions of their forefathers into a rejected past, that it may embrace the 'fashionableness' of the elusive future at all costs, engrossed–nay, obsessed–with what it considers 'reformed', or else 'new', and at least 'modernized'.

Blind as bats, even the older, more stable generations of the French–for all their revolution–would shame them: *plus ça change, plus c'est la même chose.*

The *kosmos*? Fashion? But this appeared also in the old world, the world before the flood: 'And as it was in the days of Noah, so shall it be also in the days of the Son of man.

'They did eat, they drank, they married wives, they were given in marriage, until the day that Noah entered into the ark, and the flood came, and destroyed them all', Luke 17:26,27.

For 'by faith Noah, being warned of God of things not seen as yet, moved with fear, prepared an ark to the saving of his house; by the which he condemned the world'–condemned the *kosmos*–'and became heir of the righteousness which is by faith', Hebrews 11:7.

'Whereby the *kosmos* that then was, being overflowed with water, perished.' That is, as saith Peter, 'bringing in the flood upon the world of the ungodly.'

James instructs us that pure religion and undefiled before God and the Father is this: to visit the fatherless and widows in their affliction, and to keep oneself *unspotted from the world.* Neither one without the other, nor the other without the one.

Of course not, for, having extolled the showing of mercy, sternly he adds, 'Ye adulterers and adulteresses'– that is, against God, a-whoring in worldliness–'know ye not that the friendship of the world is enmity with God? whosoever therefore will be a friend of the world'–the *kosmos*–'is the enemy of God.'

The entire *kosmos*? Yes, the *kosmos* in its entirety: 'But the heavens and the earth, which are now, by the same word'–that is, of judgment against the condemned heavens and earth before the flood–'are kept in store, *reserved unto fire* against the day of judgment and perdition of ungodly men.'

Wherein 'the heavens shall pass away with a great noise, and the elements shall melt with fervent heat, the earth also and the works that are therein shall be burned up. Seeing then that all these things shall be dissolved, what manner of persons ought ye to be in all holy conversation and godliness,

'Looking for and hasting unto the coming of the day of God, wherein the heavens being on fire shall be dissolved, and the elements shall melt with fervent heat? Nevertheless we, according to his promise, look for new heavens and a new earth, wherein dwelleth righteousness.'

And what Saviour but Jesus Christ could save and bring us through and to all that, or what salvation shall once be likened unto the salvation of our God, a just God and a Saviour?

'Love not the world' the last apostle exhorts and warns in his extreme age, in view of all that was to come as an ever-increasing and overwhelming danger to the remnant that should be left after his decease, and till this day. So much the more until this very day.

By the *kosmos* John does not mean the outwardly apparent and differing countries, nations, peoples, classes, societies, conditions, states, confederacies, occupations, or even generations that exist in the world. These distinctions create multiple diversities. But in I John 2:15 the whole world is seen as one.

No distinctions are envisaged. John here sums up the world as an entity. The *kosmos* is seen spiritually as a system that is both unified and seamless: it is a whole.

The world does not know the Father. The Father begat his own children in Christ *out* of the world. Of these Jesus says, 'Ye are not of the world'. And again, 'O righteous Father, the world hath not known thee.' Hence the world has nothing to do with the Father.

Then how can those begotten of the Father love that which denies and wilfully rejects the light–for God *is* light–to which the blinded world is in thick darkness?

The world knows not the Son. Concerning those that are of the world Jesus states, 'The world cannot hate *you*; but me it hateth', John 7:7.

And again, '*Ye* are of this world; I am not of this world', John 8:23.

Hence the world has nothing to do with the Son *as he is in reality*. That is, as opposed to the false image which they give to him, lying against the truth.

Thus in verity–contrary to these delusions–Jesus says, 'I pray not for the world', John 17:9. Then how *could* the children of God do *other* than 'love not the world', I John 2:15?

Again, the world knows nothing of the Holy Ghost. 'Whom the world cannot receive', John 14:17. But the children of God receive him: and if so, how could they love that which rejects the Spirit of truth who quickened them?

Indeed, the Holy Ghost, when he came, immediately reproved the entire *kosmos*: 'When he is come, he will reprove the world', John 16:8.

And shall those born from above, begotten of the Father, made alive in Christ, quickened by the Spirit of God, love a world that is reproved by the Holy Ghost? How can those chosen out of the world possibly love that which despises the Father; is at enmity against the Son; and always resists the Holy Ghost?

The children of God hear the voice of the Son: 'If the world hate you, ye know that it hated me before it hated you', John 15:18.

Once more, 'If ye were of the world, the world would love his own: but because ye are not of the world, but I have chosen you out of the world, therefore the world hateth you', John 15:19. Now, these 'love not the world'.

It is not too much to say that these hate their life in this world, looking for the return of Christ and the world to come: 'He that loveth his life shall lose it; and he that hateth his life in this world shall keep it unto life eternal', John 12:25.

This present world, however, this *kosmos*, stands in that which is begotten of the flesh by natural generation in the Fall, condemned already, lying in moral darkness and spiritual death.

Thus the *kosmos* is oblivious to the reality of the resurrection and judgment to come after death, followed by the immutable and everlasting sentence of the wrath of God.

How can the world, how can humanity, ignore such tremendous verities? Because it is blinded by the god of this world, the prince of the power of the air, the spirit that now worketh in the children of disobedience. But not in the elect, the chosen and quickened pilgrim people of God.

As one man, these sojourners and strangers are separated from the world and from all its worldly religion, being as distinct from everything that is of this age as were the children of Israel from Egypt, the Red sea behind them, traversing the wilderness of this world on their way to the land of promise.

Thus having been crucified, dead, buried, risen, and ascended in Christ, the Spirit having descended to bear witness within them of all that had been wrought for them, longing for the Lord's return, nothing could be more conspicuous of such a united people than that they 'love not the world'.

'Neither the things that are in the world', I John 2:15. Whatever things they may be, if they are of the world, if they are in this present evil age, if they pertain to the fallen creation, the saints are warned not to love them.

The admonition could not be broader or more all-embracing. 'Things' are not intangible; they are not abstracts; they are tangible; they are materialistic.

This does not refer to the world itself, it points to that which clothes it, that of which it is comprised, that which enriches it, that with which it is adorned.

It comprehends all that is outward, visible, and material. It is the fashion, the form, which the world takes at any given time or place, that goes to make up its 'things'.

But the spiritual, heavenly-minded, godly, separated pilgrims, self-denying, cross-bearing, following Jesus, desire a better country, that is, an heavenly; and another creation, namely, the world to come, filled with 'the things which are Jesus Christ's'.

They will not, do not, and cannot love the things of this world, no, nor the world itself: they love it not.

After this John brings the matter to a summary conclusion, allowing of no loophole for the love of the world, of worldliness, or of the things of this world: 'If any man love the world, the love of the Father is not in him', I John 2:15. How could it be in him? the two are wholly incompatible.

All that the Father is, the Son makes manifest. He and his Father are one. But the world hates the Son, John 7:7. Then – given the nature of the unity of the Father and the Son – the world must hate the Father also.

Then if any man loves the world, by so much he excludes the love of the Father and of the Son.

How can the love of God dwell in such a man? 'I know you, that ye have not the love of God in you.' It is impossible. What dwells in these is the love of the world. Besides, how can the world love the Father, when it neither sees him nor knows him?

'O righteous Father, the world hath not known thee', saith the Son, and, 'They said unto him, Where is thy Father?' The world could neither see nor know, despite its scripture and religion.

And the reason is, they know not the Son – in fact, now they *re-invent* both the Father and the Son, and to *that* fiction they pay the lip-service of 'love' – but verily, verily, in truth they hate him without a cause.

And if the world hate the Son, it hates the Father also. His love is not in them.

He is from above; they are from beneath. He is heavenly; they are earthly. He is Spirit; they are flesh. He is light; they are darkness. He is living; they are dead. He is righteous; they are sinful. He is good; they are evil.

He is the Father of the Son; they are of their father the devil. Then how could the love of the Father be in such a world?

The world knows neither the Father nor the Son, but such speech and doctrine that it cannot but hear from the Son, that the world hates.

If so, it hates the Father. But whoso loves what hates the Father, loves the world. Then, 'If any man love the world, the love of the Father is not in him', I John 2:15.

Next John passes to a threefold admonition, and, finally, to the conclusion. 'For all that is in the world, the lust of the flesh, and the lust of the eyes, and the pride of life, is not of the Father, but is of the world', I John 2:16.

Here John shows that which fills the *kosmos*, the world, in its entirety: '*All* that is in the world.' There is nothing else in the world.

For all the delusions of the world, and for all that it is deluded, it is the truth of God that nothing exists in the world save that which John describes.

And nothing of it is of the Father. It is wholly of the world. Whence it is plain, the world and the Father are entirely incompatible, irrevocably incompatible, and everlastingly incompatible.

Three factors comprise the whole of that which is in the world: *all* that is in the world. These factors are not material. They are not even exterior. Neither are they visible. They are all *within man.*

It is *this* that John means when he says 'all that is in the world'. He means *morally*. This is what epitomizes the world, all the world, the world in its entirety, namely, *the things that are within the souls of men.*

Not the things exterior to man. There are things, things of the world, exterior to man. But John does not refer to these in this place. He refers to the *interior* desires, swellings, covetings, workings of lust in man's heart. That which is within. That which corresponds inwardly with outward and visible 'things'.

It is this threefold interior state that makes up the parts which together constitute *all that is in the world.*

Consider the first: 'the lust of the flesh.' It is not in the plural, lusts, in which case there would appear an inward correspondence with various and diverse material forms. No. John puts the word in the singular, lust, the essence of the thing, desire in and of itself.

This is the insatiable craving for gratification, seated in the sensibility, and impossible of satisfaction, being like the horse-leach that hath two daughters, crying, Give, give, Proverbs 30:15.

Why two daughters? Because no sooner is the desire of the one granted, than the rising cry of the other clamours for gratification. So lust in itself continues unabated with mounting voracity. Nor can it ever once be pacified or sated. It is like a bottomless pit: nothing will suffice to fill the yawning void.

This is the inward lust of the flesh. To change the metaphor, whatever its tentacles, reaching out to the creature and in the creation, there is this undying head within, called, The lust of the flesh. Of this the world is composed with a witness, and by it, the world is driven.

The next factor is called, The lust of the eyes. Whereas the lust of the flesh yearns for gratification in itself, the lust of the eyes creates a craving at the heart for outward things which, once seen, excite an interior covetousness. This inward appetite is gendered by what appears to the sight of the eyes.

Be it riches, houses, lands, women, men, status, power: the thing is seen to be desirable, whether in itself, or in the possession of others, and the inwardness of the fire of lust is kindled, till the craving swells as leavened bread in the baker's oven.

The eyes rove over that which is not one's own, not given to one, and by lighting upon the object of desire, covetousness is inflamed. This is called, The lust of the eyes.

The world is full of this. It is of the world. But it is not in the saints, not in the brethren, not in the pilgrims, not in the elect.

Nor is this once to be imagined, entertained, or conceived by those who 'love not the world, neither the things that are in the world', because 'if any man love the world, the love of the Father is not in him'.

'And the pride of life.' This completes the sum. Here are all the vanities and gloryings; all the boastings and conceits; all the vauntings and exaltings; all the attainments and disdainments, that fill the heart.

Here are all the presumptions and despisings; all the flattery and contempt; all the bribery and exploitation; all the posturing and deceiving, with which the earth has been burdened, the world filled, and man enamoured since the Fall.

But to what does it all amount, this pride of life that lifts up the interior heart of man? It amounts to this: 'Surely men of low degree are vanity, and men of high degree are a lie: to be laid in the balance, they are altogether lighter than vanity', Psalm 62:9.

The world is filled with these three inward movings, that puff up the soul of mankind as leaven in the baker's oven.

There is nothing *else* in the world, for there is nothing at all of the Father that is in the world.

'For all that is in the world, the lust of the flesh, and the lust of the eyes, and the pride of life, is not of the Father, but is of the world.'

And what has all this to do with those to whom the Father in heaven reveals the Son, who love the Father who begat them, who are heavenly, spiritual, holy, separate; who are pilgrims, strangers, sojourners, and wayfarers? Nothing at all.

It has nothing to do with them. They have come out; they have departed; they are separated; they are holiness to the Lord. They 'love not the world, neither the things that are in the world: the lust of the flesh, and the lust of the eyes, and the pride of life.'

For they that are Christ's have cleansed themselves from all filthiness of the flesh and of the spirit. They have crucified the flesh, with the affections and lusts.

The world is crucified unto them, and they unto the world. All the world, with all, but all, its things. Though they must pass through the world on their way to glory, it is to them a barren wilderness, a place of desolation and death.

They know inwardly and experimentally, as the nature of this life, that 'if any man love the world, the love of the Father is not in him'. The Saviour has saved them from the world, and by the salvation of God they are destined for glory.

These, the children of God, the Lord's own sheep and lambs, can cry with one voice, as one body, one flock, 'We know that we are of God, and the whole world lieth in wickedness', I John 5:19.

First, 'We.' That is, by definition, 'we', as opposed to 'the whole world'. Note that there are but two states under which all classes and kinds of persons must fall of necessity.

All other distinctions are entirely irrelevant. But two states alone exist in the sight of God, whether for time or eternity.

These two states do not refer to persons in an individualistic way, as if any from either party were disconnected from all others of that party. Each is a *united* party. It does not imply persons in an isolated way, or singularly considered. It is persons *collectively* and *corporately* considered.

Here are two distinct *bodies*. Not innumerable merged yet distinguishable individuals. Each of the two – the *only* two – states is wholly separate from the other, visibly corporate, and each united respectively as an entity in and of itself.

Consider the first body, that embraced by the words of John, 'We are of God'. No question. No one else is: *we* are; none other. Moreover, *we* are *one*. What makes us one? 'We are *of* God.' That makes us one: it constitutes our unity. John's words will suffer no other, and no lesser, meaning.

Being *of God* makes us one, according to the holy apostle, abiding in the unity of the Father, and of the Son, and of the Holy Ghost. 'And truly our fellowship' – in one Spirit – 'is with the Father, and with his Son Jesus Christ', I John 1:3. 'That ye also may have fellowship with us.'

We are of God, and we know that we are of God, because we have received that which was seen and heard by the apostles, and declared unto us. Thus we are one in the apostles' fellowship: 'and truly our fellowship' – that in which we are gathered together in one – 'is with the Father, and with his Son Jesus Christ', I John 1:3.

We are of God, and know that we are of God, because we walk in the light, and dwell in the life, and the love of God is perfected in us.

Not in some of us, or in one or two of us, utterly apart, and scattered abroad in the worldly and divided congregations.

We are *one*, abiding in him, and he in us, in the oneness of divine unity, united in assembly, and united in all the assemblies as one, wherever we are on the earth, all having been baptized in one Spirit into one body.

We are of God, and know that we are of God, because the anointing which we have received of him abideth in us, and we know that he has given us of his Spirit, so that we abide in him, and he in us.

We are not of this world. Entirely apart from it, all its 'things'– its environment, course, fashions, education, ways, habits, politics, ideals, diversions, entertainments, imaginations, and devices– we are of God, and love not the world, neither the things that are in the world.

On the contrary, we are separate from the world, and we eschew its things, because the whole would rob us of the love of God, and the fellowship that is in the Father and the Son.

We are of God, and know that we are of God, because we have the victory over the world, and that by the faith of God's elect.

Likewise we are of God, and know that we are of God, because 'whosoever is born of God doth not commit sin; for his seed abideth in him: and he cannot sin, because he is born of God', I John 3:9. 'We know that whosoever is born of God sinneth not', I John 5:18.

But the whole world sins, sins inwardly, and inwardly sins continually, because the whole world is governed by the god of this world, the spirit that now worketh in the children of disobedience.

The entirety of the *kosmos* is under the blinding delusion of *ho diabolos*: 'In this the children of God are manifest, and the children of *ho diabolos*: whosoever doeth not righteousness is not of God.'

Then, a people joined in one appears as utterly separate from
the world, called 'We': We know that *'we'* are of God, and the
whole world lieth in the Wicked One.

Only one other body exists *besides the visible unity of the 'we' who
are of God*. Which other body? It is vastly greater than the other,
and hugely more widespread.

None the less, in the sight of God, and of the holy apostles
of the Lamb, it is *still a single entity*. It is called the *kosmos*: 'the
whole world.' Mark that: the *whole* world, I John 5:19.

In every way 'the whole world' is opposite to the 'we' who
'are of God'. The world is in darkness, and walks in darkness.
The world is dead towards God, and under the sentence of
death. If any man love the world, the love of the Father is not
in him.

All that is in the world—and there is nothing else in the
world—the lust of the flesh, the lust of the eyes, and the pride
of life, is not of the Father. All is of the world. And the world
passeth away, and the lust thereof, but he that doeth the will
of God abideth for ever.

The world hearkens to worldly, false religion: 'They are of the
world: therefore speak they of the world, and the world heareth
them', I John 4:5.

But the world is deceived: 'that old serpent, called the Devil,
and Satan, which deceiveth the whole'—*whole*—'world', Revelation
12:9. Hence Satan is called by John three times over, 'the prince
of this world'.

Paul is even stronger, declaring him to be 'the god of this
world [who] hath blinded the minds of them which believe not.'

Satan, the prince, or god, of the whole world, deludes and
draws all after him 'according to the course of this world,

according to the prince of the power of the air, the spirit that now worketh in the children of disobedience', Ephesians 2:2.

As to the religious that are of the world—evangelical, evangelistic, biblical, reformed—so-called—orthodox, charismatic, or otherwise, it maketh no difference—the blind are led by the blind.

Hence Jesus describes in his day those who follow them in this day: 'Ye are of your father the devil, and the lusts of your father ye will do.

'He was a murderer from the beginning, and abode not in the truth, because there is no truth in him. When he speaketh a lie, he speaketh of his own: for he is a liar, and the father of it. And because I tell you the truth, ye believe me not', John 8:44,45.

This is the world, and the whole world. Its bible, its religion, and all that is in the world, is of one character. In the sight of God it is an entity, and that entity is of one unified nature. Hence it is written, 'the *whole* world lieth in the Wicked One', I John 5:19.

Completely apart from the world, entirely separate from all that is in the world, having another origin altogether, there stands the only other entity in existence. This also is of one unified character, no matter where it may be found: it is all of one: 'We *know* that we are *of God*', I John 5:19.

'There is *one* body, and *one* Spirit, even as ye are called in *one* hope of your calling; *one* Lord, *one* faith, and *one* baptism,

'*One* God and Father of all, who is above all, and through all, and in *you all*', Eph. 4:4-6. These are of God, and abide in him together as one, and abide together as one. One *ecclesia*. 'I pray for *them*: I pray *not for the world*', John 17:9.

'I in them, and thou in me, that they may be made perfect in one; and that'–by this spiritual unity *being made manifest*–'the world may know that thou hast sent me, and hast loved them'–it being *evident* that *they* are of God–'as thou hast loved me', John 17:23.

Thus, 'We *know* that we are of God.' And we know that we are *united* in the Father and the Son by one Spirit *in one body.*

Then, these things being so, and it being a truth also that there is nothing *else* except the entity of the world, Why is it that the worldly ask the question of the godly–who *know* that they are of God–querying what is *utterly to the contrary of the truth that is so obvious in I John 5:19?*

What is that question? It is this: 'What *denomination* are you?'

Some, like the multiple divisions of Brethrenism, or else the charismatics, or those in house-meetings, or other 'bible-pattern' independents, will protest, 'But we are *not* a denomination.'

But they are. They are divided. They are out of the unity. They are of the world, and speak of the world, and the world heareth them.

All these, of whatever persuasion, being of the world, agree that we who know that we are of God, whose fellowship is with the Father, and with his Son Jesus Christ, who abide in him, and he in us, to them, to the whole world–religious or otherwise–Oh, we are just another cult.

In fact, in their indignation against us, the worst and most presumptuous cult: The sect that is everywhere spoken against, Acts 28:22.

Since we receive 'the testimony of Jesus', which 'is the spirit of prophecy', and since prophecy came neither in old time nor at the present time other than by 'holy men of God', the world and its religion lampoons us for 'following a man'.

But we are not following a man. We *know* that we are *of God*. That is what we are following. As to the prophetic speech of his Son through his servants, this is our witness: 'We are of God: he that knoweth God heareth us; he that is not of God heareth not us', I John 4:6.

And that speech, agreeable to the apostles' doctrine, by one Spirit in the anointing, sounds to this day. We who are of God hear that, and hear it with a witness.

And since we know that in these last times God has reiterated his prophetic word, to bring us back again to that which was from the beginning, we know also that the world will make diligent search for those through whom this heavenly word sounds.

And, should it find any, the religious world–backed by the secular world–will both lie, slander, and invent fables, to discredit them, hoping by this means to hinder the work of God.

Indeed, if permitted, they will lay hands upon such, and draw them before their councils–or to their worldly authorities: it is all of one.

All alike are of the world–crying out with great indignation: 'We have found this man a pestilent fellow, and a mover of sedition among all the Jews'–and 'Christians'–'*throughout the world*, and a ringleader of the *sect* of the Nazarenes', Acts 24:5.

Nevertheless the counsel of the Lord shall stand. And the word that proceedeth out of the mouth of the Lord abideth for ever. Take heed then to *his* counsel; mark diligently *his* word. Which counsel? What word?

This: 'We *know* that *we* are of God, and *the whole world* lieth in wickedness', or, 'in the Wicked One', I John 5:19.

Therefore it is of necessity, if we are to be saved at all, that the Saviour must needs deliver us by the salvation of God from the world as an entity, and from all that is in the world in the entirety of its parts.

And such a work expresses the very nature of what he has done in saving his people from the *kosmos*, and the prince of this world, and all the beguiling influences that go to make up the world in its entirety, so that the Son of God separates us from it as one people: his *own* people.

Hence he declares unto us, 'If ye were of the world, the world would love his own: but because ye are not of the world, but I have chosen you out of the world, therefore the world hateth you', John 15:19.

And this we must suffer and bear to the end in the joy of the Lord, earnestly awaiting his coming again, whilst sojourning as strangers on our pilgrimage to the heavenly country, and to the world to come, whereof we speak. Amen.

'Now unto him that is able to keep you from falling, and to present you faultless before the presence of his glory with exceeding joy.

'To the only wise God our Saviour, be glory and majesty, dominion and power, both now and ever. Amen.'

PART FOUR

SALVATION FROM
THE WRATH TO COME

SALVATION FROM THE WRATH TO COME

XII
'Thumos' and 'Orgē'

FIRST, there is a day of wrath, called the day of judgment, the last day, and, inexorably, inevitably, immutably it draws closer and closer, as time runs out to its destined end.

Of this, God's holy prophets have spoken since the world began. And since in turn every last word of each prophetic utterance has assuredly come to pass as a matter of indisputable historical record, What could be more certain of fulfilment?

The more so, since the millennia of prophecy preceding the first advent of Christ certainly came to pass at the precise time, to the exact detail, in the predicted order, How much more incontestable must be the one event of commensurate importance, namely, the second coming of Christ at the day of judgment?

How much? As much as the historic fact of his coming into the world, foretold from the beginning of the ages.

Hence, the day of wrath, the day of judgment, predicted by all the holy prophets, has been proven by precedent to be as certain to follow, as surely as day following night. And if so, there can be no question regarding the indisputability of the future *Dies Irae*: Day of Wrath.

By faith Noah, being warned of God of things not seen as yet, moved with fear, prepared an ark to the saving of his house; by which he condemned the world, and became heir of the right-eousness which is by faith.

Thus he foretold of the judgment of the old world by flood, and surely made clear that the end of this world shall be by fire.

Abel also, being dead, yet speaketh of that judgment of God which can never fail of avenging his own elect.

Likewise Enoch condemns this present world in the judgment to come at the last day: 'And Enoch also, the seventh from Adam, prophesied of these' – very things, especially the judgment of the hypocrites mingled with the elect – 'saying, Behold, the Lord cometh with ten thousands of his saints.'

But when? And why? To do what? 'To execute judgment upon all, and to convince all that are ungodly among them' – that is, among the godly – 'of all their ungodly deeds which they have ungodly committed, and of all their hard speeches which ungodly sinners have spoken against him.'

And this, among those who profess godliness. Then what of the openly godless? And the seventh from *Adam*? Is that not from the beginning of the age? And concerning what? Why, *Dies Irae*.

But of all the prophets, Isaiah is the most evangelical. Yet he speaks more eloquently of the day of judgment than any other, before or since.

Isaiah looked through time as if it were a vast corridor, stretching ahead, and seeing the burning furnace at the end, cried aloud, 'Howl ye; for the day of the LORD is at hand; it shall come as a destruction from the Almighty.

'Therefore shall all hands be faint, and every man's heart shall melt: and they shall be afraid: pangs and sorrows shall take hold of them; they shall be in pain as a woman that travaileth: they shall be amazed one at another; their faces shall be as flames.

'Behold, the day of the LORD cometh, cruel both with wrath and fierce anger, to lay the land desolate: and he shall destroy the sinners thereof out of it.

'For the stars of heaven and the constellations thereof shall not give their light: the sun shall be darkened in his going forth, and the moon shall not cause her light to shine.

'And I will punish the world for their evil, and the wicked for their iniquity; and I will cause the arrogancy of the proud to cease, and will lay low the haughtiness of the terrible.'

'Therefore I will shake the heavens, and the earth shall remove out of her place, in the wrath of the LORD of hosts, and in the day of his fierce anger.'

And again, 'Fear, and the pit, and the snare, are upon thee, O inhabitant of the earth.

'And it shall come to pass, that he who fleeth from the noise of the fear shall fall into the pit; and he that cometh up out of the midst of the pit shall be taken in the snare: for the windows from on high are open, and the foundations of the earth do shake.

'The earth is utterly broken down, the earth is clean dissolved, the earth is moved exceedingly. The earth shall reel to and fro like a drunkard, and shall be removed like a cottage; and the transgression thereof shall be heavy upon it; and it shall fall, and not rise again.' This prophecy is of *Dies Irae*.

Such prophecies and foreshadowings the Lord Jesus himself confirms, saying, 'As it was in the days of Noah, so shall it be also in the days of the Son of man.

'They did eat, they drank, they married wives, they were given in marriage, *until the day* that Noah entered into the ark, and the flood came, and destroyed them all.'

This is that *day* of judgment, of which the Saviour speaks, saying, 'Many will say to me in that day, Lord, Lord, have we not prophesied in thy name? and in thy name have cast out devils? and in thy name done many wonderful works?'

And, if they say this in *that* day, then they must have been raised from the dead, thus to be called to account in the resurrection.

So Jesus confirms elsewhere, 'That every idle word that men shall speak, they shall give account thereof in the day of judgment.' 'But of that day and hour knoweth no man, no, not the angels which are in heaven, neither the Son, but the Father only.'

Then, 'Take heed to yourselves, lest at any time your hearts be overcharged with surfeiting, and drunkenness, and cares of this life, and so that day come upon you unawares. For as a snare shall it come on all them that dwell on the face of the whole earth.

'Watch ye therefore, and pray always, that ye may be accounted worthy to escape all these things that shall come to pass, and to stand before the Son of man.'

'Marvel not at this: for the hour is coming, in the which all that are in the graves shall hear his voice, and shall come forth; they that have done good, unto the resurrection of life; and they that have done evil, unto the resurrection of damnation.'

Of those who have done good, whom the Son will raise up unto the resurrection of life, he says, 'And this is the Father's will which hath sent me, that of all which he hath given me I should lose nothing, but should raise it up again at the last day.'

The Lord repeats this assurance three times over in the same context. Nor is there any lack of further passages, whether of the resurrection unto life, or that to damnation.

However, what has been said is more than enough to demonstrate that the Son of God forewarned of a coming day of judgment, and of the absolute necessity of being prepared to face it.

So Peter testified to Cornelius of the parting commandment of the risen Lord to his apostles, just before the ascension: 'And he commanded us to preach unto the people, and to testify that it is he which was ordained of God to be the Judge of quick and dead.'

Wherefore also Paul affirms, 'Because he hath appointed a day, in the which he will judge the world in righteousness by that man whom he hath ordained; whereof he hath given assurance unto all men, in that he hath raised him from the dead', Acts 17:31.

Given the *day* of judgment, the agonizing question follows: *What* is judged? what is the *standard* of judgment?

Yet this is a question already made clear from the day itself: 'And shall come forth; *they that have done good*, unto the resurrection of life; and *they that have done evil*, unto the resurrection of damnation', John 5:29.

Here there can be no question but that the *doing* of 'good' or of 'evil', respectively, in this life, provide the sole issues of resurrection and the judgment to come in the next.

What one professes about religion does not enter into the question. *The character produced* is the sole issue. Then, judgment is according to *the nature of one's life* according to the exact words of Jesus, John 5:29.

'For we must all appear before the judgment seat of Christ; that every one may receive the things done in his body, according to that he hath done, whether it be good or bad', II Corinthians 5:10.

Attempting to wriggle out of the very context, dispensationalists and premillennialists—particularly those who call themselves 'Brethren'—make great play of the Greek word *bēma*, 'the judgment seat', as though this sophistry dispensed with the force of the passage.

'Oh, it is merely a tribunal.' Is that so? Were that so, does that make Christ's judgment from it 'merely' some kind of solvent?

It was not solvent enough to dispense with the death penalty. For example, when Christ appeared before Pilate as he sat at the tribunal of Roman justice, the *bēma*.

Nor was it when Paul was arraigned before the supreme tribunal of Caesar. It was a matter of life and death.

Not to become entangled in the snares of foolish subterfuges, it is enough to see that the same wording, rightly taken in context—if not translation!—should be read as 'the judgment seat of God', Romans 14:10, cf. Isaiah 45:22,23 and Romans 14:11,12.

Then, this *'bēma'* is not some select discussion group for evangelicals, as these heretics would have us believe, *but the last judgment applicable to all mankind.*

And if so, the criterion at this final tribunal is 'the things done in the body' whether 'good or bad', not contradicting, but agreeing with the words of Jesus in John 5:29. In II Corinthians 5:10 also, *judgment is according to the character of the life: whether 'good' or 'bad'*.

It is not a question of whether one has been saved by grace through faith: *it is a question of the character this produces*.

It is not a question of 'Lord, Lord': *it is a question of whether one did the will of the Father throughout the life*. That is the issue at the last judgment or supreme tribunal.

Hence the apostle forewarns the entirety of humanity of the nature of the last judgment, 'In the day when God shall judge the secrets of men by Jesus Christ according to my gospel'.

That is *one* day, the last day; *one* resurrection, though of the just and unjust respectively, sheep and goats distinctly; nevertheless 'of men' that is, all mankind in the great assize.

'Behold, he cometh with clouds; and *every eye* shall see him, and they also which pierced him: and *all kindreds of the earth* shall wail because of him.'

One great general resurrection; one standard, that according to good or bad done in the body; one judgment.

Anyone who says otherwise preaches another gospel, which is not another, but a perversion of the apostolic doctrine of the Christian *ecclesia*.

Then, the last judgment is beyond this present life, after death, by resurrection, when the works and lives of men will be brought to account according to the law and righteousness of God, who will, as Judge, render to *every* man *according to his deeds*, Romans 2:6.

This is called 'the day of wrath and revelation of the righteous judgment of God', Romans 2:5.

'Render to every man according to his deeds'? What men? What deeds? But two classes of men exist before the Judge, each with their corresponding deeds.

The judgment upon these is without respect of persons. Professions of religion have nothing to do with it. *Deeds done over a lifetime* have everything to do with it. Nothing else.

The judgment is according to the righteousness of God's own nature, what he requires as Judge, what he requires to uphold the law, and what he requires according to the nature of man. These are absolutes.

They are objective, immutable requirements. The works and deeds of all men, religious or otherwise, evangelical or atheist – not what they professed to believe; what that belief *produced in character, manifest by deeds* – by the resurrection from the dead, will and must come into judgment before God.

The word 'render' confirms that the judgment is not arbitrary.

The Judge does not conjure up a judgment: sinners themselves will have provided the cause of that judgment by their own lives on earth. The Judge assesses and weighs nothing other than that life against the rule of law, passing the sentence accordingly.

That is the function of the Judge. Not to have mercy, but to pass judgment. As to appeal, the time for appeal has passed for ever.

Agreeable to what was sown in this life and on earth, the sentence for eternity in immortality will be pronounced upon what is raised up. For whatsoever a man soweth that shall he also reap.

The righteousness of God in his sentence on the day of judgment appears in Romans 2:6-8. 'Who will render to every man according to his deeds: to them who by patient continuance in well doing'–the Greek reads 'good works'–'seek for glory and honour and immortality'–God will render–'eternal life.

'But unto them that are contentious, and do not obey the truth, but obey unrighteousness'–God will render–'indignation and wrath.'

That is, 'tribulation and anguish, upon every soul of man that *doeth* evil'–irrespective of protestations of religion or of faith. 'But glory, honour, and peace, to every man that worketh good'– irrespective of protestations of religion or of faith: it is a question of 'show me thy faith by thy works'.

'For there is no respect of persons with God.' No, none whatsoever.

Say what you will; belong to what you wish; recite all you please: *it will have no effect at all upon the Judge of all the earth, who will do right, and judge righteously, according to thy works.*

First, the lives of the righteous are described by the apostle from their existence and character in this present world, as will come to light in the resurrection at the day of judgment.

Their life was one characterized by patient continuance, an enduring whilst waiting. The words mean 'a remaining under anything'.

The impression is one of a life of hope and patient waiting under present suffering.

Their life appears to be one of affliction whilst patiently continuing in hope. Why? Because this world to them was a place of harsh pilgrimage: a wilderness to be endured.

They looked for a world to come, and they lived for it. This is taken account of in the day of strict and impartial judgment.

The 'patient continuance' of these, the righteous, is said to be in 'well doing'. That is, literally, 'good works'. What is profitable, virtuous, of goodness or excellence in the issue of their lives.

They continually acted in virtue, and with good will, in the tenor of their lives, selfless, and with a view to the judgment, and the glory thereafter.

This is what they lived for. That cut clean across the way of the world. Like Moses, they esteemed the reproach of Christ, in the promise, of 'greater riches than the treasures in Egypt'. Then, they were 'persecuted for righteousness' sake.'

This caused much suffering, but they endured meekly, looking for a city and a country, that is, an heavenly; continuing in benevolence, good works of virtue, endeavouring to keep a conscience void of offence before God and man.

However such patient continuance in good works could not be acceptable before the righteous judgment of God in and of itself: the spring and motive of all must be pleasing in his sight.

That is, the patient continuance in well doing acceptable to God must not be with an eye to man, or the praise of men, neither must it be with a view to this world, or to time.

There must be a higher motive, a deeper purpose, than the thing in and of itself. It must be through 'seeking for glory and honour and immortality', Romans 2:7.

That is, the patient continuance in well doing acceptable before God must be in pursuit of a heavenly end, the motive must be to appear before the eye of God; to please him, and to dwell with him in immortality in the glory of the world to come.

In that day it will be found that the righteous sought for glory. That is, in the land that is very far off. It is in the heavenly country, the holy city, having the glory of God. In new Jerusalem it shall be seen, effulgent with the glory of God's outshining for ever and ever in the world to come.

They sought for it, they lived for it, and they continued patiently in good works with the eye of faith fixed upon that glory yet to be revealed, enduring 'as seeing him who is invisible'.

Likewise those approved at the last judgment, the righteous, had, in the nature of their having been righteous, sought not only for glory but for honour also.

Honour? That is, Weightiness: worth. The very opposite to the vacant, chaffy, light, and empty religion of the fool. The righteous were sober, serious, weighty, and earnest. They were deep, they were of the circumcised heart.

And this depth and inwardness was what they sought all their lives, lamenting their relative shallowness, despising the honour that comes from man, that is of the world, seeking the honour that comes from God only.

Moreover, the righteous sought by patient continuance in well doing likewise for immortality.

'Glory and honour and *immortality*.' The righteous sought constantly, consistently, zealously, with all their heart and mind and strength and understanding for immortality. That is, for incorruption, which is what cannot be attained whilst in this present body.

For incorruption, immortality, the language of the soul must be 'If by any means I might attain unto the resurrection of the dead'. It is a yearning to put off mortality, to be taken out of this world; to put on incorruption, to be brought into the world to come.

Then, it is to seek a better resurrection. The resurrection of the just.

This is the character that the justice of God will seek out in righteousness in the day of judgment. For this is the character of the just. It is not a question of *how* they attained to this character. It is a question of *that* they attained to this character.

It is not a matter of *what* they believed. It is a matter of what was *effected* by what they believed. They *are* righteous.

The judgment is entirely on character, life, and work, to the exclusion of all else. This divides mankind, as it justifies God in his judgments.

The character approved by the righteous sentence of God in that day is one in which by patient continuance in well doing the just are found to have sought for glory and honour and immortality.

The sentence that follows, Romans 2:7, is that of God's righteous judgment upon such character. Persons of this character can have but one sentence from the righteous judgment of God in that day: it is written; it is certain.

The Judge does not view how such a character was developed, but that it was developed. Not the means by which patient continuance in well doing was secured, but that it was secured.

What is judged is not the feeling that they should seek for glory and honour and immortality, but that they did seek for glory and honour and immortality. Continually.

The sentence, the righteous sentence, is pronounced, and must be pronounced, upon all possessed of such a character in the resurrection of the dead. And that sentence is, Eternal life, Romans 2:7.

Then, they will receive that for which they had sought. Those who suffered in this world, looking for the world to come, have the desire of their hearts. What could be more just?

With equal justice appears the sentence of God upon the wicked. What is it that marks the wicked? In what does their wickedness consist? The lives which they lived upon the earth before their death – religious or not – appear at the resurrection as lives precisely the opposite to those of the just.

The character of the wicked is described firstly as 'contentious', Romans 2:8. Contention characterizes the wicked. Men might well think contentiousness a strange thing to select as that which distinguishes the wicked, but whatever men think, according to the apostles' doctrine it is so.

Designating the wicked, men would say, murderers, whore-mongers, fornicators, thieves, frauds, wastrels, and the like. And, indeed, some might have been, but then again others not.

However, irrespective of anything else, what God emphasizes about the wicked is that they were *contentious*. Now, this the rather focusses upon the religious, upon those who justify themselves rather than admit the truth.

Contention against the truth is stressed above all, whether outwardly corrupt or outwardly religious, what classified men as wicked or unjust was, firstly, that they were contentious.

They contended against the word and truth of God, when it convicted *them*. This was the *worst* sin. They despised the truth that inspired the just.

Almost as a matter of course, an attitude of know-all in religion followed. Against promise and prophecy they wrangled, they argued, they debated, they strove. Every revelation of God must submit to them, rather than they to the revelation of God: in their own eyes they knew everything.

Hence they contended, and more especially against the very notion of the righteous judgment of God in the day of wrath.

Again, 'they obeyed not the truth.' Not 'they professed not the truth.' What truth? Whatever truth God had revealed, that had inspired the just. Truth within, truth without; truth from creation, truth from consciousness; truth by revelation, truth from the ministers of God.

Truth about glory, truth concerning honour, truth declaring immortality. They may have known it; they may even have confessed it; but they did not obey it. Contentious persons, who obeyed not the truth, may well have gone so far as to contend for what they did not obey.

They would argue for truths, contend for creeds, stand for schools of thought, for interpretations, traditions, parties. They were not as other men were, they would not just accept matters as did the unlearned and ignorant, or even as this publican.

No, they had a background: some were even intellectuals, academics, and, pray, who can teach them?

Teach them? No, they taught others, they contended, to make others twofold more the children of hell than themselves, they knew everything. Hence, they contended, and justified their contention.

But in that day, God condemns that above all. In the resurrection, at the last judgment, God calls it disobedience to the truth.

Disobedience? Yes, because, for all their contention, what they actually obeyed was 'unrighteousness', Romans 2:8. They contradicted revealed righteousness, whether that righteousness was revealed under the law or promised in the evangel.

But God calls that 'unrighteousness', and now they are going to account for it, for it was the consistent course of their lives, set of their minds, and haughtiness of their hearts.

They laid a crooked line to God's rectitude, and clave to their crookedness, and now the God of truth requires it of them in righteousness. They obeyed unrighteousness; had they owned and obeyed the revelation of God's righteous judgments, they would have fled from the wrath to come, as did the just.

To the contrary, the unrighteous, ignoring the wrath to come, let alone fleeing from it, or seeking a Saviour from it, fled from righteousness instead. And in the day of judgment, at the resurrection of the dead, God will call this 'obeying unrighteousness'.

That is the character, and the whole of the character, brought to light in the wicked in the day of wrath. It is how they will appear: they are contentious, they obey not the truth.

All that they said or did in religion, evangelical or otherwise; or all that they did in drunkenness, whoredoms, or depravity, was subsidiary to the heart of it. Contentiousness and disobedience to the truth is the judgment and the whole of the judgment.

Here is the *full* description of those persons that bring forth such a sentence from the judgment of God in that day, according to the apostolic doctrine of the evangel. But what is the sentence?

The sentence is 'indignation and wrath', and, of course, given the undying nature of the soul, the immortality of the body in the resurrection, and the endlessness of the life to come in eternity, it will be for ever and ever, world without end.

It is a troublous thing that the reader must be distracted from the awful solemnity of the eternal state by having to draw attention – once again: but here, of all places – to the ineptitude of the translators.

However, it is obligatory to enlighten the reader as to the mind of the Spirit in the word of God: 'Words which the Holy Ghost useth.'

First, 'Indignation.' In the Greek this word is θυμός, *thumos*, occurring eighteen times in the new testament, but translated Wrath, fifteen times; Indignation, once; and Fierceness, twice. None of these is accurate. Not even Wrath.

As to the alternative fancies of these clergy, 'Indignation' being their arbitrary choice in Romans 2:8, the single use of such an English word out of the eighteen times *thumos* appears, speaks for itself.

The rule is clear and unambiguous in such a case: one Greek word; one English equivalent. There are no complications at all with the Greek *thumos*.

It is not my intention to get involved with etymology over so momentous a question as the eternal fixed state of the soul, and hence, reducing comments on the family of words concerned to an absolute minimum, I concentrate upon *thumos* itself.

This Greek word is used eight times about God. Seven such occurrences are found in John's writings, one in Paul's. That once is the–so-called–'indignation' of Romans 2:8.

The root of *thumos* is *thuō*, a word used fifteen times, denoting 'to kill' especially in the context of sacrifice. From *thuō* is derived the word 'altar'–the place of slaying and burning the sacrifice– occurring twenty-three times in the Greek.

Likewise 'sacrifice' itself, which appears twenty-nine times. The concept is *to burn*, associated mainly with the burning of the slain sacrifice, although another important branch refers to burning incense.

The question is, How should the word *thumos* be translated?

The word which would satisfy the root and its derivatives would at the same time indicate the smoke ascending from the burning sacrifice, or from that issuing from the burning incense in the censer.

To this corresponds the fury burning with rage within the heart of God or man.

What English word best serves the purpose consistently? 'Wrath' is unsuitable for reasons which shall appear shortly. 'Rage' or 'Fury' imply the *expression* of *thumos*, whereas – whilst that may be implied – the source, the inward passion, the burning *within* is the thing that must be emphasized.

From this – agreeable with the associated derivatives – the word 'Fume' would appear to be most suitable, the more especially as it is derived directly from the Latin *fumus, fumare*, Smoke. The liability of this would be the lack of application to fury breaking out.

Nevertheless, I would favour 'Fume', and, on occasion 'Fuming' as the most suitable all-round English equivalent to translate with uniformity the Greek *thumos*.

In the extreme instance, 'fuming with rage' or 'fury', may be understood as the meaning given that an outburst is intended: but if so, that must not be assumed as necessarily extinguishing the fire that smokes. That may burn for ever.

But to return: Used in all eighteen times, of these *thumos* refers to the fuming or fury of God eight times, seven of which are from the pen of John, all in the Book of the Revelation.

Then, metaphors are employed to describe God's fuming at that which incurs his anger. Whilst noting these passages, for a fuller exposition I refer the reader to my book 'The Revelation of Jesus Christ'.

All who worship 'the beast and his image', receiving his 'mark' in his forehead or in his hand, incur the perpetual fuming of God, and 'shall be tormented with fire and brimstone in the presence of the holy angels, and in the presence of the Lamb: and the smoke of their torment ascendeth up for ever and ever:

'And they have no rest day nor night, who worship the beast and his image, and whosoever receiveth the mark of his name', Revelation 14:9-11.

This is a measure—however figurative—of what Paul calls the fuming of God, Romans 2:8, in the eternal sentence passed in the last judgment upon 'them that are contentious, and do not obey the truth, but obey unrighteousness.'

This is likened to 'the great winepress of God's fury'—or 'fuming'—Revelation 14:19, and, in another figure, the 'seven last plagues' which are filled up with the fuming—or 'fury'—of God.

These are the seven vials poured out by the seven angels from heaven, to engulf the earth below, leading to the conflagration and final dissolution at the resurrection and the last judgment.

This terrifying and cataclysmic symbolism shows the reality of the fuming of God, from the curse at the beginning till the last day at the end. No lesser figures adequately portray God's fury against the earth and its inhabitants, who 'are contentious, and do not obey the truth, but obey unrighteousness', Romans 2:8.

However, 'the fuming of God' is not all. The verse goes on to read 'and wrath'. In context, 'But unto them that are contentious, and do not obey the truth, but obey unrighteousness, *fuming and wrath*' will be rendered by God, without respect of persons, world without end.

But what of the word translated 'wrath'? The Greek reads οϱγή, *orgē*, used thirty-six times in the new testament. Yet – once again – misleading us by the inconsistent translation.

Instead of being uniformly translated by one equivalent word for the benefit of the English reader, the clerical doctors have managed four separate alternatives.

Why, but out of perversity? It is a matter otherwise inconceivable, given that *twice* over only *one* use of a *different* English 'translation' occurs; and on another occasion, yet another alternative *thrice*.

But yet the main translation – thirty-one times – is the perfect English equivalent! Then why mar this by three incongruities, two of them once only, and the last but thrice?

The Greek *orgē* appears in the English as Anger, three times; Indignation, once; Vengeance, once; and Wrath, thirty-one times. 'Wrath' is perfect. Then, 'Wrath' should have been used on all thirty-six occasions. Not infrequently – as in Romans 2:8 – *thumos* and *orgē* are coupled together.

Used of God, it may be recalled that *thumos* occurs eight times, once in Paul's writings, and seven in John's. In the case of *orgē*, referring to the wrath of God, there are twenty-seven such occurrences, fourteen from Paul, seven from John, and six others.

Whereas it may appear that there is a certain overlapping in the meaning of the two words, obviously there must be that which is distinctive in each case.

If the reader follows the rule that *thumos* encompasses the idea of the billowing forth of smoke from the flaming fire of God's fury, whereas *orgē* embraces the settled habit and intent of the abiding and interior burning heat of wrath, this distinction will serve sufficiently to mark the difference.

There is ambiguity with the Lexicons. However Liddell and Scott, whilst leaving room for either definition to serve both Greek words for anger–they *will* do it!–nevertheless use the terms 'propensity' 'disposition' in relation to *orgē*.

In which case 'wrath'–far and away the choice of the translators, regarded as an abiding interior disposition–serves the purpose of providing the best English equivalent.

Wrath is of the Lord. 'When he had looked with anger', Mark 3:5. What filled the Lord with wrath? 'being grieved for the *hardness of their hearts*', which came about as a result of their settled forms of religion and creed, quite petrifying all compassion and mercy in their interior heart.

The Lord loathed this, and loathes it. Where the form quenches the spirit. Having the form of godliness but denying the power thereof. Punctilious observance but heartless coldness. This genders the Lord's wrath.

John the Baptist, though heralding the Lord's coming, yet looks through it to his coming again to judgment, and the *orgē* of God at the last day thunders and flashes through his preaching. 'Who hath warned you to flee from the wrath to come?', Matthew 3:7; Luke 3:7.

Then wrath, *orgē*, sustained for eternity, *is* yet *to come*. And come it will.

The epistle to the Romans, revealing God's salvation through the evangel of Christ, some ten times over warns of the wrath of God, and his coming vengeance in the resurrection, for ever to abide in eternity. Indeed, the epistle reveals the righteousness of faith to the believer, and the wrath of God upon the impenitent.

'The wrath of God is revealed from heaven', Romans 1:18, but what does man, earthy, of the earth, covetous eyes set on the world, see of *that* heavenly vision? It is made manifest in Creation;

it is pronounced in the law; it is revealed in the evangel. Then, man is without excuse.

Creation revealed the eternal power and Godhead of the Creator. Man was formed to worship and glorify the God of heaven and earth. The law taught man to love the Lord his God with all his heart, mind, strength, and understanding. And the evangel enables him to do so.

Then where is the excuse for a wasted life of ungodliness and unrighteousness? nay: for so much as a wasted day?

As the seconds tick on; as the minutes pass; as the hours are chimed; as the days fall; as the years accrue: *every moment is recorded as to what was owed to God, body, soul, and spirit.* This is called 'treasuring up wrath unto thyself against the day of wrath and revelation of the righteous judgment of God', Romans 2:5.

The recompense of vengeance for eternity appears in Romans 2:8, as has been seen: *thumos* and *orgē.* Where 'indignation' billowing forth from God, may be understood as 'fury': fuming against such impenitent, contentious, disobedient, and incorrigible rebels. Where then shall they appear in the day of judgment?

What recompense is due, for what was stolen from God, in life, strength, time, obligation, and continual worship? All was *his*, not *theirs.* But they stole it, as if it were *theirs*, not *his*, as if he did not so much as warrant attention at all.

But now comes the day of recompense: of the revelation of *orgē.*

This is a sustained, abiding anger. It is an inexorable wrath that cannot be changed, upon an immortal state that can never be altered.

The everlasting judgment of God follows upon the sentence of righteousness declared in Romans 2:8. After that sentence this is the judgment: 'tribulation and anguish, upon every soul of man that doeth evil, of the Jew'–or so-called Christian–'first, and also of the Gentile'–or so-called heathen–Romans 2:9.

The judgment of God, according to the law–and, now, according to the gospel–falls for eternity first upon those reckoned of God as evil. This judgment declares that the sentence of justice, after death, and in the resurrection, ushers in a fixed eternal state.

However the apostle here declares in the evangel the unending interior condition–'every *soul* of man'–of those who, irrespective of their religious creed or profession, actually *did* evil in this present life.

It is described first as 'tribulation', *thlipsis*, Romans 2:9. This refers to pressure, as the corn under the millstone, the grapes in the winepress.

Next this everlasting vengeance of punishment is defined as 'anguish', *stenos*, straitness. This indicates constriction, confinement, as when one is immoveably trapped in the narrowness of a dark underground tunnel.

The very same words are used to describe the conditions on earth, and in time, of those who in their pilgrimage sought for glory, and honour, and immortality.

They passed through the strait–*stenos*–gate. They walked in the narrow–*thlipsis*–way.

'But Abraham said, Son, remember that thou in thy lifetime receivedst thy good things, and likewise Lazarus evil things: but now'–in the next, unending life of eternity–'he is comforted, and thou art tormented', Luke 16:25.

Yet the light affliction of the strait gate and narrow way was but for a moment–though that moment was a lifetime on earth–

but they knew that it worked for them a far more exceeding and eternal weight of glory, II Corinthians 4:17.

To the contrary, the pressure and confinement of the impenitent, who shunned the strait gate and narrow way to enjoy the width and breadth of the world, and worldly religion, during this passing lifetime, shall in the life that is to come be magnified exceedingly. It shall last for ever. It is world without end.

This is the judgment of the righteousness of God.

Likewise the judgment of God's righteousness upon the just shall stand for ever. This follows: 'Glory, honour, and peace, to every man that worketh good, to the Jew first, and also to the Gentile: *for there is no respect of persons with God*', Romans 2:10,11.

The sentence having been passed, the everlasting judgment commences in those who by patient continuance in well doing sought for glory and honour and immortality. The glory which they sought is the glory that they are given. They *are* glorified; raised to glory; and they inherit an everlasting glorious possession.

Their God is their glory, and the God of glory appears unto them, and they shall dwell in the house of the LORD for ever, and find in his presence fulness of joy, and at his right hand pleasures for evermore.

This is their glorious portion, and, since it is appointed by the righteous judgment of God, it can never be taken away from them.

Honour is theirs, and weightiness; dignity rests upon them. They are approved of God, they attain the resurrection: thus shall it be done unto the man whom the King delighteth to honour.

Furthermore, the peace which they sought becomes theirs, and peace like a river flows over them. Their enemies have perished, their warfare is accomplished, nothing offends.

'Peace be unto you' said Jesus unto them then; and now it is theirs for evermore. The peace of God, which passeth all understanding, enfolds them in the arms of everlasting love.

In this present life, they had not merely sought, they had striven to enter in the strait gate, and had with much affliction traversed the narrow way. It had been a pilgrimage of great tribulation, the world was at enmity with them whilst it enjoyed its days of glory and honour and peace from the glory of man.

Then, it was 'And he lifted up his eyes on his disciples, and said, Blessed be ye poor: for your's is the kingdom of God. Blessed are ye that hunger now: for ye shall be filled. Blessed are ye that weep now: for ye shall laugh.

'Blessed are ye, when men shall hate you, and when they shall separate you from their company, and shall reproach you, and cast out your name as evil, for the Son of man's sake.

'Rejoice ye in that day, and leap for joy: for, behold, your reward is great in heaven: for in the like manner did their fathers unto the prophets.

'But woe unto you that are rich! for ye have received your consolation. Woe unto you that are full! for ye shall hunger. Woe unto you that laugh now! for ye shall mourn and weep. Woe unto you, when all men shall speak well of you! for so did their fathers to the false prophets.'

Whence you see, even as was prophesied by Jesus in this present world of that which was to come; and during the life that is now, of the life that shall follow after death in eternity: all shall be reversed.

Well? What could be more just? And this is *experimental religion* of which he speaks, not dead, theoretic, repetitive meetings divorced from one's actual way of life and passage of time.

The sentence and judgment of God respect character, and the *life* lived in consequence of that character, as it is written, 'There is no respect of persons with God', Romans 2:11. This is impartial, objective, universal, inexorable, immutable, and eternal.

It is not an enquiry into the *means* by which the just were brought to that life and walk; or the *way* by which they attained to that character and behaviour, but into the *result*, into *the character itself*. Here there is no excuse; no appeal; no difference.

There is *no* respect of persons. It is but a question of strict, impartial justice: 'That thou mightest be justified when thou speakest, and be clear when thou judgest.'

If God were to condemn one for what was winked at and condoned in another, 'How shall God judge the world?' 'Shall not the Judge of all the earth do right?'

Then, 'there is *no* respect of persons with God.' It is the *actual life and character* that is judged universally, according to the *nature* of that life and character. Nothing else. That is the doctrine of the evangel on the wrath to come, Romans 2:6-11.

None, not even the most contentious, could question God's judgment upon the righteous, or raise the faintest doubt about its fairness. It is so impartial and just, relative to his judgment upon the evil: all can see that. They were righteous, just as these were evil.

And so the judgment falls: 'Who will render to *every* man according *to his deeds*', Romans 2:6. 'For there is *no* respect of persons with God', Romans 2:11. And if it were not so, where were the righteousness of God under the law, and from the Creation?

Or what else does the apostle mean by this holy doctrine of the evangel, Romans 1:18 to 3:20?

There is, and there can be, no other meaning than that which is enforced in this apostolic doctrine inspired for eternity by the Holy Ghost below; delivered for ever by the Son from glory on high; and endorsed to everlasting by the Father in heaven above. World without end. Amen.

In many places and consistently throughout every phase of his ministry on earth the Son of man, Jesus, spoke directly or obliquely of the resurrection, the judgment, and the wrath to come.

For example 'hell', and again, 'hell', once more 'hell fire' in the so-called 'Sermon on the Mount', the danger being the greatest where the religion waxed the warmest.

Once more, 'As therefore the tares'—but they *looked* like wheat—'are gathered and burned in the fire; so shall it be in the end of this world.

'The Son of man shall send forth his angels, and they shall gather out of his kingdom'—so they *appeared* in it—'all things that offend, and them which *do* iniquity; and shall cast them into a furnace of fire'—*after* which; *eternally* after which—'there shall be wailing and gnashing of teeth.'

Likewise the words, form, feelings of religion, and moving of the affections are not enough. One such *entered as guest into the very wedding feast*. But his appearance was inappropriate.

'Bind him hand and foot', said the king, 'and cast him into outer darkness; there shall be weeping and gnashing of teeth.' After the casting. For ever. This is the wrath to come.

Jesus affirmed in prophecy, 'When'—not *if*; when—'they shall rise from the dead.'

And what of those, quite convinced that they were Christ's, who called him 'Lord', yet were so astonished, crying 'Lord, when saw we thee an hungred, or athirst, or a stranger, or naked, or sick, or in prison, and did not minister unto thee?'

When? When this was the impoverishment of the few elect, whom they hated, as opposed to the whole world, which they loved. But the King ruled in the kingdom *within his brethren*, not in the world.

Hence 'Inasmuch as ye have done it unto one of the least of these *my brethren*'—and none other—'ye have done it *unto me*.' But they never did anything to the elect, these worldly religious universal lovers, except despise, reject, and persecute them.

Then what shall be the judgment upon these so-religious worldlings, in the resurrection from the dead? This is the sentence:

'Depart from me, ye cursed, into everlasting fire, prepared for the devil and his angels.' And this is the judgment: 'And these shall go away into everlasting punishment: but the righteous into life eternal.'

Thus the Saviour declares of the righteous—*in character*, who by patient continuance in well doing sought for glory, and honour, and immortality—that these '*shall be accounted worthy* to obtain that world', namely, the world to come.

Wherefore the apostle Paul, with such utter guileless zeal, at all costs, cries, 'If by any means I might attain unto the resurrection of the dead'. That is, of the righteous.

And what of the man who was rich in this world? for where his treasure was, or riches were, there was his heart also. But he died and was buried. Then whose shall those things be? As to him, 'in hell he lifted up his eyes, being in torments.' But he lifted them up too late.

He cried for one to dip his finger in water, and cool his tongue; 'for I am tormented in this flame'. But none came, nor could come, no, not over the 'great gulf fixed' which can never be crossed in time or for eternity.

But 'if only.' No 'if only.' The scriptures were available in this life. He took no hold on them, nor they on him. Then, knowingly, he sinned away his soul past redemption.

This is called 'the wrath to come'.

But for those, the righteous, there is a deliverance from the wrath to come. This is salvation. 'Jesus saith unto her, Thy brother shall rise again. Martha saith unto him, I know that he shall rise again in the resurrection at the last day.

'Jesus said unto her, I am the resurrection, and the life: he that believeth in me, though he were dead, yet shall he live: and whosoever liveth and believeth in me shall never die.

'Believest thou this? She saith unto him, Yea, Lord: I believe that thou art the Christ, the Son of God, which should come into the world.' This is the resurrection of life.

'For the hour is coming, in the which all that are in the graves shall hear his voice, and shall come forth; they that have done good, unto the resurrection of life; and they that have done evil, unto the resurrection of damnation.'

The latter brings down the wrath to come for ever, as Jesus said in another place, 'This is the condemnation, that light is come into the world, and men loved darkness rather than light, because their deeds were evil.

'For every one that doeth evil hateth the light, neither cometh to the light, lest his deeds should be reproved. But he that doeth truth cometh to the light, that his deeds may be made manifest, that they are wrought in God.'

This determines in which resurrection – whether that of life, or of damnation – men shall rise, hear the sentence, and receive their everlasting judgment accordingly.

As to those who hated the light, they are in the resurrection of the damned, and 'the wrath of God abideth' – everlastingly – 'on them'. This is called 'the wrath to come'. It abides perpetually. It is fixed for eternity: '*abideth* on them.'

Let none think that a professed 'conversion', or the so-called 'eternal security of the believer' as these self-deceivers invent the term, much less some fictitious 'committal' *will avoid or escape this everlasting truth, on which hangs the veracity of God's word and the impartiality of his judgment.*

'Let no man' – idolized evangelical speaker or not: *no man* – 'let no man deceive you with vain words: for because of these things cometh the wrath of God upon the children of disobedience' – *whatever* they profess, Ephesians 5:6.

But because of what things cometh this wrath, irrespective of who commits them? These things: 'fornication, and all uncleanness, or covetousness, let it not be once named among you, as becometh saints; neither filthiness, nor foolish talking, nor jesting, which are not convenient: but rather giving of thanks.'

'For this ye know' – but *do* you know, in practice, you evangelicals, as you call yourselves: *do you know?* – 'that no whoremonger, nor unclean person, nor covetous man, who is an idolater, hath any inheritance in the kingdom of Christ and of God', Ephesians 5:3-5.

'For we must *all* appear before the judgment seat of Christ.' And let no vain deceiver try to wriggle out of *that*, what with gross errors about the translation and meaning of '*Bēma*'. The '*bēma*' or 'judgment seat' was that tribunal at which Pilate condemned Christ to death.

Besides which the quotation from Isaiah puts it beyond question that it is the last judgment to which Paul alludes.

'That *every one* may receive the things *done* in his body, according to that he hath *done*, whether it be good or bad. Knowing therefore the terror of the Lord, we persuade men.'

Men? Which men? Well, for example, the saints at Ephesus, whom Paul addressed, and all others, unto this day, who are not contentious, but obey the truth, II Corinthians 5:10,11; Romans 2:8.

This is confirmed in experience – if confirmation were necessary–of old time, when God took himself to oath, swearing by himself in the matter, since he could swear by no greater, testifying of the fathers, 'They do alway err *in heart*; and they have *not known my ways*.

'So I sware in my wrath, They shall not enter into my rest', Hebrews 3:10,11.

But God's rest, though inwardly in heart now, is in glory for ever. If God sware that they should not enter into the *figure* of that rest then, how much more shall the oath stand concerning exclusion from God's rest for ever in the wrath to come?

If so – knowing that *to the saints* the same *terror of the Lord* is signified, as it was to Israel then– the writer applies the warning to us, saying, 'Take heed, brethren'–brethren; mark it, *Brethren*– 'lest there be in any of *you* an evil heart of unbelief, in departing from the living God', Hebrews 3:12.

Where *life* is the issue, the certain death of which is an *inward* 'evil heart of unbelief'–for all the outward show–the inevitable consequence of such hypocrisy being dead brethren without a hope.

Wherefore the apostle strips brethren of all outward forms, such as baptism and 'breaking bread'—as they call it—addressing the spiritual heart, when speaking of them, as of the fathers.

They 'did all eat the same spiritual meat; and did all drink the same spiritual drink: for they drank of that spiritual Rock that followed them: *and that Rock was Christ.*

'But with many of them God was not well pleased: for they were overthrown in the wilderness'—by wrath then sworn, and for ever assured by an immutable oath—Why? Because of the nature and character of their life, heart, works, and capacity for self-deception in religion, I Corinthians 10:1-10.

'Now all these things happened unto them for ensamples: and they are written for *our* admonition, upon whom the ends of the world are come. Wherefore let him that thinketh he standeth take heed lest he fall', I Corinthians 10:11,12.

Ensamples? Examples? Fall? Fall into what? Elementary, my dear brethren: *the curse now, and the wrath to come thereafter.*

'For we know him'—who *do* know him, and delude not ourselves with an imaginary idol, made up in our minds and by our wishes, which blasphemously we call *Jesus*—'that hath said, Vengeance belongeth unto me, I will recompense, saith the Lord.

'And again, The Lord shall judge *his people*. It is a fearful thing to fall into the hands of the living God', Hebrews 10:30,31.

Why fearful for his people? Because they have fallen under the judgment of the *living* God. And he lives for ever. Then, his judgment is for evermore. If so, it is the curse now, and the wrath to come for ever.

Unbelief and hardness of heart were the cause. Deadness was the effect. It needed no more than that to gender his wrath.

Save they kept up the form and the letter after they had lost faith, heart, and life, and their pretence but adding to the wrath.

Examples to the brethren. No more. No less. No others. Receive and obey, and righteousness is obeyed. Deny it and contend, and unrighteousness is committed. Never mind the outward form and letter. When will you people who profess the Christian religion WAKE UP?

'Wherefore he saith, Awake thou that sleepest, and arise from the dead, and Christ shall give thee light', Ephesians 5:14.

Flee from the wrath to come! For it is almost upon us. And to those who flee, suffering ridicule and persecution, the apostle says, 'And to you who are troubled rest with us, when the Lord Jesus shall be revealed from heaven with his mighty angels.

'In flaming fire taking vengeance on them that know not God, and that obey not'– *obey* not–'the gospel of our Lord Jesus Christ: who shall be punished with everlasting destruction'–the *destruction* never ends: it is not *annihilation*–'from the presence of the Lord, and from the glory of his power', II Thessalonians 1:7-9.

'The wrath of God is revealed from heaven against all ungodliness and unrighteousness of men', but never more finally than at the last judgment, depicted in figure and metaphor seven times over in the Book of Revelation.

But if in figure, figurative of reality. If in metaphor, metaphorical of the actuality. If in shadow, then of the substance.

'And, lo, there was a great earthquake; and the sun became black as sackcloth of hair, and the moon became as blood; and the stars of heaven fell unto the earth, even as a fig tree casteth her untimely figs, when she is shaken of a mighty wind.

'And the heaven departed as a scroll when it is rolled together; and every mountain and island were moved out of their places.

'And the kings of the earth, and the great men, and the rich men, and the chief captains, and the mighty men, and every bondman, and every free man, hid themselves in the dens and in the rocks of the mountains; and said to the mountains and rocks, Fall on us, and hide us from the face of him that sitteth on the throne, and from the wrath of the Lamb:

'For the great day of his wrath is come; and who shall be able to stand?', Revelation 6:12-17. Now, this is the day on which falls the wrath to come, and, once come, abides for ever. And, observe, it is the wrath *of the Lamb*.

Again: 'If any man worship the beast and his image, and receive his mark in his forehead, or in his hand, the same shall drink of the wine of the wrath of God, which is poured out without mixture into the cup of his indignation;

'And he shall be tormented with fire and brimstone in the presence of the holy angels, *and in the presence of the Lamb*:

'And the smoke of their torment ascendeth up for ever and ever: and they have no rest day nor night, who worship the beast and his image, and whosoever receiveth the mark of his name', Revelation 14:9-11. This is called, The wrath to come.

Escape it? The next verse shows who shall escape it: 'Here is the patience of *the saints*'–the holy ones: for without holiness no man shall see the Lord–'here are they that keep the commandments of God, and the faith of Jesus.

'And I heard a voice from heaven saying unto me, Write, Blessed are the dead which die in the Lord from henceforth: Yea, saith the Spirit, that they may rest from their labours; and their works do follow them.'

Did you read that? and observe it? 'their works do follow them', Revelation 14:12,13. These are the blessed dead that die in the Lord. They are saved from the wrath to come.

The wrath to come? When? After the resurrection. Where? At the last judgment. For how long? For ever and ever.

'And I saw the dead, small and great, stand before God; and the books were opened: and another book was opened, which is the book of life: and the dead were judged out of those things which were written in the books, according to their works.

'And the sea gave up the dead which were in it; and death and hell delivered up the dead which were in them: and they were judged every man according to their works.

'And death and hell were cast into the lake of fire. This is the second death. And whosoever was not found written in the book of life was cast into the lake of fire', Revelation 20:12-15.

This passage depicts the general resurrection of the dead, precisely as did that of the parable of the sheep and the goats. Just and unjust, righteous and wicked, from the beginning of time to the end of it, all stand before God in the searing purity of the radiance of that great white throne.

All, but all humanity, first and last, stand in the risen body at one and the same time. Premillennialists, Futurists, and Dispensationalists crown the destructive nature of their heresy by denying this transparent truth, so vital to sanctification of the Spirit and belief of the truth.

But their heresy is confounded by the word of the Lord: if all the dead are judged at once in one resurrection from the same opened books, the book of life being opened at one and the same time, How can their erroneous scheme set all sorts of 'resurrections' apart the one from the other by uncounted ages?

What kind of heresy is this, and what sort of beguiled blind follow these blind leaders of the blind, all to end up in the ditch?

The names of the saints, of the righteous, of those dwelling in that eternal life which was with the Father and with his Son, Jesus Christ, which was manifested unto the apostles, in which was their fellowship, all these, I say—every last one by name—shall be found written in the book of life.

But this book is opened at the same time as the other books out of which the goats, the wicked, the unjust, the contentious, those who disobey the truth, who obey unrighteousness, besides every hypocrite in Zion, are judged simultaneously.

'And the books were opened: and another book was opened, which is the book of life: and the dead were judged out of those things which were written in the books, according to their works', Revelation 20:12.

Here observe two paramount truths. First, that the resurrection of the dead is general, and that *all* dead bodies are raised together. Second, that all the dead are judged by one standard, 'according to their works', Revelation 20:12.

And lest there be any doubt about it, this is repeated, 'according to their works', Revelation 20:13.

This is indisputable. To dispute it is to contend against the truth: to disobey the truth. Here is infallible testimony that cannot be denied. To deny it is to obey unrighteousness.

Finally; although all the dead are judged out of the books, a distinction is made between the book of life and the rest of the books. But this distinction makes no difference to the overriding standard of judgment, no matter which book or books.

The dead are judged, and all the dead are judged 'according to their works'. How is this?

This was made clear from the word of the truth of the evangel at the beginning, when God made known the immutable truth:

'Who will render to every man according to his deeds: to them who by patient continuance in well doing seek for glory and honour and immortality, eternal life:

'But unto them that are contentious, and do not obey the truth, but obey unrighteousness, indignation and wrath,

'Tribulation and anguish, upon every soul of man that doeth evil, of the Jew first, and also of the Gentile; but glory, honour, and peace, to every man that worketh good, to the Jew first, and also to the Gentile:

'For there is no respect of persons with God', Romans 2:6-11.

Now, this is being judged according to works with a witness, Revelation 20:12, and again, 13, and this twofold witness is universal, impartial, immutable, irrevocable, and everlasting. It is written in the books that are opened in that day.

Then what of the book of life? The case is precisely the same as with the other books that were opened: 'the dead were judged out of those things which were written in the books'–that is, all the books before mentioned including the book of life – 'according to their works.'

What was in these books? The record of the past lives of all the dead, whilst yet they were upon the earth. If such a written record had not been kept, how then could the dead be judged out of the books according to their works? But they are judged out of the books 'according to their works'.

That being so, I will be asked, How is the life of those written in the book of life recorded? The life of all those who are named in this book has the like testimony: 'by patient continuance in well doing' these all sought for 'glory and honour and immortality.'

That is the invariable and inevitable effect of life from God, for 'the just shall *live* by faith'. Given that life of faith–for to 'seek for glory and honour and immortality' must demand faith, and at that, of a better resurrection, in the world to come after the judgment – such living consequences must follow.

This is the issue of life. Hence it is called 'the book of life'. All the quickened are written therein, all their works do follow them, and all the living agree in this: they condemn the world, and become heirs of the righteousness which is by faith. The just therefore literally *stand out* at the last judgment.

Someone will say, But are we not justified by faith? And is that belief not in the imputed righteousness of God by faith of Jesus Christ? Yes; but why say it? It is made abundantly clear in all our doctrine.

For however we are justified *before God*, John assures us that we are judged according to our works *impartially before men*. 'As it is written, That thou mightest be justified in thy sayings, and mightest overcome when thou art judged.' How? By strict impartiality, and incontrovertible fairness.

As James insists, saying, 'Faith, if it hath not works, is dead, being alone. Yea, a man may say, Thou hast faith, and I have works: show me thy faith without thy works, and I will show thee my faith by my works.

'Thou believest that there is one God; thou doest well: the devils also believe, and tremble'–which is more than thou dost–'But wilt thou know, O vain man, that faith without works is dead?', James 2:17-20.

If thou sayest, I am justified by faith, then show me your justification by your life, for it is the book of *life*, not the book of *justification*. Then, the *life* of the just–for the just shall live by faith–is the evangelical criterion now, as it is the standard of judgment in that day: 'according to their works.'

If so, now, as then, you will bring forth the record of your patient continuance in well doing, as, having been justified, that righteousness of faith brings forth life, as it must, in the which it follows of necessity you seek all the days of your life henceforth, for glory and honour and immortality.

But know this for certain: the greater multitude that profess justification by faith – even if they get so far as to use the only sound apostolic term – have no life, but only emotional pretence, excitement, or the mere form of words.

They never continue patiently in the good works described, they are void of them, and, moreover, enamoured of this world, the things that can be seen, the praise of man, and worldliness, they never once sought for glory and honour and immortality. Religion to them stands in word only: not power.

Nevertheless, whatever their false hopes, in the day of judgment the works of their lives shall be judged by the same criteria as all others: not by their confession, excitement, pretence, profession, creed, or committal, but 'every man according to his works'.

This is equally true of those who were of God justified by faith only, and, receiving life because of righteousness, brought forth the living fruits thereof, in sanctification of the Spirit and belief of the truth.

These stand out in that day, they are distinct from all mankind, and agree in their lives with what is written in the Lamb's book of *life*.

Nothing in time or eternity, this world or the next, makes the least iota of difference, nor can anything change by one jot or tittle, the immutability of the word, counsel, will, covenant, oath, purpose, and judgment of God written in his holy word: 'judged *according to their works*', Revelation 20:12,13.

What astounding visions had broken upon the wondering eyes of the Seer! He had viewed the metaphoric vision of Satan being bound; of the souls of the saints reigning; the abyss being opened; and of Satan ascending.

His visions opened the figurative enormity of the last great battle against the besieged but united remnant that was left; of fire falling from heaven.

Then appeared the dread lake of fire and brimstone; of its fearsome fumes, its erupting turbulence, its livid and searing effluent closing over the mystic form of the dragon, called the Devil, and Satan, for ever to sink and be tormented in its depths.

And now before his eyes the very heavens themselves melt with fervent heat; the earth dissolves; the universe passes away with a great noise.

In sheets of fire the astounding scene, from zenith to nadir, stands poised in a stupendous impression of the molten elements in their entirety dissolving in the fervent heat of the vanishing old heavens and old earth.

Even as John—trembling with awe—beholds clearer and clearer the flaming cosmos resolve itself in an incandescent effulgence, so the vision forms of a great—so vast, so titanic—white—so dazzling, so pure—throne—so sovereign, so majestic.

And now the dead, from the first man at the dawn of time to the last man at the end of the world, all generations; all mankind; high and low; rich and poor; young and old; male and female; alike are raised in the body to throng a boundless infinity before that immeasurable throne.

The books are opened. The book of life is opened.

The secrets of the heart; the seconds of a lifetime; every inward thought; all inmost desires; each hidden imagination;

the deepest intentions; the outward actions; from the entire lifetime: all, all are intoned one by one from the books opened before all humanity.

Yet so solemnly declared to each one as if none other were present, the voice of God pronouncing the everlasting sentence again and again.

As John beheld, astounded beyond all measure, the dead were judged in the unbearable light of that radiant throne, out of those things which were written in the books, according to their works.

So limitless a concourse, nevertheless, judged every man according to his works.

And death and hell were cast into the lake of fire. John saw it. And what he saw must, but must, come to pass in reality. And whosoever was not found written in the book of life was cast into the lake of fire.

XIII
'Sheol'; 'Hadēs'; 'Gehenna'

IT is evident that man was created to worship and live for God in this present life and world, as opposed to living for himself in selfishness and worldliness.

Such worship in its nature demands all the heart, and life, and strength, and understanding, and that continually.

It follows that *not* to do so, *but* to do the opposite, of necessity breaches obligation, abnegates responsibility, demands punishment, and brings down vengeance.

Did man suppose that rebellion had no consequences? The difference is this: rebellion is during this life, and in this world, which has an end. But vengeance and punishment is throughout the life to come, and is in eternity.

Wherefore since man is immortal, and God from everlasting to everlasting, obligation *must* be absolute. Then it follows that the judgment is and must be commensurate.

This awaits the sentence at the day of judgment: but death does not. Then, what lies between death, and the resurrection in the last day?

As to the body, it rots and decays, either in the grave, or where it falls, or else it is destroyed. As to the immortal, undying, ever conscious soul, it descends to what is called in the Hebrew *Sheol*, and in the Greek *Hadēs*.

The English word 'Hell' might have been allowable – but not in my judgment – as a kind of 'translation' of either Hebrew or Greek, were it not for the confusion sown by the translators, especially over another Greek word not yet mentioned.

'Hell is derived through the Old English *hel* from the Old Teutonic *halja*, 'the coverer up or hider', from *hel-, hal-, hul-,* 'to hide', *hele*. The abode of the dead, or (covered; hidden) place of departed spirits: *hadēs*.' Quote, Oxford English Dictionary.

XIV
The Meaning of the Words

THE Hebrew *Sheol* occurs sixty-five times in the old testament, being translated Grave on thirty-one occasions – meaning 'the unseen state' – and Hell thirty-one times; still referring to 'the underworld', Pit has been selected by the translators thrice. But why not one word for all sixty-five references?

Although 'grave' or 'pit' has a certain bearing, it is only because it was regarded as the way down for *the soul*, which, having departed from the body, went down into the hidden 'underworld'.

This is called '*Sheol*'. Thence went the departed souls of all, irrespective of state, throughout the old testament.

The Greek ἅδης, *hadēs*, gives the precise equivalent in that language to the Hebrew *sheol*, and 'the underworld' is as correct a translation as any for both tongues. Without doubt this conveys the *idea* better than any other English word.

'*Hadēs*' has been translated 'grave' once, and 'hell' ten times. Given the circumstances of a further Greek word – yet to be mentioned – besides the totally unnecessary English alternatives to the single Greek or Hebrew, the universal use of 'underworld' would have given a helpfully balanced understanding.

The fact to grasp at this point is that whether *Sheol* or *Hadēs*, both refer to the place of departed souls immediately after death.

With the resurrection and ascension of Christ, who abolished death at the cross *for his own*, a new situation exists for those who die *in the Lord* thereafter. Likewise for the old testament saints.

Impenitent souls still descend into *Hadēs* even though the souls of those who die in Christ go to be with him in glory, together with all the old testament saints delivered when Christ died, descended, rose, and ascended.

Nevertheless this *still* refers to states *up to* the day of judgment and the resurrection of the dead.

Thereafter, another situation altogether comes into existence, to be explained shortly. But first, to clear the ambiguity created by the translators' indiscriminate use of the word 'hell' for *hadēs*, it is necessary to give the passages in order, so that the reader may clearly discriminate.

I suggest that the tract 'The Mystery of Godliness' may be consulted with profit.

The first two references to *hadēs* are parallel in the gospels, in which Jesus affirms that Capernaum—for its blind impenitence—shall be thrust down into *hadēs*, Matthew 11:23; Luke 10:15. The gates of *hadēs* shall not prevail against Christ's *ecclesia*, Matthew 16:18.

Peter quotes the psalmist twice over to affirm that the soul of Jesus would not be left in *hadēs*, Acts 2:27,31.

The parable of the rich man and Lazarus shows that *hadēs* is not, and was not, undivided. The heirs of promise, whose affliction was in this life, were carried by angels into Abraham's bosom. But across a fixed and infinite gulf, those whose portion was in this life were—and are—tormented already in a fearful flame.

The Lord asserts that *he* has the keys of death and of *hadēs*, and, opening the seal, shows that Death was followed by *hadēs*. At the last, death and *hadēs* delivered up their dead – from the first day to the last – and death and *hadēs* were cast into the lake of fire, Revelation 1:18; 6:8; 20:13,14.

The other passage is a misleading blunder on the part of the translators: It should be, 'O *hadēs* where is thy victory?', I Corinthians 15:55.

However, this completes the identification of the eleven passages in the Greek New Testament which mention *hadēs*, which the translators have rendered 'grave', once; and 'hell', ten times.

All these references, together with those of the Hebrew *Sheol*, refer to the underworld, and anticipate the remainder of time till the last judgment and the resurrection of the dead. That is, the reuniting of the soul with the risen body at the last judgment, to begin the fixed everlasting state.

In and over all this condition – triumphantly exalted after Christ ascended up on high – the Saviour separates and saves his people with the salvation of God, even from the jaws of death, as may be seen from the case of Lazarus, and the words, 'O death, where is thy sting? O *hadēs*, where is thy victory?'

'Death is swallowed up in victory.' Thanks be to God, which giveth us the victory through our Lord Jesus Christ, with whom the souls of departed saints, now in glory, await that coming day.

The Greek word, however, which the average English speaking person misunderstands by 'Hell' – as opposed to *Sheol* and *Hadēs*, the *present* condition of departed spirits – *refers to a future everlasting condition*. It is γέεννα, *Gehenna*.

This – because it pertains to eternity, after the resurrection and the last judgment, and is unending – is another matter altogether.

Then over so solemn a matter it is really dreadful that the translators confound it with *Sheol* and *Hadēs*, deceiving the English reader. It is nothing to do with *Sheol* and *Hadēs*. Why call *Gehenna*, 'Hell', as if it were the same as *Sheol* or *Hadēs*—at their whim, randomly—as if it were some trifle of no consequence?

This has led to utter confusion among the English speaking peoples. For, practically, 'Hell' has come to be understood as '*Gehenna*' in common parlance, as if *Sheol* and *Hadēs* had neither existence nor meaning.

The Greek '*Gehenna*' has profound and complicated Hebrew roots which, given so awesome, solemn, and fearful a subject, I do not propose to enter into, lest semantics distract the senses. I will give conclusions only.

Had these 'scholars' but once been inspired to look into that fearsome and everlasting inferno, they would have laid their hands upon their mouths, trembling and aghast, putting down their pens in stunned fearfulness.

Whether or not the word in the Hebrew refers to the valley of Hinnom, what happened there, to what or whom Hinnom refers, whether there was an ever-burning fire, to what use it was put, is all academic speculation—if not sheer guesswork—to the point of folly.

Gehenna occurs twelve times in the new testament. Of these occurrences nine have been translated 'hell'; and three, 'hell fire'.

'Hell' is not correct, etymologically belonging rather to *Sheol* and *Hadēs*, if it belongs at all. Probably the best thing to have done with the Greek word *Gehenna* would have been to have transliterated it as such into the English: it is far too solemn a matter for these 'translators' and their lexicographers.

As it stands, though referring to the wrath *to come*, in flaming and everlasting fire, from English usage the word 'Hell'—or, better Hell-fire – is that which is commonly misunderstood for the Greek *Gehenna*.

Inaccurate: but regrettably a *fait accompli*. For *Sheol* and *Hadēs* – which *do* bear some etymological relationship – are barely understood at all, much less as the English misconception of 'Hell'.

All references to *Gehenna* except one fall from the lips of the Lord Jesus himself. These occur in Matthew, seven times; Mark, thrice; and in Luke, once. The last reference, the only one other than from Jesus, is to be found in James.

One may remark on the absence of passages in John. However, if the word 'fire' be included when obviously referring to 'Hell-fire', John has the most graphic and horrifying passages of all. References to fire without the addition *Gehenna*, when describing eternal punishment, must not be excluded.

Nothing *less* can describe or depict the everlasting wrath to come, after the resurrection, following the judgment, and in executing the sentence of the Eternal upon the immortal.

The twelve passages in which *Gehenna* appears now follow, but I have given a literal translation – as well as the transliteration of *Gehenna* – of the Greek.

'But whoever shall say, Fool, shall be liable to the Gehenna of fire', Matthew 5:22. 'It is profitable for thee that one of thy members should perish, and not that thy body' – mark that: *body*. If so, then, risen – 'be cast into Gehenna', Matthew 5:29.

This last is virtually repeated in the next verse: 'It is profitable for thee that one of thy members should perish, and not thy whole body be cast into Gehenna', Matthew 5:30. 'But ye should rather fear him' – as opposed to man – 'who is able to destroy both soul and body in Gehenna', Matthew 10:28.

'It is good for thee one-eyed to enter into life, than having two eyes to be cast into the Gehenna of fire', Matthew 18:9.

'Woe unto you, scribes and Pharisees, hypocrites, for ye compass the sea and the dry to make one proselyte, and when he has become one, ye make him a son of the Gehenna twofold more than yourselves', Matthew 23:15.

'Serpents, offspring of vipers, how shall you escape from the judgment of Gehenna?', Matthew 23:33.

'It is good for thee to enter into life maimed, rather than having the two hands to go away into the Gehenna, into the fire the unquenchable, where their worm dies not, and the fire is not quenched', Mark 9:43,44.

'It is good for thee to enter into life lame, than having the two feet to be cast into the Gehenna, into the fire unquench-able, where their worm dies not, and the fire is not quenched', Mark 9:45,46.

'It is good for thee with one eye to enter into the kingdom of God, than having two eyes to be cast into the Gehenna of fire, where their worm dies not, and the fire is not quenched', Mark 9:47,48.

'But I will show you whom ye should fear: Fear him who after having killed, has authority to cast into the Gehenna'—if so, to raise the once-killed, in the resurrection at the last judgment—'Yea, I say unto you, fear him', Luke 12:5.

'Thus the tongue is set in our members, defiler of the whole body, and setting on fire the course of nature, and being set on fire by Gehenna', James 3:6.

This completes the twelve passages in the new testament where the Greek '*Gehenna*'—or hell (fire)—occurs. Also the section itself includes every reference, however wrongly translated, from *Sheol* and *Hadēs*, where the English 'Hell' occurs.

This should clear the matter for the understanding of the reader.

But it is well to recall that many further references to 'fire'– without the word '*Gehenna*', much less *Hadēs*–without doubt warn of the unquenchable fire of vengeance awaiting the unrighteous, religious or not.

This is what men think of as 'hell': the wrath to come.

XV
Figures of the True

First, The unquenchable fire

'BEHOLD, the name of the LORD cometh from far, burning with his anger, and the burden thereof is heavy: his lips are full of indignation, and his tongue as a devouring fire:

'And his breath, as an overflowing stream, shall reach to the midst of the neck, to sift the nations with the sieve of vanity: and there shall be a bridle in the jaws of the people, causing them to err.'

'For Tophet is ordained of old; yea, for the king it is prepared; he hath made it deep and large: the pile thereof is fire and much wood; the breath of the LORD, like a stream of brimstone, doth kindle it', Isaiah 30:27,28,33.

These passages, full of prophetic imagery, nevertheless peer forward through the mists of time, the obscurity of the future, into eternity to come. Though graphic and figurative, they draw their character from the nature of God, and cannot fail of fulfilment in the day of judgment.

It is not necessary to give the meaning or immediate application of Tophet, which is obviously spiritualized by the prophet. Thus it is at least part of *Gehenna*.

Not now Tophet in the valley of Hinnom for those at that time; here is a much larger spiritual Tophet prepared for the world ruler and the nations. Then, not just a location at Ge-Hinnom, but *Gehenna* itself.

It is ordained and prepared of old. Through eternity for eternity because of sin and death, it is no new thing. It follows from the nature of God, the nature of the transgression, and the incorrigibility of man. It stands in the righteous, judicious, sin-hating character of God – it is immutable as is the divine being.

'He hath made it deep and large.' Not just Jerusalem then – not just Judah and Israel in their sin at that time – the prophetic vision soars into eternity to embrace the godless nations under the world ruler: to take in all flesh. O, it is deep, it is large enough, and so it was ordained of old.

'The pile thereof is fire and much wood.' It would burn till all the wicked of Jerusalem, Judah, and Israel were consumed. The wood was sufficient for so great a fire. But this is the mere figure of that which answers to what the prophet envisaged and foresaw, because it embraces the unquenchable fire.

Unforgiven sin will never cease. Incorrigible sinners can never be other than they are: their nature after death is as unchangeable as it was before death. Their immortality is as certain as their resurrection. Then for so long the fire must burn. For eternity.

'The breath of the LORD, like a stream of brimstone, doth kindle it.' As they are incorrigible, unchangeable, immortal, so he is immutable, immovable, eternal. Then, his wrath being kindled, his breath is unchangeable, as a stream of brimstone. It can never, never change.

It is in his inward eternal nature – from within himself – his breath, his very life. This, this of the eternal God faced with immortal man full of unalterable sin – this kindles 'hell' – for ever and ever.

His attributes are its unquenchable fire; his nature its everlasting wrath; his breath its ever-constant brimstone.

'And they shall go forth, and look upon the carcases of the men that have transgressed against me: for their worm shall not die, neither shall their fire be quenched; and they shall be an abhorring unto all flesh', Isaiah 66:24.

Jesus implicitly believed and took the spiritual and everlasting reality of these passages from the prophet Isaiah, using the very words and expressions to describe the *Gehenna* which he saw and knew was to come.

The wrath was to come. And seeing it, he gave himself to save men from what to them passed all imagination and comprehension in its torment and continuity.

But not to him: he endured its equivalent to save us from its inexorable inevitability.

From the fulfilment of such prophetic passages as Isaiah Jesus speaks, saying of those who offend in this life that his holy angels 'shall cast them into a furnace of fire: there shall be wailing and gnashing of teeth'.

If so, from the resurrection body of immortality in the unquenchable fire of eternity.

Hence he says 'So shall it be at the end of the world: the angels shall come forth, and sever the wicked from among the just, and shall cast them into the furnace of fire: there shall be wailing and gnashing of teeth.

'Jesus saith unto them, Have ye understood all these things? They say unto him, Yea, Lord.' And well it is for all to cease from contention, believe, understand, and flee to the Saviour from the wrath to come.

For the godless are as chaff: 'He will gather the wheat into his garner; but the chaff he will burn with fire unquenchable', Matthew 3:12; Luke 3:17.

Likewise all hypocrites–no matter how 'evangelical'–in the resurrection they shall appear in their character as goats, not sheep. And the King shall say, 'Depart from me, ye cursed, into everlasting fire, prepared for the 'devil' and his angels.'

They thought that they cast out 'devils', but the King cast them out with the 'devil'. See Matthew 25:41,46.

They said 'Lord, Lord', but the King said, 'Depart from me; I never knew you.' 'And these shall go away into everlasting punishment: but the righteous into life eternal.'

The everlasting fire was prepared not for man, but for the 'devil' and his angels. But no man can serve two masters. Neither can a sheep be a goat, or a goat a sheep: but all mankind, the whole of humanity, must be one or the other.

Goats are full of universal charity, but they know not God, neither discern nor do righteousness. They obey unrighteousness. 'The Lord Jesus shall be revealed from heaven in flaming fire taking vengeance on them that know not God, and obey not the gospel of our Lord Jesus Christ', II Thessalonians 1:7,8.

What will astound all Christendom, astonish all 'evangelicals', shock all universalists, and terrify all the double-minded among the people, is the actual discovery in that day that 'our God *is* a consuming fire', Hebrews 12:29. This is the revelation of Christ, who is the image of the invisible God.

They never expected him to be like that. But he is the brightness of his glory, the express image of his person. He dwells even now in unapproachable light. And he *is* a consuming fire. This is the wrath to come, and it comes at his coming.

Consuming fire against Satan, against all who are contentious and do not obey the truth, but obey unrighteousness. Consuming fire against all who hold the truth in unrighteousness.

Consuming fire is the everlasting issue of his character and attributes to all such, when death has settled all, and *that* is their settled character.

Two immutable opposites: one of the Eternal God; the other of immortal man. Then, such irreconcilability is that of everlasting wrath and of fire unquenchable.

The apostle Peter reveals by the Holy Ghost from heaven in the evangel of Christ that, as before the old heavens and old earth were destined for the flood to judge the wickedness of the world, the heavens and the earth which are now, are reserved unto *fire* against the day of judgment, II Peter 3:7.

Jude tells us by the same Spirit of God that Sodom and Gomorrah were set forth as an example of the vengeance of eternal fire. Neither are they built again, nor can be, being consigned to the ashes of desolation, to this day. But the 'fire of the ages' of which that was 'an example', is like that: real. Only, 'eternal.'

The beloved apostle, he whom Jesus loved, whose head was upon his bosom, assures us the world, and all the worldly, religious, 'evangelical', orthodox or not, who 'worship the beast and his image, and receive his mark in his forehead, or in his hand'—metaphorical as is the language— shall suffer the reality of the like vengeance.

'The same shall drink of the wine of the wrath of God, which is poured out without mixture into the cup of his indignation; and he shall be tormented with fire and brimstone in the presence of the holy angels, and in the presence of the Lamb:

'And the smoke of their torment ascendeth up for ever and ever: and they have no rest day nor night, who worship the beast and his image, and whosoever receiveth the mark of his name', Revelation 14:9-11.

I entreat the reader to consult 'The Revelation of Jesus Christ' for the opening of this solemn passage.

Consider the consequences in the world to come of being of this world, or of being worldly in this life; as opposed to being of the Lamb, and of being spiritual, in the everlasting glory.

The one endure a certain torment in this world, and for a short duration. But the other, having shut themselves off from God, are tormented–tortured; under acute pains–for the ages of the ages. That is, their immortal beings are fixed for everlasting eternity.

This is the wrath to come, and there is no escape, save by the Saviour.

Graphically and in terrifyingly awakening imagery the beloved disciple warns of the wrath to come, describing it as 'the lake which burneth with fire and brimstone' for ever and ever. 'And whosoever was not found written in the book of life was cast into the lake of fire', Revelation 20:15.

'The fearful, and unbelieving, and the abominable, and murderers, and whoremongers, and sorcerers, and idolaters, and all liars, shall have their part in the lake which burneth with fire and brimstone', Revelation 21:8.

This is the wrath to come. Would to God, that not only my reader, but all men, were to flee from it. For whatever the figure, it is a figure of the true. No matter the imagery, it is an image of the reality. However it is a shadow, it is a shadow of the substance.

The prophets foretold of it; Jesus believed and preached it; the apostles were given by the Holy Ghost to hold it as an essential part of the evangel of Christ.

And not for time. For eternity. Because it is not temporal. It is everlasting. Oh, that the Spirit awaken the reader to the verity of things assuredly to come, of things to come beyond death, of things to come unseen as yet.

Second, *The undying worm*

Whereas the fire is without the body, the worm is within: it causes constant gnawing at the vitals of the inward parts, an insufferable irritation of pain inside the organs and vessels of the body, impossible to reach or relieve.

This is taken metaphorically to describe the agonies of the soul – if not the body of the resurrection of the wicked – which cannot be eased, world without end. It is an *undying* worm.

Of this terrible and unending state of torment in the life to come, of those who in the life now present were contentious, and did not obey the truth, but obeyed unrighteousness, Isaiah foresees and prophesies in a mystical allusion: 'the worm is spread under thee, and the worms cover thee', Isaiah 14:11.

And again he saith 'for their worm shall not die', Isaiah 66:24.

No, neither shall it: crawling out of their skin, over their misshapen bodies in the resurrection of the damned, burrowing with anguished irritation and pain to the inmost soul, for ever and ever, nothing less could describe the torment of the godless and wicked.

Hence Jesus cries out in warning three times over, 'Go into the *Gehenna*, into the fire that never shall be quenched: where their worm dieth not, and the fire is not quenched.'

This is the eternal vengeance abiding on those who offend Christ's little ones.

Once more. These, that despise, condemn, offend, and persecute the 'babes', that is, the elect, in this life, in the next God shall avenge these afflicted faithful, because those that scorned them shall 'be cast into the *Gehenna*, into the fire unquenchable, where their worm dieth not, and the fire is not quenched.'

Again. The world, with contemptuous resentment against the children of God, whom he had chosen out of the world–and *because* he had chosen them out of the world–shall, in the world to come, for a recompense, 'be cast into the *Gehenna* of fire: where their worm dieth not, and the fire is not quenched.'

Here is a threefold testimony from the lips of Jesus, with a witness, according to the prophecy of Isaiah.

And, since this comes from the mouth of the Lord, the tongue of Jesus, above all else heed this testimony, and be warned, for *it cannot fail of fulfilment*. O earth, earth, earth, hear the word of the Lord: O, be warned; Mark 9:44,46,48.

Flee; flee; flee from the wrath to come, and rest not, till thou be sure of righteousness in Christ; union with him; and of life everlasting by the salvation of God.

Third, The bottomless pit

This is the dreaded shaft of the abyss, to which there is no bottom.

Therefore those figured as cast into it, must turn, twist, and wheel for ever, endlessly falling further and further into an infinity away from God, and from all that could ever bring relief from the horrifying and unceasing descent.

Thus it is that the psalmist prays so earnestly, 'Let me not sink: neither let the deep swallow me up, and let not the pit shut her mouth upon me', Psalm 69:14,15.

And again, 'Be not silent to me; lest I become like them that go down into the pit.'

Hence he praises God for salvation, 'O LORD, thou hast brought up my soul from the grave: thou hast kept me alive, that I should not go down to the pit', Psalm 30:3.

No wonder he is full of praise, for the prophet assures us 'they that go down into the pit cannot hope for thy truth.'

No, for then 'the pit and the snare, are upon thee', and, 'he who fleeth shall fall into the pit', yea, they shall 'go down quick into the pit', and, whosoever they be, or however religious, they shall find no Saviour.

Most new testament references are in Revelation, and refer to the Adversary as being the king of the bottomless pit; a fallen star being given its key; of the pit being opened, and vast enveloping clouds of smoke as of a great furnace billowing out to obscure the heavens and the earth.

No wonder men take no alarm till it is too late: they are blinded by the smoke. They cannot see through the–spiritual–obscurity, neither can they discern whence it comes, nor the invisible Adversary who ensures their blindness to the wrath to come.

Apart from some ten or eleven references to the bottomless pit, couched in the allegorical language of the Book of the

Revelation–but terrifying enough, and none the less descriptive of the wrath to come–only one clear passage occurs in the new testament.

This place refers to Christ, and is put in the form of a rhetorical question.

'Say not in thine heart, Who shall ascend into heaven? (that is, to bring Christ down from above:) or, Who shall descend into the deep? (that is, to bring up Christ again from the dead.)', Romans 10:(6)7.

Say it not in thine heart, much less express it by thy mouth. For he *did* come down from heaven. And he *did* ascend from the abyss.

But his descent into the abyss after his death was not as with all mankind: *his* descent was unique.

It was to proclaim his triumph in death, to lead captivity captive, to preach to the spirits in prison, to descend into the lower parts of the earth, to deliver those who–though they had died in faith–were yet all their lifetime subject to bondage.

He went to the deepest depth, where even the spirits of just men made perfect were held, till his victory on the cross, to cause them to ascend in him with himself, was accomplished.

Oh, the Saviour had the victory, having destroyed him that had the power of death, and, taking the keys of hell and of death, delivered every soul of his believing people, to live and reign with him above.

So why say, Who shall descend into the deep, the abyss?

In victory the Saviour made *diabolos* null and void, took the keys, abolished death, delivered them that died trusting in him, announced his triumph to trembling wicked spirits, and, from the depths, ascended up on high, with the sound of the trump of salvation.

See how great is the Saviour, how mighty the salvation of God, in the tract 'The Mystery of Godliness'.

But for all that, rather say not in thine heart words that deny his descent, resurrection, and ascension, but rather echo the shout of a King, and say, Christ is risen this day, and is glorified indeed, having saved his people from the deep, to reign in spirit with him in glory.

Fourth, The outer darkness

Darkness, in and of itself, is diametrically opposed to the nature of God, for God *is* light, and this is the message which the apostles heard from the Son, I John 1:5, and in him is no darkness at all.

Then, in eternity, banishment from the presence of God can only mean everlasting darkness.

This is true of the angels that sinned: For God spared not the angels that sinned, but cast them down into *tartarus*–the deepest abyss–and delivered them into chains of darkness–*zophos*, gloom; darkness–to be reserved unto judgment; and spared not the old world, II Peter 2:4,5.

Then how much more ought *we* to be careful to walk in the light?

'And the angels which kept not their first estate, but left their own habitation, he hath reserved in everlasting chains under darkness unto the judgment of the great day', Jude 6.

Then they, with all the old world save Noah and those in the ark, have begun to experience the fearful judgment of outer darkness for ever that awaits them after the last judgment. And so shall it be upon all the ungodly.

Thus it shall be with all who walk after the flesh in the lust of uncleanness, and despise government; presumptuous and self-willed; they fear not to speak evil of dignities: 'to whom is reserved the mist'–*zophos*, gloom–'of darkness'–*skotos*, the black darkness– 'for ever', II Peter 2:17.

Likewise certain ungodly men–and women!–who have crept in unawares among the godly, who were before of old ordained to this condemnation, turning the grace of our God into lasciviousness, blaspheming the Lord Jesus Christ.

These are 'wandering stars, to whom is reserved the gloom'–*zophos*, gloom, darkness–'of dark blackness'–*skotos*–'for ever', Jude 13.

And of this end, inconceivable to the senses, or to any present consciousness, blinded by the god of this world, lest the light of the glorious evangel should break in unto them that believe not, the Adversary hides the heinous enormity of their rebellion.

Even more, he does so of the fearful nature of the wrath to come, men being immortal, God everlasting, and eternity immutable.

Hence the Saviour himself warns the complacent in religion, secure in their positional apathy, 'But the children of the kingdom shall be cast out into outer darkness: there shall be weeping and gnashing of teeth', Matthew 8:12.

Here is the darkness–*skotos*, blackness, darkness–following the sentence of everlasting judgment upon immortal souls as a consequence of *their actual life and works* in this present world.

This is the darkness farthest out; the darkness beyond darkness; the outermost, uttermost darkness for ever.

God is light, his love is warmth: these 'sons of the kingdom' for all their profession, were not like him; they were bastards, not sons. They were *liars* in heart against the evangel they professed by mouth so enthusiastically and fulsomely to others.

For they lived in this life to save their lives, they existed for the things that can be seen, and they craved for the world that now is, though they did it for self-glory in evangelicalism.

Then, in the life to come, after the day of judgment, the justice of God metes out to them what is agreeable to all that they chose for themselves in time: for eternity, they shall have what they lived for in time. They hated *the light*, neither would come to it, lest their deeds be reproved.

Then, they shall have the outer darkness in the world to come. It follows of course. It is the necessary consequence of the conflict between *his* nature, and *theirs*. Total alienation. Utter opposition. As opposed to the radiance of the glory, the blackness of outer darkness.

Nevertheless, one actually entered the wedding feast. He was a *guest*. He was a *friend*. Yes, but *he was unprepared in this life in terms of experience*. So he lacked no more than a wedding garment. A mere trifle, beside the enormous privilege and position?

Oh? But, 'Friend, how camest thou in hither?'–Ah, but he got in there–'not having a wedding garment? And he was speechless', Matthew 22:12. And so will multitudes, multitudes upon multitudes, abundantly assured and persuaded of 'the eternal security of the believer', be equally speechless.

Yes, assured, persuaded, secure; but none of these things is a wedding garment. Even if they *could* get so far in reality: *Where is their wedding garment?* For all of these shall verily hear the words of the King to his servants, 'Bind him hand and foot, and take him away, and cast him into outer darkness;

'There shall be weeping and gnashing of teeth. For many are called, but few are chosen', Matthew 22:13,14.

Oh, these were unprofitable servants in this life, living out to save their lives in trivial pursuits punctuated by meetings but filled with worldliness. They never lost their lives; they never took up the daily cross; they never denied themselves; they were never profitable servants; much less were they ever disciples.

'And cast ye the unprofitable servant into outer darkness'– shall resonate from the highest heaven to the lowest hell, from the thunderous voice of the Judge at the last Assize on the day of judgment, passing the everlasting sentence. 'There shall be weeping and gnashing of teeth', Matthew 25:30.

Yes, there shall, and be sure it is not your eyes, or your teeth, because what is certain is that *none of these expected that*. Nevertheless, that is what they got, for everlasting eternity. Nor is there any remission from this eternal sentence.

Therefore, be ye also ready, and flee from the wrath to come. For there is a Saviour from the wrath to come, with his own terms, now admonishing you from your bible, and witnessing by his Spirit, faithfully recorded in this ministry which he hath given, namely, that of 'Salvation'.

Therefore take heed whom ye hear; what ye hear; and how ye hear. 'For how shall they hear without a preacher?'

And know ye this day that Christ hath forewarned you in his evangel that there *is* a salvation of God; that he is the Saviour, and that you are commanded to hear, and bring forth fruits meet for repentance. Now: this day and hour.

'Today if ye will hear his voice'–not your opinion, or your sect's interpretation, of the dead letter: rather and only, *his voice*– 'harden not your *hearts*', Hebrews 3:7,13,15; and 4:7.

'For he saith, I have heard thee in a time accepted, and in the day of salvation have I succoured thee: *behold, now is the accepted time; behold, now is the day of salvation*', II Corinthians 6:2.

XVI
Salvation from Wrath

IN emphasizing that *judgment* is according to works it is of paramount importance never to lose sight of the all-important truth that *justification* is by faith, and by faith *without works*.

Hence the judgment vividly contrasts the lives on earth of the righteous and those of the wicked; of saints and sinners; of the just and the unjust; of the godly and the ungodly.

And so they appear, respectively, in the resurrection of damnation, and the resurrection of life. Their opposite *character* appears. This justifies God in his judgments.

However, *Justification* is beyond any relative comparison between the just and the unjust, the godly and the ungodly.

What comparison, between men, any men, all men, and Almighty God, the Eternal, the invisible, from everlasting to everlasting, dwelling in the light which no man can approach unto, whom no man hath seen, nor can see?

What comparison, before whom even the cherubims must hide their faces, crying, Holy, holy, holy, Lord God Almighty?

Comparison? There *is* no comparison. He is incomparable. Then, if men are to dwell with him, a justification must be wrought for them in righteousness that is *all of God, all of grace, and all of faith.*

This righteousness of God, by faith of Jesus Christ, imputed to all the heirs of faith, fully wrought out by the death of Christ, and by his blood, is wholly commensurate with the everlasting righteousness of the divine nature.

That justifies. Nothing else does, and nothing else can: 'even the righteousness *of God* which is by faith of Jesus Christ unto all and upon all them that believe', Romans 3:22.

It is a matter of balance. That each part of the evangel is balanced properly and in proportion with every other part. God justifying by faith is one thing. God being justified in his judgments is another thing.

However sanctified the righteous, the just, the godly, there is absolutely no comparison between *that* and the ineffable righteousness of God.

But there *is* a comparison between the righteous, the holy, and the godly, over against the unrighteous, the wicked, and the ungodly. *That comparison, in the last day, justifies God in his judgments.*

As to the righteousness of the law, or the righteousness of God, 'enter not into judgment with thy servant: for in thy sight shall no man living be justified', Psalm 143:2.

But as to the righteousness of those *whom God has justified,* and thus quickened, 'ye know that every one that doeth righteousness is born of him', I John 2:29.

Whence it follows that all, but all, from the beginning of time to the end of it, under whatever testament, or in how little or great a light on or from the Saviour, all 'who by patient continuance in well doing seek for glory and honour and immortality' *did not do so from birth.*

Such seeking *never came from nature.* It was not, it could not, and it never will be *from the flesh.* For 'that which is born of the flesh is flesh; and that which is born of the Spirit is spirit', John 3:6.

'Because the fleshly mind is enmity against God: for it is not subject to the law of God, *neither indeed can be.* So then they that are in the flesh *cannot please God*', Romans 8:7,8. Then, neither of birth; nature; or the flesh.

Yet without controversy there *were* and *are* those 'who by patient continuance in well doing seek for glory and honour and immortality.'

These shine as the stars in the firmament. Then, if not of birth; neither nature; nor the flesh: Whence came they, and what brought them so to seek all the days of their life?

It is certain that, like David, they were shapen in iniquity, and in sin did their mother conceive them; that they were fallen in Adam; that they were by nature the children of wrath, even as others, that 'every mouth may be stopped, and all the world may become guilty before God'.

For 'there is none righteous, no, not one: there is none that understandeth, there is none that seeketh after God. They are all gone out of the way, they are together become unprofitable; there is none that doeth good, no, not one.'

Then, *at one time* those, all those without exception, who *afterwards* 'by patient continuance in well doing seek for glory and honour and immortality', were as sinful and sinning as any and all of mankind.

What made the difference?

Being justified made the difference. Abraham was justified by faith; Noah became heir of the righteousness which is by faith; David describeth the blessedness of the man unto whom God imputeth righteousness without works. God justified Paul. Righteousness was imputed to Peter.

And so to all the chosen seed, and faithful in Christ Jesus. *That* made the difference.

Then, then, 'by patient continuance in well doing' they sought 'for glory and honour and immortality', *and not till then*. No, *not till the Saviour was revealed to them, and the salvation of God had arrested them.*

They were not *born* like it: they were *saved* like it.

They did not patiently continue in well doing, seeking for glory and honour and immortality *to be saved*. They sought for it *because they were saved*.

Not *to be justified*. But because *they had been justified*.

They *had been* saved from the wrath to come. The divinely conveyed, spiritually witnessed, inwardly revealed knowledge of *that*, in the revelation of the Son by the Father, was what caused the *total change in their life, conversation, and behaviour*.

That was what began their work of faith, labour of love, and patience of hope in our Lord Jesus Christ.

And that endurance and continuance of the saints in their salvation—who *had* been saved, and that by the evangel of Christ, which is the power of God unto salvation—caused the apostle to exult, 'Knowing, brethren beloved, your election of God', I Thessalonians 1:4.

They had turned to God from idols; then they had been idolaters. They now served the living and true God; then they had served the law of sin and death, with every dark error in the falsity of their invented gods.

Now continually they waited for God's Son from heaven; but they never looked heavenward before, expecting only wrath and fire, diverting their lusts to the earth the meantime.

What changed them, converted them 180°, utterly altered their course? Why, that Jesus *had saved* them from the wrath to come. Believing this evangel, they turned, that is, to 'patient continuance in well doing, seeking for glory and honour and immortality.'

Not *to be* saved from the coming wrath. But because Jesus *had saved them* from the wrath to come: 'how ye turned to God from idols to serve the living and true God; and to wait for his Son from heaven, whom he raised from the dead, even Jesus, which delivered us from the wrath to come', I Thessalonians 1:9,10.

But how did Jesus deliver them—and save us—from the wrath to come? By bearing it himself on our behalf. That was what *had taken place* on the cross at Golgotha, in the salvation of God.

Take in all the agony of the crucifixion itself: the being suspended in shame and degradation in uttermost physical pain, hanging between heaven and earth, mocked and derided for three hours in the light.

Nevertheless it was in the three hours of darkness, when men saw nothing, that the ultimate and absolute substitutionary sufferings of the Saviour took place.

'And it was the sixth hour, and there was darkness over all the land until the ninth hour.'

It is by the cries from the cross in these selfsame hours, that we are pointed to the sin-bearing of the Son of man, and to his taking away the immeasurable wrath of God on behalf of all those for whom he died.

This darkness indicates that the reality of what took place on the cross was impenetrable to the natural sight of men. *Because what took place, took place between God and the Saviour, in the outworking of the covenant between the Father and the Son.*

And that is as invisible as it is incomprehensible. No more can it be penetrated by reading the scriptures.

For if the events themselves were shrouded from the eye and incomprehensible to the mind of the men actually present, how much more is the written record of the invisible work of God to all merely reading about that from which they were absent?

As for the one, the darkness was without; so for the other the blindness is within.

Only the direct inshining of God by interior revelation can dispel the darkness, and radiate the spiritual, invisible, divine, and supernatural truth.

'The god of this world hath blinded the minds of them which believe not, lest the light of the glorious gospel of Christ, who is the image of God, should shine unto them.'

'For God, who commanded the light to shine out of darkness, hath shined in our hearts, to give the light of the knowledge of the glory of God in the face of Jesus Christ.'

Yet for all that, a deeper darkness, and a horror of great darkness, transcended all: this was the darkness that descended from God upon the Saviour, when, having been made sin, and bearing sins, the wrath fell upon him in the stead of the sinner.

Then, in the place of vicarious substitution, when he was compassed with the pangs of darkness and death, the Saviour entered into the words of the prophet, He hath set me in dark places, as they that be dead of old. How else could we be delivered from outer darkness?

Thus, when the light was darkened in the heavens, and the sun darkened in his going forth, the day was darkened, for God darkened the earth in a clear day, a sign of what the Saviour must endure on our behalf to deliver us from that to which naturally we had consigned ourselves world without end.

Through the wrath is the land darkened, for as Abraham felt aforetime in measure, so without measure, on behalf of those whom he would save, 'an horror of great darkness fell upon him'.

As saith the psalmist, 'Thou hast laid me in the lowest pit, in darkness, in the deeps.'

But why? Because, speaking in the Spirit of the sufferings of Christ, who should save his people from their sins, and, if so, from wrath, the Spirit revealed that the Saviour was to suffer our punishment vicariously, to deliver us from the wrath to come.

This is nothing to do with man. Man has neither part nor lot in the matter. This is wholly to do with the covenant–the new testament–between the Father and the Son. Salvation is of the LORD. It is not that we loved God. It is that he loved us.

It was God that laid our iniquities upon our Saviour, as he was transfixed as the Substitute of his people. And, God being a Spirit, and the work supernatural, spiritually our iniquities were gathered up and laid upon him *within*, that is, upon his interior soul.

This was the work of God: the Son was passive. Never does it say that our iniquities were *imputed* to him, as if it were an

391

exterior calculation. That would take away nothing. They were *borne*, having been laid upon his interior soul, an entirely different thing.

He 'bare our sins in'—mark that: *in*—'his own body on the tree', I Peter 2:24. And, again, 'The LORD hath laid on him'—note that: 'laid on him'—'the iniquity of us all', Isaiah 53:6.

As the Son of man hung on the tree, God 'made' him to be sin—the verb is ποιέω, *poieō*, to make, create, cause—for us, who knew no sin. That is, God wrought creatively upon his manhood so that he became identified and united with the real condition of that people whom he would save.

Otherwise there could *be* no salvation.

By the mysterious and supernatural work of God, a vast weight of divers and innumerable sins was laid upon him—within his sinless soul—whilst, withal, God wrought in his humanity—in and of itself spotless, impeccable—so that he was *made to be sin*, offered up instead of his people in the place of judgment.

This *thorough exchange of places* is what has been called 'reconciliation', though that word is hardly an accurate translation of the Greek. But, save for such a 'thorough exchange' there was no other way of remission of sins, of salvation from wrath, or of deliverance from outer darkness.

But Jesus took the place of his people and bore all on their behalf.

The burnt offering, the meat offering, the peace offering, the sin offering, the trespass offering, all these might imperfectly set forth substitutionary atonement in an outward figure, but the reality, no mere shadow could possibly depict.

Totally and experimentally identified with the elect, Jesus entered into thick darkness, into sufferings beyond description, into torment defying imagination, into depths of agony that beggar definition.

Why? In order to take upon himself the cause and thus bear the effect of that which alone could 'deliver us from the wrath to come'.

Nothing of this was of man, or could be perceived by men. All that God wrought lay hidden behind the blackness of darkness. No mortal vision beheld the transaction between the Father and the Son for the salvation of his people.

But the Son of man believed God in the place of judgment, and in those dreadful hours when his sore ran in the night, and ceased not, his faith was not disappointed.

Whilst Jesus hung there, steeped in a dread darkness far beyond that which obscured the sun, 'God spared not his own Son, but delivered him up for us all'.

All our uncleanness, defilement, corruption, iniquity, and sinfulness broke in waves to submerge his blameless soul, yea, he sank in deep mire: the waters came into his soul.

Upon him was laid a multitude of transgressions, sins innumerable, and errors past number, answering to all that the only wise God saw from Adam, from birth, throughout life, in death, at the very judgment, on the part and behalf of every last one of his people.

That this should be laid upon the Son of man—withal *made* sin—the suffering Saviour of his people, entailed the divine and creative work of the stupendous love of God, besides the love of Christ which passeth knowledge.

At last came the cause of his bearing iniquity: to bear it away. Not now its being laid upon him, but, being laid, its being punished and avenged in his soul and body. To this end he received the wrath of God against all that and all those with which and with whom he had become identified.

Worse than the judgment by flood of the old world, in the sensation of the horror of outer darkness, the overwhelming fires of wrath roared down upon the vicarious sacrifice of his humanity. Worse than the yawning pit, the bottomless abyss gaped beneath the suffering soul of the Substitute.

Worse than the searing fire and brimstone – in a figure, suffering the vengeance of eternal fire – that rained upon Sodom and Gomorrah, the wrathful indignation and fury of Almighty God issued as a deluge from the heavens upon the saving Substitute of his people.

He passed through fire and flood, darkness and gnawing torment, poured out from on high to engulf the lonely sin-bearer, hung in shameful degradation between heaven and earth in the midst of time at the end of the world.

The pangs of hell gat hold of him; the sorrows of death compassed him about.

Though an equivalent of unquenchable fire, the undying worm, outer darkness, and endless torment seized upon his unique humanity, as he bore the just punishment, the equal wrath, the equivalent vengeance, due to his people, all present – all humanity – stood completely uncomprehending and indifferent about what was taking place in the darkness of Golgotha.

In a mystery, the seven heavenly vials of the wrath and vengeance of Almighty God were emptied and exhausted upon him, in the hours of the horror of thick darkness upon the cross. But men saw nothing. They heard not a sound.

Yet all the while, ringing in his ears with a continual roar that crashed and reverberated from the vaults of heaven to the caverns of hell, the thunders, lightnings, and voices of the broken law sounded with outraged indignation and unabated strength, as, without remission, the curse fell upon the crucified.

And men saw nothing? heard not a sound? stood oblivious in the darkness? Yet it was for men that he bore the dreadful penalty, for man that he was charged with so vast a number of transgressions, so great a multitude of trespasses, against the holy commandments of God.

But at the end, with the uttermost execration exhausted, the last bolt of retributive justice shot, and the final sentence of vindictive judgment executed, when the law could say no more, and the curse could find no further cause of vengeance, when the sounding trumpet ceased to utter: *then*.

Then, when peace reigned on earth, and good will toward men, the heavens rejoiced, and the earth rang again for gladness. Nothing but satisfaction remained in the judgment of God; and there was a great calm.

Justice passed over, requited to the last mite. Nothing was seen to offend. The Almighty viewed, he looked down from heaven, but there was no offence. Nothing. Not one spot. Not a blemish.

Not in all those countless and innumerable souls united with the sin-bearer hanging dead upon the tree. There was nothing against them: nothing in time; nothing in eternity; nothing in heaven; nothing on earth; nothing from birth; nothing after death. Nothing. Nothing at all.

The sacrifice was consumed in the flames of the wrath of God, and in the fires of everlasting justice. The sin offering was burned to ashes without the camp, and with it, all that had been laid thereon. Nothing but ashes. He had finished the work which God had given him to do, and finished it to perfection.

Thus, as with all saints; as those saved in Corinth; when these who were the called of God at Thessalonica heard the preaching of the cross, of Christ crucified, they received it, believed it, for it had entered into their hearts by the power of God.

And, believing, they *knew* that they had been delivered from the wrath to come.

Forthwith, quickened by grace, they believed, clothed with divine righteousness, filled with peace, and joy in the Holy Ghost, they turned from idols to serve the living and true God; and to wait for his Son from heaven, whom he raised from the dead.

That is, to wait abiding in him: 'even Jesus, which delivered us from the wrath to come', I Thessalonians 1:10.

Thereupon they joined and were united with that innumerable company, separate from the world, 'who by patient continuance in well doing seek for glory and honour and immortality', Romans 2:7.

How these shall shine as the stars in the firmament of heaven for brightness in the day of judgment, evident witness to and justification of the judgment of him who, without respect of persons, judgeth according to every man's work, I Peter 1:17.

The apostle Paul greatly comforts the faith of the saints in the Saviour having delivered them from the wrath to come, by the salvation of God, in the following passage: 'But God commendeth his love toward us, in that, while we were yet sinners, Christ died for us.

'Much more then, being now justified by his blood, we shall be saved from wrath through him. For if, when we were enemies, we were reconciled to God by the death of his Son, much more, being reconciled, we shall be saved by his life', Romans 5:8-10.

Here twice the apostle uses the words 'much more', and this expression is the fulcrum in his doctrine, in which he compares the certainty of what had occurred at three different points of time, in order to show *how much more* that will obtain which is *yet* to occur at a *fourth* point of time.

It is an argument reached by the comparison of three things that had taken place, each of which had assured consequences, to convince the saints that the fourth occurrence – equal in comparison with the previous three, though yet to take place – *must* have just as certain and assured a conclusion.

The four points in time, respectively, are as follows: First: from the beginning, or ever time began. Second: at the death of Christ. Third: when we ourselves were brought to faith. And Fourth: when time shall be no more, and we are raised from the dead at the last judgment.

Consider the first point in time. It is before time, from ever-lasting, that God chose and loved his people in Christ. That God *commended* such love to us *before* Christ died for us, Romans 5:8. This means that God's love for us *preceded* Christ's dying for us, so as to be the prior moving cause of that death.

Preceded by how long? Preceded by so long as the nature of the unchangeable God. Then, from everlasting. If so, throughout time, from before it, to await the commendation of such love from the beginning, prior to the cross.

As to us, in our time, before we came to the knowledge of God at all, we were 'yet without strength', Romans 5:6. We were 'yet sinners', Romans 5:8. And we were 'enemies' of God, Romans 5:10.

All this time – yea, before time began – unknown to us, dis-believed by us, God loved us. Yes, and had done so since before either the world or time yet existed.

Secondly: consider the death of Christ on the cross. As to all the old testament saints, these died in faith. Yes, but all were born in sin, and, sinning, brought down wrath and the curse upon themselves. True, they were quickened to faith in him who was yet to come, but they were in sin before that faith was given.

As to all the new testament saints, few were alive in the event. Of these, fewer were called. Of the called, 'they all forsook him, and fled.' 'All ye shall be offended because of me this night.' An apostle betrayed him, and the chiefest denied him. None penetrated the darkness.

Of the new testament saints since, most were not yet born. Of those born, they were 'without strength'; 'ungodly'; 'sinners', and 'enemies'. But, elect of the love of God in Christ, he *still* died for them. *All* of them. And, whether old or new testament, all, before the coming of faith, and all in their prior evil condition.

That was our condition when he was crucified: 'while we were yet sinners, Christ died for us', Romans 5:8. If so, he being without sin, who knew no sin, who did no sin, then, as the Substitute, unknown in place of the unwitting sinners for whom he died.

'Christ died for our sins according to the scriptures.' 'Who his own self bare our sins in his own body on the tree.' 'This is my blood of the new testament, which is shed for many for the remission of sins.' 'And without shedding of blood is no remission.'

But his blood was shed. Then there is remission. Then *whilst we were yet sinners; ungodly; without strength; enemies; unknown to us, God laid our sins upon him, and, an equivalent price of suffering unto death having been paid, they* – old and new testament alike – *were all remitted.*

Then. And there. No ifs or buts. All the sins of all the elect were actually and effectually taken away for ever. And not only those without the law; neither yet those under the law; but all sins measured even unto the very righteousness of God from the first to the last.

This is called 'Justification'. And it, the whole of it, the unconditional completeness of it, took place at the cross, and at the cross alone, when 'Christ died for our sins according to the scriptures'.

'So Christ was once offered to bear the sins of many', and, if so, they *were* – past tense – borne away *when that one offering was made.*

On this basis, that Christ died for us *while we were yet sinners,* so that *when he did so* our sins were taken away in the judgment of the righteousness of God, which Paul calls 'being justified by his blood', the apostle commences his first 'much more' argument.

'Much more then, being now justified by his blood', Romans 5:9. Much more *when?* When, verse 8, 'Christ died for us.' Now observe carefully, verse 9, Paul equates this precisely with 'being now justified by his blood': *then.*

That is, when he died for us: *then.* When his blood was shed: *at the time at which it was shed. Then.* The apostle declares in his doctrine that instant as 'being *now*'; *then* we were justified unconditionally, so that '*now*' that is our case: 'being *now*'.

Wherefore *by his blood alone, then,* righteousness of God was imputed to us, and we were pronounced of God to be reckoned righteous *according to the measure of his own divine righteousness,* by nothing other than the blood of Christ *when it was shed.* If so, *now*: that is 'being *now*'.

At that moment, instantly, righteousness of God was imputed to us, and we were reckoned in the sight of God to be perfectly, divinely righteous. That is what justification means. And that is what the apostle means by our 'being now justified by his blood'.

But that is only the premise, the basis, the beginning of his argument. On such a foundation he has 'much more' to conclude. About what? About the future. But what can he conclude about the future from Christ having died for us as sinners, and our now being justified in consequence?

He can conclude this: if when we were *sinners* he justified us by his blood, this being a once-and-for-all past occurrence, in consequence of which *we were no longer reckoned to be sinners*, but *then, then, then, reckoned to be righteous*, What follows?

It follows that those reckoned to be righteous, to whom the righteousness *of God himself* had been imputed, so that they were *then* accounted to be perfectly, divinely righteous, *grace is sure to do 'much more' for them*—now being reckoned righteous—*than when they were in their prior condition of sinful enmity.*

How much more? This much more: 'we shall be saved from wrath through him.'

We were sinners. He was dead. His blood had been shed in death. But that blood, shed on our behalf, not only took away our sins, it brought in to our account before God in heaven the very righteousness of God. *Then:* that is, *when* his blood was shed.

Now then that we are become the righteousness of God in him—who did *that* for us as *sinners*—how much more shall he do for us as reckoned righteous, and when shall he do it? He shall *for ever* impute the righteousness of God to us, accounting us to be perfectly righteous, *even on the very day of judgment.*

Then, 'we shall be saved from wrath through him.' Through *him?* Yes. Because he justified us by his blood when he was dead. What then shall he do for us—now being justified—as living for evermore?

For in saying 'through him', it is evident that he *is* risen again, he is alive for evermore, and *in his person* he will verify that his blood shed for us in death did all that his word assured us that it would do – much more! – once the wrath comes to pass in the day of judgment.

For the wrath will come to pass in the day of judgment. Yes, but not upon those saved from that wrath by him in his death, who is now risen from the dead, glorified in heaven, who shall in that day ratify the worth and consequences of his blood shed on earth for every one of his people.

We *then* being justified, he *now* being glorified, he shall 'much more' surely than the established certainty of what he accomplished for them in death, absolutely, indisputably, immutably save them from wrath by his own presence and person in life beyond the grave.

The second 'much more' argument of the apostle follows, and utilizes the comparison between what obtained – and must obtain – at the third and fourth points in time – and beyond it – to set forth such sure and comfortable truth from Paul to the people of God.

'For if, when we were enemies, we were reconciled to God by the death of his Son, much more, being reconciled, we shall be saved by his life', Romans 5:10.

What comparisons are here! and, these things being so, what assurance of salvation from the wrath to come springs up in joy by the Spirit at the realization of this evangelical doctrine.

The apostle first refers to the natural state of all those whom God purposes to bring to faith in Christ *before* being so awakened, quickened, and enabled to believe.

And what better example than himself? – observe: 'For if, when *we*': that is, including himself – indeed; for who would not wish to be included with the apostle? For who was more at enmity than Saul of Tarsus, fuming with rage on the Damascus road? Yet *he* was brought to faith.

'For if when *we* were enemies.' But not only Saul; ourselves also, all of us, none excluded, that should afterwards believe. 'And you, that were sometime alienated and enemies in your mind by wicked works', Colossians 1:21.

And should God love *us*? Should he bring his *enemies* to faith in him whose nature they *hated*? Yes, such is his everlasting, electing, undeserved love to his enemies, he should: '*you* hath he reconciled.'

'If, when we were *enemies*, we *were* reconciled to God by the death of his Son.'

Then, when we *were* reconciled, that work of reconciliation—the thorough exchange of places by the work of God between the Father and the Son on the cross for his own, whether dead, alive, or unborn—*irrespective of their will, choice, or existence*, was utterly and wholly completed, What now?

What now that we have been awakened, now that we are quickened, now that we do believe, now that we rejoice with joy unspeakable, and full of glory?

What now that we are lost in wonder, love, and praise, brought to believe in the Saviour, and the salvation of God on our behalf?

In a moment, in an instant, at the point of being born of God, at the moment of birth, in the twinkling of an eye, translated from the power of darkness into the glorious light of the kingdom of his own dear Son:

What? We, who only an instant before were enemies, aliens, haters of the evangel? Oh, then, so suddenly the light shining, so swiftly the voice sounding, so immediately the life quickening from glory, what prostrate, believing gratitude, what inexpressible joy, what meltedness of heart now becomes us!

How changed! From aliens to brethren; from sinners to saints; from condemned to justified; from unbelief to faith; from enmity to love; from hatefulness to sonship; from darkness to light; from the power of demons to the baptism of the Holy Ghost; from the flesh to the Spirit.

And yet it was in the *former* state that God reconciled us in Christ.

If so, in the *latter* state, being reconciled unto God, having been alarmed, awakened, convicted, quickened, converted, brought to repentance, alive with faith, joined in union, living in communion: reconciled! How pleasing must this be for God to behold, in those once wholly to the contrary.

But if so, and if *when we were enemies*, he reconciled us, now that we *are* reconciled, and he delights in his love over us, and ours for him, What must follow? Why, *much more* must follow! And when? From this day, henceforth, and for ever.

That is, 'much more, *being* reconciled', it follows that in the resurrection, at the day of judgment, raised in the salvation of God, the glory and rejoicing of the Saviour, who reconciled us by his *death*, now, risen, glorified, in that day, how much more shall we – must we – be saved by his *life*!

In fine, if when we were condemned, his blood justified us, *much more* at the last day, raised in justification, alive for evermore, he in person will show the basis and foundation of his saving us from the wrath to come.

Again, when we were enemies, *then* in death he reconciled us, *much more* at the last day he in his risen, glorified, everlasting life shall for ever uphold every single one – once at enmity –

whom he had already reconciled in his death, even unto their eternal inheritance of the glory.

This is the salvation that has been conveyed, brought home, and, engrafted, appears within the heart of the inner man of all the saints, as it is written 'for the grace of God that bringeth salvation hath appeared to all men', that is, all classes of men and women whom God has been pleased to save and call by grace.

And more: caused *that* salvation to *appear* to them by the same grace. Then, grace not only *wrought* salvation, but grace also *brought* the salvation that had been wrought, Titus 2:11. This teaches us that salvation is all of God, first and last.

By declaring that the grace of God *bringeth* salvation, it is evident that *the salvation thus brought must already have been in existence*, in order to *be* brought. And if pre-existent, *then having been previously outwrought in the covenant between the Father and the Son.*

Thus Titus 2:11, though implying the grace of the Father, is not that of which the verse speaks. The grace of the Father did not *bring* salvation in time: it purposed salvation from eternity. This is sovereign, electing, everlasting grace, in the love of God purposed in Christ before the world was.

But that grace of the Father choosing and giving a people to the Son from everlasting, which is our salvation, is not what is referred to when the apostle speaks of the grace of God *bringing* salvation, Titus 2:11.

But if not referring to salvation when it was purposed by the Father from eternity, nevertheless 'the grace of God that *bringeth* salvation' still of necessity *refers to a salvation already in existence* in order that, as an outworked entity, it should thereafter be brought.

If so, what is brought was already accomplished. By whom? and when? By the Son; at the cross. *There* the Son saved us.

Actually saved us, with the salvation of God. Not *made salvation possible*. But really, fully, finally, and eternally accomplished salvation in its entirety.

It is *that* salvation that is *brought* to every one of those for whom the Son died in substitution on the cross. Not–though implied–the grace of the Father in purposing salvation from eternity. Neither–though implied–the grace of the Son in accomplishing salvation in time.

But *the grace of the Holy Ghost* in bringing salvation to appear to every lost sinner, all those at enmity, every one of those in bleak despair, to cause the truth *that the salvation they longed for had already been purposed and outwrought and had now been brought freely to them.*

Thus the grace of God–Father, Son, and Holy Ghost–appears as that which achieves salvation from beginning to end. But here, Titus 2:11, the emphasis is upon the *work of the Holy Ghost* in *conveying* salvation; it is upon this that the apostle settles his focus in the context.

For 'Salvation is of the Lord.' It is *all* of God. It is not that the Son did a general work, and man must go and fetch it. What? Sinners under wrath; souls at enmity; those *dead* in sin go and fetch it? First, they wouldn't; Second, they couldn't.

Never. No, not condemned; bound; slaves of Satan; born in sin; under the bondage of the will; their carnal minds at enmity with God; dead before God.

Fetch salvation? They don't want it; they can't reach it; their blind eyes can't see it; and their withered arm of free will on their corpses of death are incapable of grasping it.

But the love of God can bring it. And that is the work of the Holy Ghost: to *bring* salvation, and cause it *inwardly to appear*, in the light of the glorious evangel of Christ. *Then* men believe, and, believing, rejoice with joy unspeakable and full of glory.

But just as the grace of God in the Person of the Father, and the Person of the Son, was not only different in point of time, but wholly distinctive in nature and character, so the grace of God in the Person of the Holy Ghost likewise reveals that salvation by grace in a way unique to the Spirit.

That is, as the Father gave to the Son before the world was, or time existed, all whom he had chosen to salvation; even so the Son effectually and eternally saved them by becoming their substitute at the cross. Now, in all of this, salvation was *exterior* to the persons of the saved.

That is not the case with the Spirit. He comes *to abide within*. That is, to *save* within. To do this, divinely and spiritually, he *teaches* within. With authority. To assert the reign of Christ over inbred sin and lawlessness.

Whoever does not freely and gladly submit to this interior, divine, and spiritual discipline is but a hollow, shallow hypocrite, because 'if any man have not the Spirit of Christ, he is none of his', Romans 8:9. 'For to be carnally minded is death; but to be spiritually minded is life and peace.'

Then this interior, divine, spiritual teaching is *so that one is saved*–not now before the world was; neither yet here when Christ died. But here *within oneself*. That is, salvation is *applied*.

How? First, negatively. This baptism, this anointing, this filling, this regeneration, this renewing, this quickening, this sealing, this shedding abroad, this indwelling, this earnest, yea, this abiding presence of the Spirit *teaches us to deny ourselves, and lose our lives for Christ*.

'Teaching us that, denying ungodliness and worldly lusts', Titus 2:12.

That is the *first* obvious evidence of the indwelling and salvation of the Spirit: the denial of ungodliness. Then, the relative hating of father, mother, brother, sister, wife, children, self, man, and the world, as against the quickened awareness of the uttermost love for the living God in all things.

And the denial of worldly lusts. In dress, money, the praise – or even notice – of man, of pleasures, visible things, earthly things, cosmetic things.

Oh, utterly abhorred, really denied. Now, such as are of this sort, and none other, have the evidence of being filled with the Spirit. Then where are these Pentecostals and Charismatics? Are they blind? If so, by the god of this world, through a false, deceived, and unlawful duplication, by way of strange fire.

Not even in sight. But unless *these* things, the denial of ungodliness and worldly lusts, are not only in evidence, but are the consequence of the grace of the teaching of the indwelling Spirit, let not self-deluded hypocrites suppose that *they* know anything or possess the least hint, of the salvation of God.

Nor is this teaching all negative: *but the negative is first.* Because ungodliness and worldliness were there first.

And yet ungodliness and worldliness are both things which superficial, light, chaffy pretenders to the work of the Spirit in salvation actually *practise.* As to the Spirit teaching us to *deny* ungodliness and worldly lusts, *they ignore it.*

But the first thing the grace of God that brings salvation does *is counter it by creating self-denial in the soul.* Then you can tell who are *really* saved, and who are the *antichristoi.*

Positively, that which comes second in the apostle's doctrine – the indwelling grace of God by the Holy Ghost having first taught all those in whom he abides to deny the lusts of the body of sin

and of worldliness, to which they are to reckon themselves dead –
is to live soberly, righteously, and godly, in this present world.

Sobriety: what a contrast this presents with the flippant,
superficial, uncontrolled gaiety of those who make the most noise
about being baptized in the Spirit, or having received the blessing.
Are these *sober*? Is their life one of *sobriety*?

But those in whom the Spirit dwells in truth are taught to
be sober; to be serious; to deny themselves; to take up the daily
cross; to live in the light of eternity; of the judgment to come;
of the resurrection from the dead; to look not at the things which
can be seen, but at the things which cannot be seen.

These are taught righteousness, to judge righteous judgment.
They have their senses exercised to discern between good and
evil; between the flesh and the Spirit; between what is of God
and what is not in religion.

They discern what is spurious: they have a standard from
God, and to it the Spirit leads them to judge all things by the
anointing.

The grace of God which brings salvation teaches them continually, as abiding in them, to be godly. They do not regard the
face, fear, or favour of man. Their praise is of God, not man.
They live as if man was not, but that God is, and is a rewarder
of them that diligently seek him.

To them, sober, righteous, and godly, throughout this earthly
pilgrimage, there is none to see but him who is invisible, nothing
to consider but that which is beyond death, no vision but of
the great conflagration and the dissolution of all things.

They live in the fear of God. They walk by the grace of God.
They live as loving God with all the heart, strength, mind, and
understanding. Nothing counts beside this: they are *godly*. It is

as if no man or woman by nature, yea, no present world, existed: they live unto God, their only reality.

But, in all the suffering, persecuted, ostracized, afflicted pathway such strangers, sojourners, pilgrims necessarily encountered as *thus* they endure the afflictions of this present world, a bright and blessed hope shines before them, and draws them on to the coming of Christ, and the world to come.

'Looking for that blessed hope, and the glorious appearing of the great God and our Saviour Jesus Christ', Titus 2:13.

Not looking for the wrath to come: delivered from the wrath to come. Looking for the second coming of Christ, to raise them to glory and honour and immortality.

Looking! This marks the heirs of promise, the seed of Abraham: Abraham *looked* for a city. But not on earth: 'whose builder and maker was God.' Abraham was neither a blind premillennialist nor a deluded dispensationalist. He was not stopped short by earthly figures or worldly shadows: he *looked* for a *heavenly* country.

And we look, look, look, preventing the dawning; anticipating the noonday; watching through the night, we really *look, look, look*, all the time, all our lifetime, we *look* for the appearing of the great God and our Saviour Jesus Christ.

This marks the saints! This shows whom the Spirit of God teaches by the grace of God!

But then, such a people, those who do not pretend, or put on an act because they have not the real thing, no, the rather those who *actually do have the Spirit*, whose teaching in them appears in their denying ungodliness and worldly lusts, live soberly, righteously, and godly in this present world.

And they look all the time for the end of this world and the coming of the world to come.

That is, for the appearing of the great God and our Saviour Jesus Christ.

What makes them so earnest, so zealous, so eager in this, the teaching of the Spirit within? Why, *what Christ has done to save them.*

'Who gave himself for us, that he might redeem us from all iniquity, and purify unto himself a peculiar people, zealous of good works. These things speak, and exhort, and rebuke with all authority. Let no man despise thee', Titus 2:14,15.

O, note these words: 'Who gave himself for us.' Here is the past work in redemption, when we were saved for eternity: when, 'he gave himself for us.' When did he do that? At Golgotha. It did not appear that he did so: It appeared that he was crucified.

And that is all the world, the religious world, the pseudo-evangelical sees: He was crucified. It is all that the modernist, the liberal, the ecumenicalist, the progressive sees: He was crucified. But the light from heaven reveals to the chosen that *while* he was crucified, *'he gave himself for us'*.

Then, at Golgotha; in those hours on the cross; when all that men saw in the light, and supposed in the dark, was that he was crucified.

What they did not see was that *in* that crucifixion, unseen, divinely, spiritually, in the covenant between the Father and the Son, *God had given us to him; and he gave himself for us.*

To save us from the wrath to come.

Had he not, we would have been lost. But the love of God was set upon a people foreknown, predestinated, chosen, and elect, of whom it was said 'he gave himself for us'. Otherwise, our sin and our sins would have condemned us to wrath.

He gave himself for us when he cried in Hebrew, 'Eli'. He gave himself for us when he cried in Aramaic, 'Eloi'. He gave himself for us when he prayed, 'Father, forgive them; for they know not what they do'.

He gave himself for us when he affirmed, 'Verily I say unto thee, Today shalt thou be with me in paradise.' He gave himself for us when he cried, 'Father, into thy hands I commend my spirit.'

He gave himself for us when he said, 'Woman, behold thy son'. And commanded, 'Behold thy mother'. He gave himself for us when he cried out, 'I thirst'. And he had given himself for us when he affirmed, 'It is finished'.

In those hours, when all that appeared to take place was the crucifixion, what did not appear, what was not seen, neither was it understood, was that *during* that crucifixion 'He gave himself for us'.

However, the apostle makes it clear that his giving himself for us was to an end. An end *actually realized* in all those for whom *in fact* he gave himself.

But *never realized* in any of those who emptily *say* he gave himself for them, *despite that their barren, worldly, disobedient hypocrisy bears witness, giving the lie to their meaningless claim.*

'Who gave himself for us, *that he might redeem us from all iniquity.*' That is, all *lawlessness.* Namely, all 'the motions of sin.' From every class of action of the will in all the interior ungovernable rebelliousness of the unregenerate.

Let the sober, righteous, godly reader carefully read with an open bible the appropriate opening of I John 3:4-10 in my book

'The First Epistle of John', and, I trust in the Lord, there will be no doubt then what it is to have been redeemed from *all* iniquity.

Not in the future. It is *now*. He gave himself for us in the past, that he might redeem us from all lawlessness *now*, as I John 3:4-10 – quite apart from the obvious Titus 2:14 – teaches beyond all question. Not *some* lawlessness, *sometime*. But *all* lawlessness *at this time*.

As to *anomia*, lawlessness, this refers to being void of law: without restraint. As in 'Ye stiffnecked and uncircumcised in heart and ears, ye do *always* resist the Holy Ghost.' *Anomia* is not strictly outward action – as in 'whited sepulchres' – but inward intention; proximate resolution; and ultimate purpose.

This, in the will, is the whole of sin, and sin without intermission or cessation. It is irrespective of outward appearance, which in the externally religious or apparently charitable gives precisely the opposite impression.

'For the LORD seeth not as man seeth; for man looketh on the outward appearance, but the LORD looketh on the heart.' Within. Where the will is, which *every class of its action, to the very depths, does nothing but anomia*.

This genders the wrath to come.

But Christ the Saviour gave himself for his people at Golgotha *then*, to utterly, wholly, and completely redeem them from *all* lawlessness *now*. That is the work of the Holy Ghost.

He gave his Spirit to us, that we should give ourselves to the Spirit. He gave himself for us, that we should give ourselves for him. The grace of God that bringeth salvation teaches us that denying ungodliness and worldly lusts, we should live soberly, righteously, and godly *in this present world*.

Christ's death in the past transforms our life in the present, looking for that blessed hope, and the glorious appearing of our great God and Saviour Jesus Christ.

His giving of himself for us *then* was to redeem us *now*. To set us loose, free us, from all defiance of authority, all resisting of the Holy Ghost, all self-will, all living for self-gratification, in religion or out of it.

To bring in a meek and contrite spirit that trembleth at his word. Continually. From the inmost hidden parts. Evidently.

This tells you—and makes abundantly manifest before your eyes and judgment—those for whom he *really* gave himself.

But it is not all. Yet there is more. *Having been thus redeemed from all iniquity*, it follows that *this was for himself, not ourselves*.

'Who gave himself for us, that he might redeem us from all iniquity, and'—O, mark that *and*—'purify unto himself a peculiar people, zealous of good works', Titus 2:14.

Then, this *which is for himself*, must, but must, follow and act in concert with being redeemed from all iniquity.

To be redeemed from all iniquity is not for oneself, or one's so-called service, or individual pathway: it must, but must, issue in a company, a gathered out people, *for himself.* To 'purify unto *himself* a peculiar *people.*'

And there is only one company like that under heaven, wherever gathered; for ever united; called 'purified unto himself': from the world, from worldly religion, from the flesh, from worldliness. That is, *purified*: without mixture: the word is 'purified'.

Called 'purified unto himself': from the flesh, the flesh being constantly judged. Walking not in the flesh, but in the Spirit;

dwelling not in the flesh, but in the Spirit. Abiding not in the flesh, but in the Spirit.

Not minding the things of the flesh, but minding the things of the Spirit. Without mixture: the word is 'purified'.

Purified *unto himself.* 'That they which live should not henceforth live unto themselves, but unto him which died for them, and rose again.' 'For ye are dead, and your life is hid with Christ in God.' 'Ye are not your own: ye are bought with a price.'

'A peculiar people.' Called 'the body of Christ.' 'The temple of God', with 'the Spirit of God dwelling in you.' 'The house of God, the *ecclesia* of the living God, the pillar and ground of the truth.' Singular: beyond the ordinary: indeed, unique.

Such a peerless people is zealous of good works. Such a matchless company is subject and obedient to Christ in his ministers, sent to the whole body to bring all into the fellowship of the mystery:

'These things speak, and exhort, and rebuke with all authority. Let no man despise thee', Titus 2:15.

And what will such sound doctrine, not to be condemned, bring in but this: a people who by patient continuance in good works seek for glory and honour and immortality?

Not to *be* saved, but because they *are* saved. Not to *obtain* his giving himself for them, but because he *has* given himself for them.

That kind of people: A people saved from the wrath to come.

But how is so great salvation brought to such a people? By appointment. Since man cannot reach to it, the grace of God must bring it, if ever men are to be saved.

Bring it how? Bring it by appointment. There is no other way that salvation will come to sinners, but by the appointment of the Majesty on high. This saves from the wrath to come.

'For God hath not appointed us to wrath, but to obtain salvation by our Lord Jesus Christ, who died for us, that, whether we wake or sleep, we should live together with him', I Thessalonians 5:9,10.

This verse shows that beyond all question of doubt *God is the author of salvation, first and last.* It is not of man, no, not in any part of it, in its accomplishment, application, or consummation.

Salvation is of the LORD, and it is *all* of the LORD, nothing of man at any stage enters into the matter, from beginning to end. It is God's appointment.

Then, he has not 'deposited' salvation in the 'church'–so-called–so that the 'church' should dispense salvation. It is his own appointment *individually, personally, and directly:* 'Neither is there salvation in any other: for there is none other name under heaven given among men, whereby we must be saved.'

God saves, by appointment, directly.

Much less is salvation dispensed by a 'priesthood' not so much as envisaged in the new testament, but which has been invented since in the apostasy, copying the voided and abolished old testament priesthood in vestment, function, architecture, and mediatorship. This is a lie.

Supposing God to have deposited salvation in the 'church'– as they call their bricks, stones, wood, and mortar–they then foist upon the superstitious the notion that none but their man-made priests are authorized to dispense it. And *where is God's appointment in that?* Nowhere.

Neither is salvation within the reach of the withered arm of free will, as though it were 'offered'–a term foreign to the whole bible, and alien to the entire evangel–to all.

Verily, verily, I say unto you, *Salvation is appointed to whom God will.*

The saved are 'appointed' of God to salvation, I Thessalonians 5:9.

Much less is salvation—falsely supposed to be 'deposited' in the church, and 'dispensed' by the humanly imposed 'priesthood'—administered, conveyed, or communicated by 'sacraments' as the apostasy erroneously and deceitfully invent, having perversely mangled the ordinances.

The appointment is *direct* from God to the sinner. Neither more nor less.

It is none of man's things, but *God himself in person* who has appointed us *personally and individually* to obtain salvation.

It is *there*: Salvation is *there*. The question is, How is it obtained? The answer is before you: 'God *hath appointed us* to obtain salvation.'

Then who is the 'us' to whom the apostle refers? Those of whom Paul declares, 'knowing, brethren beloved, your election of God.' About whom he recalls 'our gospel came not unto you in word only, but also in power, and in the Holy Ghost, and in much assurance', I Thessalonians 1:4,5.

Those to whom the apostle bears record, 'Ye became followers of us, and of the Lord', testifying 'what manner of entering in we had unto you, and how ye turned to God from idols to serve the living and true God;

'And to wait for his Son from heaven, whom he raised from the dead, even Jesus, which delivered us from the wrath to come', I Thessalonians 1:9,10. These are the 'us' whom God has appointed to obtain salvation.

And *that* was the manner of appointment, described in the first chapter, and summarized later: 'For God hath not appointed us to wrath, but to obtain salvation by our Lord Jesus Christ', I Thessalonians 5:9.

These were prefigured by the publicans and sinners; the lepers; the lame; the blind; the deaf; the dumb; the palsied; the dead.

These were personified by the foolish; the weak; the base; the despised; those who are nothing. These labour and are heavy laden. These are the poor, the meek, the mourning, the hungering after righteousness, the broken and contrite in spirit.

God has not appointed these to wrath, but to obtain salvation by our Lord Jesus Christ, to whom he draws them. And the Saviour never, no, never casts them out. He brings them in. He saves them *himself*. By *his* having borne *their* sin and wrath.

'To appoint unto them that mourn in Zion, to give unto them beauty for ashes, the oil of joy for mourning, the garment of praise for the spirit of heaviness; that they might be called trees of righteousness, the planting of the LORD, that he might be glorified', Isaiah 61:3.

'In that day shall this song be sung in the land of Judah; We have a strong city; salvation will God appoint for walls and bulwarks. Open ye the gates, that the righteous nation which keepeth the truth may enter in', Isaiah 26:1,2.

But there are others, who have a different appointment. Of these the apostle Peter speaks when referring to Jesus Christ in relation to the self-righteous.

To these Christ is 'a stone of stumbling, and a rock of offence, even to them which stumble at the word, being disobedient: whereunto also they were appointed', I Peter 2:8.

417

John speaks of such, saying, 'Therefore they could not believe, because that Esaias said again, He hath blinded their eyes, and hardened their heart; that they should not see with their eyes, nor understand with their heart, and be converted, and I should heal them', John 12:39,40.

As Jesus says in another place, 'But ye believe not, because ye are not of my sheep.' Wherefore you see that there is one appointment for the sheep, who hear his voice and obediently follow him, and another for the goats, who hear no voice at all, but disobediently stumble at the word.

Of these Christ declares, 'For this people's heart is waxed gross, and their ears are dull of hearing, and their eyes they have closed; lest at any time'–at *any* time–'they should see with their eyes, and hear with their ears, and should understand with their heart, and should be converted, and I should heal them', Matthew 13:15.

Note that 'at *any* time': whence you see that God keeps his appointments, and *never* breaks them, neither with his sheep, who hear his voice, and follow him in the obedience of faith:

Nor yet with the goats, who hear nothing, profess everything, but stumble in the disobedience of unbelief at the word of faith which we preach.

Seeing, they see not; hearing, they hear not; and understand they cannot.

That was the appointment, and God will keep it of a truth.

But who are these that are so appointed? Thieves, murderers, harlots, publicans? No, the rather those who, being ignorant of God's righteousness, go about to establish their own righteousness. The self-righteous, who justify themselves.

'Jesus saith unto *them*, Verily I say unto you, That the publicans and the harlots go into the kingdom of God before *you*', Matthew

21:31. 'And he spake this parable unto certain which trusted in themselves that they were righteous, and despised others:

'Two men went up into the temple to pray; the one a Pharisee, and the other a publican. The Pharisee stood and prayed thus with himself, God, I thank thee, that I am not as other men are, extortioners, unjust, adulterers, or even as this publican.

'I fast twice in the week, I give tithes of all that I possess. And the publican, standing afar off, would not lift up so much as his eyes unto heaven, but smote upon his breast, saying, God be merciful to me a sinner.

'I tell you, this man went down to his house justified rather than the other: for every one that exalteth himself shall be abased; and he that humbleth himself shall be exalted', Luke 18:9-14.

Mary saw this very thing, saying of God's appointments, respectively, 'His mercy is on them that fear him from generation to generation.

'He hath showed strength with his arm; he hath scattered the proud in the imagination of their hearts. He hath put down the mighty from their seats, and exalted them of low degree.

'He hath filled the hungry with good things; and the rich he hath sent empty away. He hath holpen his servant Israel, in remembrance of his mercy; as he spake to our fathers, to Abraham, and to his seed for ever', Luke 1:50-55.

Pointing to the stone of offence, and rock of stumbling, Paul emphasizes precisely the same thing, saying, 'For the preaching of the cross is to them that perish foolishness; but unto us which are saved it is the power of God.

'For it is written, I will destroy the wisdom of the wise, and will bring to nothing the understanding of the prudent. Where is the wise? where is the scribe? where is the disputer of this world?

hath not God made foolish the wisdom of this world? For after that in the wisdom of God the world by wisdom knew not God,

'It pleased God by the foolishness of preaching to save them that believe. For the Jews require a sign, and the Greeks seek after wisdom: but we preach Christ crucified, unto the Jews a stumblingblock, and unto the Greeks foolishness;

'But unto them which are called, both Jews and Greeks, Christ the power of God, and the wisdom of God. Because the foolishness of God is wiser than men; and the weakness of God is stronger than men.

'For ye see your calling, brethren, how that not many wise men after the flesh, not many mighty, not many noble, are called: but God hath chosen the foolish things of the world to confound the wise; and God hath chosen the weak things of the world to confound the things which are mighty;

'And base things of the world, and things which are despised, hath God chosen, yea, and things which are not, to bring to nought things that are: that no flesh should glory in his presence.'

Now, these are the marks of God's appointments respectively, whether to wrath, or to salvation. The ability of man does not come into it: but the resultant character speaks for itself, and it is brought to light by those sent to preach, teach, and establish the evangel.

'For we are unto God a sweet savour of Christ, in them that are saved, and in them that perish: to the one we are the savour of death unto death; and to the other the savour of life unto life. And who is sufficient for these things?

'For we are not as many, which corrupt the word of God: but as of sincerity, but as of God, in the sight of God speak we in Christ', II Corinthians 2:15-17.

The character of those appointed unto wrath is more often than not those who cloak themselves with the form of religion. They search the scriptures, but their hearts are covetous. They have the form of religion, but they are devoid of its power.

They make clean the outside of the cup and platter, but within they are full of extortion and excess. They are like unto whited sepulchres, which indeed appear beautiful outward, but are within full of dead men's bones, and of all uncleanness.

These are not the poor in spirit; they never mourn; they are not the meek; neither do they hunger and thirst after righteousness. Mercy is far from them, and they sow discord among brethren, being talebearers, knowing nothing of making peace.

How then can they be vessels of mercy, appointed to salvation? They have not the sacrifices of God, that is, a broken spirit, namely, a broken and a contrite heart which weeps now, and shall never be refused or despised of God.

Not that the vessels of mercy appointed themselves, or were any better. They were worse. But it pleased God to take these despised, contemptible things, and make of them vessels of mercy, to show forth his glory, that no flesh should glory in his presence.

'For he saith to Moses, I will have mercy on whom I will have mercy, and I will have compassion on whom I will have compassion.

'So then it is not of him that willeth, nor of him that runneth, but of God that showeth mercy.

'For the scripture saith unto Pharaoh, Even for this same purpose have I raised thee up, that I might show my power in thee, and that my name might be declared throughout all the earth.

'Therefore hath he mercy on whom he will have mercy, and whom he will he hardeneth. Thou wilt say then unto me, Why doth he yet find fault? For who hath resisted his will?

'Nay but, O man, who art thou that repliest against God? Shall the thing formed say to him that formed it, Why hast thou made me thus?

'Hath not the potter power over the clay, of the same lump to make one vessel unto honour, and another unto dishonour?

'What if God, willing to show his wrath, and to make his power known, *endured with much longsuffering* the vessels of wrath fitted to destruction:

'And that he might make known the riches of his glory on the vessels of mercy, which he had afore prepared unto glory, even us, whom he hath called, not of the Jews only, but also of the Gentiles?', Romans 9:15-24.

Now these are his appointments, to wrath and salvation respectively, and if, under the longsuffering of God, men choose to fit themselves on the one hand, Why should they complain if God chooses to prepare the unfit, who can do nothing, on the other?

For we, whom they despise, know that God prepared us by an eternal election in Christ before the world was. We know that he accomplished salvation in everlasting righteousness by the blood of Christ in the midst of time.

And we know that the grace of God that bringeth salvation hath appeared unto us to apply that salvation in our lifetime, 'teaching us that, denying ungodliness and worldly lusts, we should live soberly, righteously, and godly, in this present world;

'Looking for that blessed hope, and the glorious appearing of the great God and our Saviour Jesus Christ; who gave himself for us, that he might redeem us from all lawlessness, and purify unto himself a peculiar people, zealous of good works.'

It was the Father who predestinated us in Christ to salvation; it was the Son who gave himself for us to accomplish salvation; and it is the Spirit who indwells us to apply salvation.

Wherefore we fall on our faces and cry out in thanksgiving, 'Salvation belongeth unto the LORD: thy blessing is upon thy people', Psalm 3:8. Amen and amen.

JOHN METCALFE

INDEX

TO OTHER PUBLICATIONS

PSALMS, HYMNS AND SPIRITUAL SONGS

Thoroughly revised second edition

THE PSALMS

OF THE

OLD TESTAMENT

The Psalms of the Old Testament, the result of years of painstaking labour, is an original translation into verse from the Authorized Version, which seeks to present the Psalms in the purest scriptural form possible for singing. Here, for the first time, divine names are rendered as and when they occur in the scripture, the distinction between LORD and Lord has been preserved, and every essential point of doctrine and experience appears with unique perception and fidelity.

The Psalms of the Old Testament is the first part of a trilogy written by John Metcalfe, the second part of which is entitled *Spiritual Songs from the Gospels*, and the last, *The Hymns of the New Testament*. These titles provide unique and accurate metrical versions of passages from the psalms, the gospels and the new testament epistles respectively, and are intended to be used together in the worship of God.

Price £2.50 (*postage extra*)
(hard-case binding, dust-jacket)
Printed, sewn and bound
by the John Metcalfe Publishing Trust
ISBN 1 870039 75 0

SPIRITUAL SONGS

FROM

THE GOSPELS

The *Spiritual Songs from the Gospels*, the result of years of painstaking labour, is an original translation into verse from the Authorized Version, which seeks to present essential parts of the gospels in the purest scriptural form possible for singing. The careful selection from Matthew, Mark, Luke, and John, set forth in metrical verse of the highest integrity, enables the singer to sing 'the word of Christ' as if from the scripture itself, 'richly and in all wisdom'; and, above all, in a way that facilitates worship in song of unprecedented fidelity.

The *Spiritual Songs from the Gospels* is the central part of a trilogy written by John Metcalfe, the first part of which is entitled *The Psalms of the Old Testament*, and the last, *The Hymns of the New Testament*. These titles provide unique and accurate metrical versions of passages from the psalms, the gospels and the new testament epistles respectively, and are intended to be used together in the worship of God.

Price £2.50 *(postage extra)*
(hard-case binding, dust-jacket)
Printed, sewn and bound
by the John Metcalfe Publishing Trust
ISBN 0 9506366 8 1

THE HYMNS

OF THE

NEW TESTAMENT

The Hymns of the New Testament, the result of years of painstaking labour, is an original translation into verse from the Authorized Version, which presents essential parts of the new testament epistles in the purest scriptural form possible for singing. The careful selection from the book of Acts to that of Revelation, set forth in metrical verse of the highest integrity, enables the singer to sing 'the word of Christ' as if from the scripture itself, 'richly and in all wisdom'; and, above all, in a way that facilitates worship in song of unprecedented fidelity.

The Hymns of the New Testament is the last part of a trilogy written by John Metcalfe, the first part of which is entitled *The Psalms of the Old Testament*, and the next, *Spiritual Songs from the Gospels*. These titles provide unique and accurate metrical versions of passages from the psalms, the gospels and the new testament epistles respectively, and are intended to be used together in the worship of God.

Price £2.50 (*postage extra*)
(hard-case binding, dust-jacket)
Printed, sewn and bound
by the John Metcalfe Publishing Trust
ISBN 0 9506366 9 X

'THE APOSTOLIC FOUNDATION
OF THE
CHRISTIAN CHURCH' SERIES

Third Printing

FOUNDATIONS UNCOVERED

THE APOSTOLIC FOUNDATION
OF THE
CHRISTIAN CHURCH

Volume I

Foundations Uncovered is the introduction to the major series: 'The Apostolic Foundation of the Christian Church'.

Rich in truth, the Introduction deals comprehensively with the foundation of the apostolic faith under the descriptive titles: The Word, The Doctrine, The Truth, The Gospel, The Faith, The New Testament, and The Foundation.

The contents of the book reveal: The Fact of the Foundation; The Foundation Uncovered; What the Foundation is not; How the Foundation is Described; and, Being Built upon the Foundation.

'This book comes with the freshness of a new Reformation.'

Price 75p *(postage extra)*
Paperback 110 pages (Laminated cover)
Printed, sewn and bound
by the John Metcalfe Publishing Trust
ISBN 0 9506366 5 7

*Thoroughly revised and extensively rewritten
second edition (Hardback)*

Third Printing

THE MESSIAH

THE APOSTOLIC FOUNDATION
OF THE
CHRISTIAN CHURCH

Volume III

The Messiah is a spiritually penetrating and entirely original
exposition of Matthew chapter one to chapter seven from the
trenchant pen of John Metcalfe.

Matthew Chapters One to Seven

GENEALOGY · BIRTH · STAR OF BETHLEHEM
HEROD · FLIGHT TO EGYPT · NAZARETH
JOHN THE BAPTIST · THE BAPTIST'S MINISTRY
JESUS' BAPTISM · ALL RIGHTEOUSNESS FULFILLED
HEAVEN OPENED · THE SPIRIT'S DESCENT
THE TEMPTATION OF JESUS IN THE WILDERNESS
JESUS' MANIFESTATION · THE CALLING · THE TRUE DISCIPLES
THE BEATITUDES · THE SERMON ON THE MOUNT

'Something of the fire of the ancient Hebrew prophet ......
Metcalfe has spiritual and expository potentials of a high order.'

The Life of Faith.

Price £7.75 (*postage extra*)
Hardback 420 pages
Laminated bookjacket
Printed, sewn and bound
by the John Metcalfe Publishing Trust
ISBN 1 870039 51 3

Second Edition (Hardback)

THE SON OF GOD AND SEED OF DAVID

THE APOSTOLIC FOUNDATION
OF THE
CHRISTIAN CHURCH

Volume IV

The Son of God and Seed of David is the fourth volume in the major work entitled 'The Apostolic Foundation of the Christian Church'.

'The Author proceeds to open and allege that Jesus Christ is and ever was *The Son of God*. This greatest of subjects, this most profound of all mysteries, is handled with reverence and with outstanding perception.

'The second part considers *The Seed of David*. What is meant precisely by 'the seed'? And why 'of David'? With prophetic insight the author expounds these essential verities.'

Price £6.95 *(postage extra)*
Hardback 250 pages
Laminated bookjacket
Printed, sewn and bound
by the John Metcalfe Publishing Trust
ISBN 1 870039 16 5

CHRIST CRUCIFIED

THE APOSTOLIC FOUNDATION
OF THE
CHRISTIAN CHURCH

Volume V

Christ Crucified, the definitive work on the crucifixion, the blood, and the cross of Jesus Christ.

The crucifixion of Jesus Christ witnessed in the Gospels: the gospel according to Matthew; Mark; Luke; John.

The blood of Jesus Christ declared in the Epistles: the shed blood; the blood of purchase; redemption through his blood; the blood of sprinkling; the blood of the covenant.

The doctrine of the cross revealed in the apostolic foundation of the Christian church: the doctrine of the cross; the cross and the body of sin; the cross and the carnal mind; the cross and the law; the offence of the cross; the cross of our Lord Jesus Christ.

Price £6.95 (*postage extra*)
Hardback 300 pages
Laminated bookjacket
Printed, sewn and bound
by the John Metcalfe Publishing Trust
ISBN 1 870039 08 4

JUSTIFICATION BY FAITH

THE APOSTOLIC FOUNDATION
OF THE
CHRISTIAN CHURCH

Volume VI

The Heart of the Gospel · The Foundation of the Church
The Issue of Eternity
Clearly, Originally and Powerfully Opened

The basis · The righteousness of the law
The righteousness of God · The atonement · Justification
Traditional views considered · Righteousness imputed to faith
Faith counted for righteousness · Justification by Faith

'And it came to pass, when Jesus had ended these sayings, the people
were astonished at his doctrine: for he taught them as one having
authority, and not as the scribes', Matthew 7:28,29.

Price £7.50 (postage extra)
Hardback 375 pages
Laminated bookjacket
Printed, sewn and bound
by the John Metcalfe Publishing Trust
ISBN 1·870039 11 4

THE CHURCH: WHAT IS IT?

THE APOSTOLIC FOUNDATION
OF THE
CHRISTIAN CHURCH

Volume VII

The answer to this question proceeds first from the lips of Jesus himself, Mt. 16:18, later to be expounded by the words of the apostles whom he sent.

Neither fear of man nor favour from the world remotely affect the answer.

Here is the truth, the whole truth, and nothing but the truth.

The complete originality, the vast range, and the total fearlessness of this book command the attention in a way that is unique.

Read this book: you will never read another like it.

Outspokenly devastating yet devastatingly constructive.

Price £7.75 (*postage extra*)
Hardback 400 pages
Laminated bookjacket
Printed, sewn and bound
by the John Metcalfe Publishing Trust
ISBN 1 870039 23 8

THE REVELATION OF JESUS CHRIST

THE APOSTOLIC FOUNDATION
OF THE
CHRISTIAN CHURCH

Volume VIII

Uniquely perceptive and original, the result of decades alone in the secret place of the most High, abiding under the shadow of the Almighty, this peerless work on the Revelation of Jesus Christ will stand the test of time and eternity for its heavenly, spiritual, and divine opening into the last book of the last apostle of the new testament, for all who have an ear to hear what the Spirit saith unto the churches.

Here is the transcript of the series of addresses delivered over some eighteen months during 1997 and 1998, in the Assembly Hall, Church House, Westminster, London, by John Metcalfe.

The famed Assembly Hall is used as the Synod Chamber of the Church of England as occasion requires.

Price £9.25 (*postage extra*)
Hardback 640 pages
Laminated bookjacket
Printed, sewn and bound
by the John Metcalfe Publishing Trust
ISBN 1 870039 77 7

THE MINISTRY OF RECONCILIATION

THE APOSTOLIC FOUNDATION
OF THE
CHRISTIAN CHURCH

Volume IX

THE MINISTRY OF RECONCILIATION

The Implication of Reconciliation · The Ministry of Reconciliation
The Tenses in Reconciliation · The Scope of Reconciliation
The Ground of Reconciliation

THE MEANING OF 'RECONCILIATION'

THE NATURE OF RECONCILIATION

The Substitution · The Doctrine
The Premise: Adam and Christ, Romans 5:12-14
The Three Comparisons, Romans 5:15-17
The Two Deductions, Romans 5:18-19
Parenthesis: The Law, verse 20 · The Conclusion, Romans 5:21

Price £6.95 (postage extra)
Hardback 270 pages
Laminated bookjacket
Printed, sewn and bound
by the John Metcalfe Publishing Trust
ISBN 1 870039 87 4

NEWLY PUBLISHED

SALVATION

THE APOSTOLIC FOUNDATION
OF THE
CHRISTIAN CHURCH

Volume X

SALVATION FROM SIN

Wilful Sins · The Remission of Sins · Inbred Sin

SALVATION FROM SATAN

The 'Satan' · The 'Devil' · The 'Prince' · The 'Serpent'

SALVATION FROM THE WORLD

Salvation from the World:
'Aiōn' · 'Gē' · 'Oikoumenē' · 'Kosmos'

SALVATION FROM THE WRATH TO COME

'Thumos' and 'Orgē' · 'Sheol'; 'Hadēs'; 'Gehenna'
The Meaning of the Words
Figures of the True · Salvation from Wrath

Price £9.25 (postage extra)
Hardback 500 pages
Laminated bookjacket
Printed, sewn and bound
by the John Metcalfe Publishing Trust
ISBN 1 870039 88 2

LECTURES
FROM
CHURCH HOUSE, WESTMINSTER

COLOSSIANS

This concise and unique revelation of the Epistle to the Colossians has the hallmark of spiritual originality and insight peculiar to the ministry of John Metcalfe. It is as if a diamond, inert and lifeless in itself, has been divinely cut at great cost, so that every way in which it is turned, the light from above is enhanced and magnified to break forth with divine radiance showing colour and depth hitherto unsuspected.

Price 95p *(postage extra)*
Paperback 135 pages (Laminated cover)
Printed, sewn and bound
by the John Metcalfe Publishing Trust
ISBN 1 870039 55 6

MATTHEW

This concise revelation of the essence and structure of the Gospel according to Matthew, the culmination of years of prayer and devotion, retreat and study, opens the mind of the Spirit in the unique vision of Jesus Christ, the son of David, the son of Abraham, recorded in the first gospel.

Price 95p *(postage extra)*
Paperback 135 pages (Laminated cover)
Printed, sewn and bound
by the John Metcalfe Publishing Trust
ISBN 1 870039 61 0

PHILIPPIANS

The Epistle of Paul the Apostle to the Philippians is opened by this work from the pen of John Metcalfe with that lucid thoroughness which one has come to expect from a ministry received 'not of men, neither by man, but by the revelation of Jesus Christ'.

The work of God at Philippi is traced 'from the first day' until the time at which the epistle was written. Never was Lydia or the Philippian jailor drawn with more lively insight. The epistle itself is revealed in order, with passages–such as 'the mind that was in Christ Jesus'–that evidence the work of no less than a divine for our own times.

Price £1.90 (*postage extra*)
Paperback 185 pages (Laminated cover)
Printed, sewn and bound
by the John Metcalfe Publishing Trust
ISBN 1 870039 56 4

PHILEMON

This penetrating revelation of the Epistle to Philemon opens the substance of four consecutive lectures given by John Metcalfe in The Hoare Memorial Hall, Church House, Westminster, London.

Price £1.90 (*postage extra*)
Paperback 190 pages (Laminated cover)
Printed, sewn and bound
by the John Metcalfe Publishing Trust
ISBN 1 870039 66 1

FIRST TIMOTHY

This penetrating revelation of the First Epistle to Timothy opens the substance of five consecutive lectures given by John Metcalfe in The Hoare Memorial Hall, Church House, Westminster, London.

Price £2.00 *(postage extra)*
Paperback 220 pages (Laminated cover)
Printed, sewn and bound
by the John Metcalfe Publishing Trust
ISBN 1 870039 67 X

Fourth Printing

CREATION

Genesis 1:1, 'In the beginning God created the heaven and the earth.'

This spiritually penetrating and outstandingly original revelation of the Creation from Genesis chapters 1 and 2 opens the substance of five consecutive lectures given by John Metcalfe, commencing in the Hoare Memorial Hall and later moving to the central Assembly Hall, Church House, Westminster, London.

The Hoare Memorial Hall was used as the House of Commons at various times during the Second World War. Many of Sir Winston Churchill's renowned war time speeches were delivered in this Hall. The famed Assembly Hall is used as the Synod Chamber of the Church of England as occasion requires.

Price £2.00 *(postage extra)*
Paperback 230 pages (Laminated cover)
Printed, sewn and bound
by the John Metcalfe Publishing Trust
ISBN 1 870039 71 8

MARK

This penetrating revelation of the Gospel according to Mark opens the substance of seven consecutive lectures given by John Metcalfe in The Hoare Memorial Hall, Church House, Westminster, London.

Price £2.35 (*postage extra*)
Paperback 290 pages (Laminated cover)
Printed, sewn and bound
by the John Metcalfe Publishing Trust
ISBN 1 870039 70 X

THE FIRST EPISTLE OF JOHN

Deeply spiritual and of the very essence, it is as if one heard the apostle himself taking and opening the book in a way that is unprecedented.

THE BEGINNING . THE MESSAGE . THE COMMANDMENTS

THE LITTLE CHILDREN . THE ABIDING

THE WITNESS . THE CONCLUSION

Price £9.25 (*postage extra*)
Hardback 585 pages
Laminated bookjacket
Printed, sewn and bound
by the John Metcalfe Publishing Trust
ISBN 1 870039 78 5

OTHER TITLES

Second Edition

Fourth Printing

NOAH AND THE FLOOD

Noah and the Flood expounds with vital urgency the man and the message that heralded the end of the old world. The description of the flood itself is vividly realistic. The whole work has an unmistakable ring of authority, and speaks as 'Thus saith the Lord'.

'Mr. Metcalfe makes a skilful use of persuasive eloquence as he challenges the reality of one's profession of faith ... he gives a rousing call to a searching self-examination and evaluation of one's spiritual experience.'

The Monthly Record of the Free Church of Scotland.

Price £1.90 (*postage extra*)
Paperback 155 pages (Laminated cover)
Printed, sewn and bound
by the John Metcalfe Publishing Trust
ISBN 1 870039 22 X

DIVINE FOOTSTEPS

Divine Footsteps traces the pathway of the feet of the Son of man from the very beginning in the prophetic figures of the true in the old testament through the reality in the new; doing so in a way of experimental spirituality. At the last a glimpse of the coming glory is beheld as his feet are viewed as standing at the latter day upon the earth.

Price 95p (*postage extra*)
Paperback 120 pages (Laminated cover)
Printed, sewn and bound by
the John Metcalfe Publishing Trust
ISBN 1 870039 21 1

Second Edition
Third Printing

THE RED HEIFER

The Red Heifer was the name given to a sacrifice used by the children of Israel in the Old Testament – as recorded in Numbers 19 – in which a heifer was slain and burned. Cedar wood, hyssop and scarlet were cast into the burning, and the ashes were mingled with running water and put in a vessel. It was kept for the children of Israel for a water of separation: it was a purification for sin.

In this unusual book the sacrifice is brought up to date and its relevance to the church today is shown.

Price 95p *(postage extra)*
Paperback 120 pages
ISBN 1 870039 89 0

OF GOD OR MAN?

LIGHT FROM GALATIANS

The Epistle to the Galatians contends for deliverance from the law and from carnal ministry.

The Apostle opens his matter in two ways:

Firstly, Paul vindicates himself and his ministry against those that came not from God above, but from Jerusalem below.

Secondly, he defends the Gospel and evangelical liberty against legal perversions and bondage to the flesh.

Price £1.45 *(postage extra)*
Paperback 190 pages (Laminated cover)
ISBN 0 9506366 3 0

THE BOOK OF RUTH

The Book of Ruth is set against the farming background of old testament Israel at the time of the Judges, the narrative – unfolding the work of God in redemption – being marked by a series of agricultural events.

These events – the famine; the barley harvest; the wheat harvest; the winnowing – possessed a hidden spiritual significance to that community, but, much more, they speak in figure directly to our own times, as the book reveals.

Equally contemporary appear the characters of Ruth, Naomi, Boaz, and the first kinsman, drawn with spiritual perception greatly to the profit of the reader.

Price £4.95 *(postage extra)*
Hardback 200 pages
Laminated bookjacket
Printed, sewn and bound
by the John Metcalfe Publishing Trust
ISBN 1 870039 17 3

A QUESTION FOR POPE JOHN PAUL II

As a consequence of his many years spent apart in prayer, lonely vigil, and painstaking study of the scripture, John Metcalfe asks a question and looks for an answer from Pope John Paul II.

Price £1.25 *(postage extra)*
Paperback 105 pages (Laminated cover)
ISBN 0 9506366 4 9

DIVINE MEDITATIONS

OF

WILLIAM HUNTINGTON

Originally published by Mr. Huntington as a series of letters to J. Jenkins, under the title of 'Contemplations on the God of Israel', the spiritual content of this correspondence has been skilfully and sympathetically edited, abridged, and arranged so as to form a series of meditations, suitable for daily readings.

Mr. Huntington's own text is thereby adapted to speak directly to the reader in a way much more suited to his ministering immediately to ourselves, in our own circumstances and times.

It is greatly hoped that many today will benefit from this adaptation which carefully retains both the spirit and the letter of the text. If any prefer the original format, this is readily available from several sources and many libraries.

Nevertheless, the publishers believe the much more readable form into which Mr. Huntington's very words have been adapted will appeal to a far wider audience, for whose comfort and consolation this carefully edited work has been published.

Price £2.35 (*postage extra*)
Paperback 300 pages (Laminated cover)
Printed, sewn and bound
by the John Metcalfe Publishing Trust
ISBN 1 870039 24 6

Second Edition
Third Printing

THE WELLS OF SALVATION

The Wells of Salvation is written from a series of seven powerful addresses preached at Tylers Green. It is a forthright and experimental exposition of Isaiah 12:3, 'Therefore with joy shall ye draw water out of the wells of salvation.'

John Metcalfe is acknowledged to be perhaps the most gifted expositor and powerful preacher of our day and this is to be seen clearly in The Wells of Salvation.

Price £2.35 *(postage extra)*
Paperback 285 pages (Laminated cover)
Printed, sewn and bound
by the John Metcalfe Publishing Trust
ISBN 1 870039 72 6

Second Printing

SAVING FAITH

The sevenfold work of the Holy Ghost in bringing a sinner to saving faith in Christ opened and enlarged.

True faith is the work of God. False faith is the presumption of man. But where is the difference? *Saving Faith* shows the difference.

Price £2.25 *(postage extra)*
Paperback 250 pages (Laminated cover)
Printed, sewn and bound
by the John Metcalfe Publishing Trust
ISBN 1 870039 40 8

DELIVERANCE FROM THE LAW
THE WESTMINSTER CONFESSION EXPLODED

Deliverance from the Law. A devastating vindication of the gospel of Christ against the traditions of man.

Price £1.90 *(postage extra)*
Paperback 160 pages (Laminated cover)
Printed, sewn and bound
by the John Metcalfe Publishing Trust
ISBN 1 870039 41 6

PRESENT-DAY CONVERSIONS
OF THE NEW TESTAMENT KIND

FROM THE MINISTRY OF
JOHN METCALFE

The outstandingly striking presentation of this fascinating paperback will surely catch the eye, as its title and contents will certainly captivate the mind: here is a unique publication.

Woven into a gripping narrative, over twenty-one short life stories, all centred on conversions that simply could not have happened had not God broken in, and had not Christ been revealed, the book presents a tremendous challenge, at once moving and thrilling to the reader.

Price £2.25 *(postage extra)*
Paperback 240 pages (Laminated cover)
Printed, sewn and bound
by the John Metcalfe Publishing Trust
ISBN 1 870039 31 9

THE BEATITUDES

A unique insight destined to be the classic opening of this wonderful sequence of utterances from the lips of Jesus.

The reader will discover a penetration of the spiritual heights and divine depths of these peerless words in a way ever fresh and always rewarding though read time and time again.

Price £1.90 (*postage extra*)
Paperback 185 pages (Laminated cover)
Printed, sewn and bound
by the John Metcalfe Publishing Trust
ISBN 1 870039 45 9

PASTORAL LETTERS TO THE FAR EAST

Feeling the abiding spiritual value of letters written by John Metcalfe in his absence from the Far East, Miss Sie Siok Hui cherished the correspondence to her, and at the same time was moved to seek for similar writings to some of her closest sisters in Christ.

Gathering these letters together, it was her earnest desire that such an enduring testimony should be made available to all the faithful remnant in our own day. The result of her prayers and spiritual exercise appears in the publication 'Pastoral Letters to the Far East'.

Price £2.00 (*postage extra*)
Paperback 240 pages (Laminated cover)
Printed, sewn and bound
by the John Metcalfe Publishing Trust
ISBN 1 870039 74 2

LAW AND GRACE CONTRASTED

A SERIES OF ADDRESSES

BY

WILLIAM HUNTINGTON

The Child of Liberty in Legal Bondage · The Bondchild
brought to the Test · The Modern Plasterer Detected
Not under Law · The Law a Rule of Life?

Mr. Huntington's own text is adapted to speak directly to the
reader in a way much more suited to his ministering immediately to ourselves, in our own circumstances and times.

It is greatly hoped that many today will benefit from this
adaptation which carefully retains both the spirit and the letter
of the text. If any prefer the original format, this is readily
available from several sources and many libraries.

Nevertheless, the publishers believe the much more readable
form into which Mr. Huntington's very words have been
adapted will appeal to a far wider audience, for whose comfort
and consolation this carefully edited work has been published.

Price £2.35 *(postage extra)*
Paperback 265 pages (Laminated cover)
Printed, sewn and bound
by the John Metcalfe Publishing Trust
ISBN 1 870039 76 9

THE GIFTS AND BAPTISM
OF THE SPIRIT

For so long confusion has reigned in respect of THE GIFTS AND
BAPTISM OF THE SPIRIT. Here at last is that spiritual, sound, and
balanced opening of the Holy Scripture from I Corinthians 12:1-13.

This gives the unmistakable ring of apostolic authority, puts the
matter beyond the realm of speculation or experiment, past all
doubt bringing the text into the light of revelation of Jesus Christ.

Price 95p (*postage extra*)
Paperback 128 pages (Laminated cover)
Printed, sewn and bound
by the John Metcalfe Publishing Trust
ISBN 1 870039 80 7

THE BODY OF CHRIST
AND THE GIFTS

For so long confusion has reigned in respect of THE BODY OF CHRIST
AND THE GIFTS. Here at last is that spiritual, sound, and balanced
opening of the Holy Scripture from I Corinthians 12:14-13:13.

This gives the unmistakable ring of apostolic authority, puts the
matter beyond the realm of speculation or experiment, past all
doubt bringing the text into the light of revelation of Jesus Christ.

Price 95p (*postage extra*)
Paperback 140 pages (Laminated cover)
Printed, sewn and bound
by the John Metcalfe Publishing Trust
ISBN 1 870039 82 3

THE COMING RESURRECTION
OF THE DEAD

For so long confusion has reigned in respect of THE COMING RESURRECTION OF THE DEAD. Here at last is that spiritual, sound, and balanced opening of the Holy Scripture from I Corinthians 15.

This gives the unmistakable ring of apostolic authority, puts the matter beyond the realm of speculation or prejudice, past all doubt bringing the text into the light of revelation of Jesus Christ.

Price 95p (*postage extra*)
Paperback 145 pages (Laminated cover)
Printed, sewn and bound
by the John Metcalfe Publishing Trust
ISBN 1 870039 85 8

THE GIFTS OF TONGUES
AND OF PROPHECY

For so long confusion has reigned in respect of THE GIFTS OF TONGUES AND OF PROPHECY. Here at last is that spiritual, sound, and balanced opening of the Holy Scripture from I Corinthians 14.

This gives the unmistakable ring of apostolic authority, puts the matter beyond the realm of speculation or experiment, past all doubt bringing the text into the light of revelation of Jesus Christ.

Price 95p (*postage extra*)
Paperback 90 pages (Laminated cover)
Printed, sewn and bound
by the John Metcalfe Publishing Trust
ISBN 1 870039 86 6

OPENINGS IN
FIRST CORINTHIANS

The Beginning · The Vision
The Opening: The Testimony of Christ

Judgment concerning the Testimony:

Judgment concerning divisions; Judgment concerning the wicked; Judgment pertaining to the saints; Judgment concerning questions of marriage; Judgment concerning meats offered to idols; Judgment concerning headship.

Judgment concerning assembling together:

The Lord's Supper; The Unity of the Spirit in the Body of Christ; The manifestation of the Gifts in the Assembly; The Evangelical Truth of the Resurrection of the Dead.

The Conclusion

Price £9.25 (*postage extra*)
Hardback 495 pages
Laminated bookjacket
Printed, sewn and bound
by the John Metcalfe Publishing Trust
ISBN 1 870039 84 X

'TRACT FOR THE TIMES' SERIES

'TRACT FOR THE TIMES' SERIES

The Gospel of God by John Metcalfe. No. 1 in the Series. Laminated cover, price 25p.

The Strait Gate by John Metcalfe. No. 2 in the Series. Laminated cover, price 25p.

Eternal Sonship and Taylor Brethren by John Metcalfe. No. 3 in the Series. Laminated cover, price 25p.

Marks of the New Testament Church by John Metcalfe. No. 4 in the Series. Laminated cover, price 25p.

The Charismatic Delusion by John Metcalfe. No. 5 in the Series. Laminated cover, price 25p.

Premillennialism Exposed by John Metcalfe. No. 6 in the Series. Laminated cover, price 25p.

Justification and Peace by John Metcalfe. No. 7 in the Series. Laminated cover, price 25p.

Faith or Presumption? by John Metcalfe. No. 8 in the Series. Laminated cover, price 25p.

The Elect Undeceived by John Metcalfe. No. 9 in the Series. Laminated cover, price 25p.

Justifying Righteousness by John Metcalfe. No. 10 in the Series. Laminated cover, price 25p.

Righteousness Imputed by John Metcalfe. No. 11 in the Series. Laminated cover, price 25p.

The Great Deception by John Metcalfe. No. 12 in the Series. Laminated cover, price 25p.

A Famine in the Land by John Metcalfe. No. 13 in the Series. Laminated cover, price 25p.

Blood and Water by John Metcalfe. No. 14 in the Series. Laminated cover, price 25p.

Women Bishops? by John Metcalfe. No. 15 in the Series. Laminated cover, price 25p.

The Heavenly Vision by John Metcalfe. No. 16 in the Series. Laminated cover, price 25p.

The Mystery of Godliness by John Metcalfe. No. 17 in the Series. Laminated cover, price 25p.

EVANGELICAL TRACTS

EVANGELICAL TRACTS

1. **The Two Prayers of Elijah.** Light green card cover, price 10p.

2. **Wounded for our Transgressions.** Gold card cover, price 10p.

3. **The Blood of Sprinkling.** Red card cover, price 10p.

4. **The Grace of God that brings Salvation.** Blue card cover, price 10p.

5. **The Name of Jesus.** Rose card cover, price 10p.

6. **The Ministry of the New Testament.** Purple card cover, price 10p.

7. **The Death of the Righteous** (*The closing days of J.B. Stoney*) by A.M.S. (his daughter). Ivory card cover, price 10p.

8. **Repentance.** Sky blue card cover, price 10p.

9. **Legal Deceivers Exposed.** Crimson card cover, price 10p.

10. **Unconditional Salvation.** Green card cover, price 10p.

11. **Religious Merchandise.** Brown card cover, price 10p.

12. **Comfort.** Pink card cover, price 10p.

13. **Peace.** Grey card cover, price 10p.

14. **Eternal Life.** Cobalt card cover, price 10p.

15. **The Handwriting of Ordinances.** Fawn card cover, price 10p.

16. **'Lord, Lord!'.** Emerald card cover, price 10p.

17. **Conversion.** Wedgewood card cover, price 10p.

ECCLESIA TRACTS

ECCLESIA TRACTS

The Beginning of the Ecclesia by John Metcalfe. No. 1 in the Series, Sand grain cover, price 10p.

Churches and the Church by J.N. Darby. Edited. No. 2 in the Series, Sand grain cover, price 10p.

The Ministers of Christ by John Metcalfe. No. 3 in the Series, Sand grain cover, price 10p.

The Inward Witness by George Fox. Edited. No. 4 in the Series, Sand grain cover, price 10p.

The Notion of a Clergyman by J.N. Darby. Edited. No. 5 in the Series, Sand grain cover, price 10p.

The Servant of the Lord by William Huntington. Edited and Abridged. No. 6 in the Series, Sand grain cover, price 10p.

One Spirit by William Kelly. Edited. No. 7 in the Series, Sand grain cover, price 10p.

The Funeral of Arminianism by William Huntington. Edited and Abridged. No. 8 in the Series, Sand grain cover, price 10p.

One Body by William Kelly. Edited. No. 9 in the Series, Sand grain cover, price 10p.

False Churches and True by John Metcalfe. No. 10 in the Series, Sand grain cover, price 10p.

Separation from Evil by J.N. Darby. Edited. No. 11 in the Series, Sand grain cover, price 10p.

The Remnant by J.B. Stoney. Edited. No. 12 in the Series, Sand grain cover, price 10p.

The Arminian Skeleton by William Huntington. Edited and Abridged. No. 13 in the Series, Sand grain cover, price 10p.

FOUNDATION TRACTS

liv

FOUNDATION TRACTS

1. **Female Priests?** by John Metcalfe. Oatmeal cover, price 25p.

2. **The Bondage of the Will** by Martin Luther. Translated and Abridged. Oatmeal cover, price 25p.

3. **Of the Popish Mass** by John Calvin. Translated and Abridged. Oatmeal cover, price 25p.

4. **The Adversary** by John Metcalfe. Oatmeal cover, price 25p.

5. **The Advance of Popery** by J.C. Philpot. Oatmeal cover, price 25p.

6. **Enemies in the Land** by John Metcalfe. Oatmeal cover, price 25p.

7. **An Admonition Concerning Relics** by John Calvin. Oatmeal cover, price 25p.

8. **John Metcalfe's Testimony Against Falsity in Worship** by John Metcalfe. Oatmeal cover, price 25p.

9. **Brethrenism Exposed** by John Metcalfe. Oatmeal cover, price 25p.

10. **John Metcalfe's Testimony Against The Social Gospel** by John Metcalfe. Oatmeal cover, price 25p.

MINISTRY BY JOHN METCALFE

THE MINISTRY OF THE NEW TESTAMENT

The purpose of this substantial A4 gloss paper magazine is to provide spiritual and experimental ministry with sound doctrine which rightly and prophetically divides the word of truth.

Readers of our books will already know the high standards of our publications. They can be confident that these pages will maintain that quality, by giving access to enduring ministry from the past, much of which is derived from sources that are virtually unobtainable today, and publishing a living ministry from the present. Selected articles from the following writers have already been included:

ELI ASHDOWN · JOHN BERRIDGE · ABRAHAM BOOTH
JOHN BRADFORD · JOHN BUNYAN · JOHN BURGON
JOHN CALVIN · DONALD CARGILL · JOHN CENNICK · J.N. DARBY
GEORGE FOX · JOHN FOXE · WILLIAM GADSBY · BERNARD GILPIN
JOHN GUTHRIE · WILLIAM GUTHRIE · GREY HAZLERIGG · JOHN HICKS
WILLIAM HUNTINGTON · WILLIAM KELLY · JOHN KENNEDY
JOHN KERSHAW · JOHN KEYT · HANSERD KNOLLYS · JOHN KNOX
JAMES LEWIS · MARTIN LUTHER · ROBERT MURRAY MCCHEYNE
JOHN METCALFE · BROWNLOW NORTH · THOMAS OXENHAM
ALEXANDER–SANDY–PEDEN · J.C. PHILPOT · J.K. POPHAM
JAMES RENWICK · J.B. STONEY · HENRY TANNER · WILLIAM TIPTAFT
ARTHUR TRIGGS · JOHN VINALL · JOHN WARBURTON
JOHN WELWOOD · GEORGE WHITEFIELD · J.A. WYLIE

Price £1.75 (*postage included*)
Issued Spring, Summer, Autumn, Winter.

Magazine Order Form

Name and address (in block capitals)

....

....

....

Please send me ...... current copy/copies of The Ministry of the New Testament.

Please send me ...... year/s subscription.

I enclose a cheque/postal order for £......

(Price: including postage, U.K. £1.75; Overseas £1.90)
(One year's subscription: including postage, U.K. £7.00; Overseas £7.60)

Cheques should be made payable to The John Metcalfe Publishing Trust, and for overseas subscribers should be in pounds sterling drawn on a London Bank.

10 or more copies to one address will qualify for a 10% discount.

Some back numbers from Spring 1986 available.

Please send to The John Metcalfe Publishing Trust, Church Road, Tylers Green, Penn, Bucks, HP10 8LN, U.K.

All publications of the Trust are subsidised by the Publishers

Book Order Form

Please send to the address below:

	Price	Quantity
A Question for Pope John Paul II	£1.25	......
Of God or Man?	£1.45	......
Noah and the Flood	£1.90	......
Divine Footsteps	£0.95	......
The Red Heifer	£0.95	......
The Wells of Salvation	£2.35	......
The Book of Ruth (Hardback edition)	£4.95	......
Divine Meditations of William Huntington	£2.35	......
Present-Day Conversions of the New Testament Kind	£2.25	......
Saving Faith	£2.25	
Deliverance from the Law	£1.90	......
The Beatitudes	£1.90	......
Pastoral Letters to the Far East	£2.00	......
Law and Grace Contrasted by William Huntington	£2.35	......
The Gifts and Baptism of the Spirit	£0.95	......
The Body of Christ and the Gifts	£0.95	......
The Coming Resurrection of the Dead	£0.95	......
The Gifts of Tongues and of Prophecy	£0.95	......
Openings in First Corinthians (Hardback edition)	£9.25	......

Lectures from Church House, Westminster

	Price	Quantity
Colossians	£0.95	......
Philippians	£1.90	......
Matthew	£0.95	......
Philemon	£1.90	......
First Timothy	£2.00	......
Mark	£2.35	......
Creation	£2.00	......
The First Epistle of John (Hardback edition)	£9.25	......

Psalms, Hymns & Spiritual Songs (Hardback edition)

	Price	Quantity
The Psalms of the Old Testament	£2.50	......
Spiritual Songs from the Gospels	£2.50	......
The Hymns of the New Testament	£2.50	......

'Apostolic Foundation of the Christian Church' series

		Price	Quantity
Foundations Uncovered	Vol. I	£0.75	......
The Birth of Jesus Christ	Vol. II	£0.95	......
The Messiah (Hardback edition)	Vol. III	£7.75	......
The Son of God and Seed of David (Hardback edition)	Vol. IV	£6.95	......
Christ Crucified (Hardback edition)	Vol. V	£6.95	......
Justification by Faith (Hardback edition)	Vol. VI	£7.50	......
The Church: What is it? (Hardback edition)	Vol. VII	£7.75	......
The Revelation of Jesus Christ (Hardback edition)	Vol. VIII	£9.25	......
The Ministry of Reconciliation (Hardback edition)	Vol. IX	£6.95	......
Salvation (Hardback edition)	Vol. X	£9.25	......

Name and address (in block capitals)

....

....

....

If money is sent with order please allow for postage. Please address to:- The
John Metcalfe Publishing Trust, Church Road, Tylers Green, Penn, Bucks, HP10 8LN, U.K.

Tract Order Form

Please send to the address below:

		Price	Quantity
Evangelical Tracts			
The Two Prayers of Elijah		£0.10	......
Wounded for our Transgressions		£0.10	......
The Blood of Sprinkling		£0.10	......
The Grace of God that brings Salvation		£0.10	......
The Name of Jesus		£0.10	......
The Ministry of the New Testament		£0.10	......
The Death of the Righteous by A.M.S.		£0.10	......
Repentance		£0.10	......
Legal Deceivers Exposed		£0.10	......
Unconditional Salvation		£0.10	......
Religious Merchandise		£0.10	......
Comfort		£0.10	......
Peace		£0.10	......
Eternal Life		£0.10	......
The Handwriting of Ordinances		£0.10	......
'Lord, Lord!'		£0.10	......
Conversion		£0.10	......
'Tract for the Times' series			
The Gospel of God	No. 1	£0.25	......
The Strait Gate	No. 2	£0.25	......
Eternal Sonship and Taylor Brethren	No. 3	£0.25	......
Marks of the New Testament Church	No. 4	£0.25	......
The Charismatic Delusion	No. 5	£0.25	......
Premillennialism Exposed	No. 6	£0.25	......
Justification and Peace	No. 7	£0.25	......
Faith or Presumption?	No. 8	£0.25	......
The Elect Undeceived	No. 9	£0.25	......
Justifying Righteousness	No.10	£0.25	......
Righteousness Imputed	No.11	£0.25	......
The Great Deception	No.12	£0.25	......
A Famine in the Land	No.13	£0.25	......
Blood and Water	No.14	£0.25	......
Women Bishops?	No.15	£0.25	......
The Heavenly Vision	No.16	£0.25	......
The Mystery of Godliness	No.17	£0.25	......

Name and address (in block capitals)

....

....

....

If money is sent with order please allow for postage. Please address to:- The
John Metcalfe Publishing Trust, Church Road, Tylers Green, Penn, Bucks, HP10 8LN, U.K.

cut here

Tract Order Form

Please send to the address below:

		Price	Quantity
Ecclesia Tracts			
The Beginning of the Ecclesia	No. 1	£0.10	......
Churches and the Church (J.N.D.)	No. 2	£0.10	......
The Ministers of Christ	No. 3	£0.10	......
The Inward Witness (G.F.)	No. 4	£0.10	......
The Notion of a Clergyman (J.N.D.)	No. 5	£0.10	......
The Servant of the Lord (W.H.)	No. 6	£0.10	......
One Spirit (W.K.)	No. 7	£0.10	......
The Funeral of Arminianism (W.H.)	No. 8	£0.10	......
One Body (W.K.)	No. 9	£0.10	......
False Churches and True	No.10	£0.10	......
Separation from Evil (J.N.D.)	No.11	£0.10	......
The Remnant (J.B.S.)	No.12	£0.10	......
The Arminian Skeleton (W.H.)	No.13	£0.10	......
Foundation Tracts			
Female Priests?	No. 1	£0.25	......
The Bondage of the Will (Martin Luther)	No. 2	£0.25	......
Of the Popish Mass (John Calvin)	No. 3	£0.25	......
The Adversary	No. 4	£0.25	......
The Advance of Popery (J.C. Philpot)	No. 5	£0.25	......
Enemies in the Land	No. 6	£0.25	......
An Admonition Concerning Relics (John Calvin)	No. 7	£0.25	......
John Metcalfe's Testimony Against Falsity in Worship	No. 8	£0.25	......
Brethrenism Exposed	No. 9	£0.25	......
John Metcalfe's Testimony Against The Social Gospel	No.10	£0.25	......

Name and address (in block capitals)

....

....

....

If money is sent with order please allow for postage. Please address to:- The
John Metcalfe Publishing Trust, Church Road, Tylers Green, Penn, Bucks, HP10 8LN, U.K.

cut here